OXFORD WORLD'S CLASSICS

THE WOODLANDERS

THOMAS HARDY was born in Higher Bockhampton, Dorset, on 2 June 1840; his father was a builder in a small way of business, and he was educated locally and in Dorchester before being articled to an architect. After sixteen years in that profession and the publication of his earliest novel *Desperate Remedies* (1871), he determined to make his career in literature; not, however, before his work as an architect had led to his meeting at St Juliot in Cornwall Emma Gifford, who became his first wife in 1874.

In the 1860s Hardy had written a substantial amount of unpublished verse, but during the next twenty years almost all his creative effort went into novels and short stories. *Jude the Obscure*, the last-written of his novels, came out in 1895, closing a sequence of fiction that includes *Far from the Madding Crowd* (1874), *The Return of the Native* (1878), *Two on a Tower* (1882), *The Mayor of Casterbridge* (1886), and *Tess of the d'Urbervilles* (1891).

Hardy maintained in later life that only in poetry could he truly express his ideas; and the more than nine hundred poems in his collected verse (almost all published after 1898) possess great individuality and power.

In 1910 Hardy was awarded the Order of Merit; in 1912 Emma died and two years later he married Florence Dugdale. Thomas Hardy died in January 1928; the work he left behind—the novels, the poetry, and the epic drama *The Dynasts*—forms one of the supreme achievements in English imaginative literature.

DALE KRAMER teaches English literature at the University of Illinois at Urbana-Champaign. He has edited *The Woodlanders* for the Clarendon Press and *The Mayor of Casterbridge* for Oxford World's Classics, and is the author of *Thomas Hardy: The Forms of Tragedy*.

OXFORD WORLD'S CLASSICS

For almost 100 years Oxford World's Classics have brought
readers closer to the world's great literature. Now with over 700
titles—from the 4,000-year-old myths of Mesopotamia to the
twentieth century's greatest novels—the series makes available
lesser-known as well as celebrated writing.

The pocket-sized hardbacks of the early years contained
introductions by Virginia Woolf, T. S. Eliot, Graham Greene,
and other literary figures which enriched the experience of reading.
Today the series is recognized for its fine scholarship and
reliability in texts that span world literature, drama and poetry,
religion, philosophy and politics. Each edition includes perceptive
commentary and essential background information to meet the
changing needs of readers.

OXFORD WORLD'S CLASSICS

THOMAS HARDY

The Woodlanders

Edited with an Introduction and Notes by
DALE KRAMER

OXFORD
UNIVERSITY PRESS

OXFORD
UNIVERSITY PRESS

Great Clarendon Street, Oxford OX2 6DP

Oxford University Press is a department of the University of Oxford.
It furthers the University's objective of excellence in research, scholarship,
and education by publishing worldwide in

Oxford New York

Athens Auckland Bangkok Bogotá Buenos Aires Calcutta
Cape Town Chennai Dar es Salaam Delhi Florence Hong Kong Istanbul
Karachi Kuala Lumpur Madrid Melbourne Mexico City Mumbai
Nairobi Paris São Paulo Singapore Taipei Tokyo Toronto Warsaw

with associated companies in Berlin Ibadan

Oxford is a registered trade mark of Oxford Univeristy Press
in the UK and in certain other countries

Published in the United States
by Oxford University Press Inc., New York

First published 1981 by the Clarendon Press
First issued as a World's Classics paperback 1985
Reset with new bibliography 1996
Reissued as an Oxford World's Classic paperback 2000

British Library Cataloguing in Publication Data

Data available

Library of Congress Cataloging in Publication Data

Hardy, Thomas, 1840–1928.
The woodlanders.
(Oxford World's classics)
Bibliography: p.
I. Kramer, Dale, 1936– . II. Title.
PR4750.W7 1985   823'.8 84–25422
ISBN 0–19–283504–1

1 3 5 7 9 10 8 6 4 2

Typeset by Graphicraft Ltd, Hong Kong
Printed in Great Britain by
Cox & Wyman Ltd.
Reading, Berkshire

CONTENTS

GENERAL EDITOR'S PREFACE

THE first concern in The World's Classics editions of Hardy's works has been with the texts. Individual editors have compared every version of the novel or stories that Hardy might have revised, and have noted variant readings in words, punctuation, and styling in each of these substantive texts; they have thus been able to exclude much that their experience suggests that Hardy did not intend. In some cases this is the first time that the novel has appeared in a critical edition purged of errors and oversights; where possible Hardy's manuscript punctuation is used, rather than what his compositors thought he should have written.

Some account of the editors' discoveries will be found in the Note on the Text in each volume, while the most interesting revisions their work has revealed are included as an element of the Explanatory Notes. In some cases a Clarendon Press edition of the novel provides a wealth of further material for the reader interested in the way Hardy's writing developed from manuscript to final collected edition.

I should like to thank Shirley Tinkler for her help in drawing the maps that accompany each volume.

SIMON GATRELL

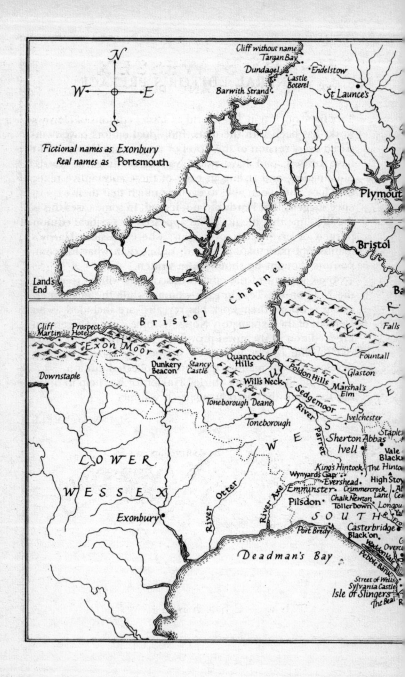

HARDY'S WESSEX
OF THE NOVELS AND POEMS

0   10   20
Miles

Lumsdon•   •Christminster

River Thames

NORTH

•Alfredston
The Brown House
•Cresscombe
•Marygreen

River Thames

Castle
Royal

MID-

WESSEX

Marlbury Downs

Gaymead
•Aldbrickham
•Kennetbridge

WESSEX

•Inkpen Beacon

Stoke Barehills•

Quartershot

The Great
Plain

•Weydon
Priors

Icenway
House

Stonehenge•

:our Head

UPPER

Melchester•
Leddenton•
Shaston
Marlott   •Wingreen
The Chase•   The Slopes
Trantridge Cross Chaseborough
:tourcastle
Knollingwood Hall
ilbarrow Shottsford 'Lornton
•Forum   Inn
ntcombe
:h   ersholt •Warborne
•Kingsbere •Welland R. Stour
WESSEX   •Sandbourne
Egdon Heath
lbo:hays Anglebury• :renpool
ries• Wellbridge
•Nether Mington
ll A: Corvesgate
:lmind   •Knollsea
Cove

Fernel Hall•

Wintoncester

•Deansleigh
Park

WESSEX

•Southampton

Portsmouth

Chene Manor

Solentsea

The
Island

ghtship

The   Channel

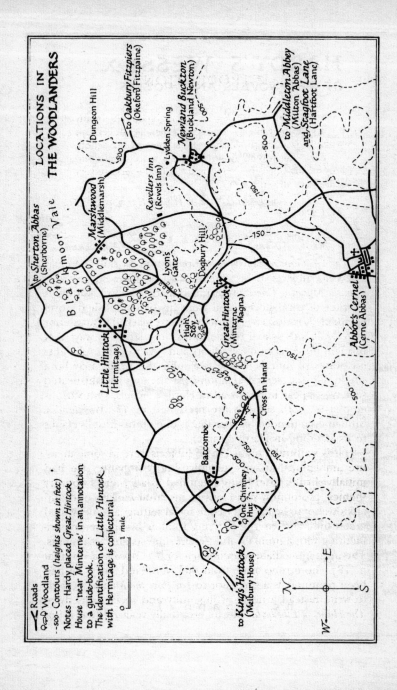

LOCATIONS IN
THE WOODLANDS

Notes: Hardy placed *Great Hintock* House 'near *Minterne*' in an annotation to a guide-book.
The identification of *Little Hintock* with *Hermitage* is conjectural.

〜 Roads
ᵔᵔ Woodland
--500- Contours (heights shown in feet) •

to Sherton Abbas
(Sherborne)

Dungeon Hill

to Oakbury Fitzpiers
(Okeford Fitzpaine)

500

Marshwood
(Middlemarsh)

Revellers Inn
(Revels Inn)

Lydden Spring

Newland Buckton
(Buckland Newton)

500

to Middleton Abbey
(Milton Abbas) and
Scagfoot Lane
(Hartfoot Lane)

B l a c k m o o r   V a l e

Lyon's Gate

Dogbury Hill

-150-

500

Great Hintock
(Minterne Magna)

High Stoy
225

150

Little Hintock
(Hermitage)

Batcombe

Cross in Hand
+

One Chimney Hut

500

150

Abbot's Cernel
(Cerne Abbas)

500

to King's Hintock
(Melbury House)

N
W ⊕ E
S

0   1 mile

INTRODUCTION

On taking up *The Woodlanders* and reading it after many years I think I like it, *as a story*, the best of all. Perhaps that is owing to the locality and scenery of the action, a part I am very fond of. It seems a more quaint and fresh story than the *Native*, and the characters are very distinctly drawn.

(*Life and Work of Thomas Hardy*, p. 520)

I

In *The Woodlanders* Hardy develops with great skill the characteristic subjects of his career. His first large success, *Far from the Madding Crowd* (1874), had made him well known as a writer of rural stories; and from his first published novel (*Desperate Remedies*, 1871) onward he was marked as an author who dealt with sexual relationships, frequently in ways that brought into question for editors and reviewers his reliability on points of morals. These two subjects—which may be a single subject, sexual relationships in an unsophisticated society—appear in nearly all of Hardy's novels, with various emphases. Both subjects are presented in *The Woodlanders* with an even-handed balance that is one of this novel's claims to its standing in Hardy's career.

Hardy's attitudes toward these subjects were in some measure ambiguous, at once tentative and combative. He had initially shrunk from being identified as a writer of country themes, profoundly conscious of his rural background and anxious not to be limited to one social setting; and he wasted much time and energy in trying to alter his image, experimenting with a number of different subjects and treatments. The most immediate consequence for *The Woodlanders* is that in 1874 he turned aside from the 'woodland story' he had been planning as a successor to *Far from the Madding Crowd*, to write instead a novel of ingenuity and social comedy in *The Hand of Ethelberta*. But he eventually realized that it was

the land and people of southern England that he knew about,
and for the next decade novels ranging in seriousness from
The Return of the Native to *The Trumpet-Major* are set in various
parts of Wessex; eventually Hardy returned to the woodland
setting he had abandoned.

The Woodlanders takes place in a fictional part of Wessex
resembling a small area in the north-west portion of Dorset,
in a landscape of well-forested gentle hills connected by narrow lanes. It was an area in which Hardy's mother's family had
lived (Millgate, *Thomas Hardy: A Biography*, pp. 9, 12–13),
and the harshness of his mother's existence while a member
of a poverty-stricken family on poor relief and later while in
service is perhaps reflected in the frequent reminders of the
cruelty that nature imposes upon itself: lichen as a parasite of
trees ('Here, as everywhere, the Unfulfilled Intention, which
makes life what it is, was as obvious as it could be among the
depraved crowds of a city slum. The leaf was deformed, the
curve was crippled, the taper was interrupted; the lichen ate
the vigour of the stalk, and the ivy slowly strangled to death
the promising sapling' (p. 53)); trees assaulting other trees
('two over-crowded branches . . . were rubbing each other into
wounds' (p. 16)); the various animals feeding on each other
('Owls . . . had been catching mice in the outhouses, rabbits
. . . had been eating the winter-greens in the gardens, and
stoats . . . had been sucking the blood of the rabbits' (pp. 23–
4)). But it is also an area where people with dedication and
persistence can be rewarded in worldly terms, as Melbury is
and as Giles is in way of being, despite the loss of his cottages.
The area's visual beauty and the delicate odours of flowering
fruit trees and their produce permeate the progress of the
novel, to an extent that many early readers, overlooking all
the evidences of an unremitting struggle for survival, thought
of this novel as offering Hardy's most benevolent landscape.

The second subject for which he was famous—the 'coarse-
ness' of his stories—gave Hardy greater trouble. While writing the serial versions of several of his novels, including *The
Return of the Native* (1878) and *Tess of the d'Urbervilles* (1891),
Hardy was forced either by the periodicals' editors, or by
his own sense of the prudishness of the readers of English

periodicals, to replace scenes and explanations containing sexual implications with less lubricious ones, sometimes far-fetched: a mock marriage was used more than once in place of a seduction bringing a woman to grief. He reinserted into the book versions many of the original passages; but he could not entirely separate his magazine and book audiences or completely obliterate evidences of his sense of his characters' motivations. *The Woodlanders* was more strongly condemned for its author's apparent approval of the immorality of his characters (especially Fitzpiers) than his earlier works; and it is quite reasonable to believe that the reviewers of *Tess of the d'Urbervilles* were primed by the example of *The Woodlanders*.

Although he resented the reviews that criticized him for portraying sexual dilemmas, the 1895 Preface to *The Woodlanders* acknowledges Hardy's awareness that more than one of his works centres on the problem of regulating sexual relations in the context of unhappy marriages. He believed that a good story required the honest treatment of human problems, a belief that led him throughout his career to depict situations that challenged orthodox or pious resolution. In 'Candour in English Fiction' (1890), written shortly after *The Woodlanders* and while *Tess of the d'Urbervilles* was much in his mind, Hardy declares his belief that fiction is best suited of all forms of education to deal with the interaction between the individual personality and the sexual impulse. This belief no doubt exacerbated his frustration as a 'true artist' upon first discovering 'the fearful price that [one] has to pay for the privilege of writing in the English language—no less a price than the complete extinction, in the mind of every mature and penetrating reader, of sympathetic belief in his personages'. Hardy's career, especially in his finer novels, is a record of his evasion of this extinction: his protestations in the essay to the contrary, he does not shy from allowing his characters a full range of sexual impulses. Certainly his adept use of euphemisms does not disguise the subject in *The Woodlanders*, as Giles resists sexual passion and Fitzpiers camouflages it in Shelleyan language; Grace's sexual urges, which grow in intensity through Hardy's successive revisions to the novel, are in all versions imaged through a 'tearfulness' and 'intoxication' of 'brain', the significance of which Victorians would have recognized at once.

In *The Mayor of Casterbridge* sexuality is seen in its implications for the myth of society that the novel projects. Through selling his sexual partner and their child, Henchard refuses the consequences of sexuality and thereby rejects a crucial link between the individual and society. Sexual liaisons in *The Woodlanders* reflect Hardy's perception of an evolving society, with an acceptance of traditional prohibitions and class exploitativeness (the affair between Fitzpiers and Suke Damson) contrasted with the possibility of counteracting those hierarchical exclusions (Fitzpiers's courtship of Grace). In *Tess of the d'Urbervilles* and *Jude the Obscure* the emphasis in the treatment of sex is on its basis in physicality, tempered though it may be by affection, a shift paralleled by the changed emphasis in these four novels' tragedies from mythic resonance to individual subjectivity.

In *The Woodlanders* the balance of forces affecting manifestations of sexuality—community and individual, authority and impulse, role and self-concept, love and passion—is more finely struck than in any of Hardy's other novels. Mrs Charmond's cry—'Oh why were we given hungry hearts and wild desires if we have to live in a world like this?'—may flout the truisms of respectability and marriage, but its impact is countered by Fitzpiers, who, although the object of this outburst of passion, reflects as a doctor that her unhappiness is probably caused by staying indoors too much. When Giles allows Grace to deceive herself about the possibility of divorce from Fitzpiers in order to kiss her one last time passionately, Hardy brilliantly reveals the physicality of the purest love (which scarcely needs Giles's subsequent implausibly managed self-sacrificial expiation to underscore its quality).

Such balance shapes *The Woodlanders* throughout; and perhaps this explains in part why the novel has never had so wide a readership, and has never aroused critics' disputatiousness as have Hardy's other generally acknowledged masterpieces. Put simply, no feature and no character in this novel stands out in our memory, as does Egdon Heath in *The Return of the Native* and as do Eustacia, Henchard, Tess, Jude, and Sue.

Even the woodland, which comes the closest to providing this kind of focus, in the complexity of its presentation lacks the strong and stark aspects of such settings as Egdon Heath or Casterbridge. Balance implies understanding and care or thoroughness, but it seems to prohibit, by its very nature, the concentration upon one or two elements with such intensity as to reveal their universal aspects and even to mythologize them. Myth is not dominant in the effect of *The Woodlanders*, despite references to Giles as wood god and despite Hardy's ostentatious centring of his novel in 'one of those sequestered spots outside the gates of the world where . . . from time to time, dramas of a grandeur and unity truly Sophoclean are enacted in the real'. Certainly there are echoes of myth and of literary formulas in the novel—of the pastoral, of the elegy, of the use of natural forces as signifiers, all consonant with mythic connotations—but there is little of the decisive mysteriousness of myth, of the sort we find in Tess's obdurant tolerance to pain and rejection, of Egdon Heath's embrace of and indifference to all human activity on its surface. *The Woodlanders*, instead, portrays the need for accommodation within the limits of normal human options.

The balance colours nearly every aspect of the novel, even the plot, as if *The Woodlanders* was intended to refute Hardy's own idea that the writer of fiction ought to offer the reader something exceptional or unusual to merit attention. The narrative is superbly plotted, with preparation, development, initial dénouements or plot-turns leading naturally into new complications, with the outcome determined by the characters' essential qualities. Grace, hapless through role demands and self-repression and confusion about her sexuality; Marty, self-sacrificial and patient, with only one chance to rebel against the limitations of her situation, a chance which when taken brings on consequences only long after they could have advanced Marty's own interests; Giles, noble and concerned for others' wishes and perceptions—not just Grace's but also Mr Melbury's (only Marty's wishes are ignored by Giles—which gives him humanity and increases the poignancy of her loyalty); Mrs Charmond, torn by impulse and passion in conflict with a desire for stability and love. This is not to say that the plot is faultless in detail: Hardy occasionally while writing and revising the novel had his eye so firmly on large patterns that he created inconsistencies. But these are all minor, and seldom noticed in first readings (several of these are mentioned in the Note on the Text and detailed in the Explanatory Notes).

The plotting is marked also by a structural kind of symmetry. It takes half the novel to wed Grace and Fitzpiers, another half to separate and reunite them; Marty appears here and there through the novel to confirm the values she represents; one character after another—Grammer Oliver, Melbury, Marty, John South, Fitzpiers—emerges to direct an action to shape the plot and then withdraws again, waiting as it were in the background: it is not Grace alone who waits 'for others' deeds before her own doings'. The plot is moved forward by characters whose participation may be only indirect: Melbury serves as a focus of ambition and social mobility although completely lacking in such ambition for himself; indeed, his vanity at being trusted by Mrs Charmond is that of the contented subordinate.

Perhaps what primarily keeps the plot meditative rather than energetic and propulsive is that actions intended to be decisive frequently serve only for the short term, and that the character the reader naturally expects to be forceful and pre-eminent turns out to be the most short-sighted of heroes. What characterizes Giles most pointedly is his keeping his lease-deeds under his mattress for years without having read them. Without an occasion for action Giles merely follows the seasons, in taking his apple-press around the countryside or in planting trees at someone else's behest. In tracing many characters' actions, the plot draws off some of the customary reader involvement with the romance triangles, further keeping the novel on an even keel and distributing the interest through the story. Finally, there are many passages of nature description and lengthy scenes occurring in clearings and woods, which by placing the narrative within a context of repetitive rural patterns diminish the sense of urgency felt by the egoistic characters.

One of these nature passages, when Winterborne outbids Melbury for the faggots in Chapter VII, is one of the perfectly realized scenes in the novel, although one easily overlooked. Readers have been trained by generations of teachers and critics to read Hardy for his gloominess, his powerful scenes that impart a pessimism that often passes for tragic force, for concatenations of circumstances that prevent the characters from shaping their own destinies, for suggestions of sexual energies capable of disrupting a traditional but increasingly incoherent social morality. But Hardy's quiet and lasting genius, and perhaps a large explanation for his approval of this novel, appears in scenes like the faggot-sale. This scene is a paradigm for the novel. It takes place within the woods of the title; it contains unforced imagery of the strain between the rural (presumably traditional and reassuring) and the fashionable (thus transient and shallow—but also immensely attractive to many of the characters); it shows Giles to be simultaneously hesitant, aggressive, fatally detached from the immediate scene, and slow to make up for his error; and it shows Melbury to be dominant in his woodlands milieu and kowtowing outside it. (It is true that as far as one character is concerned the scene is not adumbrative. Grace here is moved along by other people's personalities, while later in the novel an awakened sexuality gives an edge to her behaviour.)

Few of these aspects are made explicit, but they are what Hardy expects the reader to grasp. In his 'The Profitable Reading of Fiction' (1888) Hardy describes how insight or knowledge does not depend on a 'finish of phraseology or incisive sentences of subtle definition' but can arise from a baldly incidental treatment. Scenes like that in the wood—underdramatized but telling in every detail—appear throughout the novel. Giles preparing for—or failing to prepare for—the Christmas party (Chapter IX); Fitzpiers watching passersby open the newly painted gate (Chapter XVI); the lengthy portrayal of the meetings in the wood at the barking site with Fitzpiers, Melbury, and Grace (Chapter XIX)—all these moments offer similar opportunities for insight. Through such scenes as these Hardy impresses on the reader a sense of the 'locality and scenery of the action', and also allows his characters to reveal their traits through unstressed behaviour.

The novel contains no character that has become part of our literary heritage like Tess or Clym Yeobright or Jude. What distinguishes the characterization in *The Woodlanders* is the variety of personalities that Hardy develops within his constricted framework. Although possessing traits and concerns in common, they are all clearly different from each other; this can be seen, for example, in the various mixtures of selflessness and self-concern within the female characters, in the male characters' attitudes and reactions towards the traditions and laws that guide their society, as well as in the wide but not unsubtly demarcated differences in the handling of sexual passion by individuals of both sexes. Their behaviour, their thoughts, and others' feelings about them are shaped by inner qualities that are carefully drawn, varied, and 'true'—thus meeting Hardy's own criterion that any strangeness in fiction should be in the action, not the characters. Indeed, the characters seem so ordinary that the skill required to portray them can easily escape appreciation. Their traits are normal, not exotic or eccentric, and their developments are in accord with their initial personalities.

Callous and selfish though he is, Fitzpiers seems human—someone whose flaws are not over-dramatized, whose emotional life is so much on the surface that it almost seems the fault of others when they credit to him emotions and loyalties that he is at best able to experience for only short durations. Grace, in contrast, scarcely knows her own emotions, and infrequently, if ever, acknowledges them. (Does she, at the end, for example?) Giles knows his emotions, but because his dominating characteristic is principled living he refuses to live by them; indeed, during his best opportunities for wooing Grace—the Christmas party and the post-elopement courtship—he proceeds hesitantly and apparently reluctantly. Fitzpiers also understands his emotions and his instability for what they are, but he still engages others' feelings, which must inevitably be disappointed: because he thus acts selfishly despite his self-knowledge, he is not only ultimately contempt-ible but the primary destructive agent in the novel.

Particularly influential in bringing about the balanced tone of the novel is the manner of narration. Hardy's narrator normally imparts a distinctive shape to his novels, and over his career his narrators evolve in step with the changes of emphasis in his concerns. The narrator of *The Woodlanders* is at a mid-point, between the traditional and external teller of Hardy's early stories and the manager of the complex subjec-tive perspectives of *Tess of the d'Urbervilles* and *Jude the Obscure*. The narrator in *The Woodlanders* is closer to the earlier 'voice', no surprise in view of the 1874 origin of the novel. Whereas in *Tess of the d'Urbervilles* and *Jude the Obscure* the handling of disparate evidence creates apparent inconsistency, in *The Woodlanders* conflicting energies are incorporated into the patterns of balance we have been considering. In addition, the narrator of *The Woodlanders* enhances the novel's even-handedness by subordinating the individual to vision, por-traying nearly every situation and character in an abstract manner that reduces the specialness of any single act or person. Some instances: the meditations about thumbs now bony in the grave that had handled the decks of cards, im-plicitly reflecting on the triviality of Giles's anxiety that his Christmas party make a good impression; the portrayal of the boy carrying the horse-collar, which in stressing the super-stitiousness of the rural community supports its belief in man-killing trees and devilish doctors; the meditations on the flowers being crushed by the wheels of Melbury's gig; the uncertainty as to whose consciousness reflects on the vanish-ing Fitzpiers as he rides to visit Mrs Charmond at Milton Abbey with references to acorns and chestnuts that look fine but are as unsound as Grace's own situation. Such a narrator is a reminder that in fiction characters represent abstract values, as counters in an intellectual perception. More richly, such a narrator creates or shapes a context that conforms, in anticipation so to speak, to the discoveries about life made by the characters, so that earned wisdom in Hardy is not so much a matter of predetermination but of inevitability—in a far more complex way than in Trollope, for example, where the narrator and the characters simultaneously speak in the same terminology, with the same concerns.

The method of narration further reduces the reader's concern with any single character by its manner of dispersing attention, in that the focus upon events may be a character who is not then one of the persons most directly involved in those events. The clearest instance of this technique is the use of Melbury's thought processes to trace the suspicion and revelation that Fitzpiers is having an affair with Mrs Charmond. It is during this time that Melbury is most closely before the reader. Clearly he is anxious about his daughter's happiness, but of course he is tangential to the significance of the drama, even allowing that it is his anger with Fitzpiers that literally catapults the doctor into his elopement with Mrs Charmond. Giles seems to be the dominating character, and the one who embodies the novel's—and presumably the narrator's—values. But in fact he is absent for long stretches, and even when present he seldom provides the focus for the narrator's meditations on the ironies of a life presumably paced by woodland rhythms. It is Marty South who interprets the sighing of trees as reluctance to participate in life—Giles chastises her for the thought. As interpreter of the pain and complexities arising from the modern clash between tradition and the individual, Mrs Charmond's rebelliousness makes her a more poignant character than Giles, with his phlegm and endurance.

How to explain Hardy's achievement of this balance? First, perhaps, there is the long gestation of the novel. If the 'woodland story' abandoned in 1874 in the effort to escape reviewers' labelling survives in some way in the novel begun more than a decade later, the balance may be the result of Hardy's longer familiarity with and curiosity about the scene and characters—points reflected in Hardy's explanation, given as the epigraph to this introduction, of his preference for this novel. Second, Hardy reports in his autobiography that on 17–19 November 1885 he has 'gone back to [his] original plot for "The Woodlanders" after all' and that he is working over thirteen hours a day 'to get [his] mind made up on the details' (*Life and Work of Thomas Hardy*, p. 182). If he knew from the beginning of composition all, or nearly all, the turns his plot would take, he would have known the kinds of information needed at each juncture. That such indeed appears to be the case is seen from the very few alterations in plot detectable in the manuscript (see the Note on the Text). Of course, there may have been earlier drafts that have not survived; but this would not change the point that, once engaged in the final months-long development of the surviving manuscript, Hardy knew what he was trying to achieve. In *The Woodlanders* Hardy was dealing with a subject with which he felt comfortable; he had the plot's details early and well in hand; and his handling of sentences and words was never more assured.

II

Hardy's early interest in writing had included a strong political bent. Macmillan's decision not to publish his first story, *The Poor Man and the Lady*, was based in part on their feeling that not only was it fiercely radical, but inartistically so. By the time of *The Woodlanders*, Hardy had learned to phrase his views with general rather than immediate or temporal stresses. His concern with the relations of individual and society had slackened but little; but now he demonstrates and analyses the relationship within the main lines of a story rather than imposing a dogmatism upon the story. In keeping with the balance of shaping the novel as a whole, characters individually can represent both sides of a problematic issue, embodying moral and ideological values that are at once conflicting and complementary. Giles is on the one hand projected as a mythic enforcer of established and traditional authority, of dignity and conformity to universal law that is distinguishable from ordinary convention mostly because it is areligious. But likewise, and more powerfully, he represents that which undercuts external value systems—individual integrity. In his embodying so thoroughly (and unreflectingly) these contradictory postures toward authority, Giles's dilemma provides most of the deep-seated tension in the novel. Mrs Charmond, although less personally stable, is nearly as significant as Giles, representing both Bohemia and opportunism, unconventionality and helplessness before convention. Melbury's sense of values resembles Giles's, but he lacks that internal coherence upon which Giles's essential worth rests, and upon which depends any substantial positive stance towards an external or even hierarchical source of authority. Indeed, the pathos in Melbury's characterization stems from his self-created and disabling alienation from the traditional sources of his own beliefs: the things he does that are significant he does to improve Grace's standing in society and, later, for the sake of salvaging what happiness he can for his daughter—not for any non-personal value for which one can say he 'stands' in a positive way. As for Fitzpiers, it is clear that Hardy intends him as one of those outsiders in Wessex whose indifference to the emotions and inherent worth of the persons he encounters in the rural setting marks a destructive self-isolation. He is one of Hardy's more ambivalent characters, an admirer of Shelley but transitory in any identity, too shifting to project a significant intellectual posture—unless it is the hedonism and cynicism that undercuts all effort to build a community of mutual understanding. On the assumption that Hardy intends Fitzpiers to be intellectually brilliant, it is clear that improvement in social morality will not be based on superior rationality, but on qualities less readily definable and less reducible to a programme. To put it more directly, whatever his intentions had been in *The Poor Man and the Lady*, in *The Woodlanders* Hardy is not a practical reformer: he is rather an artist, one who portrays a situation pressing upon his society without suggesting specific remedies.

Nonetheless, in this novel Hardy perhaps comes closer to deliberate social criticism than he had done in his earlier published work. The conflict between love and society's laws and customs anticipates both the wider psychological concerns and the near-theological approach in *Tess of the d'Urbervilles* and the more narrow but also more devastating attack in *Jude the Obscure*. In *The Mayor of Casterbridge*, the opposition of Henchard's and Farfrae's situations had been incorporated within an established social scene and solid basis of economic productivity, even though both scene and basis are evolving. The poetic evocativeness of *The Woodlanders* (effective in spite of the framing Darwinism) nearly masks the political energy expressed through the interactions of Fitzpiers and Grace, of Melbury and Mrs Charmond, of Suke and Giles. (The latter is one of Hardy's more startling but subtle oppositions. The two do not interact within the novel, but as representatives of the will-less rural underclass and the principled but nonetheless equally helpless yeomanry, Suke and Giles develop basically contrasting, if similarly ineffectual, courses.) Although the novel contains these and other features of a society in conflict with its members, *The Woodlanders* evades the didacticism always so close to the narration of Hardy's last two great novels.

As with most novels that allude to the traditional and customary while simultaneously holding out the likelihood of change, *The Woodlanders* challenges our assumptions about time and reality. It is not an enactment of a way of life to be perceived with nostalgia, despite its delicate attentive portrayal of minutiae of nature, and despite its population of high-minded persons capable of self-sacrifice whose guiding standards are of domesticity. The novel contains these features but it simultaneously queries them. The flowers can be run over by carriage wheels, and domestic values collapse from the ambition, sympathetic in itself, to improve one's family members' social status. Most devastating to any nostalgia is the insistence that suffering pervades the animate universe. The sufferings that the trees of the title inflict upon each other in their natural setting parallel those inflicted by one well-meaning human on others in the story.

Hardy's control of his materials is sustained throughout *The Woodlanders* with a delicate and unfaltering grasp of the difference between understanding and judgement, so that the novel's balance is not distorted by the sympathy that elsewhere (as in *Tess of the d'Urbervilles* after the heroine's marriage to Angel) overwhelms Hardy. There is sympathy, certainly—towards Marty perhaps a superfluity of sympathy; but all in all Hardy clearly is well aware of humanity's way, which includes bungling, refusing to do the thing that is in one's own best interests, and doing the worst thing for the best reasons. From these manifestations of humanity neither Giles nor Fitzpiers, neither Grace nor Mrs Charmond, is exempt.

None of this is to say that all readers will respond to Hardy's characters and situations in a predictable way. For example, several reviewers of the first edition criticized Hardy for the ending, on their assumption that Grace's reacceptance of Fitzpiers was Hardy's indication that the doctor was to be forgiven by readers for his sexual laxity. This was a misapprehension that undercut one of the implicit messages of the novel about which Hardy was unwilling to be misunderstood, and in his next revision of the novel after the reviews appeared he added the statement by Melbury that Grace was doomed to live with a husband who would continue to be unfaithful. But in general, ambiguity in *The Woodlanders* leads not to misapprehension but to functional contradictoriness. It is only to the more casual reader that Hardy's novels are primarily nostalgic, or idyllic, or bitter, or settled within any single perspective; and *The Woodlanders* is at the apex of Hardy's mature vision.

The action of *The Woodlanders* is prosaic; yet perhaps this also justifies Hardy's feeling that it was his favourite 'as a story': the narrative is more suasive, precisely because less sensational, than that of any other Hardy novel. It never seems beyond hope that Giles and Grace will be able to assert their individual wills against the forces, social and universal, that constrict them. In a sense, the reader can surrender to the spectacle of Tess's helpless struggles or Jude's hapless floundering, and in a perverse way gain comfort from the very degree of desperation they experience. We do not surrender to a narrative drive in *The Woodlanders* but continue to hope to see the characters break through society's traps to gain some satisfaction or happiness, or to overcome their own trepidations and challenge society's blinkeredness. The novel's tragic tone is maintained because, in spite of this ever-present hope and possibility, no character does escape. As a tragedy, then, *The Woodlanders* fulfils a different form from any other of Hardy's great novels, for this novel portrays more finely the irresolvability of possibility and achievement.

LOCATIONS IN WESSEX AND DORSET

THE actual location of Hardy's Wessex novels 'on the ground' of Dorset interests many readers. *The Woodlanders* is more imaginatively placed than most of his novels. When first writing the story Hardy drew upon the appearance of actual houses and hills and towns, and shuffled their locations as the plot and the travels of his characters required; thus, there is no locale in Dorset around which one can walk and expect to find the mentioned houses, hamlets, farms and the like precisely as juxtaposed in the novel. For example, Turnworth House, near Blandford in north-east Dorset, was fictionalized several miles westward as Hintock House, at the location of the real Melbury House west of Bubb Down Hill in north-west Dorset. Perhaps Turnworth House's situation within a declivity surrounded by overlooking trees and hills struck Hardy's fancy as a metaphor for the life of Mrs Charmond, under inspection by her society. Features of scenery—houses, churches, and so forth—were borrowed according to the story's requirements from such hamlets as Hermitage, Middlemarsh, Lyons-Gate, Revels Inn, Holnest, and Melbury Bubb (see *Life and Work of Thomas Hardy*, p. 466). Hardy frequently claimed not to know the actual site of Little Hintock—for instance, in the 1912 Preface to *The Woodlanders*.

That the actual points are not located in relation to each other on the ground in Dorset as they are in the novel was not of critical importance to Hardy's imagination; but because most of his novels were situated in 'Wessex', and because they had such a high reputation, it was evident that it would be a selling point for the Osgood, McIlvaine Wessex Novels Edition (1896) if he could incorporate all of his imagined landscapes into the genuine county of Dorset and surrounding areas. Most of the topographical alterations in Hardy's novels were made for this edition.

The difficulties of establishing the 'real' setting for this novel can be eased by realizing, as the full record of revisions of the novel makes clear, that Hardy at two separate stages placed the story within two differing sitings. His original conception placed the story near Bubb Down Hill, with the location (but not the appearance) of Mrs Charmond's house identifiable as that of Melbury House. Then, anxious not to offend the Ilchester family (whose seat was Melbury House) by associating them with Mrs Charmond, he moved the action several miles eastward and centred it around High-Stoy Hill. (An account of this shift is given by F. B. Pinion in *The Thomas Hardy Yearbook*, St Peter Port, Guernsey, 1971, pp. 46–55.) Thus, the perspectives of Bubb Down Hill—which provided the backdrop for the opening description and for the characters' motions (such as Fitzpiers's riding away from his wife toward 'Middleton Abbey' [Milton Abbas]) under the names of Rub-Down and then Rubdon Hill—were also moved to another actual hill to the east, High-Stoy Hill (whose real name is used), with distances and directions appropriately altered. So the sightseer today has a choice. The original siting, with Melbury Osmund as Great Hintock and with an imaginary setting in the vicinity of Bubb Down Hill as Little Hintock, has one kind of validity, while Hardy's later revisions put the novel within a region more of whose points are locatable on a map.

Hardy's statement of uncertainty about the topographical location of Little Hintock has caused confusion even among people who presumably work with Hardy's later versions as to which of two Dorset villages, Minterne Parva or Hermitage, 'is' Little Hintock. As Carl Weber has pointed out (*Hardy of Wessex*, 2nd edn., New York, 1965, p. 155), the 'names "Little Hintock" and "Great Hintock" were obviously suggested by Minterne Parva and Minterne Magna'. But Hermitage has the better claim for Hardy's final siting, as will be seen by the reader who notices in the initial pages of all versions of the novel that Mrs Dollery's van is travelling south from Sherton and that Little Hintock always comes before Great Hintock on her route. The actual Minterne Parva is south of Minterne Magna. Hermitage, on the other hand, is north of Minterne Magna. Also, a revision for the Osgood edition identifies Little Hintock more precisely as being north of High-Stoy Hill (see note to p. 8). Both of the actual

Minternes in Dorset are south of High-Stoy Hill, while Hermitage is north of it. Hermann Lea's *Thomas Hardy's Wessex* (London, 1913), which was prepared under the occasional advice of Hardy, essentially corroborates these placements (Lea, pp. 108, 110).

NOTE ON THE TEXT

I

THIS text is based on the Clarendon Press edition of the novel, published in 1981. That edition employs as copy-text the manuscript (which is in the Thomas Hardy Memorial Room at the Dorset County Museum, Dorchester), emended according to current generally accepted editing practice. Of the ten versions of *The Woodlanders* listed at the head of the Explanatory Notes, nine were prepared by Hardy or contain his revisions of a preceding version. (The Colonial Library Edition is of uncertain provenance.)

The textual history of *The Woodlanders* increases our knowledge about Hardy's manner of creating, especially the ways he seized the opportunities offered by conventional practices of novel-publishing in the late nineteenth and early twentieth centuries to reshape his work. He had planned 'a woodland story' in 1874, to follow *Far from the Madding Crowd*, but he put it aside; and when ten years later a serial was wanted by *Macmillan's Magazine* he decided to take it up again. *Macmillan's Magazine* did not circulate widely enough in America to justify Macmillan's also paying for American serial rights, so Hardy wrote to several American magazines to offer the story for sale; it was eventually accepted by *Harper's Bazar*, whose parent firm, Harper & Brothers, also agreed to publish the novel as a book upon completion of the serialization. To Harper were sent galleys that had been prepared by Macmillan's printers, Hardy revising lightly the set used for the serial, and somewhat more heavily the set used for the Harper book version, whose hardcover and paperback versions were identical. (There were also in America numerous 'pirated' book versions of *The Woodlanders*—International Copyright did not come into effect until 1891—but naturally Hardy made no contribution to any of these.) Hardy revised the galleys further before returning a third set to *Macmillan's Magazine*. He made still more revisions on pages of the printed instalments and, for the last two instalments, on magazine proofs for the English first edition, printed in three volumes. The Colonial Library Edition was prepared at nearly the same time; possibly its very few variants in wording are by Hardy, but more probably they were caused by the compositors, who were in haste to prepare plates for Macmillan's offices in the colonies in order to cut the ground from under editions imported from America. (Colonial Library Edition variants are excluded from this World's Classics edition.)

Within months of the three-volume first edition, Hardy was again revising the novel for its appearance in a single volume to be sold at six shillings—the so-called cheap format, a standard move in publishing. Within a few years, Hardy signed with a new publisher, Osgood, McIlvaine and Co., whose particular desire was to bring out a collected edition, the Wessex Novels. For this edition (1896), Hardy gave the novel a thoroughgoing revision. One of the firm's founders, James Ripley Osgood, died before the Wessex Novels appeared, and eventually the Osgood, McIlvaine firm was absorbed into the English branch of Harper & Brothers. At this, Hardy decided he wanted a publisher whose head office was in England, and so he returned to the Macmillan firm, which announced the event by issuing the Wessex Novels Edition under a different name, the Uniform Edition of 1903, an edition whose significance in the history of *The Woodlanders* is that Hardy revised a copy of this edition for use as printer's copy for his next (and last) version. Publishing elaborate de luxe editions, as memorials of living authors, became the thing to do around the turn of the century; Hardy was eager to have one, and he gave his fiction its last thorough revision for a projected de luxe edition. The de luxe aspect of the production was abandoned when the intended American co-publisher proved not to be up to the job; but Macmillan brought out the freshly revised texts anyway, in an attractively printed and serviceably bound edition that until recently has been felt to represent Hardy's 'definitive' text: the Wessex Edition. The de luxe edition itself materialized in 1920 in the Mellstock Edition, but for this edition Hardy made a careful revision only of *A Pair of Blue Eyes; The Woodlanders* text in the Mellstock edition has only minor variants, which may or may not be Hardy's. The present edition accepts two Mellstock variants, and a further alteration written by Hardy in his 'study copy' of the Wessex Edition.[1]

II

A conscientious craftsman, Hardy planned his novels before beginning to write, and worked hard to achieve soundly paced, block-structured plots that well answered instalment readers' desires for a recurring pattern of suspense, moments of partial resolution, and ensuing complications. (That he was willing to allow editors to divide his novels to fit available space shows his practicality, not a disregard for structure while writing.) The pragmatic and even mechanical flair of much of his plotting is countered by a bent towards poetry and coloured by a sober assessment of humanity's chances for happiness. He was conscious of fiction's high responsibilities, stressing that its purpose is 'mental enlargement' ('On the Profitable Reading of Fiction'), while maintaining that as long as the personalities and emotions ring 'true', freshness and novelty in the story line are appropriately used to attract readers. Such attitudes are reflected in the characteristic contradictions of Hardy's art, early and late: passages of stiff writing and implausibilities interlaced with passages of meditation about nature and fate, and with delineations of subtle feelings and conflicts. In *The Woodlanders*, a more quietly plotted story than usual with Hardy, these patterns hold, although there are more passages of meditation than of strained action.

A principal point to be drawn from the history of the text of the story is that all the surviving evidence shows Hardy from the beginning in control of his intentions and materials. The manuscript generally fixes the plot, the characters,

---

[1] Details of these minor alterations, further alterations I am not able to discuss here for reasons of space, as well as the mass of evidence on which the present edition is founded, may be found in my critical edition of *The Woodlanders* (Clarendon Press, 1981), and in my 'Revisions and Vision: Thomas Hardy's *The Woodlanders*', *Bulletin of the New York Public Library*, 75 (1971), 195–230, 248–82.

the emphases: in the numerous subsequent stages of revision Hardy attempted to realize better his original conceptions, not to resolve divergences and unintended contradictions and certainly not to alter the novel's purposes. Remarkably, surviving cancellations in the manuscript itself reveal only one marked difference from the final manuscript version. A nearly illegible, crossed-out passage seems to reveal that the character who became Fitzpiers had originally been intended to be a 'land agent' at 'my lords' (presumably the Charmonds), a characterization that—had it held, instead of the sophisticated doctor entering the cast of characters—might well have led to a lesser overall concentration on the impact of London- and Continent-based culture upon the rustic woodlanders than is present in the novel as we have it.

Two further qualifications might be made of the confident assertion that when Hardy began the novel he had firmly in mind the directions he wanted it to take. One concerns the still influential piety and prudery of much of the reading public in the 1880s, who spoke to Hardy through letters to the editor of *Macmillan's Magazine*, Mowbray Morris. When Morris realized that Fitzpiers was carrying on an affair with Suke Damson while engaged to Grace, he cautioned Hardy 'not to bring the fair Miss Suke to too open shame'. Possibly Hardy altered the fate of Suke Damson as a result of this caution; but as far as sexual issues are concerned it is clear that he ignored Morris's tremors, because the seduction of Suke is a comparatively pallid portrayal of the exploitation of the rustic by the sophisticate in comparison with the later, more carefully traced and more disruptive affair between Fitzpiers and Mrs Charmond—which Hardy almost certainly had in mind well before Morris wrote his cautionary letter. (It would seem, in fact, that Hardy had already perceived the value of discretion in portraying Suke and Fitzpiers's liaison, for he had written 'Omit for mag.' (i.e. *Macmillan's Magazine*) in the margin next to the last sentence of Chapter XX, 'It was daybreak before Fitzpiers and Suke Damson re-entered Little Hintock.')

The second qualification turns upon the kinds of responses Hardy made in his revisions to the reviewers' observations upon the first edition. The most severe criticisms were of Fitzpiers. Several reviewers felt that, by the reunion of Fitzpiers and Grace, Hardy was rewarding Fitzpiers as well as suggesting an unbelievable reformation in his character (e.g. *London Quarterly Review*, 68 (1887), 382). A similar complaint, as expressed by the reviewer for the *Spectator* (60 (1887), 419), is that Hardy 'renders it impossible for us to suppose that he entertains . . . indignation and disgust towards Fitzpiers' and thereby 'annuls all the effect of Winterborne's faithfulness, manliness, and pure disinterestedness'. Hardy's response is given most directly in the passage on page 360 (whose revisions are spread over the one-volume edition and the Osgood, McIlvaine edition)—Melbury's soliloquy pronouncing the future course of Grace's marriage with Fitzpiers. It is clear that Fitzpiers cannot 'reform'—that he is what he is; it is also clear that Grace's own sexuality (which is similarly made more explicit in post-first edition revisions) dooms her to future marital desperation. These points are evident enough in the manuscript version, but Hardy was always concerned to meet reviewers' and editors' objections if he could do so without falsifying positions about which he felt strongly. Hardy also seems willing to alter Mrs Charmond's characterization, making her more sophisticated and elegant in appearance. She thereby becomes less obviously the prey of Fitzpiers. But these revisions make her a richer and more complex character, whereas Fitzpiers's personality is essentially only diminished and mocked through post-first edition alterations, such as that turning his 'refined' face into a 'fastidious' one. But in none of these aspects are the manuscript's emphases materially altered. Hardy seems to have believed, as time went on, that changing social mores made it possible to be franker about sexual connotations and issues. As early as 1889 he wrote to a person who was thinking of turning the novel into a play that one could then make clear, in a way not possible when the novel was written, that Fitzpiers was intended to be faithless in the future. However much credence one wishes to give to this claim about a remarkable change in the reading public within a two- or three-year span, it is evident that

Hardy's concern in these revisions is to make his intentions clearer rather than to change them.

Indeed, in his eagerness or concern to clarify certain aspects of the narrative, he introduces unintentional contradictions: in the bedroom scene involving Suke Damson, Mrs Charmond, and Grace, the 1896 readings have the women going into Fitzpiers's bedroom to ruminate on his bed-linen without giving Mrs Melbury and Grammer, who had been cleaning the room, a chance to leave (see pp. 255–7); and Melbury in his soliloquy on page 360 about Fitzpiers's past and future sexual dalliances indicates knowledge about Fitzpiers and Suke Damson that previously had been held by no one but Grace, Fitzpiers, Mrs Charmond (after the bedroom scene), and Timothy Tangs (who complains only to Suke herself).

III

Even though the manuscript fixed the novel in its major aspects, Hardy perceived many small adjustments that could be made; and, of course, the poet in him continued through all the revisions to try to insert the right word in numerous passages. Naturally not all of these can be illustrated in the Explanatory Notes.

In the manuscript, the major alteration in addition to the transformation of Fitzpiers from an agricultural professional to a doctor is that Fitzpiers originally was to have come to reclaim Grace three 'hours' not three 'months' after the divorce attempt fails (p. 296). This makes possible Giles's serious illness in the interim (p. 291) and therefore justifies Grace's asking Fitzpiers's professional opinion of her responsibility for Giles's death. Also, Mrs Charmond's unconventionality and Fitzpiers's untrustworthiness are amplified through revisions within the manuscript. From the pagination in the manuscript it appears that Chapter VIII was placed in its present location after Hardy had written as far as Chapter XV; but having Grace's visit to Mrs Charmond occur at this point is not a major change in the plot. Rather, it suggests merely an alteration in the placement of the scene or a decision to present the visit dramatically rather than by report. A number of small developments detectable by observing deletions in the manuscript and comparing them with final manuscript versions of passages suggests something of Hardy's manner of improvising within the constraints of an established plot. One example only: originally, an allusion is made to Fitzpiers *not* having South's brain to examine, having by then passed out of that phase of his interests (p. 122), but evidently Hardy realized that actually having the brain for Grace to examine under a microscope offered a certain shock effect. (Interestingly, Hardy never reinstated any of the deleted material that would have made clearer how Fitzpiers might have obtained a section of South's brain for dissection.)

In the American serial Mrs Charmond ceases to be the 'daughter of an eminent painter' and is instead ascribed an 'adaptable, wandering *weltbürgerliche* nature'. In the American book edition Melbury loses the knowledge that the lawyer Beaucock had written to Giles informing him that a divorce for Grace is impossible, and the last sentence of Chapter XX is deleted.

As I have mentioned above, this sentence does not appear in *Macmillan's Magazine* either, Hardy having directed its removal by a marginal notation on the manuscript. Most of the revisions made for *Macmillan's Magazine* refine or clarify isolated passages. Two changes in close proximity have the effect of hinting that Mrs Charmond married for money. An interesting set of deletions are those occurring in the eighth and ninth instalments (Chapters XXX–XXXVII), both of which end flush at the bottom of their last page in the magazine; the present edition restores those readings that appear to have been made to save space—that is, to make another page unnecessary in the issues of the magazine.

Hardy wrote to Macmillan that in preparing the three-volume edition he planned to correct a 'few discrepancies here and there in the serial issue' and to 'shorten passages that seem tedious'; and he carried out his intention in his most extensive revisions for any of the printed texts of the novel. Numerous explanatory passages are deleted or shortened.

He also changed Fitzpiers's Christian name from 'Edgar' to 'Edred', and, most important, smoothed out some of the rough edges of Giles's personality, so that his cynicism and causticity are modified and his affection for Grace becomes consistently loyal and so strong it can 'enfeeble' him. These changes in Giles are concentrated in the early pages of the novel, suggesting that Hardy's concept of him evolved in this direction as he wrote the manuscript. In contrast, Grace becomes more seductive, so that it is she who becomes in large part responsible for the kisses about which Giles later comes self-destructively to feel guilty. The three-volume version also first offers the somewhat sensational possibility that Mrs Charmond was pregnant at the time of her death.

In preparing the English one-volume six-shilling edition, Hardy heeded the advice of reviewers in the ways already discussed, in making Fitzpiers less admirable and in offering Melbury's prediction of future unhappiness in Grace's marriage (p. 360).

For the Osgood, McIlvaine edition Hardy concentrated on adjusting distances and directions in his imaginary landscape of Wessex to the actual geography of Dorset (as mentioned earlier, titling the edition 'The Wessex Novels' was done in full consciousness of the commercial advantage to be gained from settling all of Hardy's novels within the region he had made famous). The overall quality of frankness is enhanced in this revision also, as Hardy underscored the sexual implications of certain scenes, made unmistakable the nature of Fitzpiers's relations with Mrs Charmond, heightened the sexual aspects of the bedroom meeting of Mrs Charmond, Suke, and Grace, and emphasized the worldliness and perhaps even promiscuity of Mrs Charmond and the sexual feelings Grace is capable of feeling for Giles. Grace and Giles's dilemma in the woods is made somewhat more plausible by the reduction of the hut's accommodation from two rooms to one. Again, however, the sexual clarifications only make clear what is present in the novel from the earliest version (note, for example, Grace's sexual feelings for Fitzpiers, which are projected through the Victorian convention of difficulty of breathing).

Hardy's last revision of the novel, for the 1912 Wessex Edition, was carried out in two stages, most of the changes being written in the copy sent to the printers (a copy of the Uniform Edition), the remainder in proofs of the edition. He clarified Fitzpiers's aristocratic background, continued to adjust distances and place-names in Wessex, and corrected left-over passages from previous versions (for example, p. 309: a reference to an 'inner' room in Giles's hut). He also made numerous minor 'touchings-up'. For example, he added a phrase in Mr and Mrs Melbury's nocturnal discussion about Grace to make clear that Mr Melbury had frequently spoken to his wife about his plan for Grace to marry Giles (p. 19; on the previous page he added in the printer's copy a second, even more explicit phrase, 'as you know very well', but modified this in the proofs to 'as you must surely see'). He made Mrs Charmond's agent responsible for the refusal to extend Giles's leases rather than Mrs Charmond herself, thereby reducing the irony of the consequences for Mrs Charmond; and he placed the story within its nineteenth-century setting of expanding estates through references to the pulling down of cottages.

So far I have considered only the changes in the wording, or the 'substantives', to use editing parlance. The 'accidentals' (that is, the punctuation, paragraphing, spelling, and the like) were also affected during each new preparation of the text. It is impossible to know how many of the changes in these areas can be laid to Hardy, because in the nineteenth century such details were commonly subject to the imposition of a printing-house style or to the interference of editors. The author's wishes in such matters often were simply ignored. A letter from the publisher Frederick Macmillan indicates that Hardy's manuscript was sent directly to the printer of *Macmillan's Magazine* before he or the magazine's editor had even read it, so it is obvious that most of the hundreds of variants in accidentals in the crucial first setting of type came from compositors, whose primary concern naturally would have been to bring the manuscript into consistency with house style. Thereafter the text of each version was set from the one preceding (with the exception of the American

texts, neither of which became part of the subsequent trans-
mission of the text). Some departures from Hardy's usages
were brought about by necessities of the trade. For example,
many long manuscript paragraphs were broken into short
paragraphs for the first English edition, which—in order to
fill the three volumes that the powerful lending libraries
wanted—was designed with generous margins and large type,
a format that would have made the original paragraphs run
on for page after page. During the new settings for the several
versions of the novel, commas were both added and deleted,
and colons and semicolons (for example) were likewise altered with no consistent pattern. *Some* of the changes in
accidentals in the novel's many revisions, of course, were
made by Hardy, a point proved by the survival of the printer's
copy for the 1912 Wessex Edition, which contains many
pencilled alterations in punctuation, especially deletions of
commas. Revisions of accidentals that have this kind of docu-
mentary support are included in this edition; otherwise the
accidentals are almost entirely those of the manuscript. Because Hardy revised the words of his novel so frequently and
so carefully, this edition accepts on general policy the substantives of the 1912 Wessex Edition (except those that appear
to be non-authorial, such as the variants in the Colonial
Library Edition and a few variants whose context indicates
they had been mis-set by compositors).

SELECT BIBLIOGRAPHY

A GOOD deal of intelligent and useful criticism about Thomas Hardy's fiction has been written, but the scholarship is of equal or even greater value in appreciating and understanding Hardy. The reason for this is that, more than with other great writers (and it is a quality of all great writers), Hardy's demands as well as his appeal for appreciation are made on a peculiarly personal level. An intelligent reader does not need critical guidance to gain the full effect of Hardy—he or she can do nearly as well just by reading the novels. Works of scholarship, on the other hand, provide significant enrichment of the fiction. Most of this material is of recent publication. Of central value are the biographies by Michael Millgate (*Thomas Hardy: A Biography*, Oxford, 1982) and by Robert Gittings (*Young Thomas Hardy*, London, 1975; *The Older Hardy*, London, 1978), which bring modern perspectives and research to bear on many features of Hardy's life which he had ignored or obscured in his own autobiography (published under the name of his second wife Florence), *The Early Life of Thomas Hardy* (London, 1928) and *The Later Years of Thomas Hardy* (London, 1930), combined as *The Life of Thomas Hardy* (London, 1962). A new edition of Hardy's autobiography, restoring passages written by Hardy that had been excised by Florence and her literary advisers, including James Barrie, and removing passages that they had added to supplement the typescript left by Hardy, has been edited by Michael Millgate (*The Life and Work of Thomas Hardy by Thomas Hardy*, London, 1985).

Hardy's non-fictional writing was collected by Harold Orel, *Thomas Hardy's Personal Writings* (London, 1966); his letters, interesting mostly for incidental information about his life and his ideas about writing, have been edited by Richard Little Purdy and Michael Millgate (Oxford, 1978–88). Hardy's notebooks have been edited by Richard H. Taylor (London, 1979), Lennart A. Björk (Gothenburg, Sweden, 1974; and London, 1984), and C. J. P. Beatty (Philadelphia, 1966).

Purdy's classic *Thomas Hardy: A Bibliographical Study* (Oxford, 1954) and Millgate's *Thomas Hardy: His Career as a Novelist* (London, 1971), which contain great amounts of original research, are—like the biographies above—indispensable works on Hardy; and Millgate, in linking critical commentary to information gained in his research, produces the most sensible as well as some of the most sensitive criticism of Hardy available. The relationship between textual details and artistic vision that forms relatively minor portions of Purdy's and Millgate's quite different works is presented with insight and empathy in Simon Gatrell's *Hardy the Creator: A Textual Biography* (Oxford, 1988).

R. B. Cox's *Thomas Hardy: The Critical Heritage* (London, 1970) reprints many of the contemporary reviews of Hardy's novels.

Of recent critical books on Hardy, those with the most interesting perspectives and commentary are: John Bayley, *An Essay on Hardy* (Cambridge, 1978); Penny Boumelha, *Thomas Hardy and Women* (Brighton, 1982); Jean Brooks, *Thomas Hardy: The Poetic Structure* (London, 1971); J. B. Bullen, *The Expressive Eye: Fiction and Perception in the Work of Thomas Hardy* (Oxford, 1986); Marjorie Garson, *Hardy's Fables of Integrity: Woman, Body, Text* (Oxford, 1991); John Goode, *Thomas Hardy: The Offensive Truth* (Oxford, 1988); Ian Gregor, *The Great Web: The Form of Hardy's Major Fiction* (London, 1974); Albert J. Guerard, *Thomas Hardy: The Novels and Stories* (Cambridge, Mass., 1949); J. Hillis Miller, *Thomas Hardy: Distance and Desire* (Cambridge, Mass., 1971); and Peter Widdowson, *Hardy in History: A Study in Literary Sociology* (London, 1989).

The most valuable articles specifically on *The Woodlanders* are George S. Fayen, 'Hardy's *The Woodlanders*: Inwardness and Memory', *Studies in English Literature*, 1 (1961), 81–100; Mary Jacobus, 'Tree and Machine: *The Woodlanders*', in *Critical Approaches to the Fiction of Thomas Hardy*, ed. Dale Kramer (1979), pp. 116–34; and John Bayley, 'A Social Comedy? On Re-reading *The Woodlanders*', in *Thomas Hardy Annual No. 5*, ed. Norman Page (London, 1987), pp. 3–21. Although the focus of Alan Manford's essay on the differences between Hardy's handwriting and Emma's is quite specialized, its

importance to all future Hardy editing projects in addition
to the history of the writing of *The Woodlanders* justifies its
notation here as one of the more significant essays on Hardy
in recent years: 'Emma Hardy's Helping Hand', *Critical Essays
on Thomas Hardy: The Novels*, ed. Dale Kramer (Boston, 1990).

A CHRONOLOGY OF THOMAS HARDY

1840   2 June: Thomas Hardy born, first child of Thomas and Jemima (Hand) Hardy, five and a half months after their marriage. His father was a builder in a small but slowly developing way of business, thus setting the family apart socially from the 'work-folk' whom they clearly resembled in financial circumstances.

1848   Entered the newly opened Stinsford National School.

1849   Sent to Dorchester British School kept by Isaac Last.

1853   Last established an independent 'commercial academy', and Hardy became a pupil there. His education was practical and effective, including Latin, some French, theoretical and applied mathematics, and commercial studies.

1856   11 July: articled to Dorchester architect John Hicks. Soon after this he became friendly with Horace Moule, an important influence on his life.

1860   Summer: Hardy's articles, having been extended for a year, completed. Employed by Hicks as an assistant.

1862   17 April: without a position; travelled to London, but soon employed by Arthur Blomfield as a 'Gothic draughtsman'. November: Elected to the Architectural Association; began to find his feet in London.

1863   Won architectural prizes; began to consider some form of writing as a means of support.

1863–7   Possibly became engaged to Eliza Nicholls.

1865   March: 'How I Built Myself a House' published in *Chambers' Journal*. Began to write poetry.

1866   Hardy's commitment to the Church and his religious belief seem to have declined, though he probably experienced no dramatic loss of faith.

1867   Returned to Dorset. Began his first unpublished novel.

1868   Sent MS of *The Poor Man and the Lady* to four publishers, where it was read by Morley and Meredith, amongst others, but finally rejected.

1869   Worked in Weymouth for the architect Crickmay; began writing *Desperate Remedies*.

1870   In order to take 'a plan and particulars' of the church, Hardy journeyed to St Juliot, near Boscastle in North Cornwall; there he met Emma Lavinia Gifford, who became his wife four years later.

1871   *Desperate Remedies* published after Hardy had advanced £75.

1872   *Under the Greenwood Tree* published; the copyright sold to
        Tinsley for £30. Hardy moved temporarily to London to
        work in the offices of T. Roger Smith. Contracted to pro-
        vide serial for *Tinsley's Magazine* for £200 (to include first
        edition rights). *A Pair of Blue Eyes* began to appear in
        September. Hardy decided to relinquish architecture and
        concentrate on writing. Leslie Stephen requested a serial
        for the *Cornhill Magazine.*

1873   *A Pair of Blue Eyes* published in three volumes; Horace Moule,
        his close adviser and friend, committed suicide in Cambridge.

1874   *Far from the Madding Crowd* begun as a serial in *Cornhill*
        under Leslie Stephen's editorship and published later in
        the year in two volumes. Hardy married Emma Gifford on
        17 September; they honeymooned in Paris and returned
        to live in London.

1875   Cornhill serialized *The Hand of Ethelberta*. The Hardys
        moved from London to Swanage in Dorset.

1876   Further moves to Yeovil and Sturminster Newton, where
        Hardy began writing *The Return of the Native.*

1878   Return to London (Tooting). *The Return of the Native*
        serialized in *Belgravia* and published in three volumes,
        to which Hardy affixed a map of the novel's environment.
        Made researches in the British Museum for the background
        of *The Trumpet-Major.*

1879   With 'The Distracted Young Preacher', began regularly to
        publish short stories.

1880   *Good Words* serialized *The Trumpet-Major*, which was also
        published in three volumes with covers designed by Hardy.
        In October he became seriously ill and believed himself
        close to death; the cause of his illness uncertain, but led
        to five months' total inactivity.

1881   *A Laodicean*, mostly written from his bed, published as a
        serial in *Harper's New Monthly Magazine* (the first in the
        new European edition), and in three volumes. The Hardys
        returned to Dorset, living at Wimborne Minster.

1882   Controversy with Pinero over Hardy's adaptation of *Far from
        the Madding Crowd* and Pinero's use of the same material.
        Hardy's third novel in three years, *Two on a Tower*, serial-
        ized in the *Atlantic Monthly* and issued in three volumes.

1883   The final move of his life—from Wimborne to Dorchester,
        though into temporary accommodation while his own
        house was being built.

1884   Made a Justice of the Peace and began to receive invitations from aristocracy. Began writing *The Mayor of Casterbridge*.

1885   Max Gate, designed by Hardy and built by his brother Henry, completed; on the outskirts of Dorchester, it remained his home for the rest of his life.

1886   *The Mayor of Casterbridge* serialized in the *Graphic* and brought out in two volumes; in the same year *The Woodlanders* began its run in *Macmillan's Magazine*. William Barnes, the Dorset poet and friend of Hardy, died.

1887   *The Woodlanders* issued in three volumes. The Hardys visited France and Italy. Began work on *Tess of the d'Urbervilles*.

1888   Hardy's first collection of short stories, *Wessex Tales*, published in two volumes. Also published the first of three significant essays on the theory of fiction, *The Profitable Reading of Fiction*.

1889   The novel that was to become *Tess* rejected by Tillotson's Fiction Bureau, which had commissioned it; subsequent further rejections fuelled the bitterness behind a second essay, *Candour in English Fiction*, published in January of the following year.

1890   *A Group of Noble Dames* appeared in the *Graphic*.

1891   *Tess of the d'Urbervilles* serialized in the *Graphic* and published in three volumes; *A Group of Noble Dames* brought out in one volume. The third important essay, *The Science of Fiction*, appeared. A Copyright Bill passed through the United States Congress in time for *Tess* to benefit from its provisions, a factor of considerable financial significance in Hardy's career.

1892   Father died 20 July. *The Pursuit of the Well-Beloved* serialized in the *Illustrated London News*.

1893   Met Florence Henniker, subject of the intensest of his romantic attachments to artistic ladies. Wrote *The Spectre of the Real* in collaboration with her. Began writing *Jude the Obscure*.

1894   Third volume of short stories, *Life's Little Ironies*, published in one volume.

1895   First collected edition of Hardy's work begun, published by Osgood, McIlvaine; it included the first edition of *Jude the Obscure*, previously serialized in *Harper's New Monthly Magazine*. Some reviews of *Jude* quite savage, a contributory factor to Hardy's writing no further novels. Hardy dramatized *Tess*.

1896   The first group of major poems with identifiable dates written since the 1860s; they included the three *In Tenebris* poems and *Wessex Heights*.

1897   *The Well-Beloved*, substantially revised from the 1892 serialization, published as part of the Osgood, McIlvaine edition. Visited Switzerland.

1898   Hardy's first collection of verse published, *Wessex Poems*; comprising mainly poems written in the 1860s and 1890s, and illustrated by himself.

1899   Boer War began, to which Hardy responded in verse. The gradual physical separation between Hardy and Emma intensified, following the mental separation that set in after the publication of *Jude the Obscure*.

1901   *Poems of the Past and the Present* published.

1902   Changed publishers for the last time, to Macmillan.

1904   First part of *The Dynasts* appeared. 3 April: Hardy's mother died, leaving a tremendous gap in his life.

1905   Met Florence Dugdale. Received LL D from Aberdeen University.

1906   Part Two of *The Dynasts* published.

1908   *The Dynasts* completed with the publication of the third part; it embodied Hardy's most complete statement of his philosophical outlook. Also published his *Select Poems of William Barnes*, undertaken as a memorial to his great predecessor. The first Dorchester dramatization of a Hardy novel, *The Trumpet Major*. Meredith and Swinburne died, leaving Hardy as the greatest living English writer.

1909   Relationship with Florence Dugdale deepened. *Time's Laughingstocks*, Hardy's third volume of poems, published.

1910   Awarded the Order of Merit, having previously refused a knighthood. Received the freedom of Dorchester.

1912   Second collected edition of Hardy's works begun, the Wessex Edition. Received the gold medal of the Royal Society of Literature. 27 November: Emma Hardy died; as a direct result Hardy began writing the poems of 1912–13.

1913   Visited Cornwall in search of his and Emma's youth. Awarded Litt.D. at Cambridge and became an Honorary Fellow of Magdalene College—a partial fulfilment of an early aspiration. His final collection of short stories published, *A Changed Man*.

1914   10 February: married Florence Dugdale. *Satires of Circumstance* published. First World War began; Hardy's attitude to the future of humanity coloured by it in a profound way.

1915   At the age of 75 Hardy began to become reclusive. Frank George, his chosen heir, killed at Gallipoli. Hardy's sister Mary died 24 November.

1916   *Selected Poems of Thomas Hardy* published.

1917   Hardy's fifth collection of verse published, *Moments of Vision*. He and Florence began work on what was eventually to become *The Life of Thomas Hardy*.

1919–20   The de luxe edition of Hardy's work issued, the Mellstock Edition.

1922   *Late Lyrics and Earlier*, with its important Preface, published.

1923   Florence Henniker died. The Prince of Wales visited Max Gate. Friendship with T. E. Lawrence developed. *The Queen of Cornwall* published.

1924   Hardy's adaptation of *Tess* acted in Dorchester with the last of his romantic attachments, Gertrude Bugler, in the title role.

1925   *Tess* acted in London, but not by Miss Bugler. *Human Shows Far Phantasies Songs and Trifles*, Hardy's seventh volume of verse, puablised.

1928   11 January: Hardy died. His final book of poems, *Winter Words*, published posthumously.

The Woodlanders

'Not boskiest bow'r,
When hearts are ill affin'd,
Hath tree of pow'r
To shelter from the wind!'

PREFACE

In the present novel, as in one or two others of this series which involve the question of matrimonial divergence, the immortal puzzle—given the man and woman, how to find a basis for their sexual relation—is left where it stood; and it is tacitly assumed for the purposes of the story that no doubt of the depravity of the erratic heart who feels some second person to be better suited to his or her tastes than the one with whom he has contracted to live, enters the head of reader or writer for a moment. From the point of view of marriage as a distinct covenant or undertaking, decided on by two people fully cognizant of all its possible issues, and competent to carry them through, this assumption is, of course, logical. Yet no thinking person supposes that, on the broader ground of how to afford the greatest happiness to the units of human society during their brief transit through this sorry world, there is no more to be said on this covenant; and it is certainly not supposed by the writer of these pages. But, as Gibbon blandly remarks on the evidence for and against Christian miracles, "the duty of an historian does not call upon him to interpose his private judgment in this nice and important controversy."

The stretch of country visible from the heights adjoining the nook herein described, under the name of Little Hintock, cannot be regarded as inferior to any inland scenery of the sort in the west of England, or perhaps anywhere in the kingdom. It is singular to find that a world-wide repute in some cases, and an absolute famelessness in others, attach to spots of equal beauty and equal accessibility. The neighbourhood of High-Stoy (I give, as elsewhere, the real names to natural features), Bubb-Down Hill, and the glades westward to Montacute; of Bulbarrow, Hambledon Hill, and the slopes eastward to Shaston, Windy Green, and Stour Head, teems with landscapes which, by a mere accident of iteration, might have been numbered among the scenic celebrities of the English shires.

September 1895.

I have been honoured by so many inquiries for the true name and exact locality of the hamlet "Little Hintock," in which the greater part of the action of this story goes on, that I may as well confess here once for all that I do not know myself where that hamlet is more precisely than as explained above and in the pages of the narrative. To oblige readers I once spent several hours on a bicycle with a friend in a serious attempt to discover the real spot; but the search ended in failure; though tourists assure me positively that they have found it without trouble, and that it answers in every particular to the description given in this volume. At all events, as stated elsewhere, the commanding heights called "High Stoy" and "Bubb-Down Hill" overlook the landscape in which it is supposed to be hid.

In respect of the occupations of the characters, the adoption of iron utensils and implements in agriculture, and the discontinuance of thatched roofs for cottages, have almost extinguished the handicrafts classed formerly as "copsework," and the type of men who engaged in them.

"The Woodlanders" was first published complete, in three volumes, in the March of 1887.

T. H.

April 1912.

THE rambler who for old association's sake should trace the forsaken coach-road running almost in a meridional line from Bristol to the south shore of England, would find himself during the latter half of his journey, in the vicinity of some extensive woodlands, interspersed with apple-orchards. Here the trees, timber or fruit-bearing as the case may be, make the wayside hedges ragged by their drip and shade; their lower limbs stretching over the road with easeful horizontality, as though reclining on the insubstantial air. At one place, on the skirts of Blackmoor Vale, where the bold brow of High-Stoy Hill is seen two or three miles ahead, the leaves lie so thick in autumn as to completely bury the track. The spot is lonely, and when the days are darkening the many gay chari-oteers now perished who have rolled along the way, the blis-tered soles that have trodden it, and the tears that have wetted it, return upon the mind of the loiterer.

The physiognomy of a deserted highway expresses solitude to a degree that is not reached by mere dales or downs, and bespeaks a tomb-like stillness more emphatic than that of glades and pools. The contrast of what is with what might be, probably accounts for this. To step, for instance, at the place under notice, from the edge of the plantation into the ad-joining thoroughfare, and pause amid its emptiness for a moment, was to exchange by the act of a single stride the simple absence of human companionship for an incubus of the forlorn.

At this spot, on the louring evening of a bygone winter's day, there stood a man who had thus indirectly entered upon the scene from a stile hard by, and was temporarily influ-enced by some such feeling of being suddenly more alone than before he had emerged upon the highway.

It could be seen by a glance at his rather finical style of dress that he did not belong to the country proper; and from his air, after a while, that though there might be a sombre beauty in the scenery, music in the breeze, and a

wan procession of coaching ghosts in the sentiment of this
old turnpike-road, he was mainly puzzled about the way.

He looked north, and south, and mechanically prodded
the ground with his cane.

At first not a soul appeared who could enlighten him as he
desired, or seemed likely to appear that night. But presently
a slight noise of labouring wheels, and the steady dig of a
horse's shoe-tips, became audible; and there loomed in the
notch of sky and plantation a carrier's van drawn by a single
horse.

The vehicle was half full of passengers, mostly women. He
held up his stick at its approach, and the woman who was
driving drew rein.

"I've been trying to find a short way to Little Hintock this
last half hour, Mrs. Dollery," he said. "But though I've been
to Great Hintock and Hintock House half-a-dozen times, on
business with the dashing lady there, I am at fault about the
small village. You can help me I dare say."

She assured him that she could—that as she went to Abbot's Cernel her van passed near it—that it was only up the
lane branching out of the road she followed. "Though,"
continued Mrs. Dollery, "'tis such a little small place that, as
a town gentleman, you'd need have a candle-and-lantern to
find it if ye don't know where 'tis. Bedad, I wouldn't live
there if they'd pay me to. Now at Abbot's Cernel you do see
the world a bit."

He mounted and sat beside her, with his feet outwards,
where they were ever and anon brushed over by the horse's
tail.

This van was rather a movable attachment of the roadway
than an extraneous object, to those who knew it well. The
old horse, whose hair was of the roughness and colour of
heather, whose leg-joints, shoulders, and hoofs were distorted
by harness and drudgery from colthood—though if all had
their rights he ought, symmetrical in outline, to have been
picking the herbage of some Eastern plain instead of tug-
ging here—had trodden this road almost daily for twenty
years. Even his subjection was not made congruous throughout, for the harness being too short his tail was not drawn

through the crupper, and the breeching slipped awkwardly to one side. He knew every subtle incline of the ten miles of ground between Abbot's Cernel and Sherton—the market-town to which he journeyed—as accurately as any surveyor could have learnt it by a Dumpy level.

The vehicle had a square black tilt which nodded with the motion of the wheels, and at a point in it over the driver's head was a hook to which the reins were hitched at times, forming a catenary curve from the horse's shoulders. Somewhere about the axles was a loose chain, whose only known function was to clink as it went. Mrs. Dollery, having to hop up and down many times in the service of her passengers, wore, especially in windy weather, short leggings under her gown for modesty's sake, and instead of a bonnet a felt hat tied down with a handkerchief, to guard against an ear-ache to which she was frequently subject. In the rear of the van was a glass window, which she cleaned with her pocket-handkerchief every market-day before starting. Looking at the van from the back the spectator could thus see, through its interior, a square piece of the same sky and landscape that he saw without, but intruded on by the profiles of the seated passengers; who, as they rumbled onward, their lips moving and heads nodding in animated private converse, remained in cheerful unconsciousness that their mannerisms and facial peculiarities were sharply defined to the public eye.

This hour of coming home from market was the happy one, if not the happiest, of the week for them. Snugly ensconced under the tilt they could forget the sorrows of the world without, and survey life, and discuss the incidents of the day with placid smiles.

The passengers in the back part formed a group to themselves, and while the new-comer spoke to the proprietress they indulged in a confidential chat about him, which the noise of the van rendered inaudible to himself and Mrs. Dollery sitting forward.

"'Tis Barber Percomb—he that's got the waxen woman in his window," said one. "What business can bring him out here at this time; and not a journeyman hair-cutter, but a master-barber that's left off his pole because 'tis not genteel?"

The barber, though he had nodded and spoken genially, seemed indisposed to gratify the curiosity that he had aroused; and the unrestrained flow of ideas which had animated the inside of the van before his arrival was checked thenceforward.

Thus they rode on, and High-Stoy Hill grew larger ahead. At length could be discerned in the dusk about half a mile to one side, gardens and orchards sunk in a concave, and as it were snipped out of the woodland. From this self-contained place rose in stealthy silence tall stems of smoke, which the eye of imagination could trace downward to their root on quiet hearthstones festooned overhead with hams and flitches. It was one of those sequestered spots outside the gates of the world where may usually be found more meditation than action, and more listlessness than meditation: where reasoning proceeds on narrow premises, and results in inferences wildly imaginative; yet where, from time to time, dramas of a grandeur and unity truly Sophoclean are enacted in the real, by virtue of the concentrated passions and closely knit interdependence of the lives therein.

This place was the Little Hintock of the master-barber's search.

The coming night gradually obscured the smoke of the chimneys, but the position of the wood-environed community could still be distinguished by a few faint lights, winking more or less ineffectually through the leafless boughs and the undiscernible songsters they bore, in the form of balls of feathers, at roost among them.

At the corner of the lane which branched to the hamlet the barber alighted, Mrs. Dollery's van going onward to the larger place, whose superiority to the despised smaller one as an exemplar of the world's movements was not particularly apparent in its means of approach.

"A very clever and learned young Doctor lives in the place you be going to—not because there's anybody for'n to cure there, but because they say he is in league with the Devil."

The observation was flung at the barber by one of the women at parting, as a last attempt to get at his errand that way.

But he made no reply and without further pause plunged

towards the umbrageous nook, and paced cautiously over the dead leaves which nearly buried the road or street of the hamlet. As very few people except themselves passed this way after dark a majority of the denizens of Little Hintock deemed window-curtains unnecessary; and on this account their visitor made it his business to stop opposite the casements of each cottage that he came to, with a demeanour which showed that he was endeavouring to conjecture, from the persons and things he observed within, the whereabouts of somebody or other who resided here.

Only the smaller dwellings interested him: one or two houses whose size, antiquity and rambling appurtenances signified that notwithstanding their remoteness they must formerly have been, if they were not still, inhabited by people of a certain social standing, being neglected by him entirely. Smells of pomace, and the hiss of fermenting cider, which reached him from the back-quarters of other tenements, revealed the recent occupation of some of the inhabitants, and joined with the scent of decay from the perishing leaves underfoot.

Half a dozen dwellings were passed without result. The next, which stood opposite a tall tree, was in an exceptional state of radiance, the flickering brightness from the inside shining up the chimney and making a luminous mist of the emerging smoke. The interior, as seen through the window, caused him to draw up with a terminative air and watch. The house was rather large for a cottage and the door, which opened immediately into the living-room, stood ajar, so that a riband of light fell through the opening into the dark atmosphere without. Every now and then a moth, decrepit from the late season, would flit for a moment across the outcoming rays and disappear again into the night.

II

IN the room from which this cheerful blaze proceeded he beheld a girl seated on a willow chair, and busily working by the light of the fire, which was ample, and of wood. With a bill-hook in one hand, and a leather glove much too large for her on the other, she was making spars—such as are used by thatchers—with great rapidity. She wore a leather apron for this purpose, which was also much too large for her figure. On her left hand lay a bundle of the straight smooth hazel rods called spar-gads—the raw material of her manufacture: on her right a heap of chips and ends—the refuse—with which the fire was maintained: in front a pile of the finished articles. To produce them she took up each gad, looked critically at it from end to end, cut it to length, split it into four, and sharpened each of the quarters with dexterous blows which brought it to a triangular point precisely resembling that of a bayonet.

Beside her, in case she might require more light, a brass candlestick stood on a little round table curiously formed of an old coffin-stool, with a deal top nailed on, the white surface of the latter contrasting oddly with the black carved oak of the substructure. The social position of the household in the past was almost as definitively shown by the presence of this article as that of an esquire or nobleman by his old helmets and shields. It had been customary for every well-to-do villager, whose tenure was by copy of court-roll, or in any way more permanent than that of the mere cotter, to keep a pair of these stools for the use of his own dead; but changes had led to the discontinuance of the custom, and the stools were frequently made use of in the manner described.

The young woman laid down the bill-hook for a moment, and examined the palm of her right hand, which unlike the other was ungloved, and showed little hardness or roughness about it. The palm was red and blistering, as if her present occupation were as yet too recent to have subdued it to what it worked in. As with so many right hands born to manual labour, there was nothing in its fundamental shape to bear out the physiological conventionalism that gradations of birth show themselves primarily in the form of this member. Nothing but a cast of the die of Destiny had decided that the girl should handle the tool; and the fingers which clasped the heavy ash haft might have skilfully guided the pencil or swept the string, had they only been set to do it in good time.

Her face had the usual fulness of expression which is developed by a life of solitude. Where the eyes of a multitude continuously beat like waves upon a countenance they seem to wear away its mobile power; but in the still water of privacy every feeling and sentiment unfolds in visible luxuriance, to be interpreted as readily as a printed word by an intruder. In years she was no more than nineteen or twenty; but the necessity of taking thought at a too early period of life had forced the provisional curves of her childhood's face to a premature finality. Thus she had but little pretension to beauty; save in one prominent particular, her hair.

Its abundance made it almost unmanageable; its colour was, roughly speaking, and as seen here by fire-light, brown; but careful notice, or an observation by day, would have revealed that its true shade was a rare and beautiful approximation to chestnut.

On this one bright gift of Time to the particular victim of his now before us the newcomer's eyes were fixed; meanwhile the fingers of his right hand mechanically played over something sticking up from his waistcoat pocket—the bows of a pair of scissors—whose polish made them feebly responsive to the light from within the house. In her present beholder's mind the scene formed by the girlish spar-maker composed itself into an impression-picture of extremest type, wherein the girl's hair alone, as the focus of observation, was depicted with intensity and distinctness, while her face, shoulders, hands, and figure in general were a blurred mass of unimportant detail lost in haze and obscurity.

He hesitated no longer, but tapped at the door and entered. The young woman turned at the crunch of his boots on the sanded floor, and exclaiming, "Oh Mr. Percomb—how you frightened me!" quite lost her colour for a moment.

He replied, "You should shut your door—then you'd hear folk open it."

"I can't," she said. "The chimney smokes so.—Mr. Percomb, you look as unnatural away from your wigs as a canary in a thorn hedge. Surely you have not come out here on my account—for——"

"Yes—to have your answer about this." He touched her

hair with his cane and she winced. . . . . "Do you agree?" he
continued. "It is necessary that I should know at once, as the
lady is soon going away, and it takes time to make up."

"Don't press me—it worries me. I was in hopes you had
thought no more of it. I can*not* part with it: so there!"

"Now look here Marty," said the other, sitting down on the
coffin-stool table. "How much do you get for making these
spars?"

"Hush—father's upstairs awake; and he don't know that I
am doing his work."

"Well, now tell me," said the man more softly. "How much
do you get?"

"Eighteen pence a thousand," she said reluctantly.

"Who are you making them for?"

"Mr. Melbury the timber-dealer, just below here."

"And how many can you make in a day?"

"In a day, and half the night, three bundles—that's a thousand and a half."

"Two-and-three-pence." Her visitor paused. "Well, look
here," he continued with the remains of a computation in
his tone, which reckoning had been to fix the probable sum
of money necessary to outweigh her present resources and
her woman's love of comeliness. "Here's a sovereign—a gold
sovereign almost new." He held it out between his finger and
thumb. "That's as much as you'd earn in a week and a half
at that rough man's-work; and it's yours for just letting me
snip off what you've got too much of."

The girl's bosom moved a very little. "Why can't the lady
send to some other girl who don't value her hair—not to
me!" she exclaimed.

"Why, simpleton, because yours is the exact shade of her
own, and 'tis a shade you can't match by dyeing. But you are
not going to refuse me now I've come all the way from
Sherton on purpose?"

"I say I won't sell it—to you or anybody."

"Now listen;" and he drew up a little closer beside her. "The
lady is very rich, and won't be particular to a few shillings; so
I will advance to this, on my own responsibility: I'll make the
one sovereign two, rather than go back empty-handed."

"No, no, no!" she cried beginning to be much agitated. "You are tempting me. You go on like the Devil to Doctor Faustus in the penny book. But I don't want your money, and won't agree. Why did you come? I said when you got me into your shop and urged me so much that I didn't mean to sell my hair!"

"Marty, now hearken. The lady that wants it wants it badly. And between you and me you'd better let her have it. 'Twill be bad for you if you don't."

"Bad for me? Who is she then?"

The wig-maker held his tongue, and the girl repeated the question.

"I am not at liberty to tell you. And as she is going abroad soon it makes no difference who she is at all."

"She wants it to go abroad wi'?"

He assented by a nod. The girl regarded him reflectively. "Now, Mr. Percomb," she said, "I know who 'tis—'Tis She at the House—Mrs. Charmond!"

"That's my secret. However, if you agree to let me have it, I'll tell you in confidence."

"I'll certainly not let you have it unless you tell me the truth. It is Mrs. Charmond?"

The man dropped his voice. "Well—it is. You sat in front of her in church the other day; and she noticed how exactly your hair matches her own. Ever since then she's been hankering for it, to help out hers, and at last decided to get it. As she won't wear it till she goes off abroad she knows nobody will recognise the change. I'm commissioned to get it for her, and then it is to be made up. I shouldn't have vamped all these miles for any less important employer. Now, mind—'tis as much as my business with her is worth if it should be known that I've let out her name; but honour between us two, Marty; and you'll say nothing that would injure me?"

"I don't wish to tell upon her," said Marty coolly. "But my hair is my own, and I'm going to keep it."

"Now that's not fair, after what I've told you," said the nettled emissary. "You see, Marty, as you are in the same parish, and in one of this lady's cottages, and your father is ill, and wouldn't like to turn out, it would be as well to oblige

her. I say that as a friend.—But I won't press you to make up
your mind to-night. You'll be coming to market to-morrow I
dare say; and you can call then. If you think it over, you'll be
inclined to bring what I want, I know."

"I've nothing more to say," she answered.

Her companion saw from her manner that it was useless
to urge her further by speech. "As you are a trusty young
woman," he said, "I'll put these sovereigns up here for ornament, that you may see how handsome they are. Bring the
article to-morrow; or return the sovereigns." He stuck them
edgewise into the frame of a small mantel looking-glass. "I
hope you'll bring it; for your sake and mine. I should have
thought she could have suited herself elsewhere; but as it's
her fancy it must be indulged if possible. If you cut it off
yourself, mind how you do it so as to keep all the locks one
way." He showed her how this was to be done.

"But I shan't," she replied with laconic indifference. "I
value my looks too much to spoil 'em. She wants my curls to
get another lover with; though if stories are true she's broke
the heart of many a noble gentleman already."

"Lord—it's wonderful how you guess things, Marty," said
the barber. "I've had it from those that know that there
certainly is some foreign gentleman in her eye. However,
mind what I ask."

"She's not going to get him through me."

Percomb had retired as far as the door; he came back,
planted his cane on the coffin-stool, and looked her in the
face. "Marty South," he said with deliberate emphasis, "*you've
got a lover yourself*; and that's why you won't let it go!"

She reddened so intensely as to pass the mild blush that
suffices to heighten beauty; she put the yellow leather glove
on one hand, took up the hook with the other, and sat down
doggedly to her work without turning her face to him again.
He regarded her head for a moment, went to the door, and
with one look back at her departed on his way homeward.

Marty pursued her occupation for a few minutes, then
suddenly laying down the bill-hook she jumped up, and went
to the back of the room; where she opened a door which
disclosed a staircase so whitely scrubbed that the grain of the

wood was well-nigh sodden away by cleansing. At the top she gently approached a bedroom, and without entering said, "Father, do you want anything?"

A weak voice inside answered in the negative; adding, "I should be all right by to-morrow if it were not for the tree!"

"The tree again—always the tree! O father, don't worry so about that. You know it can do you no harm."

"Who have ye had talking to 'ee downstairs?"

"A Sherton man called—nothing to trouble about," she said soothingly. "Father," she went on, "can Mrs. Charmond turn us out of our house if she's minded to?"

"Turn us out? No. Nobody can turn us out till my poor soul is turned out of my body. 'Tis lifehold—like Giles Winterborne's. But when my life drops 'twill be hers—not till then." His words on this subject so far had been rational and firm enough. But now he lapsed into his moaning strain: "And the tree will do it—that tree will soon be the death of me."

"Nonsense—you know better. How can it be?" She refrained from further speech, and descended to the ground floor again.

"Thank Heaven then," she said to herself. "What belongs to me I keep."

III

THE lights in the village went out, house after house, till there only remained two in the darkness. One of these came from a residence on the hill-side—that of the young medical gentleman in league with the Devil, of whom there is something to be said later on; the other shone from the window of Marty South. Precisely the same extinguished effect was produced here, however, by her rising when the clock struck ten, and hanging up a thick cloth curtain. The door it was necessary to keep ajar in hers as in most cottages, because of the smoke; but she obviated the effect of the riband of light through the chink by hanging a cloth over that also. She was one of these people who, if they have to work harder than

their neighbours, prefer to keep the necessity a secret as far
as possible; and but for the slight sounds of wood-splintering
which came from within no wayfarer would have perceived
that here the cottager did not sleep as elsewhere.

Eleven, twelve, one o'clock struck; the heap of spars grew
higher, and the pile of chips and ends more bulky. Even the
light on the hill had now been extinguished; but still she
worked on. When the temperature of the night without had
fallen so low as to make her chilly she opened a large blue
umbrella to ward off the draught from the door. The two
sovereigns confronted her from the looking-glass in such a
manner as to suggest a pair of jaundiced eyes on the watch
for an opportunity. Whenever she sighed for weariness she
lifted her gaze towards them, but withdrew it quickly, stroking her tresses for a moment as if to convince herself that
they were still secure. When the clock struck three she arose,
and tied up the spars she had last made in a bundle resembling those that lay against the wall.

She wrapped round her a long red woollen cravat and
opened the door. The night in all its fulness met her flatly
on the threshold, like the very brink of an absolute void, or
the ante-mundane Ginnung-Gap believed in by her Teuton
forefathers; for her eyes were fresh from the blaze, and here
there was no street lamp or lantern to form a kindly transition between the inner glare and the outer dark. A lingering
wind brought to her ear the creaking sound of two over-
crowded branches in the neighbouring wood which were
rubbing each other into wounds, and other vocalized sorrows of the trees, together with the screech of owls, and the
fluttering tumble of some awkward wood-pigeon ill-balanced
on its roosting-bough.

But the pupils of her young eyes soon expanded, and she
could see well enough for her purpose. Taking a bundle
of spars under each arm, and guided by the serrated line of
tree-tops against the sky, she went some hundred yards or
more down the lane till she reached a long open shed, car-
peted around with the dead leaves that lay about everywhere.
Night, that strange personality, which within walls brings
ominous introspectiveness and self-distrust, but under the

open sky banishes such subjective anxieties as too trivial for thought, gave to Marty South a less perturbed and brisker manner now. She laid the spars on the ground within the shed, and returned for more; going to and fro till her whole manufactured stock was deposited here.

This erection was the waggon-house of the chief man of business hereabout, Mr. George Melbury, the timber, bark, and copse-ware merchant for whom Marty's father did work of this sort by the piece. It formed one of the many rambling outhouses which surrounded his dwelling, an equally irregular block of building whose immense chimneys could just be discerned even now. The four huge waggons under the shed were built on those ancient lines whose proportions have been ousted by modern patterns, their shapes bulging and curving at the base and ends like Trafalgar line-of-battle ships, with which venerable hulks, indeed, these vehicles evidenced a constructive spirit curiously in harmony. One was laden with sheep-cribs, another with hurdles, another with ash poles, and the fourth, at the foot of which she had placed her thatching-spars, was half full of similar bundles.

She was pausing a moment with that easeful sense of accomplishment which follows work done that has been a hard struggle in the doing, when she heard a woman's voice on the other side of the hedge say anxiously, "George?" In a moment the name was repeated, with "Do come indoors! What are you doing there?"

The cart-house adjoined the garden, and before Marty had moved she saw enter the latter from the timber-merchant's back-door an elderly woman sheltering a candle with her hand, the light from which cast a moving thorn-pattern of shade on Marty's face. Its rays soon fell upon a man whose clothes were carelessly thrown on, standing in advance of the speaker. He was a thin slightly stooping figure, with a small nervous mouth, and a face cleanly shaven; and he walked along the path with his eyes bent on the ground. In the pair Marty South recognised her employer Melbury and his wife. She was the second Mrs. Melbury, the first having died shortly after the birth of the timber-merchant's only child.

" 'Tis no use to stay in bed," he said as soon as she came

up to where he was pacing restlessly about. "I can't sleep—
I keep thinking of things."

"What things?"

He did not answer.

"The lady at the Great House?"

"No."

"The turnpike bonds?"

"No. Though I wish I hadn't got 'em."

"The ghosts of the Two Brothers?"

He shook his head.

"Not about Grace again?"

"Yes. 'Tis she."

(Grace was the speaker's only daughter.)

"Why worry about her always?"

"First, I cannot think why she doesn't answer my letter.
She must be ill."

"No, no. Things only appear so gloomy in the night-time."

"Second, I have not invested any money specially for her,
to put her out of the reach of poverty if my affairs fail."

"They are safe. Besides, she is sure to marry well."

"You are wrong. That's my third trouble. I have, as I have
hinted to you a dozen times, that plan in my head about her,
and according to my plan she won't marry well."

"Why won't it be marrying well?" said his wife.

"Because it is a plan for her to marry that particular person Giles Winterborne, and he is poor."

"Well—it is all right. Love will make up for his want of
money. He adores the very ground she walks on."

(Marty South started; and could not tear herself away.)

"Yes," said the timber-merchant; "I know that well. There
will be no lack of that with him. But since I have educated
her so well, and so long, and so far above the level of the
daughters hereabout, it is *wasting her* to give her to a man of
no higher standing than he."

"Then why do it?" she asked.

"Why, as you must surely see, it is in obedience to that
solemn resolve I made. . . . I made it because I did his father
a terrible wrong; and it has been a weight on my conscience

ever since that time till this scheme of making amends occurred to me through seeing that Giles liked her."

"Wronged his father?" asked Mrs. Melbury.

"Yes—grievously wronged him," said her husband. "I have
spoken of it to you."

"Well don't think of it to-night," she urged. "Come indoors."

"No, no, the air cools my head—I shall not stay long." He
was silent awhile: then he reminded her that his first wife, his
daughter's mother, was first the promised of Winterborne's
father, who loved her tenderly; till he, the speaker, won her
away from him by a trick, because he wanted to marry her
himself. He went on to say that the other man's happiness
was ruined by it; that though he married Winterborne's
mother it was but a half-hearted business with him. Thus
much Marty had heard before. Melbury added that he was
afterwards very miserable at what he had done; but that as
time went on, and the children grew up, and seemed to be
attached to each-other, he determined to do all he could to
right the wrong by letting his daughter marry the lad; not
only that, but to give her the best education he could afford,
so as to make the gift as valuable a one as it lay in his power
to bestow. "I still mean to do it," said Melbury.

"Then do," said she.

"But all these things trouble me," said he; "for I feel I am
sacrificing her for my own sin; and I think of her, and often
come down here, to look at this. I have come to-night to do
so once more."

He took the candle from her hand, held it to the ground,
and removed a tile which lay in the garden-path. " 'Tis the
track of her shoe that she made when she ran down here,
the day before she went away all those months ago. I covered
it up when she was gone; and when I come here to look at
it I ask myself again, why should she be sacrificed to a poor
man?"

"It is not altogether a sacrifice," said the woman. "He is in
love with her, and he's honest and upright. If she encour-
ages him what can you wish for more?"

"I wish for nothing definite. But there's a lot of things possible for her. Why, Mrs. Charmond is wanting some refined young lady, I hear, to go abroad with her—as companion or something of the kind. She'd jump at Grace."

"That's all uncertain. Better stick to what's sure."

"True, true," said Melbury; "and I hope it will be for the best. Yes—let me get 'em married up as soon as I can, so as to have it over and done with. . . . ." He continued looking at the imprint while he added, "Suppose she should be dying, and never make a track on this path any more?"

"She'll write soon—depend upon't. Come, 'tis wrong to stay here and brood so."

He admitted it; but said he could not help it. "Whether she write or no I shall fetch her in a few days." And thus speaking he covered the shoe-track, and preceded his wife indoors.

Melbury perhaps was an unlucky man in having the sentiment which could make him wander out in the night to regard the imprint of a daughter's footstep. Nature does not carry on her government with a view to such feelings, and when advancing years render the opened hearts of those that possess them less dexterous than formerly in shutting against the blast, they must inevitably, like Little Celandines, suffer "buffeting at will by rain and storm."

But her own existence, and not Mr. Melbury's, was the centre of Marty's consciousness, and it was in relation to this that the matter struck her as she slowly withdrew.

"That, then, is the secret of it all," she said. "I had half thought so. And Giles Winterborne is not for me!"

She returned to her cottage. The sovereigns were staring at her from the looking-glass as she had left them. With a preoccupied countenance, and with tears in her eyes, she got a pair of scissors and began mercilessly cutting off the long locks of her hair, arranging and tying them with their points all one way as the barber had directed. Upon the pale scrubbed deal of the coffin-stool-table they stretched like waving and ropy weeds over the washed white bed of a stream.

She would not turn again to the little looking-glass, out of humanity to herself, knowing what a deflowered visage would look back at her and almost break her heart; she dreaded it as much as did her own ancestral goddess the reflection in the pool after the rape of her locks by Loke the Malicious. She steadily stuck to business, wrapped the hair in a parcel, and sealed it up; after which she raked out the fire and went to bed, having first set up an alarum made of a candle and piece of thread with a stone attached.

But such a reminder was unnecessary to-night. Having tossed about till five o'clock Marty heard the sparrows walking down their long holes in the thatch above her sloping ceiling to their exits at the eaves; whereupon she also arose and descended to the ground floor.

It was still dark, but she began moving about the house in those automatic initiatory acts and touches which represent among housewives the installation of another day. While thus engaged she heard the rumbling of Mr. Melbury's waggons and knew that there, too, the day's toil had begun.

An armful of gads thrown on the still-hot embers caused them to blaze up cheerfully, and bring her diminished headgear into sudden prominence as a shadow. At this a step approached the door.

"Are folk astir here yet?" enquired a voice she knew well.

"Yes, Mr. Winterborne," said Marty, throwing on a tilt bonnet, which completely hid the recent ravages of the scissors. "Come in."

The door was flung back, and there stepped in upon the mat a man, not particularly young for a lover, nor particularly mature for a person of affairs—each of which functions he in some degree discharged. There was reserve in his glance, and restraint upon his mouth. He carried a perforated lantern which hung upon a swivel and wheeling as it dangled marked grotesque shapes upon the shadier part of the walls and ceiling.

He said that he had looked in on his way down to tell her that they did not expect her father to make up his contract if he was not well. Mr. Melbury would give him another week, and they would go their journey with a short load that day.

"They are done," said Marty. "And lying in the cart-house."

"Done?" he repeated. "Your father has not been too ill to work after all, then?"

She made some evasive reply. "I'll show you where they be, if you are going down," she added.

They went out and walked together, the pattern of the air-holes in the top of the lantern rising now to the mist overhead, where they appeared of giant size, as if reaching the tent-shaped sky. They had no remarks to make to each other, and they uttered none. Hardly anything could be more isolated, or more self-contained, than the lives of these two walking here in the lonely hour before day, when grey shades, material and mental, are so very grey. And yet their lonely courses formed no detached design at all, but were part of the pattern in the great web of human doings then weaving in both hemispheres, from the White Sea to Cape Horn.

The shed was reached, and she pointed out the spars. Winterborne regarded them silently, then looked at her.

"Now Marty—I believe . . . . ." he said, and shook his head.

"What?"

"That you've done the work yourself."

"Don't you tell anybody, will you, Mr. Winterborne," she pleaded by way of answer. "Because I am afraid Mr. Melbury may refuse the work if he knows it is mine."

"But how could you learn to do it? 'Tis a trade."

"Trade!" said she. "I'd be bound to learn it in two hours."

"Oh no you wouldn't, Miss Marty." Winterborne held down his lantern, and examined the cleanly split hazels as they lay. "Marty," he said with dry admiration, "your father with his forty years of practice never made a spar better than that. They are too good for the thatching of houses, they are good enough for the furniture. But I won't tell. Let me look at your hands—your poor hands!"

He had a kindly manner of quietly severe tone; and when she seemed reluctant to show her hands he took hold of one and examined it as if it were his own. Her fingers were blistered.

"They'll get harder in time," she said. "For if father continues ill I shall have to go on wi' it. Now I'll help put 'em up in waggon."

Winterborne without speaking set down his lantern, lifted her like a baby as she was about to stoop over the bundles, dumped her down behind him, and began throwing up the bundles himself. "Rather than you should do it I will," he said. "But the men will be here directly. . . . . Why, Marty—whatever has happened to your head. Lord, it has shrunk to nothing—it looks like an apple upon a gate-post."

Her heart swelled, and she could not speak. At length she managed to groan, looking on the ground, "I've made myself ugly—and hateful—that's what I've done!"

"No, no," he answered. "You've only cut your hair—I see now."

"Then why must you needs say that about apples and gate-posts!"

"Let me see?" He moved to lift her bonnet.

But she ran off into the gloom of the sluggish dawn. He did not attempt to follow her. When she reached her father's door she stood on the step and looked back. Mr. Melbury's men had arrived, and were loading up the spars, their foggy lanterns appearing from the distance at which she stood to have wan circles round them, like eyes weary with watching. She observed them for a few seconds as they set about harnessing the horses, and then went indoors.

IV

THERE was now a distinct manifestation of morning in the air, and presently the bleared white visage of a sunless winter day emerged like a dead-born child. The woodlanders everywhere had already bestirred themselves, rising this month of the year at the far less dreary time of absolute darkness. It had been above an hour earlier, before a single bird had untucked his head, that twenty lights were struck in as many bedrooms, twenty pairs of shutters opened, and twenty pairs of eyes stretched to the sky to forecast the weather for the day.

Owls that had been catching mice in the outhouses, rabbits that had been eating the winter-greens in the gardens, and stoats that had been sucking the blood of the rabbits, discerning that their human neighbours were on the move discreetly withdrew from publicity, and were seen and heard no more till nightfall.

The daylight revealed the whole of Mr. Melbury's homestead, of which the waggon sheds had been an outlying erection. It formed three sides of an open quadrangle, and consisted of all sorts of buildings, the largest and central one being the dwelling itself. The fourth side of the quadrangle was the public road.

It was a dwelling-house of respectable, roomy, almost dignified aspect; which, taken with the fact that there were the remains of other such buildings hereabout, indicated that Little Hintock had at some time or other been of greater importance than now. The house was of no marked antiquity; yet of a well-advanced age; older than a stale novelty, but no canonized antique; faded, not hoary; looking at you from the still distinct middle-distance of the early Georgian time, and awakening on that account the instincts of reminiscence more decidedly than the remoter, and far grander memorials which have to speak from the misty reaches of mediævalism. The faces, dress, passions, gratitudes, and revenges of the great-great-grandfathers and grandmothers who had been the first to gaze from those rectangular windows, and had stood under that keystoned doorway, could be divined and measured by homely standards of to-day. It was a house in whose reverberations queer old personal tales were yet audible if properly listened for; and not, as with those of the castle and cloister, silent beyond the possibility of echo.

The garden-front remained much as it had always been and there was a porch and entrance that way. But the principal house-door opened on the square yard or quadrangle towards the road, formerly a regular carriage entrance; though the middle of the area was now made use of for stacking timber, faggots, hurdles, and other products of the wood. It was divided from the lane by a lichen-coated wall, in which hung a pair of gates, flanked by piers out of the perpendicular, with a round white ball on the top of each.

The building on the left of the enclosure was a long-backed

erection now used for spar-making, sawing, crib-framing, and copse-ware manufacture in general. Opposite were the waggon-sheds where Marty had deposited her spars.

Here Winterborne had remained after the girl's abrupt departure, to see that the loads were properly made up. Winterborne was connected with the Melbury family in various ways. In addition to the sentimental relationship which arose from his father having been the first Mrs. Melbury's lover Winterborne's Aunt had married and emigrated with the brother of the timber-merchant many years before—an alliance that was sufficient to place Winterborne, though the poorer, on a footing of social intimacy with the Melburys. As in most villages so secluded as this intermarriages were of Hapsburgian frequency among the inhabitants, and there were hardly two houses in Little Hintock unrelated by some matrimonial tie or other.

For this reason a curious kind of partnership existed between Melbury and the younger man—a partnership based upon an unwritten code, by which each acted in the way he thought fair towards the other, on a give-and-take principle. Melbury, with his timber and copse-ware business, found that the weight of his labour came in winter and spring. Winterborne was in the apple and cider trade, and his requirements in cartage and other work came in the Autumn of each year. Hence horses, waggons, and in some degree men, were handed over to him when the apples began to fall; he in return, lending his assistance to Melbury in the busiest wood-cutting season, as now.

Before he had left the shed a boy came from the house to ask him to remain till Mr. Melbury had seen him. Winterborne thereupon crossed over to the spar-house where some journeymen were already at work, two of them being travelling spar-makers from Stagfoot Lane, who, when the fall of the leaf began, made their appearance regularly, and when winter was over disappeared in silence till the season came again.

Fire-wood was the one thing abundant in Little Hintock; and a blaze of gad-ends made the outhouse gay with its light, which vied with that of the day as yet. In the hollow shades of the roof could be seen dangling and etiolated arms of ivy which had crept through the joints of the tiles and were groping in vain for some support, their leaves being dwarfed and sickly for want of sunlight; others were pushing in with such force at the eaves as to lift from their supports the shelves that were fixed there.

Besides the itinerant journey-workers there were also present John Upjohn, Melbury's regular man; a neighbour engaged in the hollow-turnery trade; Old Timothy Tangs and young Timothy Tangs, top and bottom sawyers at work in Mr. Melbury's pit outside, Farmer Cawtree, who kept the cider-house, and Robert Creedle, an old man who worked for Winterborne, and stood warming his hands; these latter having been enticed in by the ruddy blaze though they had no particular business there. None of them calls for any remark, except perhaps Creedle. To have completely described him it would have been necessary to write a military memoir, for he wore under his smockfrock a cast-off soldier's jacket that had seen hot service, its collar showing just above the flap of the frock; also a hunting memoir, to include the top-boots that he had picked up by chance; also chronicles of voyaging and ship-wreck, for his pocket-knife had been given him by a weather-beaten sailor. But Creedle carried about with him on his uneventful rounds these silent testimonies of war, sport, and adventure, and thought nothing of their associations or their stories.

Copse-work, as it was called, being an occupation which the secondary intelligence of the hands and arms could carry on without the sovereign attention of the head, allowed the minds of its professors to wander considerably from the objects before them; hence the tales, chronicles, and ramifications of family history which were recounted here were of a very exhaustive kind.

Winterborne, seeing that Melbury had not arrived, stepped back again outside the door; and the conversation interrupted by his momentary presence flowed anew, reaching his ears as an accompaniment to the regular dripping of the fog from the plantation boughs around.

The topic at present handled was a highly popular and

frequent one—the personal character of Mrs. Charmond, the owner of the surrounding glades and groves.

"My brother-in-law told me, and I have no reason to doubt it," said Creedle, "that she'll sit down to her dinner with a gown hardly higher than her elbows. 'O you wicked woman!' he said to hisself when he first see her, 'you go to the Table o' Sundays, and kneel, as if your knee-jints were greased with very saint's anointment, and tell off your hear-us-good-Lords as pat as a business-man counting money; and yet you can eat your victuals a-stript to such a wanton figure as that!' Whether she's a reformed character by this time I can't say; but I don't care who the man is, that's how she went on when my brother-in-law lived there."

"Did she do it in her husband's time?"

"That I don't know—hardly, I should think, considering his temper. Ah! . . . ." Here Creedle threw grieved remembrance into physical form by resigning his head to obliquity and letting his eyes water. "That man! 'Not if the angels of heaven come down, Creedle,' he said, 'shall you do another day's work for me!' Yes—he would as soon take a winged angel's name in vain as yours or mine!—Well, now I must get these spars home-along, and to-morrow, thank God, I must see about using 'em."

An old woman now entered upon the scene. She was Mr. Melbury's servant, and passed a great part of her time in crossing the yard between the house-door and the spar-shed, whither she had come now for fuel. She had two facial aspects: one of a soft and flexible kind, which she used indoors; the other, with stiff lines and corners, which she assumed when addressing the men outside.

"Ah, Grammer Oliver," said John Upjohn, "it do do my heart good to see a old woman like you so dapper and stirring, when I bear in mind that, after fifty, one year counts as two did afore! But your smoke didn't rise this morning till twenty minutes past seven by my beater; and that's late, Grammer Oliver."

"If you was a full-sized man, John, I might take notice of your scornful meanings. But really a woman couldn't feel

hurt if such smallness were to spit fire and brimstone itself
at her. . . . . Here," she added, holding out a spar-gad to one
of the workmen, from which dangled a long black-pudding;
"here's something for thy breakfast; and if you want tea you
must fetch it from indoors."

"Mr. Melbury is late this morning," said the bottom-sawyer.

"Yes. 'Twas a dark dawn," said Mrs. Oliver. "Even when I
opened the door, so late as I was, you couldn't have told
poor men from gentlemen, or John from a reasonable-sized
object. And I don't think maister's slept at all well to-night.
He's anxious about his daughter; and I know what that is, for
I've cried bucketfuls for my own."

When the old woman had gone Creedle said;—"He'll fret
his gizzard green if he don't soon hear from that maid of
his. Well, learning is better than houses and lands. But to
keep a maid at school till she is taller out of pattens than her
mother was in 'em—'tis tempting Providence."

"It seems no time ago that she was a little playward girl,"
said young Timothy Tangs.

"I can mind her mother," said the hollow-turner. "Alway a
teuny, delicate piece; her touch upon your hand was like the
passing of wind. She was inoculated for the small-pox and
had it beautiful-fine, just about the time that I was out of
my apprenticeship. . . Ay, and a long apprenticeship 'twas. I
served that master of mine six years, and three hundred and
fourteen days." The hollow-turner pronounced the days with
emphasis, as if, considering their number, they were a rather
more remarkable fact than the years.

"Mr. Winterborne's father walked with her at one time,"
said old Timothy Tangs. "But Mr. Melbury won her. She was
a child of a woman, and would cry like rain if so be he
huffed her. Whenever she and her husband came to a puddle
in their walks together he'd take her up like a halfpenny doll,
and put her over without dirting her a speck. And if he keeps
the daughter so long at boarding-school he'll make her as
nesh as her mother was. But here he comes."

Just before this moment Winterborne had seen Melbury
crossing the court from his door. He was carrying an open

letter in his hand, and came straight to Winterborne. His gloom of the preceding night had quite gone.

"I'd no sooner made up my mind, Giles, to go and see why Grace didn't come or write than I get a letter from her.— 'My dear Father,' says she. 'I'm coming home to-morrow (that's to-day), but I didn't think it worth while to write long beforehand.' The little rascal, and didn't she! Now, Giles, as you are going to Sherton market to-day with your appletrees, why not join me and Grace there, and we'll drive home all together?"

He made the proposal with cheerful energy; he was hardly the same man as the man of the small dark hours. Even among the moodiest, the tendency to be cheered is stronger than the tendency to be cast down; and a soul's specific gravity constantly re-asserts itself as less than that of the sea of troubles into which it is thrown.

Winterborne, though not demonstrative, replied to this suggestion with alacrity. There was not much doubt that Marty's grounds for cutting off her hair were substantial enough, if this man's eyes had been a reason for keeping it on. As for the timber-merchant, his invitation had been given solely in pursuance of his scheme for uniting the pair. He had made up his mind to the course as a duty; and was strenuously bent upon following it out.

Accompanied by Winterborne he now turned towards the door of the spar-house, when his footsteps were heard by the men as aforesaid. "Well John, and Robert," he said, nodding, as he entered. "A rimy morning."

"'Tis, sir!" said Creedle energetically, for not having as yet been able to summon force sufficient to go away and begin work he felt the necessity of throwing some into his speech. "I don't care who the man is, 'tis the rimiest morning we've had this fall."

"I heard you wondering why I've kept my daughter so long at boarding-school," resumed Mr. Melbury, looking up from the letter which he was reading anew by the fire, and turning to them with the suddenness that was a trait in him. "Hey?" he asked with affected shrewdness. "But you did, you know.

Well now, though it is my own business more than anybody else's, I'll tell ye. When I was a boy another boy—the pa'son's son along with a lot of others—asked me 'Who dragged Whom round the walls of What?' and I said, 'Sam Barret, who dragged his wife in a wheeled chair round the tower when she went to be churched.' They laughed at me so much that I went home and couldn't sleep for shame; and I cried that night till my pillow was wet: till I thought to myself: 'They may laugh at me for my ignorance; but that was father's fault, and none o' my making, and I must bear it. But they shall never laugh at my children, if I have any: I'll starve first!' Thank God I've been able to keep her at school at the figure of near a hundred a year; and her scholarship is such that she has stayed on as governess for a time. Let 'em laugh now if they can: Mrs. Charmond herself is not better informed than my girl Grace."

There was something between high indifference and humble emotion in his delivery, which made it difficult for them to reply. Winterborne's interest was of a kind which did not show itself in words: listening, he stood by the fire, mechanically stirring the embers with a spar-gad.

"You'll be ready, then, Giles?" Melbury continued, awaking from a reverie. "Well, what was the latest news at Shottsford yesterday, Mr. Cawtree?"

"Oh, well, Shottsford is Shottsford still—you can't victual your carcase there unless you've got money; and you can't buy a cup of genuine there, whether or no.... But as the saying is, Go abroad and you'll hear news of home. It seems that our new neighbour, this young Doctor What's-his-name, is a strange, deep, perusing gentleman; and there's good reason for supposing he has sold his soul to the wicked-one."

"'Od name it all," murmured the timber-merchant, unimpressed by the news but reminded of other things by the subject of it: "I've got to meet a gentleman this very morning; and yet I've planned to go to Sherton Abbas for the maid."

"I won't praise the doctor's wisdom till I hear what sort of bargain he's made," said the top-sawyer.

"'Tis only an old woman's tale," said Cawtree. "But it seems that he wanted certain books on some mysterious black art, and in order that the people hereabout should not know anything about them he ordered 'em direct from London, and not from the Sherton bookseller. The parcel was delivered by mistake at the pa'son's, and as he wasn't at home his wife opened it; and went into hysterics when she read 'em, thinking her husband had turned heathen and 'twould be the ruin of the children. But when he came he knew no more about 'em than she; and found they were this Mr. Fitzpiers's property. So he wrote 'Beware!' outside, and sent 'em on by the sexton."

"He must be a curious young man," mused the hollow-turner.

"He must," said Timothy Tangs.

"Nonsense," said Mr. Melbury. "He's only a gentleman fond of science, and philosophy, and poetry, and, in fact, every kind of knowledge; and being lonely here he passes his time in making such matters his hobby."

"Well," said old Timothy, "'tis a strange thing about doctors that the worse they be the better they be. I mean that if you hear anything of this sort about 'em, ten to one they can cure 'ee as nobody else can."

"True," said Cawtree emphatically. "And for my part I shall take my custom from old Jones and go to this one directly I've anything the matter inside me. That last medicine old Jones gave me had no taste in it at all."

Mr. Melbury, as became a well informed man, did not listen to these recitals, being moreover preoccupied with the business appointment which had come into his head. He walked up and down looking on the floor—his usual custom when undecided. That stiffness about the arm, hip, and knee-joint which was apparent when he walked was the net product of the divers sprains and over-exertions that had been required of him in handling trees and timber when a young man, for he was of the sort called self-made, and had worked hard. He knew the origin of every one of these cramps: that in his left shoulder had come of carrying a pollard, unassisted, from Tutcombe Bottom home; that in one leg was caused by the crash of an elm against it when they were felling; that in the other was from lifting a bole. On many a morrow after wearying himself by these prodigious muscular efforts, he had risen from his bed fresh as usual; and confident in the recuperative power of his youth he had repeated the strains anew. But treacherous Time had been only hiding ill results when they could be guarded against for greater effect when they could not. Now in his declining years the store had been unfolded in the form of rheumatisms, pricks, and spasms, in every one of which Melbury recognised some act which, had its consequences been contemporaneously made known, he would wisely have abstained from repeating.

On a summons by Grammer Oliver to breakfast he went to the kitchen, where the family breakfasted in winter to save house-labour; and sitting down by the fire looked a long time at the pair of dancing shadows cast by each fire iron and dog-knob on the whitewashed chimney-corner—a yellow one from the window, and a blue one from the fire.

"I don't quite know what to do to-day," he said to his wife at last. "I've recollected that I promised to meet Mrs. Charmond's steward in Round Wood at twelve o'clock; and yet I want to go for Grace."

"Why not let Giles fetch her by himself. 'Twill bring 'em together all the quicker?"

"I could do that—but I always have gone without fail, every time hitherto, and perhaps she'll be disappointed if I stay away."

"You may be disappointed, but I don't think she will, if you send Giles," said Mrs. Melbury drily.

"Very well—I'll send him."

Melbury was often persuaded by the quiet of his wife's words when strenuous argument would have had no effect. This second Mrs. Melbury was a placid woman who had been nurse to his child Grace after her mother's death. Little Grace had clung to the nurse with much affection; and ultimately Melbury, in dread lest the only woman who cared for the girl should be induced to leave her, persuaded the mild Lucy to marry him. The arrangement—for it was little more—had worked satisfactorily enough; Grace had thriven, and Melbury had not repented.

He returned to the spar-house and found Giles near at hand, to whom he explained the change of plan. "As she won't arrive till five o'clock you can get your business very well over in time to receive her," said Melbury. "The green gig will do for her—you'll spin along quicker with that, and won't be late upon the road. Her boxes can be called for by one of the waggons."

Winterborne, knowing nothing of the timber-merchant's restitutory aims, quietly thought this to be a kindly chance. Wishing even more than her father to despatch his apple-tree business in the market before Grace's arrival, he prepared to start at once.

Melbury was careful that the turn-out should be seemly. The gig-wheels, for instance, were not always washed during winter-time before a journey, the muddy roads rendering that labour useless; but they were washed to-day. The harness was polished, and when the grey horse had been put in and Winterborne was in his seat, ready to start, Mr. Melbury stepped out with a blacking-brush and with his own hands touched over the yellow hoofs of the animal.

"You see, Giles," he said as he blacked, "coming from a fashionable school she might feel shocked at the homeliness of home; and 'tis these little things that catch a dainty woman's eye if they are neglected. We living here alone don't notice how the whitey-brown creeps out of the earth over us; but she, fresh from a city—why, she'll notice everything."

"That she will," said Giles.

"And scorn us if we don't mind."

"Not scorn us."

"No, no, no—that's only words. She's too good a girl to do that. But when we consider what she knows, and what she has seen since she last saw us, 'tis as well to meet her views. Why 'tis a year since she was in this old place, owing to her going abroad in the summer: and naturally we shall look small—just at first—I only say just at first."

Mr. Melbury's tone evinced a certain exultation in the very sense of that inferiority he affected to deplore; for this advanced and refined being, was she not his own all the time? Not so Giles; he felt doubtful. He looked at his clothes with misgiving; but said nothing.

It was his custom during the planting season to carry a specimen appletree to market with him as an advertisement of what he dealt in. This had been tied across the gig; and mounting in front he drove away, the twigs nodding with each step of the horse. Melbury went indoors. Before the gig had passed out of sight Mr. Melbury reappeared and shouted after.

"Here, Giles," he said, breathlessly following with some wraps. "It may be very chilly to-night, and she may want something extra about her. And Giles," he added, when the young man put the horse in motion once more; "tell her that I should have come myself, but I had particular business with Mrs. Charmond's agent which prevented me. Don't forget."

He watched Winterborne out of sight under the boughs, where cobwebs glistened in the now clearing air, lengthening and shortening their shine like elastic needles; he saw the woodpigeons rise as Giles drove past them; and said to himself with a jerk—a shape into which emotion with him often resolved itself:

"There now, I hope the two will bring it to a point, and have done with it! 'Tis a pity to let such a girl throw herself away upon him—a thousand pities! . . . And yet 'tis my duty, for his father's sake."

V

WINTERBORNE sped on his way to Sherton-Abbas without elation and without discomposure. Had he regarded his inner self spectacularly, as lovers are now daily more wont to do, he might have felt pride in the discernment of a somewhat rare power in him—that of keeping not only judgment, but emotion, suspended in difficult cases. But he noted it not.

Arrived at the entrance to a long flat lane, which had taken the spirit out of many a pedestrian in times when, with the majority, to travel meant to walk, he saw before him the trim figure of a young woman in pattens, journeying with that steadfast concentration which means purpose and not pleasure. He was soon near enough to see that she was Marty South. Click click, click, went the pattens; and she did not turn her head.

Yet she had seen him, and shrank from being overtaken by him thus; but as it was inevitable she braced herself up for his inspection by closing her lips so as to make her mouth quite unemotional, and by throwing an additional firmness into her tread.

"Why do you wear pattens Marty?—The turnpike is clean enough although the lanes are muddy."

"They save my boots."

"But twelve miles in pattens—'twill twist your feet off. Come get up and ride with me."

She hesitated, removed her pattens, knocked the gravel out of them against the wheel, and mounted in front of the nodding specimen-appletree. She had so arranged her bonnet with a full border and trimmings that her lack of long hair did not much injure her appearance; though Giles of course, saw that it was gone, and may have guessed her motive in parting with it; such sales, though infrequent, being not unheard of in that locality.

But nature's adornment was still hard by, in fact within two feet of him. In Marty's basket was a brown-paper packet, and in the packet the chestnut locks which by reason of the barber's request for secrecy she had not ventured to entrust to other hands.

Giles asked with some hesitation how her father was getting on.

He was better, she said; he would be able to work in a day or two; he would be quite well but for his craze about the tree falling on him.

"You know why I don't ask for him so often as I might, I suppose?" said Winterborne. "Or don't you know?"

"I think I do."

"Because of the houses."

She nodded.

"Yes. I am afraid it may seem that my anxiety is about

those houses which I should lose by his death, more than about him. Marty, I do feel anxious about the houses, since half my income depends upon them; but I do likewise care for him; and it almost seems wrong that houses should be leased for lives, so as to lead to such mixed feelings."

"After father's death they will be Mrs. Charmond's?"

"They'll be hers."

"They are going to keep company with my hair," she thought.

Thus talking they reached the ancient town of Sherton Abbas. By no pressure would she ride up the street with him. "That's the right of another woman," she said with playful malice as she put on her pattens. "I wonder what you are thinking of! Thank you for the lift in that handsome gig. Good-bye."

He blushed a little, shook his head at her, and drove on ahead into the streets, the churches, the abbey, and other mediæval buildings on this clear bright morning having the linear distinctness of architectural drawings, as if the original dream and vision of the conceiving master-mason were for a brief hour flashed down through the centuries to an unappreciative age. Giles saw their eloquent look on this day of transparency, but could not construe it. He turned into the inn-yard.

Marty, following the same track, marched promptly to the hairdresser's. Percomb was the chief of his trade in Sherton-Abbas. He had the patronage of such county offshoots as had been obliged to seek the shelter of small houses in that venerable town, of the local clergy, and so on; for some of whom he had made wigs, while others among them had compensated for neglecting him in their lifetime by patronizing him when they were dead, and letting him shave their corpses. On the strength of all this he had taken down his pole, and called himself "Perruquier to the aristocracy."

Nevertheless this sort of support did not quite fill his children's mouths, and they had to be filled. So behind his house there was a little yard reached by a passage from the back street, and in that yard was a pole, and under the pole a shop of quite another description than the ornamental one in the front street. Here on Saturday nights from seven till ten he took an almost innumerable succession of two pences from the farm-labourers who flocked thither in crowds from the country. And thus he lived.

Marty, of course, went to the front shop, and handed her packet to him silently. "Thank you," said the barber quite joyfully. "I hardly expected it after what you said last night."

She turned aside, while a tear welled up in each eye at this reminder.

"Nothing of what I told you," he whispered. "But I can trust you I see."

She had now reached the end of this distressing business, and went listlessly along the street to attend to other errands. These occupied her till four o'clock, at which time she recrossed the marketplace. It was impossible to avoid rediscovering Winterborne every time she passed that way, for standing, as he always did at this season of the year, with his specimen appletree in the midst, the boughs rose above the heads of the farmers and brought a delightful suggestion of orchards into the heart of the town. When her eye fell upon him for the last time he was standing somewhat apart, holding the tree like an ensign, and looking on the ground instead of pushing his produce as he ought to have been doing. He was, in fact, not a very successful seller either of his trees or of his cider, his habit of speaking his mind when he spoke at all militating against this branch of his business.

While she regarded him he lifted his eyes in a direction away from Marty, and his face kindled with recognition and surprise. She followed his gaze and saw walking across to him a flexible young creature in whom she perceived the features of her she had known as Miss Grace Melbury, but now looking glorified and refined to much above her former level. Winterborne, being fixed to the spot by his appletree, could not advance to meet her: he held out his spare hand with his hat in it, and with some embarrassment beheld her coming on tip-toe through the mud to the middle of the square where he stood.

Miss Melbury, as Marty could see, had not been expected by Giles so early. Indeed her father had named five o'clock as her probable time, for which reason that hour had been looming out all the day in his forward perspective like an important edifice on a dull plain. Now here she was come, he knew not how, and his arranged welcome stultified.

His face became gloomy at her necessity for stepping into the road, and more still at the little look of shamefacedness she showed at having to perform the meeting with him under an appletree ten feet high in the middle of the marketplace. Having had occasion to take off the new gloves she had bought to come home in she held out to him a hand graduating from pink at the tips of the fingers to white at the palm; and the reception formed a scene, with the tree over their heads, which was not by any means an ordinary one in town streets.

The greeting in her looks and on her lips had a restrained shape, which perhaps was not unnatural. For true it was that Giles Winterborne, though well-attired and well-mannered for a yeoman, looked rough beside her. It had sometimes dimly occurred to him, in his ruminating silences at Little Hintock, that external phenomena—such as the lowness or height or colour of a hat, the fold of a coat, the make of a boot, or the chance attitude of a limb at the instant of view— may have a great influence upon feminine opinion of a man's worth—so frequently founded on non-essentials; but a certain causticity of mental tone towards himself and the world in general had prevented to-day, as always, any enthusiastic action on the strength of that reflection; and her momentary instinct of reserve at first sight of him was the penalty he paid for his laxness.

He gave away the tree to a bystander as soon as he could find one who would accept the cumbersome gift, and the twain moved on towards the inn at which he had put up. Marty made as if to step forward for the pleasure of being recognised by Miss Melbury; but abruptly checking herself she glided behind a carrier's van, saying drily, "No: I bain't wanted there"; and critically regarded Winterborne's companion.

It would have been difficult to describe Grace Melbury with precision, either then or at any time. Nay, from the highest point of view, to precisely describe a human being, the focus of a universe—how impossible. But, apart from transcendent-alism, there never probably lived a person who was in herself more completely a *reductio ad absurdum* of attempts to appraise a woman even externally by items of face and figure. Speaking generally it may be said that she was sometimes beautiful, at other times not beautiful, according to the state of her health and spirits.

In simple corporeal presentment she was of a fair and clear complexion, rather pale than pink, slim in build and elastic in movement. Her look expressed a tendency to wait for others' thoughts before uttering her own: possibly also to wait for others' deeds before her own doings. In her small delicate mouth, which had hardly settled down to its ma-tured curves, there was a gentleness that might hinder suffi-cient self-assertion for her own good. She had well-formed eyebrows which, had her portrait been painted, would prob-ably have been done in Prout's or Vandyke brown.

There was nothing remarkable in her dress just now be-yond a natural fitness and a style that was recent for the streets of Sherton. But, had it been quite striking, it would have meant just as little. For there can be hardly anything less connected with a woman's personality than drapery which she has neither designed, manufactured, cut, sewed, nor even seen, except by a glance of approval when told that such and such a shape and colour must be had because it has been decided by others as imperative at that particular time.

What people therefore saw of her in a cursory view was very little; in truth, mainly something that was not she. The woman herself was a conjectural creature who had little to do with the outlines presented to Sherton eyes: a shape in the gloom, whose true quality could only be approximated by putting together a movement now and a glance then, in that patient attention which nothing but watchful loving-kindness ever troubles itself to give.

There was a little delay in their setting out from the town, and Marty South took advantage of it to hasten forward with the view of escaping them on the way, lest they should feel compelled to spoil their *tête-à-tête* by asking her to ride. She walked fast, and one third of the journey was done and the evening rapidly darkening, before she perceived any sign of them behind her. Then, while ascending a hill, she dimly saw their vehicle drawing near the lowest part of the incline, their heads slightly bent towards each other; drawn together, no doubt, by their souls; as the heads of a pair of horses well in hand are drawn in by the rein. She walked still faster.

But between these and herself there was a carriage, apparently a brougham, coming in the same direction, with lighted lamps. When it overtook her—which was not soon on account of her pace—the scene was much darker, and the lights glared in her eyes sufficiently to hide the details of the equipage.

It occurred to Marty that she might take hold behind this carriage and so keep along with it, to save herself from the patronage of being overtaken and picked up for pity's sake by the coming pair. Accordingly as the carriage drew abreast of her in climbing the long ascent she walked close to the wheels, the rays of the nearest lamp penetrating her very pores. She had only just dropped behind when the carriage stopped, and to her surprise the coachman asked her over his shoulder if she would ride. What made the question more surprising was that it came in obedience to an order from the interior of the vehicle.

Marty gladly assented, for she was weary, very weary, after working all night and keeping afoot all day. She mounted beside the coachman, wondering why this good fortune had happened to her. He was rather a great man in aspect, and she did not like to inquire of him for some time.

At last she said, "Who has been so kind as to ask me to ride?"

"Mrs. Charmond," replied her statuesque companion.

Marty was stirred at the name, so closely connected with her last night's experiences. "Is this her carriage?" she whispered.

"Yes; she's inside."

Marty reflected, and perceived that Mrs. Charmond must have recognised her plodding up the hill under the blaze of the lamp; recognised, probably, her stubbly poll (since she had kept away her face) and thought that those stubbles were the result of her own desire.

Marty South was not so very far wrong. Inside the carriage a pair of deep eyes looked from a ripely-handsome face, and though behind those deep eyes was a mind of unfathomed mysteries, beneath them there beat a heart capable of quick extempore warmth—a heart which could indeed be passionately and imprudently warm on certain occasions. At present, after recognising the girl, she had acted on impulse, possibly feeling gratified at the denuded appearance which signified the success of her agent in obtaining what she had required.

"'Tis wonderful that she should ask 'ee," observed the majestic coachman presently. "I have never known her do it before; for as a rule she takes no interest in the village folk at all."

Marty said no more, but occasionally turned her head to see if she could get a glimpse of the Olympian creature who, as the coachman had truly observed, hardly ever descended from her clouds into the Tempe-vale of the parishioners. But she could discern nothing of the lady. She also looked for Miss Melbury and Winterborne. The nose of their horse sometimes came quite near the back of Mrs. Charmond's carriage. But they never attempted to pass it till the latter conveyance turned towards the park gate, when they sped by.

Here the carriage drew up that the gate might be opened; and in the momentary silence Marty heard a gentle oral sound, soft as a breeze.

"What's that?" she whispered.

"Mis'ess yawning."

"Why should she yawn?"

"Oh, because she's been used to such wonderful good life, and finds it dull here. She'll soon be off again on account of it."

"So rich, and so powerful; and yet to yawn!" the girl murmured. "Then things don't fay with her any more than with we!"

Marty now alighted; the lamp again shone upon her, and as the carriage rolled on a voice said to her from the interior, "Good night."

"Good night Ma'am," said Marty, dropping a curtsey. But she had not been able to see the woman who began so greatly to interest her—the second person of her own sex who had operated strongly on her mind that day.

VI

MEANWHILE Winterborne and Grace Melbury had also undergone their little experiences.

As he drove off with her out of the town the glances of people fell upon them, the younger thinking that Mr. Winterborne was in a pleasant place, and wondering in what relation he stood towards her. Winterborne himself was unconscious of this. Occupied solely with the idea of having her in charge he did not notice much with outward eye.

Their conversation was in briefest phrase for some time, Grace being somewhat disconcerted through not having understood, till they were about to start, that Giles was to be her sole conductor, in place of her father. When they had left Sherton Park and Castle nearly out of sight and were in the open country, he spoke.

"Don't Brownley's farm-buildings look strange to you, now they have been moved bodily from the hollow where the old ones stood to the top of the hill?"

She admitted that they did, though she should not have seen any difference in them if he had not pointed it out.

"They had a good crop of bitter-sweets—they couldn't grind them all." He nodded towards an orchard where some heaps of apples had been left lying ever since the ingathering.

She said yes, but looking at another orchard.

"Why—you are looking at John-apple-trees! You know bitter-sweets—you used to, well enough?"

"I am afraid I have forgotten—and it is getting too dark to distinguish."

Winterborne did not continue. It seemed as if the knowledge and interests which had formerly moved Grace's mind had quite died away from her. He wondered whether the special attributes of his image in the past had evaporated like these other things.

However that might be, the fact at present was merely this,

that where he was seeing John-apples and farm-buildings she was beholding a much contrasting scene: a broad lawn in the fashionable suburb of a fast city, the evergreen leaves shining in the evening sun, amid which bounding girls, gracefully clad in artistic arrangements of blue, brown, red, and white, were playing at games with laughter and chat in all the pride of life, the notes of piano and harp trembling in the air from the open windows adjoining. Moreover they were girls—and this was a fact which Grace Melbury's delicate femininity could not lose sight of—whose parents Giles would have addressed with a deferential Sir or Madam. Beside this visioned scene the homely farmsteads did not quite hold their own from her present twenty-year point of survey. For all his woodland sequestration Giles knew the primitive simplicity of the subject he had started; and now sounded a deeper note.

" 'Twas very odd—what we said to each other years ago. I often think of it. I mean our saying that if we still liked each other when you were twenty and I twenty-five we'd——"

"It was child's tattle."

"H'm?" said Giles suddenly.

"I mean we were young," said she more considerately. That abrupt manner of his in making inquiries reminded her that he was unaltered.

"Yes.—I beg your pardon, Miss Melbury; your father *sent* me to meet you to-day."

"I know it—and I am glad of it." And she looked at him affectionately.

He seemed satisfied with her and went on: "At that time you were sitting beside me at the back of your father's covered car when we were coming home from gipsying, all the party being squeezed in together as tight as sheep in an auction-pen. It got darker and darker and I said—I forget the exact words—but I put my arm round your waist, and there you let it stay till your father, sitting in front, suddenly stopped telling his story to Farmer Bollen, to light his pipe. The flash shone into the car, and showed us all up distinctly; my arm flew from your waist like lightning; yet not so quickly but that some of 'em had seen and laughed at us. Yet your father, to our amazement, instead of being angry, was mild as milk, and seemed quite pleased. Have you forgot all that, or haven't you?"

She owned that she remembered it very well, now that he mentioned the circumstances. "But I must have been in short frocks," she said slily.

"Come now, Miss Melbury; that won't do! Short frocks indeed. You know better as well as I."

Grace thereupon declared that she would not argue with an old friend she valued so highly as she valued him, but if it were as he said, then she was virtually no less than an old woman now, so far did the time seem removed from her present.

"But old feelings come to life again in some people," she added softly.

"And in others they have never died!" said he.

"Ah—they are Love's very *ownest* and best, I suppose! I don't pretend to rank so high as they."

"It's not a they—it's a he."

Grace sighed. "Shall I tell you all about Brighton or Cheltenham, or places on the Continent that I visited last summer?" she said.

"With all my heart."

She then described places and persons, avoiding, however, what he most wished to hear—everything specially appertaining to her own inner existence. When she had done she said gaily, "Now do you tell me in return what has happened in Hintock since I have been away."

"Anything to keep the conversation away from her and me," said Giles within him.

It was true. Cultivation had so far advanced in the soil of Miss Melbury's mind as to lead her to talk of anything save of that she knew well, and had the greatest interest in developing: herself. She had fallen from the good old Hintock ways.

He had not proceeded far with his somewhat bald narration when they drew near a carriage that had been preceding them for some time in the dusk. Miss Melbury enquired if he knew whose carriage it was.

Winterborne, although he had seen it, had not taken it into account. On examination he said it was Mrs. Charmond's.

Grace watched the vehicle, and its easy roll, and seemed to feel more nearly akin to it than to the one she was in.

"Pooh—we can polish off the mileage as well as they, come to that," said Winterborne reading her mind; and rising to emulation at what it bespoke he whipped on the horse. This it was which had brought the nose of Mr. Melbury's grey close to the back of Mrs. Charmond's much eclipsing vehicle.

"There's Marty South sitting up with the coachman," said he, discerning her by her dress.

"Ah—poor Marty! I must ask her to come to see me this very evening. How does she happen to be riding there?"

"I don't know. It is very singular."

Thus these people with converging destinies went along the road together, till the track of the carriage and that of Winterborne parted, and he turned into Little Hintock, where almost the first house was the timber-merchant's. Pencils of light streamed out of the windows sufficiently to show the white laurustinus flowers, and glance against the polished leaves of laurel. The interior of the rooms could be seen distinctly, warmed up by the fire-flames, which in the parlour were reflected from the pictures and book-case, and in the kitchen from the utensils and ware.

"Let us look at the dear place for a moment before we call them," she said.

In the kitchen dinner was preparing, for though Melbury dined at one o'clock at other times to-day the meal had been kept back for Grace. A rickety old spit was in motion, its end being fixed in the fire-dog, and the whole kept going by means of a cord conveyed over pulleys along the ceiling, to a large stone suspended in a corner of the room. Old Grammer Oliver came and wound it up with a rattle like that of a mill.

In the parlour a colossal shade of Mrs. Melbury's head fell on the wall and ceiling; but before the girl had regarded this room many moments their presence was discovered, and her father and step-mother came out to welcome her.

The character of the Melbury family was of that kind which

evinces some shyness in showing strong emotion among each other; a trait frequent in rural households, and one curiously inverse to most of the peculiarities distinguishing villagers from the people of towns. Thus hiding their warmer feelings under commonplace talk all round, Grace's reception produced no extraordinary demonstrations. But that more was felt than was enacted appeared from the fact that her father, in taking her indoors, quite forgot the presence of Giles without, as did also Grace herself. He said nothing; but took the gig round to the yard and called out from the spar-house the man who attended to these matters when there was no conversation among the spar-makers to particularly engage him. Winterborne then returned to the door with the intention of entering the house.

The family had gone into the parlour, and were still absorbed in themselves. The fire was as before the only light, and it irradiated Grace's face and hands so as to make them look wondrously smooth and fair beside those of the two elders; shining also through the loose hair about her temples as sunlight through a brake. Her father was surveying her in a dazed conjecture, so much had she developed and progressed in manner and in stature since he last had set eyes on her.

Observing these things Winterborne remained dubious by the door, mechanically tracing with his fingers certain timeworn letters carved in the jambs—initials of byegone generations of householders who had lived and died there.

No, he declared to himself; he would not enter and join the family; they had forgotten him, and it was enough for today that he had brought her home. Still, he was a little surprised that her father's eagerness to send him for Grace should have resulted in such indifference as this.

He walked softly away into the lane towards his own house, looking back when he reached the turning from which he could get a last glimpse of the timber-merchant's roof. He hazarded guesses as to what Grace was saying just at that moment, and murmured with some self-derision, "nothing about me!" He looked also in the other direction and saw against the sky the thatched hip and solitary chimney of

Marty's cottage, and thought of her too, struggling bravely along under that humble shelter, among her spar-gads, and pots and skimmers.

At the timber-merchant's, in the meantime, conversation flowed; and as Giles Winterborne had rightly enough deemed, on subjects in which he had no share. Among the excluding matters there was, as chief, the effect upon Mr. Melbury of the womanly mien and manners of his daughter, which took him so much unawares that it thrust back the image of her conductor homeward into quite the obscurest cellarage of his brain.

Another was his interview with Mrs. Charmond's agent that morning, at which the lady herself had been present for a few minutes. Melbury had purchased some standing timber from her a long time before, and now that the date had come for felling it he was left to pursue almost his own course. This was what the household were actually talking of during Giles's cogitation without.

"So thoroughly does she trust me," said Melbury, "that I might fell, top, or lop, on my own judgment, any stick o' timber whatever in her wood, and fix the price o't, and settle the matter. But name it all, I wouldn't do such a thing. However, it may be useful to have this good understanding with her. . . . . I wish she took more interest in the place, and stayed here all the year round."

"I am afraid 'tis not her regard for you, but her dislike of Hintock, that makes her so easy about the trees," said Mrs. Melbury.

When dinner was over Grace took a candle and began to ramble pleasurably through the rooms of her old home, from which she had latterly become well-nigh an alien. Each nook and each object revived a memory, and simultaneously modified it. The chambers seemed lower than they had appeared on any previous occasion of her return, the surfaces of both walls and ceilings standing in such near relations to the eye that it could not avoid taking microscopic note of their ir- regularities and old fashion. Her own bedroom wore at once a look more familiar than when she had left it, and yet a face estranged. The world of little things therein gazed at her in helpless stationariness, as though they had tried and been unable to make any progress without her presence. Over the place where her candle had been accustomed to stand, when she had used to read in bed till the midnight hour, there was still the brown spot of smoke. She did not know that her father had taken especial care to keep it from being cleaned off.

Having concluded her perambulation of this now uselessly-commodious edifice Grace began to feel that she had come a long journey since the morning; and when her father had been up himself, as well as his wife, to see that her room was comfortable and the fire burning, she prepared to retire for the night. No sooner, however, had she extinguished her candle, than her momentary sleepiness took itself off, and she wished she had stayed up longer. She amused herself by listening to the old familiar noises that she could hear to be still going on downstairs, and by looking towards the window as she lay. The blind had been drawn up as she used to have it when a girl, and she could just discern the dim tree-tops against the sky on the neighbouring hill. Beneath this meeting-line of light and shade nothing was visible save one solitary point of light, which blinked as the tree-twigs waved to and fro before its beams. From its position it seemed to radiate from the window of a house on the hill-side. The house had been empty when she was last at home, and she wondered who inhabited the place now.

Her conjectures, however, were not intently carried on, and she was watching the light quite idly when it gradually changed colour, and at length shone blue as sapphire. Thus it remained several minutes, and then it passed through violet to red.

Her curiosity was so widely awakened by the phenomenon that she sat up in bed, and stared steadily at the shine. An appearance of this sort, sufficient to excite attention anywhere, was no less than a marvel in Hintock, as Grace had known the hamlet. Almost every diurnal and nocturnal effect in that woodland place had hitherto been the direct result of the regular terrestrial roll which produced the season's changes; but here was something dissociated from these normal sequences, and foreign to local knowledge.

It was about this moment that Grace heard the household below preparing to retire, the most emphatic noise in the proceeding being that of her father bolting the doors. Then the stairs creaked, and her father and mother passed her chamber. The last to come was Grammer Oliver.

Grace slid out of bed, ran across the room, and lifting the latch said, "I am not asleep Grammer. Come in and talk to me."

Before the old woman had entered Grace was again under the bedclothes. Grammer set down her candlestick, and seated herself on the edge of Miss Melbury's coverlet.

"I want you to tell me what light that is I see on the hill-side," said Grace.

Mrs. Oliver looked across. "Oh, that," she said, "is from the young doctor's. He's often doing things of that sort. Perhaps you don't know that we've a doctor living here now— Mr. Fitzpiers by name?"

Grace admitted that she had not heard of him.

"Well then, miss, he's come here to get up a practice. Though he belongs to the oldest, ancientest family in the country, he's stooped to make hisself useful like any common man. I know him very well, through going there to help 'em scrub sometimes, which your father said I might do if I wanted to in my spare time. Being a bachelor-man he've only lodgings. Oh yes, I know him very well. Sometimes he'll talk to me as if I were his own mother."

"Indeed."

"Yes. 'Grammer,' he said one day when I asked him why he came here where there's hardly anybody living, 'I'll tell you why I came here. I took a map, and I marked on it where Dr. Jones's practice ends to the north of this district, and where Mr. Taylor's ends on the south, and little Jimmy Green's on the east, and somebody else's to the west. Then I took a pair of compasses, and found the exact middle of the country that was left between these bounds, and that middle was little Hintock; so here I am.' . . . But Lord, there: poor young man!"

"Why?"

"He said, 'Grammer Oliver, I've been here three months,

and although there are a good many people in the Hintocks and the villages round, and a scattered practice is often a very good one, I don't seem to get many patients; and I'm not rich. And there's no society at all; and I'm pretty near melancholy mad,' he said with a great yawn. 'I should be quite if it were not for my books, and my lab—laboratory, and what not. Grammer, I was made for higher things.' And then he'd yawn and yawn again."

"Was he really made for higher things, do you think? Is he clever?"

"Well, no. How can he be clever? He may be able to jine up a broken man or woman after a fashion, and put his finger upon an ache if you tell him nearly where 'tis; but these young men—they should live to my time of life, and then they'd see how clever they were at five-and-twenty! And yet he's a projick, a real projick, and says the oddest of rozums: 'Ah, Grammer,' he said at another time, 'Let me tell you that Everything is Nothing. There's only Me and Not Me in the whole world.' And he told me that no man's hands could help what they did, any more than the hands of a clock . . . Yes, he's a man of strange meditations, and his eyes seem to see as far as the north star."

"He will soon go away, no doubt."

"I don't think so." Grace did not say "Why?," and Grammer hesitated. At last she went on, "Don't tell your father or mother, miss, if I let you know a secret?"

Grace gave the required promise.

"Well—he talks of buying me; so he won't go away just yet."

"Buying you—how?"

"Not my soul—my body, when I'm dead. One day when I was there cleaning he said, 'Grammer, you've a large brain—a very large organ of brain,' he said. 'A woman's is usually four ounces less than a man's; but yours is man's size.' Well then—hee-hee!—after he'd flattered me a bit like that he said he'd give me ten pounds to have my head as a natomy after my death. Well, knowing I'd no chick nor chiel left, and nobody with any interest in me, I thought, faith, if I can be of any use to my fellow-creatures after I'm gone they are welcome to me; so I said I'd think it over, and would most likely agree, and take the ten pounds. Now this is a secret, miss, between us two. The money would be very useful to me; and I see no harm in it."

"Of course there's no harm. But O Grammer—how can you think to do it! I wish you hadn't told me."

"I wish I hadn't—if you don't like to know it, miss. But you needn't mind. Lord—hee-hee!—I shall keep him waiting many a year yet, bless ye!"

"I hope you will, I am sure."

The girl thereupon fell into such deep reflection that conversation languished, and Grammer Oliver, taking her candle, wished Miss Melbury good-night. The latter's eyes rested on the distant glimmer, around which she allowed her reasoning fancy to play in vague eddies that shaped the doings of the philosopher behind that light on the lines of intelligence just received. It was strange to her to come back from the world to Little Hintock, and find in one of its nooks, like a tropical plant in a hedgerow, a nucleus of advanced ideas and practices which had nothing in common with the life around. Chemical experiments, anatomical projects, and metaphysical conceptions had found a strange home here.

Thus she remained thinking, the imagined pursuits of the man behind the light intermingling with conjectural sketches of his personality; till her eyelids fell together with their own heaviness, and she slept.

VII

KALEIDOSCOPIC dreams of a weird alchemist-surgeon, Grammer Oliver's skeleton, and the face of Giles Winterborne, brought Grace Melbury to the morning of the next day. It was fine. A north wind was blowing—that not unacceptable compromise between the atmospheric cutlery of the eastern blast and the spongy gales of the west quarter. She looked from her window in the direction of the light of the previous evening, and could just discern through the trees the shape of the surgeon's house. Somehow, in the broad practical daylight, that unknown and lonely gentleman seemed to be shorn of much of the interest which had invested his personality and pursuits in the hours of darkness, and as Grace's dressing proceeded he faded from her mind.

Meanwhile Winterborne, though half-assured of her father's favour, was rendered a little restless by Miss Melbury's own behaviour. Despite his shy self-control he could not help looking continually from his own door towards the timber-merchant's, in the probability of somebody's emergence therefrom. His attention was at length justified by the appearance of two figures, that of Mr. Melbury himself, and Grace beside him. They stepped out in a direction towards the densest quarter of the wood, and Winterborne walked contemplatively behind them till all three were soon under the trees.

Although the time of bare boughs had now set in, there were sheltered hollows amid the Hintock plantations and copses in which a more tardy leave-taking than on windy summits was the rule with the foliage. This caused here and there an apparent mixture of the seasons; so that in some of the dells they passed by holly berries in full red growing beside oak and hazel whose leaves were as yet not far removed from green, and brambles whose verdure was rich and deep as in the month of August. To Grace these well-known peculiarities were as an old painting restored.

Now could be beheld that change from the handsome to the curious which the features of a wood undergo at the ingress of the winter months. Angles were taking the place of curves, and reticulations of surfaces—a change constituting a sudden lapse from the ornate to the primitive on Nature's canvas, and comparable to a retrogressive step from the art of an advanced school of painting to that of the Pacific Islander.

Winterborne followed and kept his eye upon the two figures as they threaded their way through these sylvan masses; Mr. Melbury's long legs, his gaiters drawn in to the bone at the ancles, his slight stoop, his habit of getting lost in thought and arousing himself with an exclamation of "Hah!"— accompanied with an upward jerk of the head, composed a

personage recognizable by his neighbours as far as he could
be seen. It seemed as if the squirrels and birds knew him.
One of the former would occasionally run from the path to
hide behind the arm of some tree, which the little animal
carefully edged round *pari passu* with Melbury and his daughter's movement onward, assuming a mock manner as though
he were saying, "Ho-ho: you are only a timber-merchant,
and carry no gun!"

They went noiselessly over mats of starry moss, rustled
through interspersed tracts of leaves, skirted trunks with
spreading roots whose mossed rinds made them like hands
wearing green gloves, elbowed old elms and ashes with great
forks in which stood pools of water that overflowed on rainy
days and ran down their stems in green cascades. On older
trees still than these huge lobes of fungi grew like lungs.
Here, as everywhere, the Unfulfilled Intention, which makes
life what it is, was as obvious as it could be among the depraved crowds of a city slum. The leaf was deformed, the
curve was crippled, the taper was interrupted; the lichen ate
the vigour of the stalk, and the ivy slowly strangled to death
the promising sapling.

They dived amid beeches under which nothing grew, the
younger boughs still retaining their hectic leaves, that rustled in the breeze with a sound almost metallic, like the
sheet-iron foliage of the fabled Jarnvid wood. Some flecks of
white in Grace's drapery had enabled Giles to keep her and
her father in view till this time; but now he lost sight of them
and was obliged to follow by ear—no difficult matter, for on
the line of their course every wood-pigeon rose from its perch
with a continued clash, dashing its wings against the branches
with well-nigh force enough to break every quill. By taking
the track of this noise he soon came to a stile.

Was it worth while to go further? He examined the doughy
soil at the foot of the stile, and saw amongst the large sole
and heel tracks an impression of a slighter kind from a boot
that was obviously not local. The mud-picture was enough to
make him swing himself over and proceed.

The character of the woodland now changed. The bases of
the smaller trees were nibbled bare by rabbits, and at divers

points heaps of fresh-made chips, and the newly cut stool of a tree, stared white through the undergrowth. There had been a large fall of timber this year, which explained the meaning of some sounds that soon reached him.

A voice was shouting intermittently in a sort of human bark, reminding Giles that there was a sale of trees and faggots that very day. Melbury would naturally be present. Winterborne decided that he himself wanted a few faggots; and entered upon the scene.

A large group of buyers stood round the auctioneer, or followed him when, between his pauses, he wandered on from one lot of plantation produce to another, like some philosopher of the Peripatetic school delivering his lectures in the shady groves of the Lyceum. His companions were timber-dealers, yeomen, farmers, villagers and others; mostly woodland men, who on that account could afford to be curious in their walking-sticks, which consequently exhibited various monstrosities of vegetation, the chief being corkscrew shapes in black and white thorn, brought to that pattern by the slow torture of an encircling woodbine during their growth, as the Chinese have been said to mould human beings into grotesque toys by continued compression in infancy. Two women wearing men's jackets on their gowns conducted in the rear of the halting procession a pony-cart containing bread-and-cheese, with a barrel of strong ale for the select, and cider in milking-pails into which anybody dipped who chose.

The auctioneer adjusted himself to circumstances by using his walking-stick as a hammer, and knocked down the lot on any convenient object that took his fancy, such as the crown of a little boy's head, or the shoulders of a bystander who had no business there except to taste the brew; a proceeding which would have been deemed humorous but for the air of stern rigidity which the auctioneer's face preserved, tending to show that the eccentricity was a result of that absence of mind which is engendered by the press of affairs, and no freak of fancy at all.

Mr. Melbury stood slightly apart from the rest of the Peripatetics, and Grace beside him, clinging closely to his arm;

her modern attire looking almost odd where everything else was old-fashioned, and throwing over the familiar garniture of the trees a homeliness that seemed to demand improvement by the addition of a few contemporary novelties also. Grace seemed to regard the selling with the interest which attaches to memories revived after an interval of obliviousness.

Winterborne went and stood close to them; the timber-merchant spoke, and continued his buying; Grace merely smiled. To justify his presence there Winterborne began bidding for timber and faggots that he did not want, pursuing the occupation in an abstracted mood in which the auctioneer's voice seemed to become one of the natural sounds of the woodland. A few flakes of snow descended, at the sight of which a robin, alarmed at these signs of imminent winter, and seeing that no offence was meant by the human invasion, came and perched on the tip of the faggots that were being sold, and looked into the auctioneer's face whilst waiting for some chance crumb from the breadbasket. Standing a little behind Grace Winterborne observed how one flake would sail downward and settle on a curl of her hair, and how another would choose her shoulder, and another the edge of her bonnet; which took up so much of his attention that his biddings proceeded incoherently; and when the auctioneer said every now and then with a nod towards him, "Yours, Mr. Winterborne," he had no idea whether he had bought faggots, poles, or log-wood.

He regretted that her father should show such inequalities of temperament as to keep Grace tightly on his arm to-day, when he had quite lately seemed anxious to recognise their betrothal as a fact. And thus musing, and joining in no conversation with other buyers except when directly addressed, he followed the assemblage hither and thither till the end of the auction, when Giles for the first time realized what his purchases had been. Hundreds of faggots, and divers lots of timber, had been set down to him, when all he had required had been a few bundles of spray for his man Robert Creedle's use in baking and lighting fires.

Business being over he turned to speak to the timber-merchant. But Melbury's manner was short and distant; and

Grace too looked vexed and reproachful. Winterborne then discovered that he had been unwittingly bidding against her father, and picking up his favourite lots in spite of him. With a very few words they left the spot, and pursued their way homeward.

Giles was extremely blank at what he had done, and remained standing under the trees, all the other men having strayed silently away. He saw Melbury and his daughter pass down a glade without looking back. While they moved slowly through it a lady appeared on horseback in the middle distance, the line of her progress converging upon that of Melbury's. They met, Melbury took off his hat, and she reined in her horse. A conversation was evidently in progress between Grace and her father and this equestrian, in whom he was almost sure that he recognised Mrs. Charmond, less by her outline than by the livery of the groom who had halted some yards off.

The interlocutors did not part till after a prolonged pause, during which much seemed to be said. When Melbury and Grace resumed their walk it was with something of a lighter tread than before.

Winterborne pursued his own course homeward. He was unwilling to let coldness grow up between himself and the Melburys for any trivial reason, and in the evening he went to their house. On drawing near the gate his attention was attracted by the sight of one of the bedrooms blinking into a state of illumination. In it stood Grace lighting several candles, her right hand elevating the taper, her left hand on her bosom, her face thoughtfully fixed on each wick as it kindled, as if she saw in every flame's growth the rise of a life to maturity. He wondered what such unusual brilliancy could mean to-night. On getting in-doors he found her father and step-mother in a state of suppressed excitement which he could not comprehend.

"I am sorry about my biddings to-day," said Giles. "I don't know what I was doing. I have come to say that any of the lots you may require are yours."

"Oh, never mind, never mind," replied the timber-merchant with a slight wave of his hand. "I have so much else to think of that I nearly had forgot it. Just now, too, there are matters of a different kind from trade to attend to; so don't let it concern 'ee."

As the timber-merchant spoke as it were down to him from a higher plane than his own, Giles turned to Mrs. Melbury.

"Grace is going to the House to-morrow," she said quietly. "She is looking out her things now. I daresay she is wanting me this minute to assist her." Thereupon Mrs. Melbury left the room.

Nothing is more remarkable than the independent personality of the tongue now and then. Mr. Melbury knew that his words had been a sort of boast. He decried boasting, particularly to Giles; yet whenever the subject was Grace his judgment resigned the ministry of speech in spite of him.

Winterborne felt surprise, pleasure, and also a little apprehension at the news. He repeated Mrs. Melbury's words.

"Yes," said paternal pride, not sorry to have dragged out of him what he could not in any circumstances have kept in. "Coming home from the woods this afternoon we met Mrs. Charmond out for a ride. She spoke to me on a little matter of business; and then got acquainted with Grace. 'Twas wonderful how she took to Grace in a few minutes: that free-masonry of education made 'em close at once. Naturally enough she was amazed that such an article—ha-ha!—could come out of my house. At last it led on to Mis'ess Grace being asked to the House. So she's busy hunting up her frills and furbelows to go in." As Giles remained in thought without responding Melbury continued, "But I'll call her down stairs?"

"No, no; don't do that, since she's busy," said Winterborne.

Melbury, feeling from the young man's manner that his own talk had been too much at Giles and too little to him, repented at once. His face changed and he said, in lower tones, with an effort: "She's yours Giles, as far as I am concerned."

"Thanks—my best thanks, sir. But I think, since it is all right between us about the biddings, that I'll not interrupt her now. I'll step homeward, and call another time."

On leaving the house he looked up at the bedroom again. Grace, surrounded by a sufficient number of candles to answer all purposes of self-criticism, was standing before a cheval glass that her father had lately bought expressly for her use; she was bonneted, cloaked, and gloved, and glanced over her shoulder into the mirror, estimating her aspect. Her face was lit with the natural elation of a young girl hoping to inaugurate on the morrow an intimate acquaintance with a new, interesting, and influential friend.

VIII

THE inspiriting appointment which had led Grace Melbury to indulge in a six-candle illumination for the arrangement of her attire carried her over the ground the next morning with a springy tread. Her sense of being properly appreciated on her own native soil charged her heart with expansive gratitude. She moved along, a vessel of emotion, going to empty itself on she knew not what.

Twenty minutes' walking through copses, over a stile, and along an upland lawn, brought her to the verge of a deep glen, in which Hintock House appeared immediately beneath her eye. To describe it as standing in a hollow would not express the situation of the manor-house; it stood in a hole. But the hole was full of beauty. From the spot which Grace had reached a stone could easily have been thrown over, or into the bird's-nested chimneys of the mansion. Its walls were surmounted by a battlemented parapet; but the grey lead roofs were quite visible behind it, with their gutters, laps, rolls, and skylights; together with letterings and shoe-patterns cut by idlers thereon.

The front of the house was an ordinary manorial presentation of Elizabethan windows, mullioned and hooded, worked in rich snuff-coloured freestone from Ham-hill quarries. The ashlar of the walls, where not overgrown with ivy and other creepers, was coated with lichen of every shade, intensifying its luxuriance with its nearness to the ground till, below the plinth, it merged in moss.

Above the house to the back was a dense plantation, the roots of whose trees were above the level of the chimneys.

The corresponding high ground on which Grace stood was richly grassed, with only an old tree here and there. A few sheep lay about which as they ruminated looked quietly into the bedroom windows. The situation of the house, prejudicial to humanity, was a stimulus to vegetation, on which account an endless shearing of the heavy-armed ivy went on, and a continual lopping of trees and shrubs. It was an edifice built in times when human constitutions were damp-proof, when shelter from the boisterous was all that men thought of in choosing a dwelling-place, the insidious being beneath their notice; and its hollow site was an ocular reminder by its unfitness for modern lives, of the fragility to which these have declined. The highest architectural cunning could have done nothing to make Little Hintock House dry and salubrious; and ruthless ignorance could have done little to make it unpicturesque. It was vegetable nature's own home; a spot to inspire the painter and poet of still life—if they did not suffer too much from the relaxing atmosphere—and to draw groans from the gregariously disposed. Grace descended the green escarpment by a zigzag path into the drive, which swept round beneath the slope. The exterior of the house had been familiar to her from her childhood but she had never been inside, and the first step to knowing an old thing in a new way was a lively experience. It was with a little flutter that she was shown in; but she recollected that Mrs. Charmond would probably be alone. Up to a few days before this time that lady had been accompanied in her comings, stayings, and goings by a relative, believed to be her aunt; latterly, however, the two had separated, owing, it was supposed, to a quarrel; and Mrs. Charmond had been left desolate. Being presumably a woman who did not care for solitude this deprivation might account for her sudden interest in Grace.

Mrs. Charmond was at the end of a gallery opening from the hall when Miss Melbury was announced, and saw her through the glass doors between them. She came forward with a smile on her face and told the young girl it was good of her to come.

"Ah; you have noticed those," she said seeing that Grace's eyes were attracted by some curious objects against the walls.

"They are man-traps. My husband was a connoisseur in man-traps and spring-guns and such articles, collecting them from all his neighbours. He knew the histories of all these—which gin had broken a man's leg, which gun had killed a man. I don't like them here; but I've never yet given directions for them to be taken away." She added playfully, "Man-traps are of rather ominous significance where a person of our sex lives are they not?"

Grace was bound to smile; but that side of womanliness was one which her inexperience felt no great zest in contemplating.

"They are interesting, no doubt as relics of a barbarous time happily past," she said, looking thoughtfully at the varied designs of the instruments.

"Well we must not take them too seriously," said Mrs. Charmond with an indolent turn of her head, and they moved on inwards. When she had shown her visitor different articles in cabinets that she deemed likely to interest her, some tapestries, wood carvings, ivories, miniatures and so on—always with a mien of listlessness which might either have been constitutional, or partly owing to the situation of the place—they sat down to an early cup of tea.

"Will you pour it out please—do," she said leaning back in her chair and placing her hand above her forehead, while her almond eyes—those long eyes so common to the angelic legions of early Italian art—became longer, and her voice more languishing. She showed that oblique-mannered softness which is perhaps seen oftenest in women of darker complexion and more lymphatic temperament than Mrs. Charmond's; women who lingeringly smile their meanings to men rather than speak them, who inveigle rather than prompt, and take advantage of currents rather than steer.

"I am the most inactive woman when I am here," she said. "I think sometimes I was born to live and do nothing, nothing, nothing but float about, as we fancy we do sometimes in dreams. But that cannot be really my destiny, and I must struggle against such fancies."

"I am so sorry you do not enjoy exertion—it is quite sad. I wish I could tend you and make you very happy."

There was always something so sympathetic, so responsive,

in Grace's voice, that it impelled people to overstep their customary reservations in talking to her. "It is tender and kind of you to feel that!" said Mrs. Charmond. "Perhaps I have given you the notion that my languor is more than it really is. But this place oppresses me, and I have a plan of going abroad a good deal. I used to go with a relation, but that arrangement has dropped through." Regarding Grace with a final glance of criticism she seemed to make up her mind to consider the young girl satisfactory, and continued, "Now I am often impelled to record my impressions of times and places. I have often thought of writing a *New Sentimental Journey.* But I cannot find energy enough to do it alone. When I am at different places in the South of Europe I feel a crowd of ideas and fancies thronging upon me continually; but to unfold writing materials, take up a cold steel pen, and put these impressions down systematically on cold smooth paper—that I cannot do. So I have thought that if I always could have somebody at my elbow with whom I am in sympathy, I might dictate any ideas that come into my head. And directly I had made your acquaintance the other day it struck me that you would suit me so well. Would you like to undertake it? You might read to me, too, if desirable. Will you think it over, and ask your parents if they are willing?"

"Oh yes," said Grace, "I am almost sure they would be very glad."

"You are so accomplished I hear; I should be quite honoured by such intellectual company."

Grace, modestly blushing, deprecated any such idea.

"Do you keep up your lucubrations at Little Hintock?" the lady went on.

"Oh no. Lucubrations are not unknown at Little Hintock; but they are not carried on by me."

"What—another student in that retreat?"

"There is a surgeon lately come—and I have heard that he reads a great deal—I see his light sometimes through the trees late at night."

"Oh yes—a doctor—I believe I was told of him. . . . . . It is a strange place for him to settle in."

"It is a convenient centre for a practice, they say. But he

does not confine his studies to medicine, it seems. He investigates theology, and metaphysics, and all sorts of subjects."

"What is his name?"

"Fitzpiers. He represents a very old family I believe—the Fitzpierses of Oakbury-Fitzpiers—not a great many miles from here."

"I am not sufficiently local to know the history of the family. I was never in the county till my husband brought me here." Mrs. Charmond did not care to pursue this line of investigation. Whatever mysterious merit might attach to family antiquity, it was one which her adaptable, wandering, *weltbürgerliche* nature had grown tired of caring about—a peculiarity that made her a piquant contrast to her neighbours. "It is of rather more importance to know what the man is himself than what his family is," she said, "if he is going to practise upon us as a surgeon. Heaven send him skill! Have you seen him?"

Grace had not. "I think he is not a very old man," she added.

"Has he a wife?"

"I am not aware that he has."

"Well, I hope he will be useful here. I must get to know him when I come back. It will be very convenient to have a medical man—if he is clever—in one's own parish. I get dreadfully nervous sometimes, living in such an outlandish place; and Sherton is so far to send to. No doubt you feel Little Hintock to be a great change after watering-place life."

"I do. But it is home. It has its advantages and its disadvantages." Grace was thinking less of the solitude than of the attendant circumstances.

They chatted on for some time, Grace being set quite at her ease by her entertainer. Mrs. Charmond was far too well-practised a woman not to know that to show anything like patronage towards a sensitive young girl who would probably be very quick to discern it was to demolish her dignity rather than to establish it in that young girl's eyes. So being violently possessed with her idea of making use of this gentle acquaintance, ready and waiting at her own door, she took great pains to win her confidence at starting.

Just before Grace's departure the two chanced to pause

before a mirror which reflected their faces in immediate juxtaposition, bringing into prominence their resemblances and their contrasts. Both looked attractive as glassed back by the faithful reflector; but Grace's countenance had the effect of making Mrs. Charmond appear more than her full age. There are complexions which set off each other to great advantage, and there are those which antagonize, one of such killing or damaging its neighbour unmercifully. This was unhappily the case here. Mrs. Charmond fell into a meditation, and replied abstractedly to a cursory remark of her companion's. However she parted from her young friend in the kindliest tones, promising to send and let her know as soon as her mind was made up on the arrangement she had suggested.

When Grace had ascended nearly to the top of the adjoining slope she looked back, and saw that Mrs. Charmond still stood at the door, meditatively regarding her.

Often during the previous night, after his call on the Melburys, Winterborne's thoughts had run upon Grace's announced visit to Hintock House. Why had he not proposed to walk with her part of the way? Something told him that she might not, on such an occasion, have cared for his company.

He was still more of that opinion when, standing in his garden next day, he saw her go past on the journey with such a pretty pride in the event. He questioned if her father's ambition, which had purchased for her the means of intellectual light and culture far beyond those of any other native of the village, would not operate to the flight of her future interests above and away from the local life which was once to her the movement of the world.

Nevertheless, he had her father's permission to win her if he could; and to this end it became desirable to bring matters soon to a crisis. If she should think herself too good for him he must let her go, and make the best of his loss. The question was how to quicken events towards an issue.

He thought and thought, and at last decided that as good a way as any would be to give a Christmas party, and ask Grace and her parents to come as chief guests.

These ruminations were occupying him when there became audible a slight knocking at his front door. He descended the path, and looked out, and beheld Marty South, dressed for out-door work.

"Why didn't you come, Mr. Winterborne?" she said. "I've been waiting there hours and hours, and at last I thought I must try to find you."

"Bless my soul, I'd quite forgot," said Giles.

What he had forgotten was that there were a thousand young fir trees to be planted in a neighbouring spot which had been cleared by the woodcutters, and that he had arranged to plant them with his own hands. He had a marvellous power of making trees grow. Although he would seem to shovel in the earth quite carelessly there was a sort of sympathy between himself and the fir, oak, or beech that he was operating on; so that the roots took hold of the soil in a few days. When, on the other hand, any of the journeymen planted, although they seemed to go through an identically similar process, one quarter of the trees would die away during the ensuing August.

Hence Winterborne found delight in the work even when, as at present, he contracted to do it on portions of the woodland in which he had no personal interest. Marty, who turned her hand to anything, was usually the one who performed the part of keeping the trees in a perpendicular position whilst he threw in the mould.

He accompanied her towards the spot, being inclined yet further to proceed with the work by the knowledge that the ground was close to the roadside along which Grace must pass on her way from Hintock House.

"You've a cold in the head Marty," he said as they walked. "That comes of cutting off your hair."

"I suppose it do. Yes; I've three headaches going on in my head at the same time."

"Three headaches!"

"Yes, Mr. Winterborne; a rheumatic headache in my poll, a sick headache over my eyes, and a misery headache in the middle of my brain. However I came out, for I thought you might be waiting and grumbling like anything if I was not there."

The holes were already dug, and they set to work. Winterborne's fingers were endowed with a gentle conjuror's touch in spreading the roots of each little tree, resulting in a sort of caress, under which the delicate fibres all laid themselves out in their proper directions for growth. He put most of these roots towards the south-west; for, he said, in forty years' time, when some great gale is blowing from that quarter, the trees will require the strongest holdfast on that side to stand against it and not fall.

"How they sigh directly we put 'em upright, though while they are lying down they don't sigh at all," said Marty.

"Do they?" said Giles. "I've never noticed it."

She erected one of the young pines into its hole, and held up her finger; the soft musical breathing instantly set in which was not to cease night or day till the grown tree should be felled—probably long after the two planters had been felled themselves.

"It seems to me," the girl continued, "as if they sigh because they are very sorry to begin life in earnest—just as we be."

"Just as we be?" He looked critically at her. "You ought not to feel like that, Marty."

Her only reply was turning to take up the next tree; and they planted on through a great part of the day, almost without another word. Winterborne's mind ran on his contemplated evening-party, his abstraction being such that he hardly was conscious of Marty's presence beside him. From the nature of their employment, in which he handled the spade, and she merely held the tree, it followed that he got good exercise and she got none. But she was a heroic girl, and though her outstretched hand was chill as a stone, and her cheeks blue, and her cold worse than ever, she would not complain whilst he was disposed to continue work. But when he paused she said, "Mr. Winterborne, can I run down the lane and back to warm my feet?"

"Why, yes, of course," he said, awakening to her existence. "Though I was just thinking what a mild day it is for the season. Now I warrant that cold of yours is twice as bad as it was. You had no business to chop that hair off, Marty—it serves you almost right. Look here, cut off home at once."

"A run down the lane will be quite enough."

"No it won't. You ought not to have come out to-day at all."

"But I should like to finish the——"

"Marty, I tell you to go home," said he peremptorily. "I can manage to keep the rest of them upright with a forked stick or something."

She went away without saying any more. When she had gone down the orchard a little distance she looked back. Giles suddenly went after her. "Marty, it was for your good that I was rough, you know. But warm yourself in your own way—I don't care." He took her hand kindly a moment, and then let her go.

When she had run off he fancied he discerned a woman's dress through the holly bushes which divided the coppice from the road. It was Grace at last, on her way back from the interview with Mrs. Charmond. He threw down the tree he was planting, and was about to break through the belt of holly when he suddenly became aware of the presence of another man, who was looking over the hedge on the opposite side of the way upon the figure of the unconscious Grace. The stranger appeared as a handsome and gentlemanly personage of six or eight-and-twenty, and he was quizzing her through an eyeglass. Seeing that Winterborne was noticing him he let his glass drop with a click upon the rail which protected the hedge, and walked away in the opposite direction. Giles knew in a moment that this must be Mr. Fitzpiers. When he was gone Winterborne pushed through the holly, and emerged close beside the interesting object of their contemplation.

IX

"I HEARD the bushes move long before I saw you," she began. "I said first, 'it is some terrible beast'; next, 'it is a poacher'; next, 'it is a friend!'"

He regarded her with a slight smile, weighing, not her speech, but the question whether he should tell her that she had been flatteringly watched by a gentleman. He decided in the negative.

"You have been to the House?" he said. "But I need not ask." The fact was that there shone upon Miss Melbury's face a species of exaltation which saw no environing details; not even Giles's occupation; only his bare presence.

"Why need you not ask?"

"Your face is like the face of Moses when he came down from the Mount."

She reddened a little and said, "How can you be so profane, Giles Winterborne."

"How can you think so much of that class of people!— Well, I beg pardon—I didn't mean to speak so freely. How do you like her house and her?"

"Exceedingly. I had not been near the place since I was a child, when it used to be let to strangers, before Mrs. Charmond's late husband bought the property. She is *so* nice!" And Grace fell into such an abstracted gaze at the mental image of Mrs. Charmond and her niceness that it almost conjured up a vision of that lady to Giles himself.

"She has only been here a month or two, it seems; and cannot stay much longer, because she finds it so lonely and damp in winter. She is going abroad. Only think; she would like me to go with her."

Giles's features stiffened a little at the news. "Indeed—what for?—But I won't keep you standing here.—Hoi, Robert!" he cried to a swaying collection of old clothes in the distance, which composed the figure of Creedle his man, who was looking for him. "Go on filling in there till I come back."

"I'm a coming, sir: I'm a coming."

"Well, the reason is this," continued she as they went on together. "Mrs. Charmond has a delightful side to her character—a desire to record her impressions of travel, like Alexandre Dumas, and Méry, and Sterne, and others. But she cannot find energy enough to do it herself." And Grace proceeded to explain Mrs. Charmond's proposal at large. "My notion is that Méry's style will suit her best because he writes in that soft emotional luxurious way she has," Grace said musingly.

"Indeed!" said Winterborne, sighing. "Suppose you talk over my head a little longer, Miss Grace Melbury."

"Oh—I didn't mean it!" she said repentantly looking into his eyes. "And as for myself, I hate French books. And I love dear old Hintock, *and the people in it,* fifty times better than all the Continent.—But the scheme—I think it an enchanting notion—don't you Giles?"

"It is well enough in one sense. But it will take you away," said he, mollified.

"Only for a short time. We should return in May."

"Well, Miss Melbury; it is a question for your father."

Winterborne walked with her nearly to her house. He had awaited her coming mainly with the view of mentioning to her his proposal to have a Christmas party; but homely Christmas gatherings in the jovial Hintock style seemed so primitive and uncouth beside the lofty matters of her conversation that he refrained.

As soon as she was gone he turned back towards the scene of his planting, and could not help saying to himself as he walked that this engagement of his was a very unpromising business. Her outing to-day had not improved it. A woman who could go to Hintock House, and be friendly with its mistress; enter into the views of its mistress, talk like her, and dress not much unlike her: why, she would hardly be contented with him, a yeoman, immersed in tree planting, even though he planted them well. "And yet she's a true-hearted girl," he said thinking of her words about Hintock. "I must bring matters to a point, and there's an end of it."

When he reached the place of work he found that Marty had come back, and dismissing Creedle he went on planting silently with the girl as before.

"Suppose, Marty," he said after a while, looking at her extended arm, upon which old scratches from briars showed themselves purple in the cold wind; "Suppose you know a person, and want to bring that person to a good understanding with you; do you think a Christmas party of some sort is a warming-up thing, and likely to be useful in hastening on the matter?"

"Is there to be dancing?"

"There might be, certainly."

"Will He dance with Her?"

"Well, yes."

"Then it might bring things to a head, one way or the other—I won't be the maid to say which."

"It shall be done," said Winterborne, not to her, though he spoke the words quite loudly. And as the day was nearly ended he added, "Here Marty, I'll send up a man to plant the rest to-morrow. I've other things to think of just now."

She did not inquire what other things; for she had seen him walking with Grace Melbury. She looked towards the western sky, which was now aglow like some vast foundry wherein new worlds were being cast. Across it the bare bough of a tree stretched horizontally, revealing every twig against the evening fire, and showing in dark profile every beck and movement of three pheasants, that were settling themselves down on it in a row to roost.

"It will be fine to-morrow," said Marty observing them with the vermillion light of the sun in the pupils of her eyes, "for they are a-croupied down nearly at the end of the bough. If it were going to be stormy they'd squeeze close to the trunk. The weather is almost all they have to think of, isn't it, Mr. Winterborne; and so they must be lighter-hearted than we."

"I daresay they are," said Winterborne.

Before taking a single step in the preparations Winterborne with no great hopes went across that evening to the timber-merchant's to ascertain if Grace and her parents would honour him with their presence.

Having first to set his nightly gins in the garden, to catch the rabbits that ate his wintergreens, his call was delayed till just after the rising of the moon, whose rays reached the Hintock houses but fitfully as yet, on account of the trees. Melbury was crossing his yard on his way to call on some one at the larger village, but he readily turned and walked up and down with the young man.

Giles, in his self-deprecatory sense of living on a much smaller scale than the Melburys did, would not for the world imply that his invitation was to a gathering of any importance.

So he put it in the mild form of "Can you come in for an hour when you have done business, the day after tomorrow; and Mrs. and Miss Melbury, if they have nothing more pressing to do?"

Melbury would give no answer at once. "No, I can't tell you to-day," he said. "I must talk it over with the women. As far as I am concerned, my dear Giles, you know I'll come with pleasure. But how do I know what Grace's notions may be? You see, she has been away amongst cultivated folks a good while; and now this acquaintance with Mrs. Charmond— well, I'll ask her. I can say no more."

When Winterborne was gone the timber-merchant went on his way. He knew very well that Grace, whatever her own feelings, would either go or not go, according as he suggested; and his instinct was, for the moment, to suggest staying at home. His errand took him near the church, and the way to his destination was equally easy across the churchyard or outside it. For some reason or other he chose the former way.

The moon was faintly lighting up the grave-stones, and the path, and the front of the building. Suddenly Mr. Melbury paused, turned in upon the grass, and approached a particular headstone, where he read, "In memory of John Winterborne," with the subjoined date and age. It was the grave of Giles's father.

The timber-merchant laid his hand upon the stone, and was humanized. "Jack—my wronged friend!" he said. "I'll be faithful to my plan of making amends to thee."

When he reached home that evening he said to Grace and Mrs. Melbury, who were working at a little table by the fire: "Giles wants us to go down and spend an hour with him the day after to-morrow; and I'm thinking, that as 'tis Giles who asks us, we'll go."

They assented without demur; and the timber-merchant sent Giles the next morning an answer in the affirmative.

Winterborne, in his modesty, had mentioned no particular hour in his invitation to the Melburys, though he had to the inferior guests; therefore Mr. Melbury and his family, expecting no other people, chose their own time, which chanced to be rather early in the afternoon by reason of the somewhat quicker despatch than usual of the timber-merchant's business that day.

They showed their sense of the unimportance of the occasion by walking quite slowly to the house, as if they were merely out for a ramble, and going to nothing special at all; or at most intending to pay a casual call and take a cup of tea.

At this hour stir and bustle pervaded the interior of Winterborne's domicile from cellar to apple-loft. He had planned an elaborate high tea for six o'clock or thereabouts, and a good roaring supper to come on about eleven. Being a bachelor of rather retiring habits the whole of the preparations devolved upon himself and his trusty man and familiar Robert Creedle, who did everything that required doing, from making Giles's bed to catching moles in his field. He was a survival from the days when Giles's father held the homestead and Giles was a playing boy.

These two, with a certain dilatoriness which appertained to both, were now in the heat of preparation in the bake-house, expecting nobody before six o'clock. Winterborne was standing in front of the brick oven in his shirt-sleeves, tossing in thorn-sprays, and stirring about the blazing mass with a long-handled, three-pronged, Beelzebub kind of fork, the heat shining out upon his streaming face and making his eyes like furnaces; the thorns crackling and sputtering; while Creedle, having ranged the pastry dishes in a row on the table till the oven should be ready, was pressing out the crust of a final apple-pie with a rolling-pin. A great pot boiled on the fire; and through the open door of the back-kitchen a boy was seen seated on the fender, emptying the snuffers and scouring the candlesticks, a row of the latter standing upside down on the hob to melt out the grease.

Looking up from the rolling-pin Creedle saw passing the window first the timber-merchant, in his second-best suit, next Mrs. Melbury in her best silk, and behind them Grace in the fashionable attire which, lately brought home with her from the Continent, she had worn on her visit to Mrs. Charmond's. The eyes of the three had been attracted through the window to the proceedings within by the fierce illumination which the oven threw out upon the operators and their utensils.

"Lord, Lord; if they bain't come a'ready!" said Creedle.

"No—hey?" said Giles, looking round aghast; while the boy in the background waved a reeking candlestick in his delight. As there was no help for it Winterborne hastily rolled down his shirt-sleeves and went to meet them in the door-way.

"My dear Giles—I see we have made a mistake in the time," said the timber-merchant's wife, her face lengthening with concern.

"Oh—it is not much difference. I hope you'll come in."

"But this means a regular randy-voo?" Mr. Melbury accusingly glanced round and pointed towards the viands in the bakehouse with his stick.

"Well yes," said Giles.

"And—not Great Hintock band, and dancing, surely?"

"I told three of 'em they might drop in, if they'd nothing else to do," Giles mildly admitted.

"Now, why the name didn't ye tell us afore that 'twas going to be a bouncing kind of thing! How should I know what folk mean if they don't say? Now, shall we come in, or shall we go home, and come back-along in a couple of hours?"

"I hope you'll stay, if you'll be so good as not to mind, now you are here? I shall have it all right and tidy in a very little time. I ought not to have been so backward; but Creedle is rather slow."

Giles spoke quite anxiously for one of his undemonstrative temperament; for he feared that if the Melburys once were back in their own house they would not be disposed to turn out again.

"'Tis we ought not to have been so forward; that's what 'tis," said Mr. Melbury testily. "Don't keep us here in your best sitting-room: lead on to the bake-house, man. Now we are here we'll help ye get ready for the rest. Here, mis'ess—take off your things, and help him out in his baking, or he won't get done to-night. I'll finish heating the oven, and set you free to go and skiver up them ducks." His eye had passed with pitiless directness of criticism into yet remoter recesses of Winterborne's awkwardly built premises, where the afore-said birds were hanging.

"And I'll help finish the tarts," said Grace cheerfully.

"I don't know about that," said her father. "'Tisn't quite so much in your line as it is in your mother-law's and mine."

"Of course I couldn't let you, Grace!" said Giles, with distress.

"I'll do it, of course," said Mrs. Melbury, taking off her silk train, hanging it up to a nail, carefully rolling back her sleeves, pinning them to her shoulders, and stripping Giles of his apron for her own use.

So Grace pottered idly about while her father and his wife helped on the preparations. A kindly pity of his household management, which Winterborne saw in her eyes whenever he caught them, depressed him much more than her contempt would have done.

Creedle met Giles at the pump after a while, when each of the others was absorbed in the difficulties of a *cuisine* based on utensils, cupboards, and provisions that were strange to them. He groaned to the young man in a whisper, "This is a bruckle het, maister, I'm much afeard! Who'd ha' thought they'd ha' come so soon?"

The bitter placidity of Winterborne's look hinted the misgivings he did not care to express. "Have you got the celery ready?" he asked quickly.

"Now that's a thing I never could mind: no, not if you'd pay me in silver and gold!" said Creedle. "And I don't care who the man is, I says that a stick of celery that isn't scrubbed with the scrubbing-brush, is not clean."

"*Very* well—very well!—I'll attend to it. You go and get 'em comfortable indoors."

He hastened to the garden, and soon returned, tossing the stalks to Creedle who was still in a tragic mood. "If ye'd ha' married, d'ye see, maister," he murmured, "this calamity couldn't have happened to us!"

Everything being at last under way, the oven set, and all done that could insure the supper turning up ready at some time or other, Giles and his friends entered the parlour, where the Melburys again dropped into position as guests, though the room was not nearly so warm and cheerful as the blazing bakehouse. Others now arrived, among them Farmer Cawtree and the hollow-turner, and tea went off very well.

Grace's disposition to make the best of everything, and to wink at deficiencies in Winterborne's way of living, was so uniform and persistent that he suspected her of seeing even more deficiencies than he was aware of. That suppressed sympathy which had showed in her face ever since her arrival told him as much too plainly.

"This muddling style of housekeeping is what you've not lately been used to, I suppose?" he said when they were a little apart.

"No; but I like it; it reminds me so pleasantly that everything here in dear old Hintock is just as it used to be. . . . . The oil is—not quite nice; but everything else is."

"The oil?"

"On the chairs, I mean; because it gets on one's dress. Still, mine is not a new one."

Giles found that the boy, in his zeal to make things look bright, had smeared the chairs with some greasy furniture-polish and refrained from rubbing it dry, in order not to diminish the mirror-like effect that the mixture produced as laid on. Giles apologised and scolded the boy; but he felt that the fates were against him.

X

SUPPER-TIME came, and with it the hot-baked meats from the oven, laid on a snowy cloth fresh from the press, and reticulated with folds as in Flemish Last-Suppers. Creedle and the boy fetched and carried with amazing alacrity; the latter, to mollify his superior, and make things pleasant, expressing his admiration of Creedle's cleverness when they were alone.

"I s'pose the time when you learnt all these knowing things, Mr. Creedle, was when you was in the militia?"

"Well, yes. I seed the world that year somewhat, certainly, and mastered many arts of strange dashing life. Not but that

Giles has worked hard in helping me to bring things to such perfection to-day. 'Giles,' says I, though he's maister. Not that I should call 'n maister by rights, for his father growed up side by side with me, as if one mother had twinned us and been our nourishing."

"I s'pose your memory can reach a long way back into history, Mr. Creedle?"

"Oh yes. Ancient days, when there was battles, and famines, and hang-fairs, and other pomps, seem to me as yesterday. . . . Ah, many's the patriarch I've seed come and go in this parish!—There, he's calling for more plates. Lord, why can't 'em turn their plates bottom upward for pudding, as we bucks used to do in former days!"

Meanwhile in the adjoining room Giles was presiding in a half unconscious state. He could not get over the initial failures in his scheme for advancing his suit; and hence he did not know that he was eating mouthfuls of bread and nothing else, and continually snuffing the two candles next him till he had reduced them to mere glimmers drowned in their own grease. Creedle now appeared with a specially prepared stew, which he served by elevating the little three-legged crock that contained it and tilting the contents into a platter on the table, exclaiming simultaneously, "Draw back, gentlemen and ladies, please!"

A splash followed. Grace gave a quick involuntary nod and blink and put her handkerchief to her face.

"Good heavens, what did you do that for, Creedle!" said Giles sternly, jumping up.

" 'Tis how I do it when they bain't here, maister," mildly expostulated Creedle, in an aside audible to all the company.

"Well yes—but—" replied Giles. He went over to Grace, and hoped none of it had gone into her eye.

"O no," she said. "Only a sprinkle on my face. It was nothing."

"Kiss it and make it well," gallantly observed Mr. Cawtree. Miss Melbury blushed.

The timber-merchant replied quickly, "Oh, it is nothing! She must bear these little mishaps." But there could be discerned in his face something which said, "I ought to have foreseen all this, and kept her away!"

Giles himself, since the untoward beginning of the feast, had not quite liked to see Grace present. He wished he had not asked such people as Cawtree and the hollow-turner. He had done it, in dearth of other friends, that the room might not appear empty. In his mind's eye, before the event, they had been the mere background or padding of the scene; but somehow in the reality they were the most prominent personages there.

After supper they sat down to cards, Cawtree and the hollow-turner monopolizing the new packs for an interminable game of langterloo, in which a lump of chalk was incessantly used—a game those two always played wherever they were, taking a solitary candle and going to a private table in a corner, with the mien of persons bent on weighty matters. The rest of the company on this account were obliged to put up with old packs for their round game, that had been lying by in a drawer ever since the time that Giles's grandmother was alive. Each card had a great stain in the middle of its back, produced by the touch of generations of damp and excited thumbs now fleshless in the grave; and the kings and queens wore a decayed expression of feature, as if they were rather an impecunious dethroned dynasty hiding in obscure slums than real regal characters. Every now and then the comparatively few remarks of the players at the round game were harshly intruded on by the langterloo jingle of Farmer Cawtree and the hollow-turner from the back of the room:

> "And I' will hold' a wa'-ger with you'
> That all' these marks' are thirt'-y two!"

accompanied by rapping strokes with the chalk on the table; then an exclamation, an argument, a dealing of the cards; then the commencement of the rhymes anew.

The timber-merchant showed his feelings by talking with a reserved weight in his words, and by praising the party in a patronizing tone, when Winterborne expressed his fear that he and his were not enjoying themselves.

"O yes, yes: pretty much. . . . What handsome glasses those are. I didn't know you had such glasses in the house. Now Lucy [to his wife] you ought to get some like them for ourselves."

And when they had abandoned cards, and Winterborne was talking to Melbury by the fire, it was the timber-merchant who stood with his back to the mantel in a proprietary attitude; from which post of vantage he critically regarded Giles's person, rather as a superficies than as a solid with ideas and feelings inside it; saying, "What a splendid coat that one is you have on, Giles. I can't get such coats. You dress better than I."

After supper there was a dance, the bandsmen from Great Hintock having arrived some time before. Grace had been away from home so long, and was so drilled in new dances, that she had forgotten the old figures, and hence did not join in the movement. Then Giles felt that all was over. As for her, she was thinking, as she watched the gyrations, of a very different measure that she had been accustomed to tread with a bevy of sylph-like creatures in muslin in the music-room of a large house, most of whom were now moving in scenes widely removed from this, both as regarded place, and character.

A woman she did not know came and offered to tell her fortune with the abandoned cards. Grace assented to the proposal, and the woman told her tale—unskilfully—for want of practice, as she declared.

Mr. Melbury was standing by, and exclaimed contemptuously, "Tell her fortune, indeed! Her fortune has been told by men of science—what do you call 'em—phrenologists. You can't teach her anything new. She's been too far among the wise ones to be astonished at anything she can hear among us folks in Hintock."

At last the time came for breaking up, Melbury and his family being the earliest to leave, the two card players still pursuing their game doggedly in the corner, where they had completely covered Giles's mahogany table with chalk scratches. The Melburys walked home, the distance being short and the night clear.

"Well, Giles is a very good fellow," said Mr. Melbury, as they struck down the lane under boughs which formed a black filigree in which the stars seemed set.

"Certainly he is." Grace spoke quickly, and in such a tone

as to show that he stood no lower, if no higher, in her regard than he had stood before.

When they were opposite an opening through which, by day, the doctor's house could be seen, they observed a light in one of his rooms, although it was now about two o'clock.

"The doctor is not abed yet," said Mrs. Melbury.

"Hard study, no doubt," said her husband.

"One would think that, as he seems to have nothing to do about here by day, he could at least afford to go to bed early at night. 'Tis astonishing how little we see of him."

Melbury's mind seemed to turn with much relief to the contemplation of Mr. Fitzpiers after the scenes of the evening. "It is natural enough," he replied. "What can a man of that sort find to interest him in Hintock? I don't expect he'll stay here long."

His thoughts then reverted to Giles's party, and when they were nearly home he spoke again, his daughter being a few steps in advance: "It is hardly the line of life for a girl like Grace, after what she's been accustomed to. I didn't foresee that, in sending her to boarding-school and letting her travel and what not, to make her a good bargain for Giles, I should be really spoiling her for him. Ah—'tis a thousand pities! But he ought to have her—he ought!"

At this moment the two chalk-marking, langterloo men, having at last really finished their play, could be heard coming along in the rear, vociferously singing a song to march-time, and keeping vigorous step to the same in far-reaching strides:—

> ". . . . said she,
> 'A maid again I never shall be,
> Till apples grow on an orange tree!'"

The timber-merchant turned indignantly to Mrs. Melbury. "That's the sort of society we've been asked to meet," he said. "For us old folk it didn't matter; but for Grace—Giles should have known better!"

Meanwhile, in the empty house from which the guests had just cleared out the subject of their discourse was walking from room to room surveying the general displacement of furniture with no ecstatic feeling; rather the reverse, indeed. At last he entered the bakehouse, and found there Robert Creedle sitting over the embers, also lost in contemplation. Winterborne sat down beside him.

"Well, Robert; you must be tired. You'd better get on to bed."

"Ay, ay, Giles—what do I call ye—maister, I would say. But 'tis well to think the day *is* done, when 'tis done."

Winterborne had abstractedly taken the poker, and with a wrinkled forehead was ploughing abroad the wood-embers on the wide hearth, till it was like a vast scorching Sahara, with red-hot boulders lying about everywhere. "Do you think it went off well, Creedle?" he asked.

"The victuals did; that I know. And the drink did; that I steadfastly believe, from the holler sound of the barrels. Good honest drink 'twere, the headiest drink I ever brewed; and the best wine that berries could rise to; and the briskest Horner-and-Cleeves cider ever wrung down, leaving out the spice and sperrits I put into it, while that egg-flip would ha' passed through muslin, so little criddled 'twere. 'Twas good enough to make any king's heart merry—ay, to make his whole carcase smile.—Still, I don't deny, I'm afeard some things didn't go well with He and his." Creedle nodded in a direction which signified where the Melburys lived.

"I'm afraid too that it was a failure there!"

"If so, 'twere doomed to be so. Not but what that slug might as well have come upon anybody else's plate as hers."

"What slug?"

"Well maister, there was a little small one upon the edge of her plate when I brought it out; and so it must have been in her few leaves of winter-green."

"How the deuce did a slug get there?"

"That I don't know no more than the dead; but there my gentleman was."

"But Robert, of all places, that was where he shouldn't have been!"

"Well 'twas his native home, come to that; and where else could we expect him to be? I don't care who the man is, slugs and caterpillars always will lurk in close to the stump of cabbages in that tantalizing way."

"He wasn't alive I suppose?" said Giles with a shudder on Grace's account.

"Oh no. He was well boiled—I warrant him well boiled. God forbid that a *live* slug should be seed on any plate of victuals that's served by Robert Creedle . . . . . But Lord, there; I don't mind 'em myself—them green ones; for they were born on cabbage, and they've lived on cabbage; so they must be made of cabbage. But she, the close-mouthed little lady, she didn't say a word about it; though 'twould have made good small conversation as to the nater of such creatures; especially as wit ran short among us sometimes."

"Oh yes—'tis all over!" murmured Giles to himself, shaking his head over the glooming plain of embers, and lining his forehead more than ever. "Do you know, Robert," he said, "that she's been accustomed to servants and everything superfine these many years? How, then, could she stand our ways?"

"Well, all I can say is then that she ought to hob-and-nob elsewhere. They shouldn't have schooled her so monstrous high, or else bachelor-men shouldn't give randys, or if they do give 'em, only to their own race."

"Perhaps that's true," said Winterborne, rising and yawning a sigh.

XI

"'Tis a pity—a thousand pities!" her father kept saying next morning at breakfast, Grace being still in her bedroom.

Here was the fact which could not be disguised: since seeing what an immense change her last twelvemonths of absence had produced in his daughter, after the heavy sum per annum that he had been spending for several years upon her education, he was reluctant to let her marry Giles Winterborne, indefinitely occupied as woodsman, cider-merchant, apple-farmer, and what-not, even were she willing to marry him herself.

But how could he, with any self respect, obstruct Winterborne's suit at this stage, and nullify a scheme he had laboured to promote—was, indeed, mechanically promoting at this moment? A crisis was approaching, mainly as a result of his contrivances; and it would have to be met.

"She will be his wife, if you don't upset her notion that she's bound to accept him as an understood thing," said Mrs. Melbury. "Bless you, she'll soon shake down here in Hintock and be content with Giles's way of living, which he'll improve with what money she'll have from you. 'Tis the strangeness after her genteel life that makes her feel uncomfortable at first. Why, when *I* saw Hintock the first time I thought I never could like it. But things gradually get familiar, and stone floors seem not so very cold and hard, and the hooting of owls not so very dreadful, and loneliness not so very lonely, after a while."

"Yes—I believe 'ee. That's just it. I *know* Grace will gradually sink down to our level again, and catch our manners and way of speaking, and feel a drowsy content in being Giles's wife. But I can't bear the thought of dragging down to that old level as promising a piece of maidenhood as ever lived—fit to ornament a palace wi', that I've taken so much trouble to lift up. Fancy her white hands getting redder every day, and her tongue losing its pretty up-country curl in talking, and her bounding walk becoming the regular Hintock shail and wamble."

"She may shail; but she'll never wamble," replied his wife decisively.

When Grace came downstairs he complained of her lying in bed so late: not so much moved by a particular objection to that form of indulgence as discomposed by these other reflections.

The corners of her pretty mouth dropped a little down. "You used to complain with justice when I was a girl," she said. "But I am a woman now, and can judge for myself. . . . But it is not that: it is something else!" Instead of sitting down she went outside the door.

He was sorry. The petulance that relatives show towards each other is in truth directed against that intangible Cause which has shaped the situation no less for the offenders than the offended, but is too elusive to be discerned and cornered

by poor humanity in irritated mood. Melbury followed her.
She had rambled on to the paddock, where the white frost
lay, making the grass rustle like paper-shavings under their
feet; and where starlings in flocks of twenties and thirties
were walking about, watched by a comfortable family of sparrows perched in a line along the string-course of the chimney, and preening themselves in the rays of the sun.

"Come in to breakfast, my girl," he said. "And as to Giles,
use your own mind. Whatever pleases you will please me."

"I am promised to him, father; and I cannot help thinking
that in honour I ought to marry him, whenever I do marry."

He had a strong suspicion that somewhere in the bottom
of her heart there pulsed an old simple indigenous feeling
favourable to Giles, though it had become overlaid with
implanted tastes. "Very well," he said. "But I hope I shan't
lose you yet. Come in to breakfast.—What did you think of
the inside of Hintock House the other day?"

"I liked it much."

"Different from friend Winterborne's."

She said nothing; but he who knew her was aware that
she meant by her silence to reproach him with drawing cruel
comparisons.

"Mrs. Charmond has asked you to come again—when, did
you say?"

"She thought Tuesday; but would send the day before to
let me know if it suited her." And with this subject upon
their lips they entered to breakfast.

Tuesday came; but no message from Mrs. Charmond. Nor
was there any on Wednesday. In brief, a fortnight slipped by
without a sign; and it looked suspiciously as if Mrs. Charmond
was not going further in the direction of "taking up" Grace
at present.

Her father reasoned thereon. Immediately after his daughter's two indubitable successes with Mrs. Charmond, the interview in the wood, and the visit to the House, she had attended
Winterborne's party. No doubt the out-and-out joviality of
that gathering had made it a topic in the neighbourhood,
and that every one present as guests had been widely spoken
of—Grace, with her exceptional qualities, above all. What

then so natural as that Mrs. Charmond should have heard the village news, and become quite disappointed in her expectations of Grace at finding she kept such company?

Full of this *post hoc* argument Mr. Melbury overlooked the infinite throng of other possible reasons and unreasons for a woman changing her mind. For instance, while knowing that his Grace was attractive he quite forgot that Mrs. Charmond had also great pretensions to beauty.

So it was settled in his mind that her sudden mingling with the villagers at the unlucky Winterborne's was the cause of her most grievous loss, as he deemed it, in the direction of Hintock House.

"'Tis a great sacrifice!" he would repeat to himself. "I am ruining her for conscience' sake!"

It was one morning later on, while these things were agitating his mind, that something darkened the window, just as they finished breakfast. Looking up they saw Giles in person, mounted on horseback, and straining his neck forward, as he had been doing for some time, to catch their attention through the window. Grace had been the first to see him, and involuntarily exclaimed, "There he is—and a new horse!"

On their faces as they regarded Giles, were written their suspended thoughts and compound feelings concerning him, could he have read them through those old panes. But he saw nothing: his features just now were, for a wonder, lit up with a red smile at some other idea. So they rose from breakfast and went to the door, Grace with an anxious wistful manner, her father in a reverie, Mrs. Melbury placid and enquiring. "We have come out to look at your horse," she said.

It could be seen that he was pleased at their attention, and explained that he had ridden a mile or two to try the animal's paces. "I bought her," he added, with warmth so severely repressed as to seem indifference, "because she has been used to carry a lady."

Still Mr. Melbury did not brighten. Mrs. Melbury said, "And is she quiet?"

Winterborne assured her that there was no doubt of it. "I took care of that. She's twenty-one, and very clever for her age."

"Well, get off and come in," said Melbury brusquely; and Giles dismounted accordingly.

This event was the concrete result of Winterborne's thoughts during the past week or two. The want of success with his evening-party he had accepted in as philosophic a mood as he was capable of; but there had been enthusiasm enough left in him one day at Sherton-Abbas market to purchase the mare, which had belonged to a neighbouring parson with several daughters, and was offered him to carry either a gentleman or a lady, and to do odd jobs of carting and agriculture at a pinch. This obliging quadruped seemed to furnish Giles with a means of re-instating himself in Melbury's good opinion as a man of considerateness by throwing out equestrian possibilities to Grace if she became his wife.

The latter looked at him with intensified interest this morning, in the mood which is altogether peculiar to woman's nature, and which, when reduced into plain words, seems as impossible as the penetrability of matter; that of entertaining a tender pity for the object of her own unnecessary coldness. The imperturbable poise which marked Winterborne in general was enlivened now by a freshness and animation that set a brightness in his eye and on his cheek. Mrs. Melbury asked him to have some breakfast; and he pleasurably replied that he would join them, not perceiving that they had all finished the meal, and that the tune piped by the kettle denoted it to be nearly empty; so that fresh water had to be brought in, and a general renovation of the table carried out. Neither did he know, so full was he of his tender ulterior object in buying that horse, how the morning was slipping away, nor how he was keeping the family from dispersing about their duties.

Then he told throughout the humorous story of the horse's purchase, looking particularly grim at some fixed object in the room, a way he always looked when he narrated anything that amused him. While he was still thinking of the scene he had described Grace rose and said, "I have to go and help my mother now, Mr. Winterborne."

"H'm?" he ejaculated, turning his eyes suddenly upon her. She repeated her words with a slight blush of awkwardness;

whereupon Giles becoming suddenly conscious, too conscious, jumped up saying, "To be sure, to be sure!" and wished them quickly good-morning.

Nevertheless he had upon the whole strengthened his position, with her at least. Time, too, was on his side, for (as her father saw with regret) already the homeliness of Hintock life was fast becoming lost to her observation as a singularity; as the momentary strangeness of a face from which we have for years been separated insensibly passes off with renewed intercourse, and tones itself down into identity with the lineaments of the past.

Thus Mr. Melbury went out of the house still unreconciled to the sacrifice of the gem he had been at such pains in mounting. He fain could hope, in the secret nether chamber of his mind, that something would happen before the balance of her feeling had quite turned in Winterborne's favour, to relieve his conscience and at the same time preserve her on her elevated plane.

XII

IT WAS a day of rather bright weather for the season. Miss Melbury went out for a morning walk, and her ever regardful father, having an hour's leisure, offered to walk with her. The breeze was fresh, and quite steady, filtering itself through the denuded mass of twigs without swaying them, but making the point of each ivy-leaf on the trunks scratch its underlying neighbour restlessly. Grace's lips sucked in this native air of hers like milk. They soon reached a place where the wood ran down into a corner, and they went outside it towards comparatively open ground. Having looked round they were intending to re-enter the copse when a panting fox emerged with a dragging brush, trotted past them tamely as a domestic cat, and disappeared amid some dead fern. They walked on, her father merely observing after watching the animal, "They are hunting somewhere near."

Further up they saw in the mid-distance the hounds running hither and thither, as if the scent lay cold that day.

Soon members of the hunt appeared on the scene, and it was evident that the chase had been stultified by general puzzle-headedness as to the whereabouts of the intended victim. In a minute a gentleman-farmer, panting with Acteonic excitement, rode up to the two pedestrians, and Grace being a few steps in advance he asked her if she had seen the fox.

"Yes," said she. "I saw him some time ago—just out there."

"Did you cry Halloo?"

"I said nothing."

"Then why the devil didn't you, or get the old buffer to do it for you!" said the man as he cantered away.

She looked rather disconcerted, and observing her father's face saw that it was quite red.

"He ought not to have spoken to 'ee like that!" said the old man in the tone of one whose heart was bruised, though it was not by the epithet applied to himself. "And he wouldn't if he had been a gentleman. 'Twas not the language to use to a woman of any niceness. You so well read and cultivated —how could he expect ye to go shouting a view-halloo like a farm tom-boy! Hasn't it cost me near a hundred a year to lift you out of all that, so as to show an example to the neighbourhood of what a woman can be?—Grace, shall I tell you the secret of it? 'Twas because *I* was in your company. If a black-coated squire or pa'son had been walking with you instead of me he wouldn't have spoken so."

"No, no, father; there's nothing in you rough or ill-mannered!"

"I tell you it is that! I've noticed, and I've noticed it many times, that a woman takes her colour from the man she's walking with. The woman who looks an unquestionable lady when she's with a polished-up fellow looks a tawdry imitation article when she's hobbing and nobbing with a homely blade. . . . . You shan't be treated like that for long, or at least your children shan't. You shall have somebody to walk with you who looks more of a dandy than I—please God you shall!"

"But my dear father," she said much distressed, "I don't mind at all. I don't wish for more honour than I already have!"

"A perplexing and ticklish possession is a daughter," according to the Greek poet, and to nobody was one ever more so than to Melbury. As for Grace, she began to feel troubled; she did not perhaps wish, there and then, to devote her life unambitiously to Giles Winterborne; but she was more and more uneasy at being the social hope of the family.

"You would like to have more honour, if it pleases me?" asked her father, in continuation of the subject.

Despite her feeling she assented to this. His reasoning had not been without weight upon her.

"Grace," he said, just before they had reached the house; "if it costs me my life you shall marry well! To-day has shown me that whatever a young woman's niceness, she stands for nothing alone. You shall marry well."

He breathed heavily, and his breathing was caught up by the breeze, which seemed to sigh a soft remonstrance.

She looked calmly at him. "And how about Mr. Winterborne?" she asked. "I mention it, father, not as a matter of sentiment, but as a question of keeping faith."

The timber-merchant's eyes fell for a moment. "I don't know—I don't know," he said. "'Tis a trying strait. Well, well; there's no hurry. We'll wait and see how he gets on."

That evening he called her into his room, a snug little apartment behind the large parlour. It had at one time been part of the bakehouse, with the ordinary oval brick oven in the wall; but Mr. Melbury in turning it into an office had built into the cavity an iron safe, which he used for holding his private papers. The door of the safe was now open, and his keys were hanging from it.

"Sit down Grace, and keep me company," he said. "You may amuse yourself by looking over these." He threw out a heap of papers before her.

"What are they?" she asked.

"Securities of various sorts." He unfolded them one by one. "Papers worth so much money each. Now here's a lot of turnpike-bonds, for one thing. Would you think that each of these pieces of paper is worth two hundred pounds?"

"No indeed, if you didn't say so."

"'Tis so then. Now here are papers of another sort. They are for different sums in the Three-per-cents. Now these are

Port-Breedy Harbour bonds—we have a great stake in that harbour, you know, because I send off timber there. Open the rest at your pleasure. They'll interest 'ee."

"Yes, I will—some day," said she rising.

"Nonsense—open them now. You ought to learn a little of such matters. A young lady of education should not be ignorant of money affairs altogether. Suppose you should be left a widow some day, with your husband's title-deeds and investments thrown upon your hands——"

"Don't say that, father. Title-deeds—it sounds so vain!"

"It does not. Come to that I have title-deeds myself. There—that piece of parchment represents houses in Sherton-Abbas."

"Yes; but—" She hesitated, looked at the fire, and went on in a low voice: "——if what has been arranged about me should come to anything, my sphere will be quite a middling one."

"Your sphere ought not to be middling!" he exclaimed. "You said you never felt more at home, more in your element, anywhere than you did that afternoon with Mrs. Charmond, when she showed you her house, and all her nick-nacks, and made you stay to tea so nicely in her drawing-room—surely you did!"

"Yes, I did say so," admitted Grace.

"Was it true?"

"Yes—I felt so at the time. The feeling is less strong now, perhaps."

"Ah! Now, though you don't see it, your feeling at the time was the right one, because your mind and body were just in full and fresh cultivation, so that going there with her was like meeting like. Since then you've been staying with us, and have fallen back a little, and so you don't feel your place so strongly. Now do as I tell you, and look over these papers, and see what you'll be worth some day. For they'll all be yours, you know: who have I got to leave 'em to but you? Perhaps when your education is backed up by what these papers represent, and that backed up by another such a set and their owner, men such as that fellow was this morning may think you a little more than a buffer's girl."

So she did as commanded, and opened each of the folded

representatives of hard cash that her father put before her. To sow in her heart cravings for social position was obviously his strong desire, though in direct antagonism to a better feeling which had hitherto prevailed with him, and had, indeed, only succumbed that morning during the ramble.

She wished that she was not his worldly hope; the responsibility of such a position was too great. She had made it for herself mainly by her appearance and attractive behaviour to him since her return. "If I had only come home in a shabby dress, and tried to speak roughly, this might not have happened," she thought. She deplored less the fact, however, than the contingencies.

Her father then insisted upon her looking over his cheque-book, and reading the counterfoils. This also she obediently did; and at last came to two or three which had been drawn to defray some of the late expenses of her clothes, board, and education.

"I, too, cost a good deal, like the horses and waggons and corn," she said looking up sorrily.

"I didn't want you to look at those—I merely meant to give you an idea of my investment transactions. But if you do cost as much as they, never mind. You'll yield a better return."

"Don't think of me like that!" she begged. "A mere chattel."

"A what? Oh, a dictionary word. Well as that's in your line I don't forbid it, even if it tells against me," he said good-humouredly. And he looked her proudly up and down.

A few minutes later Grammer Oliver came to tell them that supper was ready, and in giving the information she added incidentally, "So we shall soon lose the mistress of Hintock House for some time, I hear, Maister Melbury. Yes, she's going off to foreign parts to-morrow, for the rest of the winter months; and be chok'd if I don't wish I could do the same, for my wind-pipe is furred like a flue."

When the old woman had left the room Melbury turned to his daughter and said; "So Grace, you've lost your new friend; and your chance of keeping her company, and writing her travels, is quite gone from 'ee!"

Grace said nothing.

"Now," he went on emphatically, " 'tis Winterborne's affair

has done this. O yes 'tis; so let me say one word. Promise me that you will not meet him again without my knowledge."

"I never do meet him, father, either without your knowledge or with it."

"So much the better. I don't like the look of this at all. And I say it not out of harshness to him, poor fellow, but out of tenderness to you. For how could a woman brought up delicately as you have been bear the roughness of a life with him?"

She sighed; it was a sigh of sympathy with Giles, complicated by a sense of the intractability of circumstances.

At that same hour, and almost at that same minute, there was a conversation about Winterborne in progress in the village lane, opposite Mr. Melbury's gates, where Timothy Tangs the elder, and Robert Creedle, had accidentally met.

The sawyer was asking Creedle if he had heard what was all over the parish, the skin of his face being toned towards brightness in respect of it as news, and towards concern in respect of its bearings.

"Why that poor little lonesome thing Marty South is likely to lose her father. He was almost well, but is much worse again; a man all skin and grief he ever were; and if he leave Little Hintock for a better land, won't it make some difference to your good man Winterborne, neighbour Creedle?"

"Can I be a prophet in Hintock?" said Creedle. "I was only shaping of such a thing yesterday in my poor long-seeing way! It is upon John South's life that all Mr. Winterborne's houses hang. If so be South die and so make his decease, thereupon the law ordains that the houses fall without the least chance of saving 'em into Her hands at the House. I told him so; but the words of the faithful be only as wind!"

XIII

THE news was true. The Life—the one fragile life—that had been used as a measuring-tape of time by law, was in danger of being frayed away. It was the last of a group of lives which had served this purpose, at the end of whose breathings the small homestead occupied by South himself, the larger one of Giles Winterborne, and half-a-dozen others that had been in the possession of various Hintock village families for the previous hundred years, and were now Winterborne's, would fall in and become part of the encompassing estate.

Winterborne walked up and down his garden next day thinking of the contingency. The sense that the paths he was pacing, the cabbage-plots, the appletrees, his dwelling, cider-cellar, wring-house, stables, weather-cock, were all slipping away over his head and beneath his feet as if they were painted on a magic-lantern slide, was curious. In spite of John South's late indisposition he had not anticipated danger.

Whilst he was here in the garden somebody came to fetch him. It was Marty herself, and she showed her distress by her unconsciousness of a cropped poll.

"Father is still so much troubled in his mind about that tree," she said. "You know the tree I mean, Mr. Winterborne? the tall one in front of the house that he thinks will blow down and kill us. Can you come, and see if you can persuade him out of his notion? I can do nothing."

He accompanied her to the cottage, and she conducted him upstairs. John South was pillowed up in a chair between the bed and the window, exactly opposite the latter, towards which his face was turned.

"Ah, neighbour Winterborne," he said. "I wouldn't have minded if my life had only been my own to lose; I don't vallie it in much of itself, and can let it go if 'tis required of me. But to think what 'tis worth to you, a young man rising in life, that do trouble me! It seems a trick of dishonesty towards ye to go off at fifty-five! I could bear up, I know I could, if it were not for the tree—yes, the tree 'tis that's killing me. There he stands, threatening my life every minute that the wind do blow. He'll come down upon us, and squat us dead; and what will ye do when the life on your property is taken away!"

"Never you mind me—that's of no consequence," said Giles. "Think of yourself alone."

He looked out of the window in the direction of the wood-man's gaze. The tree was a tall elm, familiar to him from childhood, which stood at a distance of two-thirds its own height from the front of South's dwelling. Whenever the wind blew, as it did now, the tree rocked, naturally enough; and the sight of its motion, and sound of its sighs, had gradually bred the terrifying illusion in the woodman's mind. Thus he would sit all day, in spite of persuasion, watching its every sway, and listening to the melancholy Gregorian melodies which the air wrung out of it. This fear it apparently was, rather than any organic disease, which was eating away the health of John South.

As the tree waved South waved his head, making it his fugleman with abject obedience. "Ah—when it was quite a small tree," he said, "and I was a little boy, I thought one day of chopping it off with my hook to make a clothes-line-prop with. But I put off doing it, and then I again thought that I would; but I forgot it, and didn't. And at last it got too big; and now 'tis my enemy, and will be the death of me. Little did I think, when I let that sapling stay, that a time would come when it would torment me, and dash me into my grave."

"No, no," said Winterborne and Marty soothingly. But they thought it possible that it might hasten him into his grave, though in another way than by falling.

"I tell you what," added Winterborne. "I'll climb up this afternoon, and shroud off the lower boughs, and then it won't be so heavy, and the wind won't affect it so."

"She won't allow it—a strange woman come from nobody knows where—she won't have it done."

"You mean Mrs. Charmond? Oh, she doesn't know there's such a tree on her estate. Besides, shrouding is not felling, and I'll risk that much."

He went out, and when afternoon came he returned, took a bill-hook from the shed, and with a ladder climbed into the lower part of the tree, where he began lopping off— "shrouding" as they called it at Hintock—the lowest boughs. Each of these quivered under his attack, bent, cracked, and fell into the hedge. Having cut away the lowest tier he stepped off the ladder, climbed a few steps higher, and attacked those at the next level. Thus he ascended with the progress of his work far above the top of the ladder, cutting away his perches as he went, and leaving nothing but a bare stem below him.

The work was troublesome, for the tree was large. The afternoon wore on, turning dark and misty about four o'clock. From time to time Giles cast his eyes across towards the bedroom-window of South, where, by the flickering fire in the chamber, he could see the old man watching him, sitting motionless with a hand upon each arm of the chair. Beside him sat Marty, also straining her eyes towards the skyey field of his operations.

A curious question suddenly occurred to Winterborne, and he stopped his chopping. He was operating on another person's property to prolong the years of a lease by whose termination that person would considerably benefit. In that aspect of the case he doubted if he ought to go on. On the other hand he was working to save a man's life, and this seemed to empower him to adopt arbitrary measures.

The wind had died down to a calm, and while he was weighing the circumstances he saw coming along the road through the increasing mist a figure which, indistinct as it was, he knew well. Grace Melbury was on her way out from the house, probably for a short evening walk before dark. He arranged himself for a greeting from her, since she could hardly avoid passing immediately beneath the tree.

But Grace, though she looked up and saw him, was just at that time too full of the words of her father to give him any encouragement. The years-long regard that she had had for him was not kindled by her return into a flame of sufficient brilliancy to make her rebellious. Thinking that she might not see him he cried, "Miss Melbury; here I am."

She turned up her head again. She was near enough to see the expression of his face, and the nails in his soles, silver-bright with constant walking. But she did not reply; and dropping her glance anew went on.

Winterborne's face grew strange; he mused, and proceeded automatically with his work. Grace meanwhile had not gone far. She had reached a gate, whereon she had leant sadly and whispered to herself, "What shall I do?"

A sudden fog came on, and she curtailed her walk, passing

under the tree again on her return. Again he addressed her. "Grace," he said when she was close to the trunk, "speak to me." She gazed straight up, shook her head without stopping, and went on to a little distance, where she stood observing him from behind the hedge.

Her coldness had been kindly meant. If it was to be done, she had said to herself, it should be begun at once. While she stood out of observation Giles seemed to recognise her meaning; with a sudden start he worked on, climbing higher into the sky, and cutting himself off more and more from all intercourse with the sublunary world. At last he had worked himself so high up the elm and the mist had so thickened that he could only just be discerned as a dark grey spot on the light grey zenith; he would have been altogether out of notice but for the stroke of his bill-hook, and the flight of a bough downward, and its crash upon the hedge at intervals.

It was not to be done thus, after all: plainness and candour were best. She went back a third time; he did not see her now, and she lingeringly gazed up at his unconscious figure, loth to put an end to any kind of hope that might live on in him still. "Giles—Mr. Winterborne," she said.

His work so rustled the boughs that he did not hear. "Mr. Winterborne!" she cried again, and this time he stopped, looked down, and replied.

"My silence just now was not accident," she said in an unequal voice. "My father says it is better for us not to think too much of that—engagement, or understanding, between us, that you know of. I, too, think that upon the whole he is right. But we are friends, you know, Giles, and almost relations."

"Very well," he answered in an enfeebled voice which barely reached down the tree. "I have nothing to say, Grace—I cannot say anything till I've thought awhile."

She added, with emotion in her tone, "For myself I would have married you—some day—I think. But I give way, for I am assured it would be unwise."

He made no reply, but sat back upon a bough, placed his elbow in a fork, and rested his head upon his hand. Thus he remained till the fog and the night had completely enclosed him from her view.

Grace heaved a divided sigh with a tense pause between, and moved onward, her heart feeling uncomfortably big and heavy and her eyes wet. Had Giles, instead of remaining still, immediately come down from the tree to her, would she have continued in that filial, acquiescent frame of mind which she had announced to him as final? If it be true, as women themselves have declared, that one of their sex is never so much inclined to throw in her lot with a man for good and all as five minutes after she has told him such a thing cannot be, the probabilities are that something might have been done by the appearance of Winterborne on the ground beside Grace. But he continued motionless and silent in that gloomy Niflheim or fog-land which involved him, and she proceeded on her way.

The spot seemed now to be quite deserted. The light from South's window made rays on the fog, but did not reach the tree. A quarter of an hour passed, and all was blackness overhead. Giles had not yet come down.

Then the tree seemed to shiver, then to heave a sigh: a movement was audible, and Winterborne dropped almost noiselessly to the ground. He had thought the matter out; and having returned the ladder and bill-hook to their places pursued his way homeward. He would not allow this incident to affect his outer conduct any more than the danger to his leaseholds had done, and went to bed as usual.

Two simultaneous troubles do not always make a double trouble; and thus it came to pass that Giles's practical anxiety about his houses, which would have been enough to keep him awake half the night at any other time, was displaced and not reinforced by his sentimental trouble about Grace Melbury. This severance was in truth more like a burial of her than a rupture with her, but he did not realize so much at present; even when he arose in the morning he felt quite moody and stern: as yet the second note in the gamut of such emotions, a distracting regret for his loss, had not made itself heard.

A load of oak timber was to be sent away before dawn that morning to a builder whose works were in a town many miles off. The trunks were chained down to a heavy timber-carriage with enormous red wheels; and four of the most powerful of Melbury's horses were harnessed in front to draw them.

The horses wore their bells that day. There were sixteen to the team, carried on a frame above each animal's shoulders, and tuned to scale, so as to form two octaves, running from the highest note on the right or off-side of the leader to the lowest on the left or near-side of the shaft-horse. Melbury was among the last to retain horse-bells in that neighbourhood; for living at Little Hintock, where the lanes yet remained as narrow as before the days of turnpike-roads, these sound-signals were still as useful to him and his neighbours as they had ever been in former times. Much backing was saved in the course of a year by the warning notes they cast ahead; moreover the tones of all the teams in the district being known to the carters of each, they could tell a long way off on a dark night whether they were about to encounter friends or strangers.

The fog of the previous evening still lingered so heavily over the woods that the morning could not penetrate the trees. The load being a ponderous one, the lane crooked, and the air so thick, Winterborne set out, as he often did, to accompany the team as far as the corner where it would turn into a wider road.

So they rumbled on, shaking the foundations of the road-side cottages by the weight of their progress, the sixteen bells chiming harmoniously over all, till they had risen out of the valley, and were descending towards the more open route, sparks rising from their creaking skid as if they would set fire to the dead leaves alongside.

Then occurred one of the very incidents against which the bells were an endeavour to guard. Suddenly there beamed into their eyes, quite close to them, the two lamps of a carriage, haloed by the fog. Its approach had been quite unheard by reason of their own noise. The carriage was a covered one, while behind it could be discerned another vehicle laden with luggage.

Winterborne went to the head of the team and heard the

coachman telling the carter that he must turn back. The carter declared that this was impossible.

"You can turn if you unhitch your string-horses," said the coachman.

"It is much easier for you to turn than for us," said Winterborne. "We've five ton of timber on these wheels if we've an ounce."

"But I've another carriage with luggage at my back."

Winterborne admitted the strength of the argument. "But even with that," he said, "you can back better than we. And you ought to; for you could hear our bells half-a-mile off."

"And you could see our lights."

"We couldn't, because of the fog."

"Well; our time's precious," said the coachman haughtily. "You are only going to some trumpery little village or other in the neighbourhood; while we are going straight to Italy."

"Driving all the way, I suppose?" said Winterborne sarcastically.

The contention continued in these terms till a voice from the interior of the carriage inquired what was the matter. It was a lady's.

She was informed of the timber-people's obstinacy; and then Giles could hear her telling the footman to direct the timber-people to turn their horses' heads.

The message was brought; and Winterborne sent the bearer back to say that he begged the lady's pardon, but that he could not do as she requested; that though he would not assert it to be impossible, it was impossible by comparison with the slight difficulty to her party to back their light carriages. As fate would have it, the incident with Grace Melbury on the previous day made Giles less gentle than he might otherwise have shown himself, his confidence in the sex being rudely shaken.

In fine, nothing could move him; and the carriages were compelled to back till they reached one of the sidings or turn-outs constructed in the bank for the purpose. Then the team came on ponderously, and the clanging of its sixteen bells as it passed the discomfited carriages tilted up against the bank, lent a particularly triumphant tone to the team's progress—a tone which, in point of fact, did not at all attach to its conductor's feelings.

Giles walked behind the timber, and just as he had got past the yet stationary carriages he heard a lofty voice say, "Who is that rude man?—not Melbury?" The sex of the speaker was so prominent in the tones that Winterborne felt a pang of regret.

"No ma'am. A younger man, in a smaller way of business in Little Hintock. Winterborne is his name."

Thus they parted company. "Why, Mr. Winterborne," said the waggoner when they were out of hearing; "that was She— Mrs. Charmond! Who'd ha' thought it? What in the world can a woman that does nothing be cock-watching out here at this time o' day for?—Oh, going to Italy—yes, to be sure— I heard she was going abroad. She can't endure the winter here."

Winterborne was vexed at the incident; the more so that he knew Mr. Melbury, in his adoration of Hintock House, would be the first to blame him, if it became known. He accompanied the load to the end of the lane, and then turned back, with an intention to call at South's, to learn the result of the experiment of the preceding evening.

It chanced that a few minutes before this time Grace Melbury, who now rose soon enough to breakfast with her father, in spite of the unwontedness of the hour, had been commissioned by him to make the same inquiry at South's. Marty had been standing at the door when Miss Melbury arrived. Almost before the latter had spoken Mrs. Charmond's carriages, released from the obstruction up the lane, came bowling along, and the two girls turned to regard the spectacle.

Mrs. Charmond did not see them; but there was sufficient light for them to discern her outline between the carriage windows. A noticeable feature in her *tournure* was a magnificent mass of braided locks.

"How well she looks this morning!" said Grace, forgetting Mrs. Charmond's slight in her generous admiration. "Her hair so becomes her, worn that way. I have never seen any more beautiful!"

"Nor have I, miss," said Marty drily, and unconsciously stroking her crown.

Grace watched the carriages with lingering regret till they were out of sight. She then learnt of Marty that South was no better. Before she had come away Winterborne approached the house; but seeing that one of the two girls standing on the doorstep was Grace he turned back again, and sought the shelter of his own home till she should have gone away.

XIV

THE encounter with the carriages forced Winterborne's mind back again to the houses of his which would fall into Mrs. Charmond's possession in the event of South's death. He marvelled, as many have done since, what could have induced his ancestors at Hintock, and other village people, to exchange their old copyholds for life-leases. And he was much struck with his father's negligence in not insuring South's life.

After breakfast he went upstairs, turned over his bed, and drew out a flat canvas bag which lay between the mattress and the sacking. In this he kept his leases, which had remained there unopened ever since his father's death. It was the usual hiding-place among rural lifeholders for such documents. Winterborne sat down on the bed and looked them over. They were ordinary leases for three lives, which a member of the South family, some fifty years before this time, had accepted of the lord of the manor in lieu of certain copyholds and other rights, in consideration of having the dilapidated houses rebuilt by the said lord. They had come into his father's possession chiefly through his mother, who was a South.

Pinned to the corner of one of the indentures was a letter which Winterborne had never seen before. It bore a remote date, the handwriting being that of some solicitor or agent, and the signature the landholder's. It was to the effect that at any time before the last of the stated lives should drop, Mr. John Winterborne, or his representative, should have the privilege of adding his own and his son's life to the life remaining, on payment of a merely nominal fine; the concession being in consequence of the elder Winterborne's consent to demolish one of the houses and relinquish its site, which stood at an awkward corner of the lane, and impeded the way.

The house had been pulled down, years before. Why Giles's father had not taken advantage of his privilege to insert his own and his son's lives it was impossible to say. In all likelihood death alone had hindered him in the execution of that project, the elder Winterborne having been a man who took much pleasure in dealing with house-property in his small way.

Since one of the Souths still survived there was not much doubt that Giles could do what his father had left undone, as far as his own life was concerned. This possibility cheered him much; for by those houses hung many things. Melbury's doubt of the young man's fitness to be the husband of Grace had been based not a little on the precariousness of his holdings in Little and Great Hintock. He resolved to attend to the business at once, the fine for renewal being a sum that he could easily muster. His scheme, however, could not be carried out in a day; and meanwhile he would run up to South's as he had intended to do, to learn the result of the experiment with the tree.

Marty met him at the door. "Well, Marty," he said; and was surprised to read in her face that the case was not so hopeful as he had imagined.

"I am sorry for your labour," she said. "It is all lost. He says the tree seems taller than ever."

Winterborne looked around at it. Taller the tree certainly did seem, the gauntness of its now naked stem being more marked than before.

"It quite terrified him when he first saw what you had done to it this morning," she added. "He declares it will come down upon us and cleave us, like 'the sword of the Lord and of Gideon.'"

"Well; can I do anything else?" asked he.

"The doctor says the tree ought to be cut down."

"Oh—you've had the doctor?"

"I didn't send for him. Mrs. Charmond before she left heard that father was ill; and told him to attend him at her expense."

"That was very good of her. And he says it ought to be cut down. . . . . We mustn't cut it down without her knowledge, I suppose."

He went upstairs. There the old man sat, staring at the now gaunt tree as if his gaze were frozen on to its trunk. Unluckily the tree waved afresh by this time, a wind having sprung up and blown the fog away; and his eyes turned with its wavings.

They heard footsteps; a man's, but of a lighter weight than usual. "There is Doctor Fitzpiers again," she said, and descended. Presently his tread was heard on the naked stairs.

Mr. Fitzpiers entered the sick chamber as a doctor is wont to do on such occasions, and pre-eminently when the room is that of the humble cottager; looking round towards the patient with a preoccupied gaze which so plainly reveals that he has well-nigh forgotten all about the case and the circumstances since he dismissed them from his mind at his last exit from the same apartment. He nodded to Winterborne, who had not seen him since his peep over the hedge at Grace, recalled the case to his thoughts, and went leisurely on to where South sat.

Edred Fitzpiers was, on the whole, a finely formed, handsome man. His eyes were dark and impressive, and beamed with the light either of energy, or of susceptivity—it was difficult to say which; it might have been chiefly the latter. That quick, glittering, empirical eye, sharp for the surface of things if for nothing beneath, he had not. But whether his apparent depth of vision were real, or only an artistic accident of his corporeal moulding, nothing but his deeds could reveal.

His face was rather soft than stern, charming than grand, pale than flushed; his nose—if a sketch of his features be *de rigueur* for a person of his pretensions—was artistically beautiful enough to have been worth modelling by any sculptor not over busy, and was hence devoid of those knotty irregularities which often mean power; while the classical curve of his mouth was not without a looseness in its close. Either from his readily appreciative mien, or his reflective manner, his presence bespoke the philosopher rather than the dandy, an effect which was helped by the absence of trinkets or other trivialities from his attire, though this was more finished and up to date than is usually the case among rural practitioners.

Strict people of the highly respectable class, knowing a little about him by report, said that he seemed likely to err rather in the possession of too many ideas than too few; to be a dreamy 'ist of some sort, or too deeply steeped in some false kind of 'ism. However this may be it will be seen that he was undoubtedly a somewhat rare kind of gentleman and doctor to have descended, as from the clouds, upon Little Hintock.

"This is an extraordinary case," he said at last to Winterborne, after examining South by conversation, look, and touch, and learning that the craze about the elm was stronger than ever. "Come downstairs, and I'll tell you what I think."

They accordingly descended, and the doctor continued, "The tree must be cut down; or I won't answer for his life."

"'Tis Mrs. Charmond's tree; and I suppose we must get permission?" said Giles.

"Oh—never mind whose tree it is—what's a tree beside a life! Cut it down. I have not the honour of knowing Mrs. Charmond as yet; but I am disposed to risk that much with her."

"'Tis timber," rejoined Giles. "They never fell a stick about here without its being marked first, either by her or the agent."

"Then we'll inaugurate a new era forthwith. How long has he complained of the tree?" asked the doctor of Marty.

"Weeks and weeks, sir. The shape of it seems to haunt him like an evil spirit. He says that it is exactly his own age, that it has got human sense, and sprouted up when he was born on purpose to rule him, and keep him as its slave. Others have been like it afore in Hintock."

They could hear South's voice upstairs. "Oh—he's rocking this way; he must come! And then my poor life, that's worth houses upon houses, will be squashed out o' me. Oh—Oh."

"That's how he goes on," she added. "And he'll never look anywhere else but out of the window; and scarcely have the curtains drawn."

"Down with it, then, and hang Mrs. Charmond," said Mr. Fitzpiers. "The best plan will be to wait till the evening, when it is dark, or early in the morning before he is awake, so that he doesn't see it fall, for that would terrify him worse than ever. Keep the blind down till I come, and then I'll assure him, and show him that his trouble is over."

The doctor departed, and they waited till the evening. When it was dusk, and the curtains drawn, Winterborne directed a couple of woodmen to bring a cross-cut saw; and the tall threatening tree was soon nearly off at its base. Next morning, before South was awake they went, and lowered it cautiously, in a direction away from the cottage. It was a business difficult to do quite silently; but it was done at last; and the elm of the same birth-year as the woodman's lay stretched upon the ground. The weakest idler that passed could now set foot on marks formerly made in the upper forks by the shoes of adventurous climbers only, once inaccessible nests could be examined microscopically, and on swaying extremities where birds alone had perched the bystanders sat down.

As soon as it was broad daylight the doctor came, and Winterborne entered the house with him. Marty said that her father was wrapped up and ready as usual to be put into his chair. They ascended the stairs, and soon seated him. He began at once to complain of the tree, and the danger to his life, and Winterborne's house-property in consequence.

The doctor signalled to Giles, who went and drew back the dimity curtains. "It is gone, see," said Mr. Fitzpiers.

As soon as the old man saw the vacant patch of sky in place of the branched column so familiar to his gaze he sprang up, speechless; his eyes rose from their hollows till the whites showed all round; he fell back, and a bluish whiteness overspread him.

Greatly alarmed they put him on the bed. As soon as he came a little out of his fit he gasped, "O it is gone!—where—where?"

His whole system seemed paralysed by amazement. They were thunderstruck at the result of the experiment, and did all they could. Nothing seemed to avail. Giles and Fitzpiers went and came; but uselessly. He lingered through the day, and died that evening as the sun went down.

"Damned if my remedy hasn't killed him!" murmured the doctor.

Dismissing the subject he went downstairs. When going out of the house he turned suddenly to Giles and said, "Who was that young lady we looked at over the hedge the other day?"

Giles shook his head, as if he did not remember.

XV

WHEN Melbury heard what had happened he seemed much moved, and walked thoughtfully about the premises. On South's own account he was genuinely sorry; and on Winterborne's he was the more grieved in that this catastrophe had so closely followed the somewhat harsh suggestion to Giles to draw off from his daughter.

He was quite angry with circumstances for so heedlessly inflicting on Giles a second trouble when the needful one inflicted by himself was all that the proper order of events demanded. "I told Giles's father when he came into those houses not to spend too much money on lifehold property held neither for his own life nor his son's!" he exclaimed. "But he wouldn't listen to me. And now Giles has to suffer for it."

"Poor Giles," murmured Grace.

"Now Grace, between us two, it is very very remarkable! It is almost as if I had foreseen this; and I am thankful for your escape, though I am sincerely sorry for Giles. Had we not dismissed him already we could hardly have found it in our hearts to dismiss him now. So I say, be thankful. I'll do all I can for him as a friend; but as a pretender to the position of my son-in-law, that can never be thought of more."

And yet at that very moment the impracticability to which

poor Winterborne's suit had been reduced was touching Grace's heart to a warmer sentiment on his behalf than she had felt for years concerning him.

He, meanwhile, was sitting down alone in the familiar house which had ceased to be his; taking a calm if somewhat dismal survey of affairs. The pendulum of the clock bumped every now and then against one side of the case in which it swung, as the muffled drum to his worldly march: looking out of the window he could perceive that a paralysis had come over Creedle's occupation of manuring the garden, owing, obviously, to a conviction that they might not be living there long enough to profit by next season's crop.

He looked at the leases again and the letter attached. There was no doubt that he had lost his houses and was left practically penniless by an accident which might easily have been circumvented if he had known the true conditions of his holding. The time for performance had now lapsed, in strict law; but why should not the intention be considered by the landholder when she became aware of the circumstances, and his moral right to retain the holdings for the term of his life be conceded?

His heart sank within him, when he perceived that, despite all the legal reciprocities and safeguards prepared and written, the upshot of the matter was that it depended upon the mere caprice of the woman he had met the day before, in such an unfortunate way, whether he was to possess his houses for life or no.

While he was sitting and thinking a step came to the door, and Melbury appeared, looking very sorry for his position. Winterborne welcomed him by a word and a nod and went on with his examination of the parchments. His visitor sat down.

"Giles," he said, "this is very awkward; and I am sorry for it. What are you going to do?"

Giles informed him of the real state of affairs; and how barely he had missed availing himself of his chance of renewal.

"What a misfortune! Why was this neglected? Well, the best thing you can do is to write and tell her all about it, and throw yourself upon her generosity."

"I would rather not," murmured Giles.

"But you must," said Melbury. "Much depends on it."

In short he argued so cogently that Giles allowed himself to be persuaded, firmly believing it to be a last blow for Grace. The letter to Mrs. Charmond was written and sent to Hintock House; whence, as he knew, it would at once be forwarded to her.

Melbury, feeling that he had done so good an action in coming as to extenuate his previous arbitrary conduct, went home; and Giles was left alone to the suspense of waiting for a reply from the divinity who shaped the ends of the Hintock population. By this time all the villagers knew of the circumstances, and being well-nigh like one family a keen interest was the result all round.

Everybody thought of Giles; nobody thought of Marty. Had any of them looked in upon her during those moonlight nights which preceded the burial of her father they would have seen the girl absolutely alone in the house with the dead man. Her own chamber being nearest the stair-top the coffin had been placed there for convenience; and at a certain hour of the night, when the moon arrived opposite the window, its beams streamed across the still profile of South, sublimed by the august presence of death, and onward a few feet further upon the face of his daughter, lying in her little bed in the silence of a repose almost as dignified as that of her companion—the repose of a guileless soul that had nothing more left on earth to lose, except a life which she did not over-value.

South was buried, and a week passed, and Winterborne watched for a reply from Mrs. Charmond. Melbury was very sanguine as to its tenor; but Winterborne had not told him of the encounter with her carriage, when, if ever he had heard an affronted tone on a woman's lips, he had heard it on hers.

The postman's time for passing was just after Melbury's men had assembled in the spar-house; and Winterborne, who when not busy on his own account would lend assistance there, used to go out into the lane every morning, and meet the postman at the end of one of the green rides through the hazel-copse, in the straight stretch of which his laden figure could be seen a long way off. Grace also was very anxious; more anxious than her father, more perhaps than Winterborne himself. This anxiety led her into the spar-house on some pretext or other almost every morning whilst they were awaiting the answer.

Eleven times had Winterborne gone to that corner of the ride, and looked up its long straight slope through the wet greys of winter dawn. But though the postman's bowed figure loomed in view pretty regularly, he brought nothing for Giles. On the twelfth day the man of missives, while yet in the extreme distance, held up his hand, and Winterborne saw a letter in it. He took it into the spar-house before he broke the seal, and those who were there gathered round him while he read, Grace looking in at the door.

The letter was not from Mrs. Charmond herself, but from her agent at Sherton. Winterborne glanced it over and looked up.

"It's all over," he said.

"Ah!" said they all together.

"Her lawyer is instructed to say that Mrs. Charmond sees no reason for disturbing the natural course of things, particularly as she contemplates pulling the houses down," he said quietly.

"Only think of that," said several. "Pulling down is always the game."

Winterborne had turned away, and said vehemently to himself, "Then let her pull 'em down, and be damned to her!"

Creedle looked at him with a face of seven sorrows, saying, "Ah, 'twas that sperrit that lost 'em for ye, maister!"

Winterborne subdued his feelings, and from that hour, whatever they were, kept them entirely to himself. Yet assuming the value of taciturnity to a man among strangers, it is apt to express more than talkativeness when he dwells among friends. The countryman who is obliged to judge the time of day from changes in external nature sees a thousand successive tints and traits in the landscape which are never discerned by him who hears the regular chime of a clock, because they are never in request. In like manner do we use

our eyes on our taciturn comrade. The infinitesimal movement of muscle, curve, hair, and wrinkle, which when accompanied by a voice goes unregarded, is watched and
translated in the lack of it, till virtually the whole surrounding circle of familiars is charged with the reserved one's moods
and meanings.

So with Winterborne and his neighbours after his stroke
of ill-luck. He held his tongue; and they observed him, and
he knew that he was discomposed.

Encountering Melbury one day his manner was that of a
man who abandoned all claims. "I am glad to meet 'ee, Mr.
Melbury," he said, in a low voice whose quality he endeavoured to make as practical as possible. "I am afraid I shall
not after this be able to keep that mare I bought for the use
of—a possible wife; and as I don't care to sell her, I should
like—if you don't object—to give her to Miss Melbury.—The
horse is very quiet, and would be quite safe for her."

Mr. Melbury was rather affected at this. "You shan't hurt
your pocket like that on our account, Giles. Grace shall have
the horse, but I'll pay you what you gave for her, and any
expense you may have been put to for her keep."

He would not hear of any other terms, and thus it was
arranged. They were now opposite Melbury's house, and the
timber-merchant pressed Winterborne to enter, Grace being
out of the way.

"Pull round the settle, Giles," said the timber-merchant, as
soon as they were within. "I should like to have a serious talk
with you."

Thereupon he put the case to Winterborne frankly, and in
quite a friendly way. He declared that he did not like to be
hard on a man when he was in difficulty; but he really did
not see how Winterborne could marry his daughter now,
without even a house to take her to.

Giles quite acquiesced in the awkwardness of his situation,
but from a momentary gasp of hope—a feeling that he would
like to know Grace's mind from her own lips—he did not
speak out positively, even then. He accordingly departed
somewhat abruptly, and went home to consider whether he
would seek to bring about a meeting with her.

In the evening while he sat pondering he fancied that he heard a scraping on the wall outside his house. The boughs of a monthly rose which grew there made such a noise sometimes, but as no wind was stirring he knew that it could not be the rose-tree. He took up the candle and went out. Nobody was near. As he turned the light flickered on the whitewashed rough-cast of the front, and he saw words written thereon in charcoal, which he read as follows:

"O Giles, you've lost your dwelling-place,
    And therefore, Giles, you'll lose your Grace."

Giles went indoors. He had his suspicions as to the scrawler of those lines, but he could not be sure. What filled his heart far more than curiosity about their authorship was a terrible belief that they were turning out to be true, try to regain Grace as he might. They decided the question for him. He sat down and wrote a formal note to Melbury, stating that he shared to the full Melbury's view of his own and his daughter's promise made some years before; he wished that it should be considered as cancelled, and they themselves quite released from any obligation on account of it.

Having fastened up this their plenary absolution he determined to get it out of his hands, and have done with it; to which end he went off to Melbury's at once. It was now so late that the family had all retired; he crept up to the house, thrust the note under the door, and stole away as silently as he had come.

Melbury himself was the first to rise the next morning; and when he had read the letter his relief was great, for he knew that Giles could have made matters unpleasant if he had chosen to work upon Grace. "Very honourable of Giles; very honourable," he kept saying to himself. "I shall not forget him. . . . Now to keep her up to her own true level."

It happened that Grace went out for an early ramble that morning, and to go in her customary direction she could not avoid passing Winterborne's house. The morning sun was shining flat upon its white surface; and the words, which still remained, were immediately visible to her. She read them. Her face flushed to crimson. She could see Giles and Creedle talking together at the back; the charred spar-gad with which the lines had been written lay on the ground beneath the wall. Feeling pretty sure that Winterborne would observe her action she quickly went up to the wall, rubbed out "lose," and inserted "keep" in its stead. Then she made the best of her way home without looking behind her. Giles could draw an inference now, if he chose.

There could not be the least doubt that gentle Grace was warming to more sympathy with and interest in Winterborne than ever she had done while he was her promised lover; that since his misfortune those social shortcomings of his, which contrasted so awkwardly with her later experiences of life, had become obscured by the generous revival of an old romantic attachment to him. Though mentally trained and tilled into foreignness of view, as compared with her youthful time, Grace was not an ambitious girl; and might if left to herself have declined upon Winterborne without much discontent. Her feelings just now were so far from latent that the writing on the wall had quickened her to an unusual rashness.

Having returned from her walk she sat at breakfast silently. When her step-mother had left the room she said to her father: "I have made up my mind that I should like my engagement to Giles to continue."

Melbury looked much surprised. "Nonsense," he said sharply. "You don't know what you are talking about. Look here." He handed across to her the letter received from Giles.

She read it, and said no more. Could he have seen her write on the wall? She did not know. Fate, it seemed, would have it this way, and there was nothing to do but to acquiesce.

It was a few hours after this that Winterborne who, curiously enough, had *not* perceived Grace writing, was clearing away the tree from the front of South's late dwelling. He saw Marty standing in her doorway, a slim figure in meagre black almost without womanly contours as yet. He went up to her and said, "Marty why did you write that on my wall last night? It *was* you, you know."

"Because it was the truth."

"Having prophesied one thing, why did you alter it to another? Your predictions can't be worth much."

"I have not altered it."

"But you have."

"No."

"It is altered. Go and see."

She went, and read that in spite of losing his dwelling-place he would *keep* his Grace. Marty came back surprised. "Well," she said. "Who can have made such nonsense of it?"

"Who indeed?" said he.

"I have rubbed it all out, as the point of it is quite gone."

"You'd no business to rub it out; I meant to let it stay a little longer."

"Some idle boy altered it, no doubt," she murmured.

As this seemed very probable Winterborne said no more, and dismissed the matter from his mind.

From this day of his life onward for a considerable time Winterborne, though not absolutely out of his house as yet, retired into the background of human life and action thereabout—a feat not particularly difficult of performance anywhere when the doer has the assistance of a lost prestige. Grace, thinking that Winterborne saw her write, made no further sign, and the frail barque of fidelity that she had thus timidly launched was stranded and lost.

XVI

DR. FITZPIERS lived on the slope of the hill, in a house of much less pretension both as to architecture and as to magnitude than the timber-merchant's. The latter had without doubt been once the manorial residence appertaining to the snug and modest domain of Little Hintock, of which the boundaries were now lost by its absorption into the adjoining estate of Mrs. Charmond. Though the Melburys themselves were unaware of the fact there was every reason to believe—at least, so the parson said—that the owners of that little manor had been Melbury's own ancestors, the family name occurring in numerous documents relating to transfers of land about the time of the Civil Wars.

Mr. Fitzpiers's dwelling, on the contrary, was small, box-like, and comparatively modern. It had been occupied, and was in part occupied still, by a retired farmer and his wife, who, on the surgeon's arrival in quest of a home, had accommodated him by receding from their front rooms into the kitchen quarter, whence they administered to his wants, and emerged at regular intervals to receive from him a not unwelcome addition to their income.

The cottage and its garden were so regular in their plan that they might have been laid out by a Dutch designer of the time of William and Mary. In a low, dense hedge was a door, over which the hedge formed an arch; and from the inside of the door a straight path bordered with clipped box ran up the slope of the garden to the porch, which was exactly in the middle of the house-front, with two windows on each side. Right and left of the path were first a bed of gooseberry-bushes, next of currant, next of raspberry, next of strawberry, next of old-fashioned flowers, at the corners opposite the porch being spheres of box resembling a pair of school-globes. Over the roof of the house could be seen the orchard; on yet higher ground, and behind the orchard the forest trees, reaching up to the crest of the hill.

Opposite the garden-door into the lane, and visible from the parlour-window, was a swing-gate leading to a field, across which there ran a footpath. The swing gate had just been re-painted, and on one fine afternoon, before the paint was dry, and while gnats stuck dying thereon, the surgeon was standing in his room abstractedly looking out at an occasional pedestrian who passed along that route. Being of a philosophical stamp he perceived that the character of each of these travellers exhibited itself in a somewhat amusing manner by his or her method of handling the gate.

In the men there was not much variety: they gave the gate a kick and passed through. The women were more contrasting. To them the sticky woodwork was a barricade, a disgust, a menace, a treachery, as the case might be.

The first that he noticed was a bouncing young woman with her skirts tucked up and her hair wild. Fitzpiers knew her as Suke Damson. She grasped the gate without looking, giving it a supplementary push with her shoulder, when the white imprint drew from her an exclamation in language not too refined. She went to the green bank and sat down and rubbed herself in the grass, cursing the while.

"Ha-ha-ha," laughed the doctor.

The next was a girl with her hair cropped short in whom the surgeon recognised the daughter of his late patient the woodman South. Moreover a black gown that she wore by way of mourning unpleasantly reminded him that he had ordered a tree-felling which had caused her parent's death. She walked in thought, and not recklessly; but her preoccupation led her to grasp without suspicion the bar of the gate, and touch it with her arm. Fitzpiers felt sorry that she should have soiled that new black frock, poor as it was, for it was probably her only one. She looked at her hand and arm; seemed but little surprised; wiped off the disfigurement with an unmoved face and as if without abandoning her original thoughts. Thus she went on her way.

Then there came over the green quite a different sort of personage. She walked as delicately as if she had been bred in town, and as firmly as if she had been bred in the country; she seemed one who dimly knew her appearance to be attractive, but who retained some of the charm of ignorance by forgetting self in a general pensiveness. She approached the gate. To let such a creature touch it even with the tip of her glove was to Fitzpiers almost like letting her proceed to tragical self-destruction. He jumped up and looked for his hat; but was unable to find the right one; glancing again out of the window he saw that his assistance was unnecessary. Having come up she looked at the gate, picked up a little stick, and using it as a bayonet pushed open the obstacle without touching it at all.

He steadily watched her out of sight, recognising her as the very young lady whom he had seen once before and been unable to identify. Whose could that emotional face be? All the others he had seen in Hintock as yet oppressed him with their crude rusticity; the contrast offered by this suggested that she hailed from elsewhere.

Precisely these thoughts had occurred to him at the first

time of seeing her; but he now went a little further with them, and considered that as there had been no carriage lately in that spot she could not have come a very long distance. She must be somebody staying at Hintock House—probably Mrs. Charmond, of whom he had heard so much; and this probability was sufficient to set a mild radiance in the surgeon's somewhat dull sky.

Fitzpiers sat down to the book he had been perusing. It happened to be that of a German metaphysician for the doctor was not a practical man except by fits, and much preferred the ideal world to the real, and the discovery of principles to their application. The young lady remained in his thoughts. He might have followed her: but he was not constitutionally active, and preferred a conjectural pursuit. However when he went out for a ramble just before dusk he insensibly took the direction of Hintock House, which was the way Grace had been walking, her mind having run on Mrs. Charmond that day; though Grace had returned long since by another route.

Fitzpiers reached the edge of the glen overlooking the manor-house. The shutters were shut, and only one chimney smoked. The mere aspect of the place was enough to inform him that Mrs. Charmond had gone away, and that nobody else was staying there. Fitzpiers felt a vague disappointment that the young lady was not Mrs. Charmond; and without pausing longer to gaze at a carcase from which the spirit had flown he bent his steps homeward.

Later in the evening Fitzpiers was summoned to visit a cottage patient about five miles distant. Like the majority of young practitioners in his vicinity he was far from having assumed the dignity of being driven his rounds by a servant in a brougham that flashed the sunlight like a mirror; his way of getting about was by means of a gig which he drove himself, hitching the rein of the horse to the gate-post, shutter-hook, or garden-paling of the domicile under visitation, or giving pennies to little boys to hold the animal during his stay—pennies which were well earned when the cases to be attended were of a certain cheerful kind that wore out the patience of the little boys.

On this account of travelling alone the night-journeys which Fitzpiers had frequently to take were dismal enough, an apparent perversity in nature ruling that whenever there was to be a birth in a particularly inaccessible and lonely place that event should occur in the night. The surgeon, having been of late years a town man, hated the solitary midnight woodland. He was not altogether skilful with the reins, and it often occurred to his mind that if in some remote depths of the trees an accident were to happen his being alone might be the death of him. Hence he made a practice of picking up any countryman or lad whom he chanced to pass by, and under the disguise of treating him to a nice drive obtained his companionship on the journey, and his convenient assistance in opening gates.

The doctor had started on his way out of the village on the night in question when the light of his lamps fell upon the musing form of Winterborne, walking leisurely along as if he had no object in life. Winterborne was a better class of companion than the doctor usually could get, and he at once pulled up and asked him if he would like a drive through the wood that fine night.

Giles seemed rather surprised at the doctor's friendliness, but said that he had no objection, and accordingly mounted beside Mr. Fitzpiers.

They drove along under the black boughs which formed a tracery upon the stars. Looking up as they passed under a horizontal limb they sometimes saw objects like large tadpoles lodged diametrically across it, which Giles explained to be pheasants at roost; and they sometimes heard the report of a gun, which reminded him that others knew what those tadpole shapes represented as well as he.

Presently the doctor said what he had been going to say for some time: "Is there a young lady staying in this neighbourhood—a very attractive girl—with a little white boa round her neck, and white fur round her gloves?"

Winterborne of course knew in a moment that Grace, whom he had caught the doctor peering at, was represented by these accessories. With a wary grimness induced by the circumstances he evaded an answer by saying, "I saw a young lady talking to Mrs. Charmond the other day; perhaps it was she."

"It might have been," said Fitzpiers. "She is quite a gentle-woman—the one I mean. She cannot be a permanent resident in Hintock, or I should have seen her before. Nor does she look like one."

"She is not staying at Hintock House?"

"No: it is closed."

"Then perhaps she is staying at one of the cottages, or farm-houses?"

"Oh no—you mistake. She was a different sort of woman altogether." As Giles was nobody Fitzpiers treated him accordingly, and rhapsodised to the night in continuation:

> "She moved upon this earth a shape of brightness,
>   A power, that from its objects scarcely drew
>   One impulse of her being—in her lightness
>   Most like some radiant cloud of morning dew,
>   Which wanders through the waste air's pathless blue,
>   To nourish some far desert: she did seem
>   Beside me, gathering beauty as she grew,
>   Like the bright shade of some immortal dream
> Which walks, when tempests sleep, the wave of life's dark
>   stream."

The charm of the lines seemed to Winterborne to be some-how the result of his lost love's charms upon Fitzpiers. "You seem to be mightily in love with her, sir," he said, with a sensation of heart-sickness, and more than ever resolved not to mention Grace by name.

"Oh no—I am not that. Winterborne, people living insu-lated, as I do by the solitude of this place, get charged with emotive fluid like a Leyden jar with electric, for want of some conductor at hand to disperse it. Human love is a subjective thing—the essence itself of man, as that great thinker Spinoza says—*ipsa hominis essentia*; it is joy accompanied by an idea which we project against any suitable object in the line of our vision, just as the rainbow iris is projected against an oak, ash, or elm tree indifferently. So that if any other young lady had appeared instead of the one who did appear, I should have felt just the same interest in her, and have quoted precisely the same lines from Shelley about her, as about this one I saw. Such miserable creatures of circumstance are we all!"

"Well, it is what we call being in love down in these parts, whether or no," said Winterborne.

"You are right enough if you admit that I am in love with something in my own head, and no thing-in-itself outside it at all."

"Is it part of a country doctor's duties to learn that view of things, may I ask, sir?" said Winterborne, adopting the Socratic εἰρωνεία with such well-assumed simplicity that Fitzpiers answered readily.

"Oh no. The real truth is, Winterborne, that medical practice in places like this is a very rule-of-thumb matter: a bottle of bitter stuff for this and that old woman—the bitterer the better—compounded from a few simple stereotyped prescriptions; occasional attendance at births, where mere presence is almost sufficient, so healthy and strong are the people; and a lance for an abscess now and then. Investigation and experiment cannot be carried on without more appliances than one has here—though I have attempted a little."

Giles did not enter into this view of the case; what he had been struck with was the curious parallelism between Mr. Fitzpiers's manner and Grace's, as shown by the fact of both of them straying into a subject of discourse so engrossing to themselves that it made them forget it was foreign to him.

Nothing further passed between himself and the doctor in relation to Grace till they were on their way back. They had stopped at a wayside inn for a glass of brandy-and-cider hot, and when they were again in motion Fitzpiers, possibly a little warmed by the liquor, resumed the subject by saying, "I should like very much to know who that young lady was."

"What difference can it make, if she's only the tree your rainbow falls on?"

"Ha-ha! True."

"You have no wife, sir?"

"I have no wife; and no idea of one. I hope to do better things than marry and settle in Hintock. Not but that it is well for a medical man to be married; and sometimes, begad, 'twould be pleasant enough in this place, with the wind roaring round the house, and the rain and the boughs beating against it . . . I hear that you lost your lifeholds by the death of South?"

"I did. I lost by that in more ways than one."

They had reached the top of Hintock Lane or Street, if it could be called such where three-quarters of the road-side consisted of copse and orchard. One of the first houses to be passed was Melbury's. A light was shining from a bedroom-window facing lengthwise of the lane. Winterborne glanced at it, and saw what was coming. He had withheld an answer to the doctor's inquiry, to hinder his knowledge of Grace. But "who hath gathered the wind in his fists? who hath bound the waters in a garment?"—he could not hinder what was doomed to arrive, and might just as well have been outspoken. As they came up to the house Grace's figure was distinctly visible, drawing the two white curtains together which were used here instead of blinds.

"Why, there she is!" said Fitzpiers. "How in the name of Heaven does she come there?"

"In the most natural way in the world. It is her home. Mr. Melbury is her father."

"Indeed . . . . indeed . . . . indeed! How comes he to have a daughter of that sort?"

Winterborne laughed coldly. "Won't money do anything," he said, "if you've promising material to work upon? Why shouldn't a Hintock girl, taken early from home and put under proper instruction, become as finished as any other young lady if she's got brains and good looks to begin with."

"No reason at all why she shouldn't," murmured the surgeon with reflective disappointment. "Only I didn't anticipate quite that kind of origin for her."

"And you think an inch or two less of her now." There was a little tremor in Winterborne's voice as he spoke.

"Well," said the doctor with recovered warmth; "I am not so sure that I think less of her. At first it was a sort of blow; but dammy, I'll stick up for her. She's charming, every inch of her!"

"So she is," said Winterborne. . . . "But not for me!"

From this ambiguous expression of the reticent woodlander

Dr. Fitzpiers inferred that Giles disliked Miss Melbury, possibly for some haughtiness in her bearing towards him, and had on that account withheld her name. The supposition did not tend to diminish his admiration for her.

XVII

GRACE's exhibition of herself in the act of pulling-to the window-curtains had been the result of an unfortunate incident in the house that day—nothing less than the illness of Grammer Oliver, a woman who had never till now lain down for such a reason in her life. Like others to whom an unbroken career of health has made the idea of keeping their bed almost as repugnant as death itself, she had continued on foot till she literally fell on the floor; and though she had as yet been scarcely a day off duty she had sickened into quite a different personage from the independent Grammer of the yard and spar-house. Ill as she was, on one point she was firm. On no account would she see a doctor; in other words, Fitzpiers.

The room in which Grace had been discerned was not her own but the old woman's. On the girl's way to bed she had received a message from Grammer to the effect that she would much like to speak to her that night.

Grace entered and set the candle on a low chair beside the bed, so that the profile of Grammer as she lay cast itself in a coal-black shadow upon the whitened wall, her large head being still further magnified by an enormous turban, which was really her petticoat wound in a wreath round her temples. Grace put the room a little in order, and approaching the sick woman said, "I am come Grammer, as you wish. Do let us send for the doctor before it gets later?"

"'Ch woll not have him," said Grammer Oliver decisively.

"Then somebody to sit up with you."

"Can't abear it! No. I wanted to see you Miss Grace, because 'Ch have something on my mind. Dear Miss Grace— *I took that money of the doctor, after all!*"

"What money?"

"The ten pounds."

Grace did not quite understand.

"The ten pounds er offered me for my head, because I've a large organ of brain. I signed a paper when I took the money, not feeling concerned about it at all. I have not liked to tell 'ee that it was really settled with him, because you showed such horror at the notion. Well having thought it over more at length I wish I hadn't done it, and it weighs upon my mind. John South's death of fear about the tree makes me think that I shall die of this.... 'Ch have been going to ask him again to let me off, but I hadn't the face."

"Why?"

"I've spent some of the money—more'n two pounds o't. It do wherrit me terribly; and I shall die o' the thought of that paper I signed with my holy cross, as South died of his trouble."

"If you ask him to burn the paper he will I'm sure, and think no more of it."

"'Ch have done it once already, miss. But er laughed cruel-like. 'Yours is such a fine brain, Grammer,' er said, 'that science couldn't afford to lose you. Besides you've taken my money.' . . . . . Don't let your father know of this, please, on no account whatever!"

"No, no. I will let you have the money to return to him."

Grammer rolled the head in question negatively upon the pillow. "Even if I should be well enough to take it to him he won't like it. Though why he should so particular want to look into the works of a poor old woman's headpiece like mine, when there's so many other folks about, I don't know. I know how he'll answer me. 'A lonely person like you Grammer,' er woll say, 'what difference is it to you what becomes of 'ee when the breath's out of your body'.... Oh it do trouble me! If you only knew how he do chevy me round the chimmer in my dreams you'd pity me. How I could do it I can't think! But 'Ch war always so rackless! ... If I only had anybody to plead for me!"

"Mrs. Melbury would, I am sure."

"Ay; but he wouldn't hearken to she! It wants a younger face than hers to work upon such as he."

Grace started with comprehension. "You don't think he would do it for me?" she said.

"Oh, wouldn't he!"

"I couldn't go to him, Grammer, on any account. I don't know him at all."

"Ah, if I were a young lady," said the artful Grammer, "and could save a poor old woman's skellington from a heathen's chopper, to rest in a Christian grave, I would do it, and be glad to. But nobody will do anything for a poor old woman but push her out of the way."

"You are very ungrateful, Grammer, to say that. But you are ill, I know, and that's why you speak so. Now believe me, you are not going to die yet. Remember you told me yourself that you meant to keep him waiting many a year."

"Ay; one can joke when one is well, even in old age; but in sickness one's gaiety falters; and that which seemed small looks large; and the far-off seems near."

Grace's eyes had tears in them. "I don't like to go to him on such an errand Grammer," she said. "But I will, if I must, to ease your mind."

It was with extreme reluctance that Grace cloaked herself next morning for the undertaking. She was all the more indisposed to the journey by reason of Grammer's allusion to the effect of a pretty face upon Doctor Fitzpiers; and hence she most illogically did that which, had the doctor never seen her, would have operated to stultify the sole motive of her journey; that is to say she put on a woollen veil which hid all her face except an occasional spark of her eyes.

Her own wish that nothing should be known of this strange and gruesome proceeding, no less than Grammer Oliver's own desire, led Grace to take every precaution against being discovered. She went out by the garden-door as the safest way, all the household having occupations at the other side. The morning looked forbidding enough when she stealthily edged forth. The battle between snow and thaw was continuing in mid-air: the trees dripped on the garden-plots, where no vegetables would grow for the dripping, though they were planted year after year with that curious mechanical regularity of country people in the face of hopelessness; the moss which covered the once broad gravel terrace was swamped; and Grace stood irresolute. Then she thought of poor Grammer, and her dreams of the doctor running after her scalpel in hand, and the possibility of a case so curiously similar to South's ending in the same way; thereupon she stepped out into the drizzle.

The nature of her errand, and Grammer Oliver's account of the post-mortem compact she had made, lent a fascinating horror to Grace's conception of Fitzpiers. She knew that he was a young man; but her single object in seeking an interview with him put all considerations of his age and social aspect from her mind. Standing as she stood in Grammer Oliver's shoes, he was simply a remorseless Jehovah of the sciences, who would not have mercy, and would have sacrifice; a man whom, save for this, she would have preferred to avoid knowing. But since, in such a small village it was improbable that any long time could pass without their meeting, there was not much to deplore in her having to meet him now.

But, as need hardly be said, Miss Melbury's view of the doctor as a merciless, unwavering, irresistible scientist was not quite in accordance with fact. The real Doctor Fitzpiers was a man of too many hobbies to show likelihood of rising to any great eminence in the profession he had chosen, or even to acquire any wide practice in the rural district he had marked out as his field of survey for the present. In the course of a year his mind was accustomed to pass in a grand solar sweep throughout the zodiac of the intellectual heaven. Sometimes it was in the Ram, sometimes in the Bull; one month he would be immersed in alchemy, another in poesy; one month in the Twins of Astrology and Astronomy; then in the Crab of German literature and metaphysics. In justice to him it must be stated that he took such studies as were immediately related to his own profession in turn with the rest, and it had been in a month of anatomical ardour without the possibility of a subject that he had proposed to Grammer Oliver the terms she had mentioned to her mistress.

As may be inferred from the tone of his conversation with Winterborne, he had lately plunged into abstract philosophy with much zest; perhaps his keenly appreciative, modern, unpractical mind found this a realm more to his taste than any other. Though his aims were desultory Fitzpiers's mental constitution was not without its creditable side; a real inquirer he honestly was at times; even if the midnight rays of his lamp, visible so far through the trees of Hintock, lighted rank literatures of emotion and passion as often as, or oftener than the books and *matériel* of science.

But whether he meditated the Muses or the philosophers, the loneliness of Hintock life was beginning to tell upon his impressionable nature. Winter in a solitary house in the country, without society, is tolerable, nay even enjoyable and delightful, given certain conditions; but these are not the conditions which attach to the life of a professional man who drops down into such a place by mere accident. They were present to the lives of Winterborne, Melbury, and Grace; but not to the doctor's. They are old association—an almost exhaustive biographical or historical acquaintance with every object, animate and inanimate, within the observer's horizon. He must know all about those invisible ones of the days gone by whose feet have traversed the fields which look so grey from his windows; recall whose creaking plough has turned those sods from time to time; whose hands planted the trees that form a crest to the opposite hill; whose horses and hounds have torn through that underwood; what birds affect that particular brake; what bygone domestic dramas of love, jealousy, revenge, or disappointment, have been enacted in the cottages, the mansion, the street or on the green. The spot may have beauty, grandeur, salubrity, convenience; but if it lack memories it will ultimately pall upon him who settles there without opportunity of intercourse with his kind.

In such circumstances maybe an old man dreams of an ideal friend, till he throws himself into the arms of any impostor who chooses to wear that title on his face. A young man may dream of an ideal friend likewise; but some humour of the blood will probably lead him to think rather of an ideal mistress; and at length the rustle of a woman's dress, the sound of her voice, or the transit of her form across the field of his vision will enkindle his soul with a flame that blinds his eyes.

The discovery of the attractive Grace's name and family would have been enough in other circumstances to lead the doctor, if not to put her personality out of his head, to change the character of his interest in her. Instead of treasuring her image as a rarity he would at most have played with her as a toy. He was that kind of man. But situated here he could not go so far as amative cruelty. He dismissed all deferential thought about her, but he could not help taking her somewhat seriously.

He went on to imagine the impossible. So far, indeed, did he go in this futile direction that, as others are wont to do, he constructed dialogues and scenes in which Grace had turned out to be the mistress of Hintock Manor-house, the mysterious Mrs. Charmond, particularly ready and willing to be wooed by himself and nobody else. "Well, she isn't that," he said finally. "But she's a very sweet nice exceptional girl."

The next morning he breakfasted alone as usual. It was snowing with a fine-flaked desultoriness just sufficient to make the woodland grey without ever achieving whiteness. There was not a single letter for Fitzpiers; only a medical circular and a weekly newspaper.

To sit before a large fire on such mornings and read, and gradually acquire energy till the evening came; and then, with lamp alight, and feeling full of vigour, to pursue some engrossing subject or other till the small hours, had hitherto been his practice since arriving here. But to-day he could not settle into his chair. That self-contained position he had lately occupied, in which his whole attention was given to objects of the inner eye, all outer regard being quite disdainful, seemed to have been taken by insidious stratagem, and for the first time he had an interest without the house. He walked from one window to another, and became aware that the most irksome of solitudes is not the solitude of remoteness, but that which is just outside desirable company.

The breakfast hour went by heavily enough, and the next followed, in the same half snowy, half rainy style; the weather now being the inevitable relapse which sooner or later succeeds a time too radiant for the season, such as they had enjoyed in the late mid-winter at Hintock. To people at home there these changeful tricks had their interests; the strange mistakes that some of the more sanguine trees had made in budding before their month, to be incontinently glued up by frozen thawings now; the similar sanguine errors of impulsive birds in framing nests that were swamped by snow-water, and other such incidents, prevented any sense of wearisomeness in the minds of the natives. But these were features of a world not familiar to Fitzpiers; and the inner visions to which he had almost exclusively attended having suddenly failed in their power to absorb him he felt unutterably dreary.

He wondered how long Miss Melbury was going to stay in Hintock. The season was unpropitious for accidental encounters with her out-of-doors, and except by accident he saw not how they were to become acquainted. One thing was clear; any acquaintance with her could only, with a due regard to his future, be casual, at most of the nature of a mild flirtation; for he had high aims, and they would some day lead him into other spheres than this.

Thus desultorily thinking he flung himself down upon the couch, which, as in many draughty old country houses, was constructed with a hood, being in fact a legitimate development from the settle. He tried to read as he reclined; but having sat up till three o'clock that morning the book slipped from his hand and he fell asleep.

XVIII

GRACE approached the house. Her knock, always soft in virtue of her nature, was softer to-day by reason of her strange errand. However it was heard by the farmer's wife who kept the house, and Grace was admitted. Opening the door of the doctor's room the housewife glanced in, and imagining Fitzpiers absent asked Miss Melbury to enter and wait a few minutes whilst she should go and find him, believing him to be somewhere on the premises. Grace acquiesced, went in, and sat down close to the door.

As soon as the door was shut upon her she looked round the room, and started at perceiving a handsome man snugly ensconced on the couch, like a recumbent figure within some canopied mural tomb of the fifteenth century, except that his hands were not exactly clasped in prayer. She had no doubt that this was the surgeon. Awaken him herself she could not, and her immediate impulse was to go and pull the broad riband with a brass rosette which hung at one side of the fireplace. But expecting the landlady to re-enter in a moment she abandoned this intention, and stood gazing in great embarrassment at the reclining philosopher.

The windows of Fitzpiers's soul being at present shuttered he probably appeared less impressive than in his hours of animation; but the light abstracted from his material features by sleep was more than counterbalanced by the mysterious influence of that state, in a stranger, upon the consciousness of a beholder so sensitive. So far as she could criticize at all she became aware that she had encountered a specimen of creation altogether unusual in that locality. The occasions on which Grace had observed men of this stamp were when she had been far away from Hintock; and even then such examples as had met her eye were at a distance, and mainly of commoner fibre than the one who now confronted her.

She nervously wondered why the woman had not discovered her mistake and returned; and went again towards the bell-pull. Approaching the chimney her back was to Fitzpiers, but she could see him in the glass. An indescribable thrill passed through her as she perceived that the eyes of the reflected image were open, gazing wonderingly at her. Under the curious unexpectedness of the sight she became as if spell-bound, almost powerless to turn her head and regard the original. However by an effort she did turn, when there he lay asleep the same as before.

Her startled perplexity as to what he could be meaning was sufficient to lead her to abandon her errand precipitately. She crossed quickly to the door, opened and closed it noise-lessly, and went out of the house unobserved. By the time that she had gone down the path and through the garden-door into the lane she had recovered her equanimity. Here, screened by the hedge, she stood and considered awhile.

Drip, drip, drip, fell the rain upon her umbrella and around;

she had come out on such a morning because of the seriousness of the matter in hand; yet now she had allowed her
mission to be stultified by a momentary tremulousness concerning an incident which perhaps had meant nothing after
all.

In the meantime her departure from the room, stealthy as
it had been, had roused Fitzpiers; and he sat up. In the
reflection from the mirror which Grace had beheld there
was no mystery; he had opened his eyes for a few moments,
but had immediately relapsed into unconsciousness, if indeed
he had ever been positively awake. That somebody had just
left the room he was certain, and that the lovely form which
seemed to have visited him in a dream was no less than the
real presentation of the person departed he could hardly
doubt.

Looking out of the window a few minutes later, down the
box-edged gravel-path which led to the bottom, he saw the
garden-door open and through it enter the young girl of his
thoughts, Grace having just at this juncture determined to
return and attempt the interview a second time. That he saw
her coming instead of going made him ask himself if his first
impression of her were not a dream indeed. She came hesitat-
ingly along, carrying her umbrella so low over her head that
he could hardly see her face. When she reached the point
where the raspberry-bushes ended and the strawberry-bed
began she made a little pause.

Fitzpiers feared that she might not be coming to him even
now, and hastily quitting the room he ran down the path to
meet her. The nature of her errand he could not divine, but
he was prepared to give her any amount of encouragement.

"I beg pardon, Miss Melbury," he said. "I saw you from the
window, and fancied you might imagine that I was not at
home—if it is I you were coming for."

"I was coming to speak one word to you, nothing more,"
she replied. "And I can say it here."

"No, no. Please do come in. Well then, if you will not
come into the house come so far as the porch?" Thus pressed
she went on to the porch, and they stood together inside it,
Fitzpiers closing her umbrella for her.

"I have merely a request or petition to make," she said. "My father's servant is ill—a woman you know—and her illness is serious."

"I am sorry to hear it. I will come and see her at once."

"But I particularly wish you not to come."

"Oh indeed."

"Yes; and she wishes the same. It would make her seriously worse if you were to come. It would almost kill her. . . . My errand is of a peculiar and awkward nature. It is concerning a subject which weighs on her mind—that unfortunate arrangement she made with you, that you might have her skull after death."

"Oh—Grammer Oliver—the old woman with the fine head. Seriously ill, is she."

"And *so* disturbed by her rash compact! I have brought the money back—will you please return to her the agreement she signed?" Grace held out to him a couple of five-pound notes which she had kept ready tucked in her glove.

Without replying or considering the notes Fitzpiers allowed his thoughts to follow his eyes and dwell upon Grace's personality, and the sudden close relation in which he stood to her. The porch was narrow; the rain increased. It ran off the porch and dripped on the creepers, and from the creepers upon the edge of Grace's cloak and skirts.

"The rain is wetting your dress: please do come in," he said. "It really makes my heart ache to let you stay here."

Immediately inside the front door was the door of his sitting-room: he flung it open, and stood in a coaxing attitude. Try how she would Grace could not resist the supplicatory mandate written in the face and manner of this man, and distressful resignation sat on her as she glided past him into the room—brushing his coat with her elbow because of the narrowness.

He followed her, shut the door—which she somehow had hoped he would leave open—and placing a chair for her sat down. The concern which Grace felt at the development of these commonplace incidents was, of course, mainly owing to the strange effect upon her nerves of that view of him in the mirror gazing at her with open eyes when she had thought him sleeping, which made her fancy that his slumber might have been a feint based on inexplicable reasons.

She again proffered the notes: he awoke from looking at her as at a piece of live statuary and listened deferentially as she said, "Will you then reconsider, and cancel the bond which poor Grammer Oliver so foolishly gave?"

"I'll cancel it without reconsideration. Though you will allow me to have my own opinion about her foolishness. Grammer is a very wise woman, and she was as wise in that as in other things. You think there was something very fiendish in the compact, do you not Miss Melbury? But remember that the most eminent of our surgeons in past times have entered into such agreements."

"Not fiendish—strange."

"Yes, that may be; since strangeness is not in the nature of a thing, but in its relation to something extrinsic—in this case an unessential observer."

He went to his desk and searching awhile found a paper which he unfolded and brought to her. A thick cross appeared in ink at the bottom—evidently from the hand of Grammer. Grace put the paper in her pocket with a look of much relief.

As Fitzpiers did not take up the money (half of which had come from Grace's own purse) she pushed it a little nearer to him. "No, no. I shall not take it from the old woman," he said. "It is more strange than the fact of a surgeon arranging to obtain a subject for dissection that our acquaintance should be formed out of it."

"I am afraid you think me uncivil in showing my dislike to the notion. But I did not mean to be."

"Oh no no." He looked at her, as he had done before, with puzzled interest. "I cannot think, I cannot think," he murmured. "Something bewilders me greatly." He still reflected and hesitated. "Last night I sat up very late," he at last went on, "and on that account I fell into a little nap on that couch about half-an-hour ago. And during my few minutes of unconsciousness I dreamt—what do you think—that you stood in the room."

Should she tell? She merely blushed.

"You may imagine," Fitzpiers continued, now persuaded that it had indeed been a dream, "that I should not have dreamt of you without considerable thinking about you first."

He could not be acting; of that she felt assured.

"I fancied in my vision that you stood there," he said, pointing to where she had paused. "I did not see you directly, but reflected in the glass. I thought, what a lovely creature!— the design is for once carried out. Nature has at last recovered her lost union with the Idea! My thoughts ran in that direction because I had been reading the work of a transcendental philosopher last night; and I dare say it was the dose of Idealism that I received from it that made me scarcely able to distinguish between reality and fancy. I almost wept when I awoke, and found that you had appeared to me in Time, but not in Space, alas!"

At moments there was something theatrical in the delivery of Fitzpiers's effusion; yet it would have been inexact to say that it was intrinsically theatrical. It often happens that in situations of unrestraint, where there is no thought of the eye of criticism, real feeling glides into a mode of manifestation not easily distinguishable from rodomontade. A veneer of affectation overlies a bulk of truth, with the evil consequence, if perceived, that the substance is estimated by the superficies, and the whole rejected.

Grace, however, was no specialist in men's manners, and she admired the sentiment without thinking of the form. And she was embarrassed; "lovely creature" made explanation awkward to her gentle modesty.

"But can it be," said he suddenly, "that you really were here?"

"I have to confess that I have been in the room once before," faltered she. "The woman showed me in, and went away to fetch you; but as she did not return I left."

"And you saw me asleep," he murmured, with the faintest show of humiliation.

"Yes—*if* you were asleep, and did not deceive me."

"Why do you say if?"

"I saw your eyes open in the glass, but as they were closed when I looked round upon you I thought you were perhaps deceiving me."

"Never," said Fitzpiers fervently. "Never could I deceive you."

Foreknowledge to the distance of a year or so, in either of them, might have spoilt the effect of that pretty speech. Never deceive her! But they knew nothing, and the phrase had its day.

Grace began now to be anxious to terminate the interview; but the compelling power of Fitzpiers's atmosphere still held her there. She was like an inexperienced actress who, having at last taken up her position on the boards and spoken her speeches, does not know how to move off. The thought of Grammer occurred to her. "I'll go at once and tell poor Grammer of your generosity," she said. "It will relieve her at once."

"Grammer's is a nervous disease too—how singular," he answered, accompanying her to the door. "One moment—look at this—it is something which may interest you."

He had thrown open the door on the other side of the passage, and she saw a microscope on the table of the confronting room. "Look into it please; you'll be interested," he repeated.

She applied her eye and saw the usual circle of light patterned all over with a cellular tissue of some indescribable sort. "What do you think that is?" said Fitzpiers.

She did not know.

"That's a fragment of old John South's brain which I am investigating."

She started back, not exactly with aversion, but with wonder as to how it should have got there. Fitzpiers laughed.

"Here am I," he said, "endeavouring to carry on simultaneously the study of physiology and transcendental philosophy, the material world and the ideal, so as to discover if possible a point of contact between them; and your finer sense is quite offended!"

"Oh no, Mr. Fitzpiers," said Grace earnestly. "It is not so at all. I know from seeing your light at night how deeply you meditate and work. Instead of condemning you for your studies I admire you very much!"

Her face, upturned from the microscope, was so sweet,

sincere, and self-forgetful in its aspect that the susceptible Fitzpiers more than wished to annihilate the lineal yard which separated it from his own. Whether anything of the kind showed in his eyes, or not, Grace remained no longer at the microscope; but quickly went her way into the falling mixture of rain and snow.

XIX

INSTEAD of resuming his investigation of South's brain Fitzpiers reclined and ruminated on the interview. Grace's curious susceptibility to his presence—though it was as if the currents of her life were disturbed rather than attracted by him—added a special interest to her general charm. Fitzpiers was in a distinct degree scientific, being ready and zealous to interrogate all physical manifestations; but primarily he was an idealist. He believed that behind the imperfect lay the perfect; that rare things were to be discovered amidst a bulk of commonplace; that results in a new and untried case might be different from those in other cases where the material conditions had been precisely similar. Regarding his own personality as one of unbounded possibilities, because it was his own—notwithstanding that the factors of his life had worked out a sorry product for thousands—he saw a grand speciality in his discovery at Hintock of an altogether exceptional being of the other sex.

One habit of Fitzpiers—commoner in dreamers of more advanced age than in men of his years—was that of talking to himself. He paced round his room with a selective tread upon the more prominent blooms of the carpet and murmured. "This phenomenal girl will be the light of my life while I am at Hintock; and the special beauty of the situation is that our attitude and relations to each other will be purely casual. Socially we can never be intimate. Anything like matrimonial intentions towards her—charming as she is—would be absurd. They would spoil the recreative character of such acquaintance. And indeed I have other aims on the practical side of my life."

Fitzpiers bestowed a regulation thought on the advantageous marriage he was bound to make with a woman of family as good as his own, and of purse much longer. But as an object of contemplation for the present Grace Melbury would serve to keep his soul alive and to relieve the monotony of his days.

His first lax notion—acquired from the mere sight of her without converse—that of a vulgar intimacy with a timber-merchant's pretty daughter, grated painfully upon him now that he had found what Grace intrinsically was. Personal intercourse with such as she could take no lower form than seemly communion, mutual explorations of the world of fancy. Since he could not call at her father's, having no practical views, cursory encounters in the lane, in the wood, coming and going to and from church, or in passing her dwelling, were what the acquaintance would have to feed on.

Such anticipated glimpses of her realized themselves in the event. Rencounters of not more than a minute's duration, frequently repeated, will build up mutual interest, even warm confidence, in a lonely place. Theirs grew as imperceptibly as the twigs budded on the trees. There never was a particular moment at which it could be said they became friends; yet a delicate understanding now existed between two who in the winter had been strangers.

Spring weather came on rather suddenly, the unsealing of buds that had long been swollen accomplishing itself in the space of one warm night. The rush of sap in the veins of the trees could almost be heard. The flowers of late April took up a position unseen, and looked as if they had been blooming a long while, though there had been no trace of them the day before yesterday; birds began not to mind getting wet. Indoor people said they had heard the nightingale, to which outdoor people replied contemptuously that they had heard him a fortnight before.

The young doctor's practice being scarcely so large as a London surgeon's he frequently walked in the wood. Indeed such practice as he had he did not follow up with the assiduity that would have been necessary for developing it to exceptional proportions. One day, book in hand, he went to a part of the wood where the trees were mainly oaks. It was a calm afternoon, and there was everywhere around that sign of great undertakings on the part of vegetable nature which is apt to fill reflective human beings who are not undertaking much themselves with a sudden uneasiness at the contrast. He heard in the distance a curious sound, something like the quack of ducks, which though it was common enough here about this time was not common to him.

Looking through the trees Fitzpiers soon perceived the origin of the noise. The barking season had just commenced, and what he had heard was the tear of the ripping-tool as it ploughed its way along the sticky parting between the trunk and the rind. Melbury did a large business in bark, and as he was Grace's father, and possibly might be found on the spot, Fitzpiers was attracted to the scene even more than he might have been by its intrinsic interest. When he got nearer he recognised among the workmen John Upjohn, the two Timothys, and Robert Creedle, who probably had been "lent" by Winterborne; Marty South also assisted. A milking-pail of cider stood near, a half-pint cup floating on it, with which they dipped and drank whenever they passed the pail.

Each tree doomed to the flaying process was first attacked by Upjohn; with a small bill-hook he carefully freed the collar of the tree from twigs and patches of moss which encrusted it to a height of a foot or two above the ground, an operation comparable to the "little toilette" of the executioner's victim. After this it was barked in its erect position to a point as high as a man could reach. If a fine product of vegetable nature could ever be said to look ridiculous it was the case now, when the oak stood naked-legged, and as if ashamed; till the axe-man came and cut a ring round it; and the two Timothys finished the work with the cross-cut saw.

As soon as it had fallen the barkers attacked it like locusts; and in a short time not a particle of rind was left on the trunk and larger limbs. Marty South was an adept at peeling the upper parts, and there she stood, encaged amid the mass of twigs and buds like a great bird, running her ripping-tool into the smallest branches, beyond the furthest points to which the skill and patience of the men enabled them to proceed—branches which in their lifetime had swayed high above the bulk of the wood, and caught the earliest rays of the sun and moon while the lower part of the forest was still in darkness.

"You seem to have a better instrument than they, Marty," said Fitzpiers.

"No sir," she said, holding up the tool—a horse's leg-bone fitted into a handle and filed to an edge—"'tis only that they've less patience with the twigs, because their time is worth more than mine."

A little shed had been constructed on the spot, of thatched hurdles and boughs; and in front of it was a fire, over which a kettle sang. Fitzpiers sat down inside the shelter and went on with his reading, except when he looked up to observe the scene and the actors. The thought that he might settle here and become welded in with this sylvan life by marrying Grace Melbury crossed his mind for a moment. Why should he go further into the world than where he was? The secret of happiness lay in limiting the aspirations; these men's thoughts were conterminous with the margin of the Hintock woodlands, and why should not his be likewise limited, a small practice among the people around him being the bound of his desires?

Presently Marty South discontinued her operations upon the quivering boughs, came out from the reclining oak, and prepared tea. When it was ready the men were called; and Fitzpiers being in a mood to join sat down with them.

The latent reason of his lingering here so long revealed itself when the faint creaking of the joints of a vehicle became audible, and one of the men said, "Here's He." Turning their heads they saw Melbury's gig approaching, the wheels muffled by the yielding moss.

The timber-merchant was leading the horse past the tree-stumps, looking back at every few steps to warn his daughter, who kept her seat, when and how to duck her head so as to avoid overhanging branches. They stopped at the spot where the bark-ripping had been temporarily suspended; Melbury cursorily examined the heaps of bark, and drawing near to where the workmen were sitting down accepted their shouted invitation to have a dish of tea, for which purpose he hitched the horse to a bough. Grace declined to take any of their beverage, and remained in her place in the vehicle, looking dreamily at the sunlight that came in thin threads through the hollies with which the oaks were interspersed.

When Melbury stepped up close to the shelter he for the first time perceived that the doctor was present, and warmly appreciated Fitzpiers's invitation to sit down on the log beside him.

"Bless my heart, who would have thought of finding you here," he said, obviously much pleased at the circumstance. "I wonder now if my daughter knows you are so nigh at hand. I don't expect she do."

He looked out towards the gig wherein Grace sat, her face still turned sunward in the opposite direction. "She doesn't see us," said Melbury. "Well never mind: let her be."

Grace was indeed quite unconscious of Fitzpiers's propinquity. She was thinking of something which had little connection with the scene before her—thinking of her friend, lost as soon as found, Mrs. Charmond; of her capricious conduct, and of the contrasting scenes she was possibly enjoying at that very moment in other climes, to which Grace herself had hoped to be introduced by her friend's means. She wondered if this patronising lady would return to Hintock during the summer, and whether the acquaintance which had been nipped on the last occasion of her residence there would develope on the next.

Melbury told ancient timber-stories as he sat, relating them directly to Fitzpiers and obliquely to the men, who had heard them often before. Marty, who poured out tea, was just saying, "I think I'll take out a cup to Miss Grace," when they heard a clashing of the gig-harness and turning round Melbury saw that the horse had become restless, and was jerking about the vehicle in a way which alarmed its occupant, though she refrained from screaming. Melbury jumped up immediately; but not more quickly than Fitzpiers; and while her father ran to the horse's head and speedily began to control him, Fitzpiers was alongside the gig assisting Grace to descend. Her surprise at his appearance was so great that, far from making a calm and independent descent, she was very nearly lifted down in his arms. He relinquished her when she touched ground, and hoped she was not frightened.

"Oh no, not much," she managed to say. "There was no danger—unless the horse had run under the trees where the boughs are low enough to hit my head."

"Which was by no means impossible, and justifies any amount of alarm."

He referred to what he thought he saw written in her face, and she could not tell him that this had little to do with the horse, but much with himself. His contiguity had in fact the same effect upon her as on those former occasions when he had come closer to her than usual—that of producing in her an unaccountable tendency to tearfulness. Melbury soon put the horse to rights, and seeing that Grace was safe turned again to the workpeople. His daughter's nervous distress had passed off in a few moments, and she said quite gaily to Fitzpiers as she walked with him towards the group, "There's destiny in it you see—I was doomed to join in your picnic, although I did not intend to do so."

Marty prepared her a comfortable place and she sat down in the circle, and listened to Fitzpiers while he drew from her father and the bark-rippers sundry narratives of their fathers', their grandfathers', and their own adventures in these woods; of the mysterious sights they had seen—only to be accounted for by supernatural agency; of white witches and black witches; and the standard story of the spirits of the two brothers who had fought and fallen, and had haunted King's Hintock Court a few miles off till they were exorcised by the priest, and compelled to retreat to a swamp, whence they were returning to their old quarters at the Court at the rate of a cock's stride every new-year's-day, Old Style; hence the local saying, "On New-Year's tide, a cock's stride."

It was a pleasant time. The smoke from the little fire of peeled sticks rose between the sitters and the sun-light, and behind its blue films stretched the naked arms of the pros- trate trees. The smell of the uncovered sap mingled with the smell of the burning wood, and the sticky inner surface of the scattered bark glistened as it revealed its pale madder hues to the eye. Melbury was so highly satisfied at having Fitzpiers as a sort of guest that he would have sat on for any length of time; but Grace, on whom Fitzpiers's eyes only too frequently alighted, seemed to think it incumbent upon her to make a show of going; and her father thereupon accompanied her to the gig.

As the doctor had helped her out of it he appeared to think that he had excellent reasons for helping her in, and performed the attention lingeringly enough.

"What were you almost in tears about just now?" he asked softly.

"I don't know," she said; and the words were strictly true.

Melbury mounted on the other side, and they drove on out of the grove, their wheels silently crushing delicate-patterned mosses, hyacinths, primroses, lords-and-ladies, and other strange and common plants, and cracking up little sticks that lay across the track. Their way homeward ran along the western flank of the Vale, whence afar they beheld a wide district differing somewhat in feature and atmosphere from the Hintock precincts. It was the cider country more especially, which met the woodland district some way off. There the air was blue as sapphire—such a blue as outside that apple-region was never seen. Under the blue the orchards were in a blaze of pink bloom, some of the richly flowered trees running almost up to where they drove along. At a gate which opened down an incline a man leant on his arms, regarding this fair promise so intently that he did not observe their passing.

"That was Giles," said Melbury when they had gone by.

"Was it? Poor Giles," said she.

"All that apple-blooth means heavy autumn work for him and his hands. If no blight happens before the setting the cider yield will be such as we have not had for years."

Meanwhile, in the wood they had come from, the men had sat on so long that they were indisposed to begin work again that evening; they were paid by the ton, and their time for labour was as they chose. They placed the last gatherings of bark in rows for the curers, which led them further and further away from the shed; and thus they gradually withdrew homeward as the sun went down.

Fitzpiers lingered yet. He had opened his book again, though he could hardly see a word in it, and sat before the dying fire scarcely knowing of the men's departure. He dreamed and mused till his consciousness seemed to occupy the whole space of the woodland round, so little was there of jarring sight or sound to hinder perfect mental unity with the sentiment of the place. The idea returned upon him of sacrificing all practical aims to live in calm contentment here, and instead of going on elaborating new conceptions with infinite pains to accept quiet domesticity according to oldest and homeliest notions. These reflections detained him till the wood was embrowned with the coming night, and the shy little bird of this dusky time had begun to pour out all the intensity of his eloquence from a bush not very far off.

Fitzpiers's eyes commanded as much of the ground in front as was open. Entering upon this he saw a figure whose direction of movement was towards the spot where he sat. The surgeon was quite shrouded from observation by the recessed shadow of the hurdle-screen, and there was no reason why he should move till the stranger had passed by. The shape resolved itself into a woman's; she was looking on the ground, and walking slowly as if searching for something that had been lost, her course being precisely that of Mr. Melbury's gig. Fitzpiers by a sort of divination jumped to the idea that the figure was Grace's; her nearer approach made the guess a certainty.

Yes, she was looking for something; and she came round by the prostrate trees that would have been invisible but for their white nakedness which enabled her to avoid them easily. Thus she approached the heap of ashes, and acting upon what was suggested by a still shining ember or two she took a stick and stirred the heap, which thereupon burst into a flame. On looking around by the light thus obtained she for the first time saw the illumined face of Fitzpiers precisely in the spot where she had left him.

Grace gave a start and a scream: she had not the least expected to find him there still. Fitzpiers lost not a moment in rising and going to her side.

"I frightened you dreadfully I know," he said. "I ought to

have spoken; but I did not at first expect it to be you. I have been sitting here ever since."

He was actually supporting her with his arm, as though under the impression that she was quite overcome, and in danger of falling. As soon as she could collect her ideas she gently withdrew from his grasp and explained what she had returned for: in getting up or down from the gig, or when sitting by the hut fire, she had dropped her purse.

"Now we will find it," said Fitzpiers.

He threw an armful of last year's leaves on to the fire, which made the flame leap higher, and the encompassing shades to weave themselves into a blacker contrast, turning eve into night in a moment. By this radiance they groped about on their hands and knees; till Fitzpiers rested on his elbow, and looked at Grace. "We almost always meet in odd circumstances," he said; "and this is one of the oddest. I wonder if it means anything?"

"Oh no, I am sure it doesn't," said Grace in haste, quickly assuming an erect posture. "Pray don't say it any more."

"I hope there was not much money in the purse," said Fitzpiers, rising to his feet more slowly; and brushing the leaves from his trousers.

"Scarcely any. I cared most about the purse itself, because it was given me. Indeed, money is of little more use at Hintock than on Crusoe's island; there's hardly any way of spending it."

They had given up the search when Fitzpiers discerned something by his foot. "Here it is," he said. "So that your father, mother, friend, or *admirer* will not have his or her feelings hurt by a sense of your negligence after all."

"Oh he knows nothing of what I do now."

"The admirer?" said Fitzpiers slily.

"I don't know if you would call him that," said Grace with simplicity. "The admirer is a superficial, conditional crea- ture, and this person is quite different."

"He has all the cardinal virtues."

"Perhaps—though I don't know them precisely."

"You unconsciously practise them, Miss Melbury, which is better. According to Schleiermacher they are Self-control,

Perseverance, Wisdom, and Love; and his is the best list that I know."

"I am afraid poor—" She was going to say that she feared Winterborne—the giver of the purse years before—had not much perseverance, though he had all the other three; but she determined to go no further in this direction, and was silent.

These half-revelations made a perceptible difference in Fitzpiers. His sense of personal superiority wasted away, and Grace assumed in his eyes the true aspect of a mistress in her lover's regard.

"Miss Melbury," he said suddenly; "I divine that this virtuous man you mention has been refused by you."

She could do no otherwise than admit it.

"I did not inquire without good reason. God forbid that I should kneel in another's place at any shrine unfairly. But my dear Miss Melbury, now that he is gone from the temple, may I draw near?"

"I—I can't say anything about that!" she cried quickly. "Because when a man has been refused you feel pity for him, and like him more than you did before."

This increasing complication added still more value to Grace in the surgeon's eyes: it rendered her adorable. "But cannot you say?" he pleaded distractedly.

"I'd rather not.—I think I must go home at once."

"Oh yes," said Fitzpiers. But as he did not move she felt it awkward to walk straight away from him; and so they stood silently together. A diversion was created by the accident of two large birds, that had either been roosting above their heads or nesting there, tumbling one over the other into the hot ashes at their feet, apparently engrossed in a desperate quarrel that prevented the use of their wings. They speedily parted, however, and flew up with a singed smell, and were seen no more.

"That's the end of what is called love!" said some one.

The speaker was neither Grace nor Fitzpiers, but Marty South, who approached with her face turned up to the sky in her endeavour to trace the birds. Suddenly perceiving Grace she exclaimed, "Oh—Miss Melbury!—I have been looking at they pigeons, and didn't see you.—And here's Mr. Winterborne!" she continued shyly, as she looked towards Fitzpiers, who stood in the background.

"Marty," Grace interrupted, "I want you to walk home with me—will you? Come along." And without lingering longer she took hold of Marty's arm and led her away.

They went between the spectral arms of the peeled trees as they lay, and onward among the growing ones by a path where there were no oaks, and no barking, and no Fitzpiers— nothing but copse-wood, between which the primroses could be discerned in pale bunches. "I—didn't know Mr. Winterborne was there," said Marty, breaking the silence when they had nearly reached Grace's door.

"Nor was he," said Grace.

"But Miss Melbury—I saw him."

"No," said Grace. "It was somebody else. Giles Winterborne is nothing to me."

XX

THE leaves over Hintock unrolled their creased tissues, and the woodland seemed to change from an open filigree to a solid opaque body of infinitely larger shape and importance. The boughs cast green shades, which disagreed with the complexion of the girls who walked there; and a fringe of the same boughs which overhung Mr. Melbury's garden dripped on his seed-plots when it rained, pitting their surface all over as with pock-marks, till Melbury declared that gardens in such a place were no good at all. The two trees that had creaked all the winter left off creaking, the whirr of the night-hawk, however, forming a very satisfactory continuation of uncanny music from that quarter. Except at mid-day the sun was not seen complete by the Hintock people, but rather in the form of numerous little stars staring through the leaves.

Such an appearance it had on Midsummer eve of this year, and as the hour grew later, and nine o'clock drew on, the irradiation of the day-time became broken up by the weird shadows and ghostly nooks of indistinctness. Imagination could trace amid the trunks and boughs swarthy faces and funereal figures. This was before the moon rose. Later on, when that planet was getting command of the upper heaven, and consequently shining with an unbroken face into such open glades as there were in the neighbourhood of the hamlet, it became apparent that the margin of the wood which approached the timber-merchant's premises was not to be left to the customary stillness of that reposeful time.

Fitzpiers, having heard a voice or voices, was looking over his garden gate—where he now looked more frequently than into his books—fancying that Grace might be abroad with some friends. He was irretrievably committed in heart to Grace Melbury, though he was by no means sure that she was so far committed to him. That the Idea had for once completely fulfilled itself in the objective substance—which he had hitherto deemed an impossibility—he was enchanted enough to fancy must be the case at last. It was not Grace who had passed, however, but several of the ordinary village girls in a group—some steadily walking, some in a mood of wild gaiety. He quietly asked his landlady, who was also in the garden, what these girls were intending, and she informed him that it being old midsummer eve they were about to attempt some spell or enchantment which would afford them a glimpse of their future partners for life. She declared it to be an ungodly performance, and one that she for her part would never countenance; saying which she entered her house and retired to bed.

The young man lit a cigar, and followed the bevy of maidens slowly up the road. They had turned into the wood at an opening between Melbury's and Marty South's; but Fitzpiers could easily track them by their voices, low as they endeavoured to keep their tones.

In the meantime other inhabitants of Little Hintock had become aware of the nocturnal experiment about to be tried, and were also sauntering stealthily after the frisky maidens. Miss Melbury had been informed by Marty South during the day of the proposed peep into futurity, and, being only a girl like the rest, she was sufficiently interested to wish to see the issue. The moon was so bright and the night so calm that she had no difficulty in persuading Mrs. Melbury to accompany her; and thus, joined by Marty, these went onward in the same direction.

Passing Winterborne's house they heard a noise of hammering. Marty explained it. This was the last night on which his paternal roof would shelter him, the days of grace since it fell into hand having expired; and late as it was Giles was taking down his cupboards and bedsteads with a view to an early exit next morning. His encounter with Mrs. Charmond had cost him dearly.

When they had proceeded a little further Marty was joined by Grammer Oliver (who was as young as the youngest in such matters), and Grace and Mrs. Melbury went on by themselves till they had arrived at the spot chosen by the village daughters, whose primary intention of keeping their expedition a secret had been quite defeated. Grace and her stepmother paused by a holly tree; and at a little distance stood Fitzpiers under the shade of a young oak, intently observing Grace, who was in the full rays of the moon.

He watched her without speaking, and unperceived by any but Marty and Grammer, who had drawn up on the dark side of the same holly which sheltered Mrs. and Miss Melbury on its bright side. The two former conversed in low tones.

"If they two come up in wood *next* midsummer night they'll come as one," said Grammer, signifying Fitzpiers and Grace. "Instead of my skellinton he'll carry home her living carcase before long. But though she's a lady in herself, and worthy of any such as he, it do seem to me that he ought to marry somebody more of the sort of Mrs. Charmond, and that Miss Grace should make the best of Winterborne."

Marty returned no comment; and at that minute the girls, some of whom were from Great Hintock, were seen advancing to work the incantation, it being now about midnight.

"Directly we see anything we'll run home as fast as we can," said one, whose courage had begun to fail her. To this the rest assented, not knowing that a dozen neighbours lurked in the bushes around.

"I wish we had not thought of trying this," said another; "but had contented ourselves with the hole-digging to-morrow at twelve, and hearing our husbands' trades. It is too much like having dealings with the evil one to try to raise their forms."

However they had gone too far to recede, and slowly began to march forward in a skirmishing line through the trees, each intending to plunge alone into a deep recess of the wood. As far as the listeners could gather, the particular form of black art to be practised on this occasion was one connected with the sowing of hemp-seed, a handful of which was carried by each girl. At the moment of their advance they looked back, and discerned the figure of Miss Melbury who, alone of all the observers, stood in the full face of the moonlight, deeply engrossed in the proceedings. By contrast with her life of late years they made her feel as if she had receded a couple of centuries in the world's history. She was rendered doubly conspicuous by her light dress, and after a few whispered words one of the girls—a bouncing maiden called Suke, plighted to young Timothy Tangs—asked her if she would join in. Grace with some excitement said that she would, and moved on a little in the rear of the rest.

Soon the listeners could hear nothing of their proceedings beyond the faintest occasional rustle of leaves. Grammer whispered again to Marty: "Why didn't ye go and try your luck with the rest of the maids?"

"I don't believe in it!" said Marty shortly. "And they've spoilt it by letting people know."

"Yes, half the parish is here—the silly hussies should have kept it quiet. I see Mr. Winterborne through the leaves, just come up with Robert Creedle. Marty, we ought to act the part o' Providence sometimes—do go and tell him that if he stands just behind the bush at the bottom of the slope, Miss Grace must pass down it when she comes back, and she will most likely rush into his arms; for as soon as the clock strikes they'll bundle back home-along like hares. I've seen such larries before."

"Do you think I'd better?" said Marty reluctantly.

"Oh yes—he'll bless ye for it."

"I don't want that kind of blessing!" But after a moment's thought she went and delivered the information; and Grammer had the satisfaction of seeing Giles walk slowly to the bend in the leafy defile along which Grace would have to return.

Meanwhile Mrs. Melbury, deserted by Grace, had perceived Fitzpiers, and Winterborne, and also the move of the latter. An improvement on Grammer's idea entered the mind of Mrs. Melbury, for she had lately discerned, what her husband had not, that Grace was rapidly fascinating the surgeon. She therefore drew near to Fitzpiers.

"You should be where Mr. Winterborne is standing," she said to him significantly. "She will run down through that opening much faster than she went up it, if she is like the rest of the girls."

Fitzpiers did not require to be told twice. He went across to Winterborne, and stood beside him. Each knew the probable purpose of the other in standing there, and neither spoke, Fitzpiers scorning to look upon Winterborne as a rival, and Winterborne adhering to the off-hand manner of indifference which had grown upon him since his dismissal.

Neither Grammer nor Marty South had seen the surgeon's manœuvre, and still to help Winterborne, as she supposed, the old woman suggested to the wood-girl that she should walk forward at the heels of Grace, and "tole" her down the required way if she showed a tendency to run in another direction. Poor Marty, always doomed to sacrifice desire to obligation, walked forward accordingly, and waited as a beacon, still and silent, for the retreat of Grace and her giddy companions, now quite out of hearing.

The first sound to break the silence was the distant note of Great Hintock clock striking the significant hour. About a minute later that quarter of the wood to which the girls had wandered resounded with the flapping of disturbed birds; then two or three hares and rabbits bounded down the glade from the same direction, and after these the rustling and crackling of leaves and dead twigs denoted the hurried approach of the adventurers, whose fluttering gowns soon became visible. Miss Melbury having gone forward quite in the rear of the rest was one of the first to return, and the excitement being contagious she ran laughing towards Marty, who still stood as a hand-post to guide her; then passing on she flew round the fatal bush where the undergrowth narrowed to a gorge. Marty arrived at her heels just in time to see the result. Fitzpiers had quickly stepped forward in front of Winterborne, who, disdaining to shift his position had turned on his heel; and then the surgeon did what he would not have thought of doing but for Mrs. Melbury's encouragement and the sentiment of an eve which effaced conventionality. Stretching out his arms as the white figure burst upon him he captured her in a moment, as if she had been a bird.

"Oh!" cried Grace in her fright.

"You are in my arms, dearest," said Fitzpiers. "And I am going to claim you, and keep you there all our two lives."

She rested on him like one utterly mastered; and it was several seconds before she recovered from this helplessness. Subdued screams and struggles audible from neighbouring brakes revealed that there had been other lurkers thereabout for a similar purpose. Grace, unlike most of these companions of hers, instead of giggling and writhing said in a trembling voice, "Mr. Fitzpiers, will you let me go?"

"Certainly," he said laughing, "as soon as you have recovered."

She waited another few moments, then quietly and firmly pushed him aside and glided on her path, the moon whitening her hot blush away. But it had been enough: new relations between them had begun.

The case of the other girls was different, as has been said. They wrestled and tittered, only escaping after a desperate struggle. Fitzpiers could hear these enactments still going on after Grace had left him, and he remained on the spot where he had caught her, Winterborne having gone away. On a sudden another girl came bounding down the same descent that had been followed by Grace; a fine-framed young woman, with bare arms. Seeing Fitzpiers standing there she said with playful effrontery: "May'st kiss me if 'canst catch me, Tim!"

Fitzpiers recognized her as Suke Damson—the hoydenish maiden of the hamlet—the girl whom he had heard swear to herself when she got soiled by the newly painted gate. She was plainly mistaking him for her lover. He was impulsively disposed to profit by her error, and as soon as she began racing away he started in pursuit.

On she went under the boughs, now in light, now in shade, looking over her shoulder at him every few moments and kissing her hand; but so cunningly dodging about among the trees and moon-shades that she never allowed him to get dangerously near her. Thus they ran and doubled, Fitzpiers warming with the chase, till the sound of their companions had quite died away. He began to lose hope of ever overtaking her when all at once, by way of encouragement, she turned to a fence in which there was a stile, and leapt over it. Outside the scene was a changed one; a meadow, where the half-made hay lay about in heaps, in the uninterrupted shine of the now high moon.

Fitzpiers saw in a moment that having taken to open ground she had placed herself at his mercy, and he promptly vaulted over after her. She flitted a little way down the mead, when all at once her elusive form disappeared, as if it had sunk into the earth. She had buried herself in one of the hay-cocks.

Fitzpiers, now thoroughly excited, was not going to let her escape him thus: he approached, and set about turning over the heaps one by one. As soon as he paused tantalized and puzzled, he was directed anew by an imitative kiss which came from her hiding-place under the hay, and by snatches of a local ballad in the smallest voice she could assume:

> "O come in from the foggy foggy dew."

In a minute or two he uncovered her.

"O—'tis not Tim!" said she with a laugh, and burying her face.

Fitzpiers however disregarded her resistance by reason of its mildness, stooped, and imprinted the purposed kiss; then sank down on the same hay-cock, panting with his race.

"Whom do you mean by Tim?" he asked presently.

"My young man Tim Tangs," said she.

"Now, honour bright—did you really think it was he?"

"I did at first."

"But you didn't at last."

"No. I didn't at last."

"Do you much mind that it is not?"

"No," she answered slily.

Fitzpiers kissed her again, and pressed her close to him. He did not pursue his questioning. In the moonlight Suke looked very beautiful, the scratches and blemishes incidental to her out-door occupation being invisible under these pale rays. While they remained silent on the hay the coarse whirr of the eternal night-hawk burst sarcastically from the top of a tree at the nearest corner of the wood. Besides this not a sound of any kind reached their ears, the time of nightin-gales being now past, and Hintock lying at a distance of two miles at least. In the opposite direction the hay-field stretched away into remoteness till it was lost to the eye in a soft mist.

It was daybreak before Fitzpiers and Suke Damson re-entered Little Hintock.

XXI

WHEN the general stampede occurred Winterborne had also been looking on, and encountering one of the girls had asked her what caused them all to fly.

She said with solemn breathlessness that they had seen something very different from what they had hoped to see, and that she for one would never attempt such unholy cer-emonies again. "We saw Satan pursuing us with his hour-glass. It was terrible!"

This account being a little mixed Giles went forward to-wards the spot whence the girls had retreated. After listening there a few minutes he heard slow footsteps rustling over the leaves, and looking through a tangled screen of honeysuckle which hung from a bough he saw in the open space beyond a short stout man in evening dress, carrying on one arm a light overcoat, and also his hat, so awkwardly arranged as possibly to have suggested the "hour-glass" to his timid observers—if this were the person whom the girls had seen. With the other hand he silently gesticulated; and the moonlight, falling upon his bare brow, showed him to have dark hair, and a high forehead of the shape seen oftener in old prints and paintings than in real life. His curious and altogether alien aspect, his strange gestures, like those of one who is rehearsing a scene to himself, and the unusual place and hour, were sufficient to account for any trepidation among the Hintock daughters at encountering him.

He paused and looked round, as if he had forgotten where he was; not observing Giles, who was of the colour of his environment. The latter advanced into the light. The gentleman held up his hand and came towards Giles, the two meeting half way.

"I have lost my track," said the stranger. "Perhaps you can put me in the path again." He wiped his forehead with the air of one suffering under an agitation more than that of simple fatigue.

"The turnpike-road is over there," said Giles.

"I don't want the turnpike-road," said the gentleman impatiently. "I came from that. I want Hintock House. Is there not a path to it across here?"

"Well yes, a sort of path. But it is hard to find from this point. I'll show you the way, sir, with pleasure."

"Thanks, my good friend. The truth is that I decided to walk across the country after dinner from the Hotel at Sherton, where I am staying for a day or two. But I did not know it was so far."

"It is about a mile to the House from here."

They walked on together. As there was no path Giles occasionally stepped in front and bent aside the under-boughs of the trees to give his companion a passage, saying every now and then when the twigs, on being released, flew back like whips, "Mind your eyes sir." To which the stranger replied, "Yes, yes," in a preoccupied tone.

So they went on, the leaf-shadows running in their usual quick succession over the forms of the pedestrians, till the stranger said—"Is it far?"

"Not much further," said Winterborne. "The plantation runs up into a corner here, close behind the house." He added with hesitation: "You know, I suppose sir, that Mrs. Charmond is not at home?"

"You mistake," said the other shortly. "Mrs. Charmond has been away for some time, but she's at home now."

Giles did not contradict him, though he felt sure that the gentleman was wrong.

"You are a native of this place?" the stranger said.

"Yes."

"You are happy in having a home."

"I hope you are too, sir."

"It is what I don't possess."

"You come from far, seemingly?"

"I come now from the South of Europe."

"Oh indeed, sir. You are an Italian or Spanish or French gentleman, perhaps?"

"I am not either."

Giles did not fill the pause which ensued and the gentleman, who seemed of an emotional nature, unable to resist friendship, at length answered the question: "I am an Italianized American, a South Carolinian by birth," he said. "I left my native country on the failure of the Southern cause, and have never returned to it since."

He spoke no more about himself, and they came to the verge of the wood. Here, striding over the fence out upon the upland sward, they could at once see the chimneys of the House in the gorge immediately beneath their position; silent, still, and pale.

"Can you tell me the time?" the gentleman asked. "My watch has stopped."

"It is between twelve and one," said Giles.

His companion expressed his astonishment. "I thought it between nine and ten at latest! My! My!"

He now begged Giles to return and offered him a gold coin, which looked like a sovereign, for the assistance rendered. Giles declined to accept anything, to the surprise of the stranger, who on putting the money back into his pocket said awkwardly, "I thought it was the custom here. I offered it because I want you to utter no word about this meeting with me. Will you promise?"

Winterborne promised readily. He stood still whilst the other descended the slope. At the bottom the stranger looked back mistrustfully. Giles would no longer remain when he was so evidently desired to leave, and returned through the boughs to Little Hintock.

He suspected that this man, who seemed so distressed and melancholy, might be that lover and persistent wooer of Mrs. Charmond whom he had heard so frequently spoken of, and whom it was said she had treated cavalierly. But he received no confirmation of his suspicion beyond a report which reached him a few days later, that a gentleman had called up the servants who were taking care of Hintock House, at an hour past midnight; and on learning that Mrs. Charmond, though returned from abroad, was as yet in London, he had sworn bitterly, and gone away without leaving a card or any trace of himself.

The girls who related the story added that he sighed three times before he swore, and seemed wandering in his mind: but this part of the narrative was not corroborated. Anyhow such a gentleman drove away from Sherton next day in a carriage hired at the inn.

XXII

THE sunny leafy week which followed the tender doings of Midsummer Eve brought a visitor to Fitzpiers's door; a voice that he knew sounded in the passage. Mr. Melbury had called. At first he had a particular objection to enter the parlour because his boots were dusty; but as the surgeon insisted he waived the point and came in.

Looking neither to the right nor to the left, hardly at Fitzpiers himself, he put his hat under his chair and with a preoccupied gaze at the floor said, "I've called to ask you, doctor, quite privately, a question that troubles me. I've a daughter, Grace, an only daughter, as you may have heard. Well, she's been out in the dew—on Midsummer Eve in particular she went out in thin slippers to watch some vagary of the Hintock maids—and she's got a cough, a distinct hemming and hacking, that makes me uneasy. Now I have decided to send her away to some sea-side place for a change—"

"Send her away!" Fitzpiers's countenance had fallen.

"Yes. And the question is, where would you advise me to send her?"

The timber-merchant had happened to call at a moment when Fitzpiers was at the spring-tide of a sentiment that Grace was a necessity of his existence. The sudden pressure of her form upon his breast as she came headlong round the bush had never ceased to linger with him since he adopted the manœuvre for which the hour and the moonlight and the occasion had been the only excuse. Now she was to be sent away. Ambition?—it could be postponed. Family?—a common culture and reciprocity of tastes had taken the place of family considerations nowadays. He allowed himself to be carried forward on the wave of his desire.

"How strange, how very strange it is," he said, "that you should have come to me about her just now. I have been thinking every day of coming to you on the very same errand."

"Ah?—you have noticed, too, that her health—"

"I have noticed nothing the matter with her health because there is nothing. But Mr. Melbury, I have seen your daughter several times by accident. I have admired her infinitely; and I was coming to ask you if I may become better acquainted with her—pay my addresses to her."

Melbury was looking down as he listened, and did not see the air of half-misgiving at his own rashness that spread over Fitzpiers's face as he made this declaration.

"You have—got to know her?" said Melbury, a spell of dead silence having preceded his utterance, during which his emotion rose with almost visible effect.

"Yes," said Fitzpiers.

"And you wish to become better acquainted with her? You mean with a view to marrying o' her—is that what you mean?"

"Yes," said the young man. "I mean, get acquainted with her, with a view to being her accepted lover; and if we suited each other, what would naturally follow."

The timber-dealer was much surprised, and fairly agitated; his hand trembled as he laid by his walking-stick. "This takes me unawares," said he, his voice well-nigh breaking down. "I don't mean that there is anything unexpected in a gentleman being attracted by her; but it did not occur to me that it would be you. . . . I always said," continued he, with a lump in his throat, "that my Grace would make a mark at her own level some day. That was why I educated her. I said to myself, 'I'll do it, cost what it may'; though her mother-law was pretty frightened at my paying out so much money year after year. I knew it would tell in the end. 'Where you've not good material to work on such doings would be waste and vanity,' I said. 'But where you have that material it is sure to be worth while.'"

"I am glad you don't object," said Fitzpiers, almost wishing that Grace had not been quite so cheap for him.

"If she is willing I don't object, certainly. Indeed," added the honest man, "it would be deceit if I were to pretend to feel anything else than highly honoured by your wish; and it is a great credit to her to have drawn to her a man of such good professional station and venerable old family. That huntsman-fellow little thought how wrong he was about her! Take her and welcome, sir."

"I'll endeavour to ascertain her mind."

"Yes, yes. But she will be agreeable, I think. She ought to be."

"I hope she may. Well, now you'll expect to see me frequently."

"Oh yes. But name it all—about her cough, and her going away. I had quite forgot that that was what I came about."

"I assure you," said the surgeon, "that her cough can only be the result of a slight cold, and it is not necessary to banish her to any sea-side place at all."

Melbury looked unconvinced, doubting whether he ought to take Fitzpiers's professional opinion in circumstances which naturally led him to wish to keep her by him. The doctor saw this, and honestly dreading to lose sight of her he said eagerly, "Between ourselves, if I am successful with her I will take her away myself for a month or two, as soon as we are married, which I hope will be before the chilly weather comes on. This will be so very much better than letting her go now."

The proposal pleased Melbury much. There could be hardly any danger in postponing desirable change of air as long as the warm weather lasted, and for such a reason. Suddenly recollecting himself he said, "Your time must be precious, doctor. I'll get home-along. I am much obliged to 'ee. . . . As you will see her often you'll discover for yourself if anything serious is the matter."

"I can assure you it is nothing," said Fitzpiers, who had seen Grace much oftener already than her father knew of.

When he was gone Fitzpiers paused silent, registering his sensations, like a man who has made a plunge for a pearl into a medium of which he knows neither the density nor temperature. But he had done it, and Grace was the sweetest girl alive.

As for the departed visitor, his own last words lingered in Melbury's ears as he walked homeward; he felt that what he had said in the emotion of the moment was very stupid, ungenteel, and unsuited to a duologue with an educated gentleman, the smallness of whose practice was more than compensated by the former greatness of his family. He had uttered thoughts before they were weighed, and almost before they were shaped. They had expressed in a certain sense his feeling at Fitzpiers's news; but yet they were not right. Looking on the ground, and planting his stick at each tread as if it were a flag-staff, he reached his own precincts where, as he passed through the court, he automatically stopped to look at the men working in the shed and around. One of them asked him a question about waggon-spokes.

"Hey?" said Melbury looking hard at him. The man repeated the words.

Melbury stood; then turning suddenly away without answering he went up the court and entered the house. As time was no concern with the journeymen, except as a thing to get passed, they leisurely surveyed the door through which he had disappeared.

"What maggot has the gaffer got in his head now," said Tangs the elder. "Sommit to do with that chiel of his! When you've got a maid of yer own, John Upjohn, that costs 'ee what she costs him, that will take the squeak out of your Sunday shoes, John! But you'll never be man enough to accomplish such as she; and 'tis a lucky thing for 'ee, John, as things be. Well, he ought to have a dozen—that would bring him to reason. I see 'em walking together last Sunday, and when they came to a puddle he lifted her over like a waxen figure. He ought to have a dozen; he'd let 'em walk through puddles for themselves then."

Meanwhile Melbury had entered the house with the eye of a man who sees a vision before him. His wife was in the room. Without taking off his hat he sat down at random.

"Luce—we've done it!" he said. "Yes—the thing is as I expected. The spell, that I foresaw might be worked, has worked. She's done it, and done it well. Where is she?— Grace, I mean."

"Up in her room—what has happened?"

Mr. Melbury explained the circumstances as coherently as he could. "I told you so," he said. "A maid like her couldn't stay hid long, even in a place like this. But where is Grace? Let's have her down. Here—Gra-a-ace!"

She appeared, after a reasonable interval, for she was sufficiently spoilt by this father of hers not to put herself in a hurry, however impatient his tones. "What is it, father?" said she, with a smile.

"Why, you scamp, what's this you've been doing? Not home here more than six months, yet instead of confining yourself to your father's rank making havoc in the upper classes. . . . . ."

Though accustomed to show herself instantly appreciative of her father's meanings Grace was fairly unable to look anyhow but at a loss now.

"No, no—of course you don't know what I mean, or you pretend you don't. Though for my part I believe women can see these things through a double hedge. But I suppose I must tell 'ee. Why, you've flung your grapnel over the doctor, and he's coming courting forthwith."

"Only think of that, my dear. Don't you feel it a triumph?" said Mrs. Melbury.

"Coming courting—I've done nothing to make him!" Grace exclaimed.

" 'Twasn't necessary that you should. 'Tis voluntary that rules in these things. . . . Well, he has behaved very honourably, and asked my consent. You'll know what to do when he gets here, I daresay. I needn't tell you to make it all smooth for him."

"You mean, to lead him on to marry me?"

"I do. Haven't I educated you for it?"

Grace looked out of the window, and at the fireplace, with no animation in her face. "Why is it settled offhand in this way?" said she pettishly. "You'll wait till you hear what I think of him, I suppose?"

"Oh yes, of course. But you see what a good thing it will be."

She weighed the statement without speaking.

"You will be restored to the society you've been taken away from," continued her father; "for I don't suppose he'll stay here long."

She shyly admitted the advantage; but it was plain that though Fitzpiers when he was present exercised a certain fascination over her—or even more, an almost psychic influence, as it is called—and though his impulsive act in the wood had stirred her feelings indescribably, she had never regarded him in the light of a destined husband. "I don't know what to answer," she said. "I have learnt that he is very clever."

"He's all right, and he's coming here to see you."

A premonition that she could not resist him if he came strangely moved her. "Of course, father, you remember that it is only lately that Giles——"

"You know that you can't think of him. He has given up all claim to you."

She could not explain the subtleties of her feeling as clearly as he could state his opinion, even though she had skill in speech, and her father had none. That Fitzpiers acted upon her like a dram, exciting her, throwing her into a novel atmosphere which biassed her doings until the influence was over, when she felt something of the nature of regret for the mood she had experienced—could not be told to this worthy couple in words.

It so happened that on this very day Fitzpiers was called away from Hintock by an engagement to attend some medical meetings, and his visits therefore did not begin at once. A note however arrived from him addressed to Grace deploring his enforced absence. As a material object this note was pretty and superfine, a note of a sort that she had been

unaccustomed to see since her return to Hintock, except when
a school friend wrote to her—a rare instance, for the girls
were respecters of persons, and many cooled down towards
the timber-dealer's daughter when she was out of sight. Thus
the receipt of it pleased her, and she afterwards walked about
with a reflective air.

In the evening her father, who knew that the note had
come, said, "Why be ye not sitting down to answer your letter?
That's what young folks did in my time."

She replied that it did not require an answer.

"Oh, you know best," he said. Nevertheless he went about
his business doubting if she were right in not replying; possibly she might be so mismanaging matters as to risk the loss
of an alliance which would bring her much happiness.

Melbury's respect for Fitzpiers was based less on his professional position, which was not much, than on the standing of
his family in the county in bygone days. That touching faith
in members of long-established families, as such, irrespective
of their personal condition or character, which is still found
among old-fashioned people in the rural districts, reached
its full perfection in Melbury. His daughter's suitor was descended from a line he had heard of in his grandfather's
time as being once among the greatest, a family which had
conferred its name upon a neighbouring village; how then
could anything be amiss in this betrothal.

"I must keep her up to this," he said to his wife. "She sees
it is for her happiness; but still she's young, and may want a
little prompting from an older tongue."

XXIII

WITH this in view Melbury took her out for a walk, a custom
of his when he wished to say anything specially impressive.
Their way was towards that lofty ridge bordering their woodland and the western extremity of the Vale of Blackmoor,
the ridge culminating further on in High-Stoy Hill. They
could look back over the outskirts of the cider district, where
they had in the spring beheld the miles of appletrees in

bloom. All was now deep green. The spot recalled to Grace's mind the last occasion of her sight of it, and she said, "The promise of an enormous apple-crop is fulfilling itself, is it not? I suppose Giles is getting his mills and presses ready."

This was just what her father had not come there to talk about. Without replying he raised his arm, and moved his finger till he fixed it at a point round to the right. "There," he said, "you see that hill rising out of the level like a great whale, and just behind the hill a particularly green sheltered bottom? That's where Mr. Fitzpiers's family were lords of the manor for I don't know how many hundred years, and there stands the village of Oakbury Fitzpiers. A wonderful property 'twas—wonderful!"

"But they are not lords of the manor there now."

"Why no. But good and great folk fall as well as humble and foolish. The only ones representing the family now, I believe, are our doctor and a maiden lady living I don't know where. . . . You can't help being happy, Grace, in allying yourself with such a romantical family. Why, on the mother's side he's connected with the long line of the Lords Baxby of Sherton. You'll feel as if you've stepped into history."

"We've been at Hintock as long as they were at Oakbury; is it not so? You say our name occurs in old deeds continually."

"Oh yes—as yeomen, copyholders and such like. But think how much better this will be for 'ee. You'll be living a high, perusing life, such as has now become natural to you; and though the doctor's practice is small here he'll no doubt go to a dashing town when he's got his hand in, and keep a stylish carriage, and you'll be brought to know a good many ladies of excellent society. If you should ever meet me then, Grace, you can drive past me, looking the other way. I shouldn't expect you to speak to me, or wish such a thing— unless it happened to be in some lonely private place where 'twouldn't lower 'ee at all.—Don't think such men as neighbour Giles your equal. He and I shall be good friends enough, but he's not for the like of you. He's lived our rough and homely life here, and his wife's life must be rough and homely likewise."

So much pressure could not but produce some displacement. As Grace was left very much to herself she took advantage of one fine day before Fitzpiers's return to drive into the aforesaid vale where stood the village of Oakbury Fitzpiers. On another day she drove to the ruins of Sherton Castle, the original stronghold of the Lords Baxby, Fitzpiers's maternal ancestors.

The remains were few, and consisted mostly of remnants of the lower vaulting, supported on low stout columns surmounted by the *crochet* capital of the period. The two or three arches of these vaults that were still in position had been utilized by the adjoining farmer as shelter for his calves, the floor being spread with straw, amid which the young creatures rustled, cooling their thirsty tongues by licking the quaint Norman carving, which glistened with the moisture. It was a degradation of even such a rude form of art as this to be treated so grossly, she thought, and for the first time the aspect of Fitzpiers assumed in her imagination the hues of a melancholy romanticism.

She traversed the distance home with a preoccupied mind. The idea of so modern a man in science and æsthetics as the young surgeon springing out of relics so ancient was a kind of novelty she had never before experienced. The combination lent him a social and intellectual interest which she dreaded, so much weight did it add to the strange influence he exercised upon her whenever he came near her.

In an excitement which was not love, not ambition; rather a fearful consciousness of hazard in the air, she awaited his return.

Meanwhile her father was awaiting him also. In his house there was an old work on medicine, published towards the end of the eighteenth century, and to put himself in harmony with events Melbury spread this work on his knees when he had done his day's business, and read about Galen, Hippocrates, and Herophilus; of the dogmatic, the empiric, the hermetical, and other sects of practitioners that have arisen in history; and thence proceeded to study the classification of maladies and the rules for their treatment by copious bleeding, as laid down in this valuable book with absolute precision. Melbury regretted that the treatise was so old, fearing that he might in consequence be unable to hold as complete a conversation as he could wish with Mr. Fitzpiers, primed, no doubt, with more recent discoveries.

The day of Fitzpiers's return arrived, and he sent to say that he would call immediately. In the little time that was afforded for putting the house in order the sweeping of Melbury's parlour was as the sweeping of the parlour at the Interpreter's which well-nigh choked the Pilgrim. Motes stood in the sunbeams, which sloped visibly into the room. At the end of it Mrs. Melbury sat down, folded her hands and lips, and waited. Her husband restlessly walked in and out from the timber-yard, stared at the interior of the room, jerked out "ay; ay," and retreated again. Between four and five Fitzpiers arrived, hitching his horse to the hook under the uppingstock outside the door.

As soon as he had walked in and perceived that Grace was not in the parlour he seemed to have a misgiving. Nothing less than her actual presence could long keep him to the level of this impassioned enterprise; that lacking he appeared as one who wished to retrace his steps.

He mechanically talked at what he considered a woodland matron's level of thought till a rustling was heard on the stairs, and Grace came in. Fitzpiers was for once as agitated as she. Over and above the genuine emotion which she raised in his heart there hung the sense that he was casting a die by impulse which he might not have thrown by judgment.

Mr. Melbury was not in the room at the moment. Having to attend to matters in the yard he had delayed putting on his afternoon coat and waistcoat till the doctor's appearance, when, not wishing to be backward in receiving him, he entered the parlour hastily buttoning up those garments. Grace's fastidiousness was a little distressed that Fitzpiers should see by this action the strain his visit was putting upon her father; and to make matters worse for her just then, old Grammer seemed to have a passion for incessantly pumping in the back kitchen, leaving the doors open so that the banging and splashing were distinct above the parlour conversation. Whenever the chat over the tea sank into pleasant desultoriness Mr. Melbury broke in with speeches of laboured precision on very remote topics, as if he feared to let Fitzpiers's mind dwell critically on the subject nearest the hearts of all. In truth a constrained manner was natural enough in Melbury just now, for the greatest interest of his life was reaching its crisis. Could the real have been beheld instead of the corporeal merely, the corner of the room in which he sat would have been filled with a form typical of anxious suspense, large-eyed, tight-lipped, awaiting the issue. That paternal hopes and fears so intense should be bound up in the person of one child so peculiarly circumstanced, and not have dispersed themselves over the larger field of a whole family, involved dangerous risks to his own future happiness.

Fitzpiers did not stay more than an hour, but that time had apparently advanced his sentiments towards Grace, once and for all, from a vaguely liquescent to an organic shape. She would not have accompanied him to the door, in response to his whispered "Come!" if her mother had not said in a matter of fact way, "Of course, Grace; go to the door with Mr. Fitzpiers." Accordingly Grace went, both her parents remaining in the room. When the young pair were in the great brick-floored hall the lover took the girl's hand in his, drew it under his arm, and thus led her on to the front door, where he stealthily put his lips to her own.

She broke from him trembling, blushed, and turned aside, hardly knowing how things had advanced to this. Fitzpiers drove off kissing his hand to her, and waving it to Melbury, who was visible through the window. Her father returned the surgeon's action with a great flourish of his own hand, and a satisfied smile.

The intoxication that Fitzpiers had as usual produced in Grace's brain during the visit passed off somewhat with his withdrawal. She felt like a woman who did not know what she had been doing for the previous hour; but supposed with trepidation that the afternoon's proceedings, though vague, had amounted to an engagement between herself and the handsome, coercive, irresistible Fitzpiers.

This visit was a type of many which followed it during the long summer days of that year. Grace was borne along upon a stream of reasonings, arguments, and persuasions, supplemented, it must be added, by inclinations of her own at times. No woman is without aspirations, which may be innocent enough within limits; and Grace had been so trained socially, and educated intellectually, as to see clearly enough a pleasure in the position of wife to such a man as Fitzpiers. His material standing of itself, either present or future, had little in it to fire her ambition, but the possibilities of a refined and cultivated inner life, of subtle psychological intercourse, had their charm. It was this rather than any vulgar idea of marrying well which caused her to float with the current, and to yield to the immense influence which Fitzpiers exercised over her whenever she shared his society.

Any observer would shrewdly have prophesied that whether or not she loved him as yet in the ordinary sense, she was pretty sure to do so in time.

One evening just before dusk they had taken a rather long walk together, and for a short cut homeward passed through the shrubberies of Hintock House—still deserted, and still blankly confronting with its sightless shuttered windows the surrounding foliage and slopes. Grace was tired, and they approached the wall, and sat together on one of the stone sills—still warm with the sun that had been pouring its rays upon them all the afternoon.

"This place would just do for us, would it not, dearest," said her betrothed, as they sat, turning and looking idly at the old façade.

"Oh yes," said Grace, plainly showing that no such fancy had ever crossed her mind. "She is away from home still," Grace added in a minute rather sadly, for she could not forget that she had somehow lost the valuable friendship of the lady of this bower.

"Who is?—oh, you mean Mrs. Charmond. Do you know, dear, that at one time I thought *you* lived here."

"Indeed?" said Grace. "How was that?"

He explained, as far as he could do so without mentioning his disappointment at finding it was otherwise; and then went on: "Well, never mind that. Now I want to ask you something. There is one detail of our wedding which I am sure you will leave to me. My inclination is not to be married at the horrid little church here, with all the yokels staring round at us, and a droning parson reading."

"Where then can it be? At a church in town?"

"No. Not at a church at all. At a registry office. It is a quieter, snugger, and more convenient place in every way."

"Oh," said she with real distress. "How can I be married except at church, and with all my dear friends round me!"

"Yeoman Winterborne among them."

"Yes—why not? You know there was nothing serious between him and me."

"You see, dear, a noisy bell-ringing marriage at church has this objection in our case; it would be a thing of report a long way round. Now I would gently, as gently as possible, indicate to you how inadvisable such publicity would be if we leave Hintock, and I purchase the practice that I contemplate purchasing at Budmouth—barely twenty miles off. Forgive my saying that it will be far better if nobody there knows much of where you come from, nor anything about your parents. Your beauty and knowledge and manners will carry you anywhere if you are not hampered by such retrospective criticism."

"But could it not be a quiet ceremony, even at church," she pleaded.

"I don't see the necessity of going there!" he said a trifle impatiently. "Marriage is a civil contract, and the shorter and simpler it is made the better. People don't go to church when they take a house, or even when they make a will."

"Oh Edred—I don't like to hear you speak like that."

"Well, well—I didn't mean to. But I have mentioned as much to your father, who has made no objection; and why should you?"

She deemed the point one on which she ought to allow sentiment to give way to policy—if there were indeed policy in his plan. But she was indefinably depressed as they walked homeward.

XXIV

HE left her at the door of her father's house. As he receded and was clasped out of sight by the filmy shades he impressed Grace as a man who hardly appertained to her existence at all. Cleverer, greater than herself, one outside her mental orbit as she considered him, he seemed to be her ruler rather than her equal, protector, and dear familiar friend.

The disappointment she had experienced at his wish, the shock given to her girlish sensibilities by his irreverent views of marriage, together with the sure and near approach of the day fixed for committing her future to his keeping, made her so restless that she could scarcely sleep at all that night. She rose when the sparrows began to creep out of the roof-holes, sat on the floor of her room in the dim light, and by and by peeped out behind the window-curtains. It was even now day out-of-doors, though the tones of morning were feeble and wan, and it was long before the sun would be perceptible in this overshadowed vale. Not a sound came from any of the outhouses as yet. The tree-trunks, the road, the outbuildings, the garden, every object, wore that aspect of mesmeric passivity which the quietude of daybreak lends to such scenes. Helpless immobility seemed to be combined with intense consciousness; a meditative inertness possessed all things, oppressively contrasting with her own active emotions. Beyond the road were some cottage-roofs and orchards; over these roofs, and over the appletrees behind, high up the slope, and backed by the plantation on the crest, was the house yet occupied by her future husband, the rough-cast front showing whitely through its creepers. The window-shutters were closed, the bedroom curtains closely drawn, and not the thinnest coil of smoke rose from the rugged chimneys.

Something broke the stillness. The front door of the house she was gazing at opened softly, and there came out into the porch a female figure, wrapped in a large cloak, beneath which was visible the white skirt of a long loose garment like a night-dress. A grey arm, stretching from within the porch, adjusted the cloak over the woman's shoulders; it was withdrawn and disappeared, the door closing behind her.

The woman went quickly down the box-edged path between the raspberries and currants, and as she walked her well-developed form and gait betrayed her individuality. It was Suke Damson, the affianced one of simple young Tim Tangs. At the bottom of the garden she entered the shelter of the tall hedge, and only the top of her head could be seen hastening in the direction of her own dwelling.

Grace had recognised, or thought she recognised, in the grey arm stretching from the porch, the sleeve of a dressing-gown which Mr. Fitzpiers had been wearing on her own memorable visit to him. Her face fired red. She had just before thought of dressing herself and taking a lonely walk under the trees, so coolly green this early morning; but she now sat down on her bed, and fell into reverie. It seemed as if hardly any time had passed when she heard the household moving briskly about, and breakfast preparing downstairs; though on rousing herself to robe and descend she found that the sun was throwing his rays completely over the tree-tops, a progress in the world's diurnal turn denoting that at least three hours had elapsed since she last looked out of the window.

When attired she searched about the house for her father; she found him at last in the garden, stooping to examine the potatoes for signs of disease. Hearing her rustle he stood up and stretched his back and arms, saying, "Morning t'ye, Gracie. I congratulate 'ee. It is only a month to-day to the time!"

She did not answer, but, without lifting her dress, waded between the dewy rows of tall potato-green into the middle of the plot where he was.

"I have been thinking very much about my position this morning, ever since it was light," she began excitedly, and trembling so that she could hardly stand. "And I feel it is a false one. I wish not to marry Mr. Fitzpiers. I wish not to marry anybody; but I'll marry Giles Winterborne if you say I must as an alternative."

Her father's face settled into rigidity, he turned pale, and came deliberately out of the plot before he answered her. She had never seen him look so incensed before.

"Now, hearken to me," he said. "There's a time for a woman to alter her mind; and there's a time when she can no longer alter it, if she has any right eye to her parents' honour and the seemliness of things. That time has come. I won't say to 'ee, you *shall* marry him. But I will say that if you refuse I shall for ever be ashamed and a weary of 'ee as a daughter, and shall look upon you as the hope of my life no more. What do you know about life and what it can bring forth, and how you ought to act to lead up to best ends? Oh, you are an ungrateful maid, Grace: you've seen that fellow Giles, and he has got over 'ee; that's where the secret lies, I'll warrant me!"

"No father, no! It is not Giles—it is something I cannot tell you of——"

"Well—make fools of us all; make us laughing-stocks; break it off; have your own way!"

"But who knows of the engagement as yet—how can breaking it disgrace you?"

Melbury then by degrees admitted that he had mentioned the engagement to this acquaintance and to that, till she perceived that in his restlessness and pride he had published it everywhere. She went dismally away to a bower of laurel at the top of the garden. Her father followed her.

"It is that Giles Winterborne!" he said with an upbraiding gaze at her.

"No—it is not—though for that matter you encouraged him once!" she said, troubled to the verge of despair. "It is not Giles: it is Mr. Fitzpiers."

"You've had a tiff—a lover's tiff—that's all, I suppose?"

"It is some woman——"

"Ay, ay; you are jealous.—The old story. Don't tell me. Now do you bide here. I'll send Fitzpiers to you. I saw him smoking in front of his house but a minute bygone."

He went off hastily out of the garden-gate, and up the lane. But she would not stay where she was; and edging through a slit in the garden fence walked away into the wood. Just about here the trees were large and wide apart, and there was no undergrowth, so that she could be seen to some distance a sylph-like greenish-white creature, as toned by the sunlight and leafage. She heard a footfall crushing dead leaves behind her, and turning hastily found herself reconnoitred by Fitzpiers himself, approaching gay and fresh as the morning around them.

His remote gaze at her had been one of mild interest rather than of rapture. But she looked so lovely in the green world about her; her pink cheeks, her simple white dress, and the delicate flexibility of her movements acquired such rarity from their wildwood setting that his eyes kindled as he drew near.

"My darling, what is it? Your father says you are in the pouts, and jealous, and I don't know what. Ha-ha-ha, as if there were any rival to you except vegetable nature in this home of recluses! We know better."

"Jealous—O no—it is not so," said she gravely. "That's a mistake of his and yours sir. I spoke to him so closely about the question of marriage with you that he did not apprehend my state of mind."

"But there's something wrong—eh?" he asked, eyeing her narrowly, and bending to kiss her. She shrank away, and his purposed kiss miscarried. "What is it?" he said, more seriously for this little defeat.

She made no answer beyond, "Mr. Fitzpiers—I have had no breakfast—I must go in."

"Come!" he insisted, fixing his eyes upon her. "Tell me at once, I say."

It was the greater strength against the smaller: but she was mastered less by his manner than by her own sense of the unfairness of silence. "I looked out of the window——" she said with hesitation. "I'll tell you by and by. I must go indoors. I have had no breakfast——"

By a sort of divination his conjecture went straight to the fact. "Nor I," said he lightly. "Indeed, I rose late to-day—I have had a broken night, or rather morning. A girl of the village—I don't know her name—came and rang at my bell as soon as it was light—between four and five I should think it was—perfectly maddened with an aching tooth. As nobody heard her ring she threw some gravel at my window, till at last I heard her and slipped on my dressing-gown and went down. The poor thing had come half-dressed to beg me, with tears in her eyes, to take out her tormentor if I dragged her head off. Down she sat and out it came—a lovely molar —not a speck upon it; and off she went with it in her handkerchief, much contented, though it would have done good work for her for fifty years to come."

It was all so plausible—so completely explained! Knowing nothing of the intimacy established in the hayfield on old Midsummer eve Grace felt that her suspicions were unworthy and absurd; and with the readiness of an honest heart she jumped at the opportunity of honouring his word. At the moment of her mental libration the bushes about the garden had moved, and her father emerged into the shady glade. "Well—I hope it is made up?" he said cheerily.

"Oh yes," said Fitzpiers with his eyes fixed on Grace, whose eyes were shyly bent downwards.

"Now," said her father, "tell me, the pair of ye, that you still mean to take one another for good and all; and on the strength o't you shall have another couple of hundred paid down—I swear it by the name!"

Fitzpiers took her hand. "We declare it, do we not, my dear Grace?" said he.

Relieved of her doubt, somewhat overawed, and ever anxious to please, she was disposed to settle the matter; yet, woman-like, she would not relinquish her opportunity of asking a concession of some sort. "If our wedding can be at church, I say yes," she answered in a measured voice. "If not, I say no."

Fitzpiers was generous in his turn. "It shall be so," he rejoined gracefully. "To holy church we'll go, and much good may it do us."

They returned through the bushes indoors, Grace walking, full of thought, between the other two, somewhat comforted, both by Fitzpiers's ingenious explanation and by the sense that she was not to be deprived of a religious ceremony. "So let it be," she said to herself: "Pray God it is for the best!"

From this hour there was no serious recalcitration on her part. Fitzpiers kept himself continually near her, dominating any rebellious impulse, and shaping her will into passive concurrence with all his desires. Apart from his lover-like anxiety to possess her the few golden hundreds of the timber-dealer, ready to hand, formed a warm background to Grace's lovely face, and went some way to remove his uneasiness at the prospect of endangering his professional and social chances by an alliance with the family of a simple countryman.

The interim closed up its perspective surely and silently. Whenever Grace had any doubts of her position the sense of contracting time was like a shortening chamber: at other moments she was comparatively blithe. Day after day waxed and waned; the one or two woodmen who sawed, shaped, or spokeshaved on her father's premises at this inactive season of the year, regularly came and unlocked the doors in the morning, locked them in the evening, supped, leant over their garden-gates for a whiff of evening air, and to catch any last and furthest throb of news from the outer world, which entered and expired at Little Hintock like the exhausted swell of a wave in some innermost cavern of some innermost creek of an embayed sea; yet no news interfered with the nuptial purpose at their neighbour's house. The sappy green twig-tips of the season's growth would not, she thought, be appreciably woodier on the day she became a wife, so near was the time; the tints of the foliage would hardly have changed. Everything was so much as usual that no itinerant stranger would have supposed a woman's fate to be hanging in the balance at that summer's decline.

But there were preparations, imaginable enough by those who had special knowledge. In the remote and fashionable city of Exonbury something was growing up under the hands of several persons who had never seen Grace Melbury, never would see her, or care anything about her at all, though their creation had such interesting relation to her life that it would enclose her very heart at a moment when that heart would beat, if not with more emotional ardour, at least with more emotional turbulence than at any previous time.

Why did Mrs. Dollery's van on its return from Sherton, instead of passing along the highway to Abbot's Cernel direct, turn one Saturday night into Little Hintock Lane, and never pull up till it reached Mr. Melbury's gates? The gilding sheen of evening fell upon a large flat box, not less than a yard square and safely tied with cord, as it was handed out from under the tilt with a great deal of care. But it was not heavy for its size; Mrs. Dollery herself carried it into the house. Tim Tangs, the hollow-turner, Cawtree, Suke Damson, and others, looked knowing and made remarks to each other as they watched its entrance. Melbury stood at the door of the timber-shed in the attitude of a man to whom such an arrival was a trifling domestic detail with which he did not condescend to be concerned. Yet he well divined the contents of that box, and was in truth all the while in a pleasant exaltation at the proof that thus far at any rate no disappointment had supervened. While Mrs. Dollery remained— which was rather long, from her sense of the importance of her errand—he went into the outhouse; but as soon as she had had her say, been paid, and had rumbled away, he entered the dwelling, to find there what he knew he should find—his wife and daughter in a flutter of excitement over the wedding-gown, just arrived from the leading dressmaker of Exonbury city aforesaid.

During these weeks Giles Winterborne was nowhere to be seen or heard of. At the close of his tenure in Hintock he had sold some of his furniture, packed up the rest—a few pieces endeared by associations or necessary to his occupation—in the house of a friendly neighbour, and gone away. People said that a certain laxity had crept into his life; that he had never gone near a church latterly, and had been sometimes seen on Sundays with unblacked boots, lying on his elbow under a tree, with a cynical gaze at surrounding objects. He was likely to return to Hintock when the cidermaking season came round, his apparatus being stored there, and travel with his mill and press from village to village.

The narrow interval that stood before the day diminished yet. There was in Grace's mind sometimes a certain anticipative satisfaction, the satisfaction of feeling that she would be the heroine of an hour; moreover she was proud, as a cultivated woman, to be the wife of a cultivated man. It was an opportunity denied very frequently to young women in her position, nowadays not a few; those in whom parental discovery of the value of education has implanted tastes which parental circles fail to gratify. But what an attenuation this cold pride was of the dream of her youth, in which she had pictured herself walking in state towards the altar flushed by the purple light and bloom of her own passion, without a single misgiving as to the sealing of the bond, and fervently receiving as her due

"The homage of a thousand hearts; the fond deep love of one."

Everything had been clear then, in imagination; now something was undefined. She had little carking anxieties; a curious fatefulness seemed to rule her, and she experienced a mournful want of someone to confide in.

The day loomed so big and nigh that her prophetic ear could in fancy catch the noise of it, hear the murmur of the villagers as she came out of church, imagine the jangle of the three thin-toned Hintock bells. The dialogues seemed to grow louder, and the ding-ding-dong of those three crazed bells more persistent. She awoke: the morning had come.

Five hours later she was the wife of Fitzpiers.

XXV

THE chief hotel at Sherton-Abbas was the "Earl of Wessex"— a substantial inn of Ham-hill stone with a yawning back yard into which vehicles were driven by coachmen to stabling of wonderful commodiousness. The windows to the street were mullioned into narrow lights, and only commanded a view of the opposite houses; hence perhaps it arose that the best and most luxurious private sitting-room that the inn could afford overlooked the lateral parts of the establishment, where beyond the yard were to be seen gardens and orchards, now bossed, nay encrusted, with scarlet and gold fruit, stretching to infinite distance under a luminous lavender mist. The time was early autumn,

> When the fair apples, red as evening sky,
> Do bend the tree unto the fruitful ground,

When juicy pears, and berries of black dye
Do dance in air, and call the eyes around.

The landscape confronting the window might indeed have
been part of the identical stretch of country which the "marvellous boy" had in his mind when he penned those lines.

In this room sat she who had been the maiden Grace Melbury
till the finger of fate touched her and turned her to a wife. It
was two months after the wedding, and she was alone. Fitzpiers
had walked out to see the Abbey by the light of sunset, but she
had been too fatigued to accompany him. They had reached
the last stage of a long eight-weeks' tour, and were going on
to Little Hintock that night.

In the yard between Grace and the orchards there progressed a scene natural to the locality at this time of the year.
An apple-mill and press had been erected on the spot, to
which some men were bringing fruit from divers points in
mawn-baskets, while others were grinding them, and others
wringing down the pomace, whose sweet juice gushed forth
into tubs and pails. The superintendent of these proceedings, to whom the others spoke as master, was a young yeoman of prepossessing manner and aspect, whose form she
recognised in a moment. He had hung his coat to a nail of
the outhouse wall, and wore his shirt-sleeves rolled up beyond his elbows, to keep them unstained while he rammed
the pomace into the bags of horsehair. Fragments of apple-
rind had alighted upon the brim of his hat—probably from
the bursting of a bag—while brown pips of the same fruit
were sticking among the down upon his fine round arms,
and in his beard.

She realized in a moment how he had come there. Down
in the heart of the apple country nearly every farmer kept a
cider-making apparatus and wring-house for his own use,
building up the pomace in great straw "cheeses" as they were
called; but here, on the margin of Pomona's plain, was a
debateable land neither orchard nor sylvan exclusively, where
the apple-produce was hardly sufficient to warrant each pro-
prietor in keeping a mill of his own. This was the field of the
travelling cider-maker. His press and mill were fixed to wheels

instead of being set up in a cider-house; and with a couple of horses, buckets, tubs, strainers, and an assistant or two, he wandered from place to place, deriving very satisfactory returns for his trouble in such a prolific season as the present.

The outskirts of the town were just now abounding with apple-gatherings. They stood in the yards in carts, baskets, and loose heaps; and the blue stagnant air of autumn which hung over everything was heavy with a sweet cidery smell. Cakes of pomace lay against the walls in the yellow sun, where they were drying to be used as fuel. Yet it was not the great make of the year as yet; before the standard crop came in there accumulated in abundant times like this a large superfluity of early apples, and windfalls from trees of the later harvest, which would not keep long. Thus in the baskets, and quivering in the hopper of the mill, she saw specimens of mixed dates, including the mellow countenances of streaked-jacks, codlins, costards, stubbards, ratheripes, and other well-known friends of her ravenous youth.

Grace watched the head man with interest. The slightest sigh escaped her. Perhaps she thought of the day—not so far distant—when that friend of her childhood had met her by her father's arrangement in this same town, warm with hope, though diffident, and trusting in a promise rather implied than given. Or she might have thought of days earlier yet—days of childhood—when her mouth was somewhat more ready to receive a kiss from his than was his to bestow one. However, all that was over. She had felt superior to him then, and she felt superior to him now.

She wondered why he never looked towards her open window. She did not know that in the slight commotion caused by their arrival at the inn that afternoon Winterborne had caught sight of her through the archway, had turned red, and was continuing his work with more concentrated attention on the very account of his discovery. Robert Creedle too, who travelled with Giles, had been incidentally informed by the ostler that Dr. Fitzpiers and his young wife were in the hotel; after which news Creedle kept shaking his head and saying to himself "Ah!" very audibly, between his thrusts at the screw of the cider-press.

"Why the deuce do you sigh like that Robert?" asked Winterborne at last.

"Ah, maister—'Tis my thoughts—'tis my thoughts! . . . . Yes, ye've lost a hundred load o' timber well seasoned; ye've lost five hundred pound in good money; ye've lost the stone-windered house that's big enough to hold a dozen families; ye've lost your share of half-a-dozen good waggons and their horses:— all lost—through your letting slip she that was once yer own!"

"Good God, Creedle, you'll drive me mad!" said Giles sternly. "Don't speak of that any more!"

Thus the subject had ended in the yard. Meanwhile the passive cause of all this loss still regarded the scene. She was beautifully dressed; she was seated in the most comfortable room that the inn afforded; her long journey had been full of variety, and almost luxuriously performed—for Fitzpiers did not study economy where pleasure was in question. Hence it perhaps arose that Giles and all his belongings seemed sorry and common to her for the moment—moving in a groove so far removed from her own of late that she could scarcely believe she had ever found congruity therein. "No— I could never have married him!" she said, gently shaking her head. "Dear father was right. It would have been too rough a life for me." And she looked at the rings of sapphire and opal upon her white and slender fingers that had been gifts from Fitzpiers.

Seeing that Giles still kept his back turned, and with a little of the above-described pride of life—easily to be understood, possibly excused, in a young inexperienced woman who thought she had married well—she opened the window wider and cried, with a smile on her lips, "Mr. Winterborne!"

He appeared to take no heed, and she said a second time, "Mr. Winterborne!"

Even now he seemed not to hear, though a person close enough to him to see the expression of his face might have doubted it; and she said a third time, with a timid loudness, "Mr. Winterborne! What, have you forgotten my voice?"— She remained with her lips parted in a welcoming smile.

He turned without surprise, and came deliberately towards the window. "Why do you call me?" he said with a sternness that took her completely unawares, his face being now pale. "Is it not enough that you see me here moiling and mud-dling for my daily bread while you are sitting there in your success, that you can't refrain from opening old wounds by calling out my name?"

She flushed, and was struck dumb for some moments; but she forgave his unreasoning anger, knowing so well in what it had its root. "I am sorry I offended you by speaking, Giles," she replied. "Believe me, I did not intend to do that. I could hardly sit here so near you without a word of recognition."

Winterborne's heart had swollen big and his eyes grown moist by this time, so much had the gentle answer of that familiar voice moved him. He assured her hurriedly, and without looking at her, that he was not angry. He then managed to ask her, in a clumsy constrained way, if she had had a pleasant journey, and seen many interesting sights. She spoke of a few places that she had visited, and so the time passed till he withdrew to take his place at one of the levers which pulled round the screw.

Forgotten her voice! Indeed he had not forgotten her voice, as his bitterness showed. But though in the heat of the moment he had reproached her keenly, his second mood was a far more tender one—that which could regard her renunciation of such as he as her glory and her privilege, his own fidelity notwithstanding. He could have declared with a contemporary poet:

If I forget,
The salt creek may forget the ocean;
If I forget
The heart whence flowed my heart's bright motion,
May I sink meanlier than the worst,
Abandoned, outcast, crushed, accurst,—
If I forget!

Though you forget,
No word of mine shall mar your pleasure;
Though you forget,—
You filled my barren life with treasure,
You may withdraw the gift you gave,
You still are queen, I still am slave,
Though you forget.

She had tears in her eyes at the thought that she could not remind him of what he ought to have remembered; that not herself but the pressure of events had dissipated the dreams of their early youth. Grace was thus unexpectedly worsted in her encounter with her old friend. She had opened the window with a faint sense of triumph, but he had turned it into sadness; she did not quite comprehend the reason why. In truth it was because she was not cruel enough in her cruelty. If you have to use the knife, use it, say the great surgeons; and for her own peace Grace should have handled Winterborne thoroughly or not at all. As it was, on closing the window an indescribable—some might have said dangerous—pity quavered in her bosom for him.

Presently her husband entered the room and told her what a wonderful sunset there was to be seen.

"I have not noticed it. But I have seen somebody out there that we know," she replied, looking into the court.

Fitzpiers followed the direction of her eyes and said he did not recognise anybody.

"Why, Mr. Winterborne—there he is cider-making. He combines that with his other business, you know."

"Oh—that fellow," said Fitzpiers, his curiosity becoming extinct.

She, reproachfully; "What, call Mr. Winterborne a fellow, Edred? It is true I was just saying to myself that I never could have married him; but I have much regard for him, and always shall."

"Well, do by all means, my dear one. I dare say I am inhuman, and supercilious, and contemptibly proud of my poor old ramshackle family; but I do honestly confess to you that I feel as if I belonged to a different species from the people who are working in that yard."

"And from me too then. For my blood is no better than theirs."

He looked at her with a droll sort of awakening. It was, indeed, a startling anomaly that this woman of the tribe without should be standing there beside him as his wife, if his sentiments were as he had said. In their travels together she had ranged so unerringly at his level in ideas, tastes, and habits, that he had almost forgotten how his heart had played havoc with his ambition in taking her to him.

"Ah *you*—you are refined and educated into something quite different," he said self-assuringly.

"I don't quite like to think that," she murmured with regret. "And I think you under-estimate Giles Winterborne. Remember I was brought up with him till I was sent away to school, so I cannot be radically different. At any rate I don't feel so. That is no doubt my fault, and a great blemish in me. But I hope you will put up with it, Edred."

Fitzpiers said that he would endeavour to do so, and as it was now getting on for dusk they prepared to perform the last stage of their journey, so as to arrive at Hintock before it grew very late.

In less than half-an-hour they started, the cidermakers in the yard having ceased their labours and gone away, so that the only sounds audible there now were the trickling of the juice from the tightly screwed press, and the buzz of a single wasp, which had drunk itself so tipsy that it was unconscious of nightfall. Grace was very cheerful at the thought of being soon in her sylvan home; but Fitzpiers sat beside her almost silent. An indescribable oppressiveness had overtaken him with the near approach of the journey's-end and the realities of life that lay there. It was two months since he married her.

"You don't say a word, Edred," she observed. "Aren't you glad to get back? I am."

"You have friends here. I have none."

"But my friends are yours."

"Oh yes—in that sense."

The conversation languished, and they drew near the end of Hintock Lane. It had been decided that they should, at least for a time, take up their abode in her father's roomy house, one wing of which was quite at their service, being almost disused by the Melburys. Workmen had been painting, papering, and white-washing this set of rooms in the wedded pair's absence; and so scrupulous had been the timber-dealer that there should occur no hitch or disappointment on their arrival that not the smallest detail remained undone. To make it all complete a ground-floor room had been fitted up as a surgery, with an independent outer door, to which Fitzpiers's brass plate was screwed—for mere ornament, such a sign being quite superfluous where everybody knew the latitude and longitude of his neighbours for miles round.

Melbury and his wife welcomed the twain with affection, and all the house showed them deference. They went up to explore their rooms, that opened from a passage on the left hand of the staircase, the entrance to which could be shut off on the landing by a door that Melbury had hung for the purpose. A friendly fire was burning in the grate although it was not cold. Fitzpiers said it was too soon for any sort of meal, they having dined but shortly before leaving Sherton-Abbas; he would walk across to his old lodgings to learn how his deputy had got on in his absence.

In leaving Melbury's door he looked back at the house. There was economy in living under that roof—and economy was desirable; but in some way he was dissatisfied with the arrangement; it immersed him so deeply in son-in-lawship to Melbury. He went on to his former residence; his *locum tenens* was out, and Fitzpiers fell into conversation with his old landlady.

"Well Mrs. Cox; what's the best news?" he asked of her with cheery weariness.

She was a little soured at losing, by his marriage, so profitable a tenant as the surgeon had proved to be during his residence under her roof; and the more so in there being hardly the remotest chance of her getting such another settler in the Hintock solitudes. "'Tis what I don't wish to repeat, sir; least of all to you," she mumbled.

"Never mind me Mrs. Cox; go ahead."

"It is what people say about your hasty marrying, Dr. Fitzpiers. Whereas they won't believe you know such clever doctrines in physic as they once supposed of 'ee, seeing as you could marry into Mr. Melbury's family, which is only Hintock-born such as we."

"They are kindly welcome to their opinion," said Fitzpiers, not allowing himself to recognize that he winced. "Anything else?"

"Yes; *she's* come home at last."

"Who's she?"

"Mrs. Charmond."

"Oh indeed," said Fitzpiers with but slight interest. "I've never seen her."

"She has seen you, sir, whether or no."

"Never."

"Yes. She saw you in some hotel or street for a minute or two whilst you were away travelling, and accidentally heard your name; and when she made some remark about you, Miss Ellis—that's her maid—told her you was on your wedding-tour with Mr. Melbury's daughter; and she said, 'He ought to have done better than that. I fear he has spoilt his chances,' she says."

Fitzpiers did not talk much longer to this cheering house-wife, and walked home with no very brisk step. He entered the door quietly, and went straight upstairs to the drawing-room extemporized for their use by Melbury in his and his bride's absence, expecting to find her there as he had left her. The fire was burning still, but there were no lights; he looked into the next apartment, fitted up as a dining-room, but no supper was laid. He went to the top of the stairs, and heard a chorus of voices in the timber-merchant's parlour below, Grace's being occasionally intermingled.

Descending and looking into the room from the doorway he found quite a large gathering of neighbours and other acquaintances, praising and congratulating Mrs. Fitzpiers on her return, among them being the dairyman, Farmer Cawtree, and the relieving officer from Great Hintock; also the road contractor, the master tanner, the exciseman, and some others with their wives. Grace—girl that she was—had quite forgotten her new dignity and her husband's; she was in the midst of them blushing and receiving their compliments with all the pleasures of old comradeship.

Fitzpiers experienced a profound distaste for the situation. Melbury was nowhere in the room, but Melbury's wife, perceiving the doctor, came to him. "We thought, Grace and I," she said, "that as they have called, hearing you were come, we could do no less than ask them to supper; and then Grace proposed that we should all sup together as it is the first night of your return."

By this time Grace had come round to him. "Is it not good

of them to welcome me so warmly!" she exclaimed with tears of friendship in her eyes. "After so much good feeling I could not think of our shutting ourselves up away from them in our own dining-room."

"Certainly not—certainly not," said Fitzpiers. And he entered the room with the heroic smile of a martyr.

As soon as they sat down to table Melbury came in, and seemed to see at once that Fitzpiers would much rather have received no such demonstrative reception. He thereupon privately chid his wife for her forwardness in the matter. Mrs. Melbury declared that it was as much Grace's doing as hers, after which there was no more to be said by that young woman's tender father. By this time Fitzpiers was making the best of his position among the wide-elbowed and genial company who sat eating and drinking, laughing and joking around him, and getting warmed himself by the good cheer he was obliged to admit that after all the supper was not the least enjoyable he had ever known.

At times, however, the words about his having spoiled his opportunities, repeated to him as coming from Mrs. Charmond, haunted him like a handwriting on the wall. Then his manner would become suddenly abstracted. At one moment he would mentally put an indignant query why Mrs. Charmond or any other woman should make it her business to have opinions about his opportunities; at another he thought that he could hardly be angry with her for taking an interest in the doctor of her own parish. Then he would drink a glass of grog and so get rid of the misgiving. These hitches and quaffings were soon perceived by Grace as well as by her father; and hence both of them were much relieved when the first of the guests to discover that the hour was growing late rose and declared that he must think of moving homewards. At the words Melbury rose as alertly as if lifted by a spring; and in ten minutes they were gone.

"Now Grace," said her husband as soon as he found himself alone with her in their private apartments; "we've had a very pleasant evening, and everybody has been very kind. But we must come to an understanding about our way of living here. If we continue in these rooms there must be no mixing in with your people below. I can't stand it, and that's the truth."

She had been sadly surprised at the suddenness of his distaste for those old-fashioned woodland forms of life which in his courtship he had professed to regard with so much interest. But she assented in a moment.

"We must be simply your father's tenants," he continued, "and our goings and comings must be as independent as if we lived elsewhere."

"Certainly Edred—I quite see that it must be so."

"But you joined in with all those people in my absence, without knowing whether I should approve or disapprove. When I came I couldn't help myself at all."

She, sighing: "Yes—I see I ought to have waited; though they came unexpectedly, and I thought I had acted for the best."

Thus the discussion ended, and the next day Fitzpiers went on his old rounds as usual. But it was easy for so supersubtle an eye as his to discern, or to think he discerned, that he was no longer regarded as an extrinsic, unfathomed gentleman of limitless potentiality, scientific and social; but as Mr. Melbury's compeer, and therefore in a degree only one of themselves. The Hintock woodlanders held with all the strength of inherited conviction to the aristocratic principle, and as soon as they had discovered that Fitzpiers was one of the old Oakbury Fitzpierses they had accorded to him for nothing a touching of hat-brims, promptness of service, and deference of approach, which Melbury had to do without though he paid for it over and over. But now, having proved a traitor to his own cause by this marriage, Fitzpiers was believed in no more as a superior hedged by his own divinity; while as doctor he began to be rated no higher than old Jones whom they had so long despised.

His few patients seemed in his two-months' absence to have dwindled considerably in number; and no sooner had he returned than there came to him from the Board of Guardians a complaint that a pauper had been neglected by his substitute. In a fit of pride Fitzpiers resigned his appointment as one of the surgeons to the Union, which had been the nucleus of his practice here.

At the end of a fortnight he came indoors one evening to Grace more briskly than usual. "They have written to me again about that practice in Budmouth that I once negociated for," he said to her. "The premium asked is eight hundred pounds, and I think that between your father and myself it ought to be raised. Then we can get away from this place for ever."

The question had been mooted between them before, and she was not unprepared to consider it. They had not proceeded far with the discussion when a knock came to the door, and in a minute Grammer ran up to say that a message had arrived from Hintock House requesting Doctor Fitzpiers to attend there at once. Mrs. Charmond had met with a slight accident through the overturning of her carriage.

"This is something, anyhow," said Fitzpiers, rising with an interest which he could not have defined. "I have had a presentiment that this mysterious woman and I were to be better acquainted." The latter words were murmured to himself alone.

"Good-night," said Grace as soon as he was ready. "I shall be asleep probably when you return."

"Good-night," he replied inattentively, and went downstairs. It was the first time since their marriage that he had left her without a kiss.

XXVI

WINTERBORNE had given up his house. On this account his face was seen but fitfully in Hintock; and he would probably have disappeared from the place altogether but for his slight business connection with Melbury, on whose premises Giles kept his cider-making apparatus now that he had no place of his own to stow it in. Coming here one afternoon, on his way to a hut beyond the wood where he now slept, he noticed that the familiar brown-thatched pinion of his paternal roof had vanished from its site, and that the walls were levelled, according to the landlords' principle at this date of getting rid of cottages whenever possible. In present circumstances he had a feeling for the spot that might have been called morbid, and when he had supped in the hut aforesaid he made use of the spare hour before bedtime to return to Little Hintock in the twilight, and ramble over the patch of ground on which he had first seen the day.

He repeated this evening visit on several like occasions. Even in the gloom he could trace where the different rooms had stood; could mark the shape of the kitchen chimney-corner, in which he had roasted apples and potatoes in his boyhood, cast his bullets, and burnt his initials on articles that did and did not belong to him. The appletrees still remained to show where the garden had been, the oldest of them even now retaining the crippled slant to north-east given them by the great November gale of 1824 which carried a brig bodily over the Chesil Bank. They were at present bent to still greater obliquity by the heaviness of their produce. Apples bobbed against his head, and in the grass beneath he crunched scores of them as he walked. There was nobody to gather them now.

It was on the evening under notice that, half sitting, half leaning against one of these inclined trunks, Winterborne became lost in his thoughts as usual, till one little star after another had taken up a position in the piece of sky which now confronted him where his walls and chimneys had formerly raised their outlines. The house had jutted awkwardly into the road, and the opening caused by its absence was very distinct.

In the silence the trot of horses and the spin of carriage-wheels became audible; the vehicle soon shaped itself against the blank sky, bearing down upon him with the bend in the lane which here occurred, and of which the house had been the cause. He could discern the figure of a woman high up on the driving-seat of a phaeton, a groom being just visible behind. Presently there was a slight scrape, then a scream. Winterborne went across to the spot, and found the phaeton half overturned, its driver sitting on the heap of rubbish which had once been his dwelling, and the man seizing the horses' heads. The equipage was Mrs. Charmond's, and the unseated charioteer that lady herself.

To his inquiry if she were hurt she made some incoherent reply to the effect that she did not know. The damage in other respects was little or none: the phaeton was righted, Mrs. Charmond placed in it, and the reins given to the servant. It appeared that she had been deceived by the removal of the house, imagining the gap caused by the demolition to be the opening of the road, so that she turned in upon the ruins instead of at the bend a few yards further on.

"Drive home—drive home!" she cried impatiently; and they started on their way. They had not however gone many paces when, the air being still, Winterborne heard her say, "Stop: tell that man to call the doctor—Mr. Fitzpiers—and send him on to the House. I find I am hurt more seriously than I thought."

The seriousness seemed ludicrous to Winterborne; but he took the message from the groom and proceeded to the doctor's at once. Having delivered it he stepped back into the darkness, and waited till he had seen Fitzpiers leave the door. He stood for a few minutes looking at the window which, by its light, revealed the room where Grace was sitting; and went away under the gloomy trees.

Fitzpiers duly arrived at Hintock House, whose doors he now saw open for the first time. Contrary to his expectation there was visible no sign of that confusion or alarm which a grave accident to the mistress of the abode would have occasioned. He was shown into a room at the top of the staircase, cosily and femininely draped, where by the light of the shaded lamp he saw a woman of elegant figure reclining upon a couch in such a position as not to disturb a pile of magnificent hair on the crown of her head. A deep purple dressing-gown formed an admirable foil to the peculiarly rich brown of her hair-plaits; her left arm, which was naked nearly up to the shoulder, was thrown upwards, and between the fingers of her right hand she held a cigarette, while she idly breathed from her delicately curled lips a thin stream of smoke towards the ceiling.

The doctor's first feeling was a sense of his exaggerated prevision in having brought appliances for a serious case;

the next, something more curious. While the scene and the moment were new to him and unanticipated the sentiment and essence of the moment were indescribably familiar. What could be the cause of it? Probably a dream.

Mrs. Charmond did not move more than to raise her eyes to him, and he came and stood by her. She glanced up at his face across her brows and forehead, and then he observed a blush creep slowly over her decidedly handsome cheeks. Her eyes, which had lingered upon him with an inquiring conscious expression, were hastily withdrawn, and she mechanically applied the cigarette again to her lips.

For a moment he forgot his errand, till suddenly arousing himself he addressed her, formally condoled with her, and made the usual professional inquiries about what had happened to her, and where she was hurt.

"That's what I want you to tell me," she murmured in tones of indefinable reserve. "I quite believe in you, for I know you are very accomplished, because you study so hard."

"I'll do my best to justify your good opinion," said the young man bowing. "And none the less that I am happy to find the accident has not been serious."

"I am very much shaken," she said.

"Oh yes," he replied; and completed his examination, which convinced him that there was really nothing the matter with her, and more than ever puzzled him as to why he had been summoned since she did not appear to be a timid woman. "You must rest awhile; and I'll send something," he said.

"Oh, I forgot," she returned. "Look here." And she showed him a little scrape on her arm—the full round arm that was exposed. "Put some court plaster on that, please."

He obeyed. "And now, doctor," she said, "before you go I want to put a question to you. Sit round there in front of me, on that low chair, and bring the candles, or one, to the little table. Do you smoke? Yes? That's right—I am learning. Take one of these; and here's a light." She threw a match-box across.

Fitzpiers caught it and having lit up regarded her from his new position which, with the shifting of the candles, for the first time afforded him a full view of her face. "How many years have passed since first we met?" she resumed, in a voice which she endeavoured to maintain at its former pitch of composure, and eyeing him with daring bashfulness.

"*We* met, do you say?"

She nodded. "I saw you recently at an hotel in London, when you were passing through, I suppose, with your bride, and I recognised you as one I had met in my girlhood. Do you remember, when you were studying at Heidelberg, an English family that was staying there, who used to walk——"

"And the young lady who wore a long tail of rare-coloured hair—ah, I see it before my eyes!—who lost her handkerchief on the Great Terrace—who was going back in the dusk to find it—to whom I said, 'I'll go for it,' and who answered, 'Oh, it is not worth coming all the way up again for.' I *do* remember, and how very long we stayed talking there! I went next morning whilst the dew was on the grass: there it lay—a little morsel of damp lacework, with 'Felice' marked in one corner. I see it now! I picked it up, and then . . . . ."

"Well?"

"I kissed it," he rejoined rather shamefacedly.

"But you had hardly ever seen me except in the dusk?"

"Never mind. I was young then, and I kissed it. I wondered how I could make the most of my *trouvaille*, and decided that I would call at your hotel with it that afternoon. It rained, and I waited till next day. I called, and you were gone."

"Yes," answered she with dry melancholy. "My mother, knowing my face was my only fortune, said she had no wish for such a chit as me to go falling in love with an impecunious student, and spirited me away to Baden. As it is all over and past I'll tell you one thing; I should have sent you a line had I known your name. That name I never knew till my maid said as you passed up the hotel stairs a month ago, 'There's Dr. Fitzpiers.'"

"Good God," said Fitzpiers musingly. "How the time comes back to me! The evening, the morning, the dew, the spot. When I found that you really were gone it was as if a cold iron had been passed down my back. I went up to where you had stood when I last saw you—I flung myself on the grass, and—being not much more than a boy—my eyes were literally blinded with tears. Nameless, unknown to me as you were I couldn't forget your voice."

"For how long?"

"Oh—ever so long. Days and days."

"Days and days! *Only* days and days? Oh the heart of a man! Days and days!"

"But, my dear madam, I had not known you more than a day or two. It was not a full blown love—it was the merest bud—red, fresh, vivid, but small. It was a colossal passion in embryo. It never matured."

"So much the better perhaps."

"Perhaps. But see how powerless is the human will against predestination. We were prevented meeting; we have met. One feature of the case remains the same amid many changes. While you have grown rich, I am still poor. Better than that, you have (judging by your last remark) outgrown the foolish impulsive passions of your early girlhood. I have not outgrown mine."

"I beg your pardon," said she with vibrations of feeling in her words. "I have been placed in a position which hinders such outgrowings. Besides, I don't believe that the genuine subjects of emotion do outgrow them; I believe that the older such people get the worse they are. Possibly at ninety or a hundred they may feel they are cured: but a mere threescore and ten won't do it—at least for me, if I live so long."

He gazed at her in undisguised admiration. Here was a soul of souls! "You speak truly," he exclaimed. "But you speak sadly as well. Why is that?"

"I always am sad when I come here," she said dropping to a low tone with a sense of having been too demonstrative.

"Then may I inquire why you came?"

"A man brought me. Women are always carried about like corks upon the waves of masculine desires. . . . . . I hope I have not alarmed you; but Hintock has the curious effect of bottling up the emotions till one can no longer hold them; I am often obliged to fly away and discharge my sentiments somewhere, or I should die outright."

"There is a very good society in the county, I suppose, for those who have the privilege of entering it."

"Perhaps so. But the misery of remote country life is that your neighbours have no toleration for difference of opinion and habit. My neighbours think I am an atheist, except those who think I am a Roman Catholic; and when I speak disrespectfully of the weather or the crops they think I am a blasphemer."

"You don't wish me to stay any longer?" he inquired, when he found that she remained musing.

"No—I think not."

"Then tell me that I am to be gone."

"Why? Cannot you go without?"

"I may consult my own feelings only, if left to myself."

"Well if you do, what then? Do you suppose you'll be in my way?"

"I feared it might be so."

"Then fear no more. But good-night. Come to-morrow and see if I am going on right. This renewal of acquaintance touches me. I have already a friendship for you."

"If it depends upon myself it shall last for ever."

"My best hopes that it may."

Fitzpiers went down the stairs absolutely unable to decide whether she had sent for him in the natural alarm which might have followed her mishap, or with the single view of making herself known to him as she had done, for which the capsize had afforded excellent opportunity. Outside the house he mused over the spot under the light of the stars. It seemed very strange that he should have come there more than once when its inhabitant was absent, and observed the house with a nameless interest; that he should have assumed offhand before he knew Grace that it was here she lived; that, in short, at sundry times and seasons the individuality of Hintock House should have forced itself upon him as appertaining to some existence with which he was concerned.

The intersection of his temporal orbit with Mrs. Charmond's for a day or two in the past had created a sentimental interest in her at the time, but it had been so evanescent that in the ordinary onward roll of affairs he would scarce ever have recalled it again. To find her here, however, in these somewhat romantic circumstances, magnified that bygone and transitory tenderness to indescribable proportions.

On entering Little Hintock he found himself regarding that hamlet in a new way—from the Hintock House point of view rather than from his own and the Melburys'. The household had all gone to bed. As he went upstairs he heard the snore of the timber-merchant from his quarter of the building, and turned into the passage communicating with his own rooms in a strange access of sadness. A light was burning for him in the chamber; but Grace, though in bed, was not asleep. In a moment her sympathetic voice came from behind the curtains.

"Edred, is she very seriously hurt?"

Fitzpiers had so entirely lost sight of Mrs. Charmond as a patient that he was not on the instant ready with a reply. "Oh no," he said. "There are no bones broken, but she is shaken. I am going again to-morrow."

Another inquiry or two, and Grace said—"Did she ask for me?"

"Well—I think she did.—I don't quite remember; but I am under the impression that she spoke of you."

"Cannot you recollect at all what she said?"

"I cannot, just this minute."

"At any rate she did not talk much about me?" said Grace with disappointment.

"Oh no."

"But you did perhaps," she added innocently fishing for a compliment.

"Oh yes—you may depend upon that!" replied he warmly, though scarcely thinking of what he was saying, so vividly was there present to his mind the personality of Mrs. Charmond.

XXVII

THE doctor's professional visit to Hintock House was promptly repeated the next day and the next. He always found Mrs. Charmond reclining on a sofa, and behaving generally as became a patient who was in no great hurry to lose that title. On each occasion he looked gravely at the little scratch on her arm, as if it had been a serious wound.

He had also to his further satisfaction found a slight scar on her temple; and it was very convenient to put a piece of black plaster on this conspicuous part of her person in preference to gold-beater's skin, so that it might catch the eyes of the servants and make his presence appear decidedly necessary, in case there should be any doubt of the fact.

"Oh—you hurt me!" she exclaimed one day.

He was peeling off the bit of plaster on her arm, under which the scrape had turned the colour of an unripe blackberry previous to vanishing altogether. "Wait a moment then—I'll damp it," said Fitzpiers. He put his lips to the place and kept them there, without any objecting on her part, till the plaster came off easily. "It was at your request I put it on," said he.

"I know it," she replied. "Is that blue vein still in my temple that used to show there? The scar must be just upon it. If the cut had been a little deeper it would have spilt my hot blood indeed!" Fitzpiers examined so closely that his breath touched her tenderly, at which their eyes rose to an encounter,—hers showing themselves as deep and mysterious as interstellar space. She turned her face away. "Ah—none of that—none of that—I cannot coquet with you!" she cried. "Don't suppose I consent to for one moment. Our poor brief youthful hour of lovemaking was too long ago to bear continuing now. It is as well that we should understand each other on that point before we go further."

"Coquet! Nor I with you. As it was when I found the historic handkerchief so it is now. I might have been and may be foolish; but I am no trifler. I naturally cannot forget that little space in which I flitted across the field of your vision in those days of the past, and the recollection opens up all sorts of imaginings."

"Suppose my mother had not taken me away," she murmured, her dreamy eyes resting on the swaying tip of a distant tree.

"I should have seen you again."

"And then?"

"Then the fire would have burnt higher and higher. What would have immediately followed I know not; but sorrow and sickness of heart at last."

"Why?"

"Well—that's the end of all love, according to Nature's law. I can give no other reason."

"Oh don't speak like that," she exclaimed. "Since we are only picturing the possibilities of that time, don't for pity's sake spoil the picture." Her voice sank almost to a whisper as she added with an incipient pout upon her lips, "Let me think at least that if you had really loved me at all seriously you would have loved me for ever and ever!"

"You are right—think it with all your heart," said he. "It is a pleasant thought, and costs nothing."

She weighed that remark in silence awhile. "Did you ever hear anything of me from then till now?" she inquired.

"Not a word."

"So much the better. I had to fight the battle of life as well as you. I may tell you about it some day. But don't ever ask me to do it, and particularly do not press me to tell you now."

Thus the two or three days that they had spent in tender acquaintance on the romantic slopes above the Neckar were stretched out in retrospect to the length and importance of years; made to form a canvas for infinite fancies, idle dreams, luxurious melancholies, and pretty alluring assertions which could neither be proved nor disproved. Grace was never mentioned between them, but a rumour of his contemplated removal from the neighbourhood somehow reached Mrs. Charmond's ears.

"Doctor—you are going away," she exclaimed, confronting him with accusatory reproach in her large dark eyes no less than in her cooing voice. "Oh yes you are," she went on, springing to her feet with an air which might almost have been called passionate. "It is no use denying it. You have bought a practice at Budmouth. I don't blame you. Nobody can live at Hintock—least of all a professional man who wants to keep abreast of recent discovery. And there is nobody here to induce such a one to stay for other reasons.—That's right, that's right—go away!"

"But no—I have not actually bought the practice as yet, though I am indeed in treaty for it. And, my dear friend, if I

continue to feel about the business as I feel at this moment—
perhaps I may conclude never to go at all."

"But you hate Hintock and everything and everybody in it
that you don't mean to take away with you?"

Fitzpiers contradicted this idea in his most vibratory tones,
and she lapsed into the frivolous archness under which she
hid passions of no mean strength—strange, smouldering
erratic passions, kept down like a stifled conflagration, but
bursting out now here, now there—the only certain element
in their direction being its unexpectedness. If one word could
have expressed Felice Charmond it would have been Incon-
sequence. She was a woman of perversities, delighting in
piquant contrasts. She liked mystery, in her life, in her love,
in her history. To be fair to her, there was nothing in these
which she had any great reason to be ashamed of, and many
things of which she might have been proud; but her past had
never been fathomed by the honest minds of Hintock, and
she rarely volunteered her experiences. As for her capricious
nature, the people on her estates grew accustomed to it, and
with that marvellous subtlety of contrivance in steering round
odd tempers that is found in sons of the soil, and dependents
generally, they managed to get along under her government
rather better than they would have done beneath a more
equable rule.

Now, with regard to the doctor's notion of leaving Hintock,
he had advanced further towards completing the purchase
of the Budmouth surgeon's good-will than he had admitted
to Mrs. Charmond. The whole matter hung upon what he
might do in the ensuing twenty-four hours. The evening after
leaving her he went out into the lane, and walked and pondered between the high hedges, now greenish white with
wild clematis—here called "old-man's-beard" from its aspect
later in the year.

The letter of acceptance was to be written that night, after
which his departure from Hintock would be irrevocable. But
could he go away, remembering what had just passed? The
trees, the hills, the leaves, the grass—each had been endowed
and quickened with a subtle light since he had discovered
the person, and history, and, above all, the mood of their

owner. There was every temporal reason for leaving: it would be entering again into a world which he had only quitted in a passion for isolation, induced by a fit of Achillean moodiness after an imagined slight. His wife herself saw the awkwardness of their position here, and cheerfully welcomed the purposed change, towards which every step had been taken but the last. But could he find it in his heart—as he found it clearly enough in his conscience—to go away? No.

He drew a troubled breath and went indoors. Here he rapidly penned a letter, wherein he withdrew, once for all, from the treaty for the Budmouth practice. As the postman had already left Little Hintock for that night he sent one of Melbury's men to intercept a mail-cart on another turnpike-road; and so got the letter off.

The man returned, met Fitzpiers in the lane, and told him the thing was done. Fitzpiers went back to his house musing. Why had he carried out this impulse—taken such wild trouble to effect a probable injury to his own and his young wife's prospects? His motive was fantastic, glowing, shapeless as the fiery scenery about the western sky. Mrs. Charmond could overtly be nothing more to him than a patient, and to his wife at the outside a patron. Yet in the unattached bachelor-days of his first sojourn here how highly proper an emotional reason for lingering on would have appeared to troublesome dubiousness. Matrimonial ambition is such an honourable thing.

"My father has told me that you have sent off one of the men with a late letter to Budmouth," cried Grace coming out vivaciously to meet him under the declining light of the sky, wherein hung, solitary, the folding star. "I said at once that you had finally agreed to pay the premium they ask, and that the tedious question had been settled. When do we go, Edred?"

"I have changed my mind," said he. "They want too much—seven-hundred-and-fifty is too large a sum,—and in short I have declined to go further. We must wait for another opportunity . . . I fear I am not a good business-man." He spoke the last words with a momentary faltering at the great foolishness of his act; and as he looked in her fair and honourable face his heart reproached him for what he had done.

Her manner that evening showed her disappointment. Personally she liked the home of her childhood much; and she was not ambitious. But her husband had seemed so dissatisfied with the circumstances hereabout since their marriage that she had sincerely hoped to go for his sake.

It was two or three days before he visited Mrs. Charmond again. The morning had been windy, and little showers had scattered themselves like grain against the walls and window-panes of the Hintock cottages. He went on foot across the wilder recesses of the park, where slimy streams of fresh moisture, exuding from decayed holes caused by old amputations, ran down the bark of the oaks and elms, the rind below being coated with a lichenous wash as green as emerald. They were stout-trunked trees, that never rocked their stems in the fiercest gale, responding to it only by crooking their limbs. Wrinkled like an old crone's face, and antlered with dead branches that rose above the foliage of their summits, they were nevertheless still green—though yellow had invaded the leaves of other trees.

She was in a little boudoir or writing-room on the first floor, and Fitzpiers was much surprised to find that the window-curtains were closed and a red-shaded lamp and candles burning, though out of doors it was broad daylight. Moreover a large fire was burning in the grate, though it was not cold.

"What does it all mean?" he asked.

She sat in an easy chair, her face being turned away. "Oh," she murmured, "it is because the world is so dreary outside. Sorrow and bitterness in the sky, and floods of agonised tears beating against the panes. I lay awake last night, and I could hear the scrape of snails creeping up the window glass; it was so sad! My eyes were so heavy this morning that I could have wept my life away. I cannot bear you to see my face; I keep it away from you purposely. Oh why were we given hungry hearts and wild desires if we have to live in a world like this? Why should Death alone lend what Life is compelled to borrow—rest? Answer that, Doctor Fitzpiers."

"You must eat of a second tree of knowledge before *you* can do it, Felice Charmond."

"Then, when my emotions have exhausted themselves, I become full of fears, till I think I shall die for very fear. The terrible insistencies of society—how severe they are, and cold, and inexorable—ghastly towards those who are made of wax and not of stone. Oh I am afraid of them; a stab for this error, and a stab for that—correctives and regulations pretendedly framed that society may tend to perfection—an end which I don't care for in the least. Yet for this all I do care for has to be stunted and starved."

Fitzpiers had seated himself near her. "What sets you in this mournful mood?" he asked gently. In reality he thought that it was the result of a loss of tone from staying indoors so much; but he did not say so.

"My reflections. Doctor, you must not come here any more. They begin to think it a farce already. I say you must come no more. There—don't be angry with me." And she jumped up, pressed his hand and looked anxiously at him. "It is necessary. It is best for both you and me."

"But," said Fitzpiers gloomily, "what have we done?"

"Done—we have done nothing. Perhaps we have thought the more. However it is all vexation. I am going away to Middleton Abbey, near Shottsford, where a relative of my late husband lives, who is confined to her bed. The engagement was made in London, and I can't get out of it. Perhaps it is for the best that I go there till all this is past. . . . . When are you going to enter on your new practice, and leave Hintock behind for ever, with your pretty wife on your arm?"

"I have refused the opportunity. I love this place too well to depart."

"You *have*?" she said, regarding him with wild uncertainty. "Why do you ruin yourself in that way? Great heaven, what have I done!"

"Nothing. Besides you are going away."

"Oh yes; but only to Middleton Abbey for a month or two. Yet perhaps I shall gain strength there—particularly strength of mind—I require it. And when I come back I shall be a new woman; and you can come and see me safely then, and bring your wife with you, and we'll be friends—she and I. Oh, how this shutting up of one's self does lead to indulgence in idle sentiments. I shall not wish you to give your attendance to me after to-day. . . . . But I am glad that you are not going away—if your remaining does not injure your prospects at all."

As soon as he had left the room the mild friendliness she had preserved in her tone at parting, the playful sadness with which she had conversed with him, equally departed from her. She became as heavy as lead—just as she had been before he arrived. Her whole being seemed to dissolve in a sad powerlessness to do anything, and the sense of it made her lips tremulous and her closed eyes wet. His footsteps again startled her, and she turned round.

"I return for a moment to tell you that the evening is going to be fine. The sun is shining; so do open your curtains and put out these lights. Shall I do it for you?"

"Please—if you don't mind."

He drew back the window-curtains, whereupon the red glow of the lamp, and the two candle-flames, became almost invisible under the flood of late autumn sunlight that poured in. "Shall I come round to you?" he asked, her back being towards him.

"No," she replied.

"Why not?"

"Because I am crying, and I don't want you to see my face in the full sun's rays."

He stood a moment irresolute, and regretted that he had killed the rosy passionate lamplight by opening the curtains, and letting in garish day. "Then I am going," he said.

"Very well," she answered, stretching one hand round to him, and patting her eyes with a handkerchief held in the other.

"Shall I write a line to you at——?"

"No, no." A gentle reasonableness came into her tone as she added, "It must not be, you know. It won't do."

"Very well. Good-bye." The next moment he was gone.

In the evening, with listless adroitness, she encouraged the maid who dressed her for dinner to speak of Dr. Fitzpiers's marriage.

"Mrs. Fitzpiers was once supposed to favour Mr. Winterborne," said the young woman.

"But why didn't she marry him?" said Mrs. Charmond.

"Because you see, ma'am, he lost his houses."

"Lost his houses? How came he to do that?"

"The houses were held on lives, and the lives dropped, and your agent wouldn't renew them, though it is said that Mr. Winterborne had a very good claim. That's as I've heard it ma'am; and it was through it that the match was broke off."

Being just then distracted by a dozen emotions Mrs. Charmond sank into a mood of dismal self-reproach. "In refusing that poor man his reasonable request," she said to herself, "my agent fore-doomed my revived girlhood's romance. Who would have thought such a business matter could have nettled my own heart like this! Now for a winter of regrets, and agonies, and useless wishes—till I forget him in the spring. Oh I am glad I am going away."

She left her chamber and went down to dine with a sigh. On the stairs she stood opposite the large window for a moment, and looked out upon the lawn. It was not yet quite dark. Half-way up the steep green slope confronting her stood old Timothy Tangs, who was shortening his way homeward by clambering here where there was no road, and in opposition to express orders that no path was to be made there. Tangs had momentarily stopped to take a pinch of snuff; but observing Mrs. Charmond gazing at him he hastened to get over the top out of hail. His precipitancy made him miss his footing, and he rolled like a barrel to the bottom, his snuff-box rolling in front of him.

Her indefinite, idle, impossible passion for Fitzpiers, her constitutional cloud of misery, the sorrowful drops that still hung upon her eyelashes, all made way for the impulse started by the spectacle. She burst into an immoderate fit of laughter—her very gloom of the previous hour seeming to render it the more uncontrollable. It had not died out of her when she reached the dining-room; and even here before the servants her shoulders suddenly shook as the scene returned upon her; and the tears of her risibility mingled with the remnants of those engendered by her grief.

She resolved to be sad no more. She drank two glasses of champagne, and a little more still after those; and amused herself in the evening with singing pretty amatory songs.

"I must do something for that poor man Winterborne, however," she said.

XXVIII

A WEEK had passed, and Mrs. Charmond had left Hintock House. Middleton Abbey, the place of her sojourn, was about a dozen miles distant by road; a little less by bridle-paths and footways.

Grace observed for the first time that her husband was restless, that at moments he even was disposed to avoid her. The scrupulous civility of mere acquaintanceship crept into his manner; yet when sitting at meals he seemed hardly to hear her remarks. Her little doings interested him no longer; whilst towards her father his bearing was not far from supercilious. It was plain that his mind was entirely outside her life,—whereabouts outside it she could not tell—in some region of science possibly, or of psychological literature. But her hope that he was again immersing himself in those lucubrations which before her marriage had made his light a landmark in Hintock, was founded simply on the slender fact that he often sat up late.

One day she discovered him leaning over a gate on High-Stoy Hill, some way from Little Hintock, which opened on the brink of a declivity, slanting down directly into White-Hart or Blackmoor Vale, extending beneath the eye at this point to a distance of many miles. His attention was fixed on the landscape far away eastward, and Grace's approach was so noiseless that he did not hear her. When she came close she could see his lips moving unconsciously, as on some impassioned visionary theme.

She spoke, and Fitzpiers started. "What are you looking at?" she asked.

"Oh—I was contemplating my mother's people's old place of Sherton Abbas, in my idle way," he said.

It had seemed to her that he was looking much to the right of that cradle and tomb of his ancestral dignity, but she made no further observation, and taking his arm walked home beside him almost in silence. She did not know that Middleton Abbey lay in the direction of his gaze. "Are you going to have out Darling this afternoon?" she asked presently. Darling, the aged light grey mare which Winterborne had bought for Grace, Fitzpiers now constantly used, the animal having turned out a wonderful bargain in combining a perfect docility with an almost human intelligence; moreover she was not too young. Fitzpiers was unfamiliar with horses, and he valued these qualities.

"Yes," he replied; "but not to drive. I am riding her. I practise crossing a horse as often as I can now, for I find that I can take much shorter cuts on horseback."

He had in fact taken these riding exercises for about a week —only since Mrs. Charmond's absence, his universal practice hitherto having been to drive.

Some few days later Fitzpiers started on the back of this horse to see a patient in the aforesaid Vale. It was about five o'clock in the evening when he went away, and at bedtime he had not reached home. There was nothing very singular in this, though she was not aware that he had any patient more than five or six miles distant in that direction. The clock had struck one before Fitzpiers entered the house, and he came to his room softly, as if anxious not to disturb her.

The next morning she was stirring considerably earlier than he. In the yard there was a conversation going on about the mare; the man who attended to the horses, Darling included, insisted that the latter was "hag-rid"; for when he had arrived at the stable that morning she was in such a state as no horse could be in by honest riding. It was true that the doctor had stabled her himself when he got home, so that she was not looked after as she would have been if the speaker had groomed and fed her, but that did not account for the appearance she presented, if Mr. Fitzpiers's journey had been only where he had stated. The unprecedented exhaustion of Darling as thus related was sufficient to develope a whole series of tales about equestrian witches and demons, the narration of which occupied a considerable time.

Grace returned indoors. In passing through the outer room she picked up her husband's overcoat which he had carelessly flung down across a chair. A turnpike-ticket fell out of the breast-pocket, and she saw that it had been issued at Middleton Gate. He had therefore visited Middleton the previous night, a distance of at least four-and-twenty miles on horseback there and back.

During the day she made some inquiries and learnt for the first time that Mrs. Charmond was staying at Middleton Abbey. She could not resist an inference—strange as that inference was.

A few days later he prepared to start again, at the same time and in the same direction. She knew that the state of the cottager who lived that way was a mere pretext; she was quite sure he was going to Mrs. Charmond. Grace was amazed at the mildness of the anger which the suspicion engendered in her: she was but little excited, and her jealousy was languid even to death. It told tales of the nature of her affection for him. In truth, her ante-nuptial regard for Fitzpiers had been rather of the quality of awe towards a superior being than of tender solicitude for a lover. It had been based upon mystery and strangeness—the mystery of his past, of his knowledge, of his professional skill, of his beliefs. When this structure of ideals was demolished by the intimacy of common life, and she found him as merely human as the Hintock people themselves, a new foundation was in demand for an enduring and staunch affection—a sympathetic interdependence, wherein mutual weaknesses are made the grounds of a defensive alliance. Fitzpiers had furnished nothing of that single-minded confidence and truth out of which alone such a second union could spring; hence it was with a controllable emotion that she now watched the mare brought round.

"I'll walk with you to the hill—if you are not in a great hurry," she said, rather loth, after all, to let him go.

"Do; there's plenty of time," replied her husband. Accordingly he led along the horse and walked beside her, impatient enough nevertheless. Thus they proceeded to the turnpike-road, and ascended towards the base of High-Stoy and Dogbury Hill, till they were just beneath the gate he had been leaning over when she surprised him ten days before. This was the end of her excursion; Fitzpiers bade her adieu with affection, even with tenderness, and she observed that he looked weary-eyed.

"Why do you go to-night?" she said. "You have been called up two nights in succession already."

"I must go," he answered, almost gloomily. "Don't wait up for me."

With these words he mounted his horse, turned into a branch road by the turnpike, and ambled down the incline to the valley.

She ascended the slope of High-Stoy and watched his descent, and then his journey onward. His way was east, the evening sun which stood behind her back beaming full upon him as soon as he got out from the shade of the hill. Notwithstanding this untoward proceeding she was determined to be loyal if he proved true; and the determination to love one's best will carry a heart a long way towards making that best an ever growing thing. The conspicuous coat of the active though blanching mare made horse and rider easy objects for the vision. Though Darling had been chosen with such pains by Winterborne for Grace she had never ridden the sleek creature; but her husband had found the animal exceedingly convenient, particularly now that he had taken to the saddle, plenty of staying power being left in Darling yet for journeys of moderate length. Fitzpiers, like others of his character, while despising Melbury and his station, did not at all disdain to spend Melbury's money, or appropriate to his own use the horse which belonged to Melbury's daughter.

And so the infatuated surgeon went along through the gorgeous autumn landscape of White-Hart Vale, surrounded by orchards lustrous with the reds of apple-crops, berries, and foliage, the whole intensified by the gilding of the declining sun. The earth this year had been prodigally bountiful, and now was the supreme moment of her bounty. In the poorest spots the hedges were bowed with haws and blackberries; acorns cracked underfoot, and the burst husks of chestnuts lay exposing their auburn contents as if arranged by anxious sellers in a fruit-market. In all this proud show some kernels were unsound as her own situation, and she wondered if there were one world in the universe where the fruit had no worm, and marriage no sorrow.

Her Tannhäuser still moved on, his plodding steed rendering him distinctly visible yet. Could she have heard Fitzpiers's voice at that moment she would have found it murmuring

> "—Towards the load-star of my one desire
> I flitted, like a dizzy moth, whose flight
> Is as a dead leaf's in the owlet light."

But he was a silent spectacle to her. Soon he rose out of the valley, and skirted a high plateau of the chalk formation on his right, which rested abruptly upon the fruity district of deep loam, the character and herbage of the two formations being so distinct that the calcareous upland appeared but as a deposit of a few years' antiquity upon the level vale. He kept along the edge of this high unenclosed country, and the sky behind him being deep violet she could still see white Darling in relief upon it—a mere speck now—a Wouvermans eccentricity reduced to microscopic dimensions. Upon this high ground he gradually disappeared.

Thus she had beheld the pet animal purchased for her own use, in pure love of her, by one who had always been true, impressed to convey her husband away from her to the side of a new-found idol. While she was musing on the vicissitudes of horses and wives she discerned shapes moving up the valley towards her, quite near at hand, though till now hidden by the hedges. Surely they were Giles Winterborne, with two horses and a cider-apparatus conducted by Robert Creedle. Up, upward they crept, a stray beam of the sun alighting every now and then like a star on the blades of the pomace-shovels, which had been converted to steel mirrors by the action of the malic acid. She descended to the road when he came close, and the panting horses rested as they achieved the ascent.

"How do you do, Giles," said she, under a sudden impulse to be familiar with him.

He replied with much more reserve. "You are going for a walk, Mrs. Fitzpiers," he added. "It is pleasant just now."

"No, I am returning," said she.

The vehicles passed on, and Creedle with them, and Winterborne walked by her side in the rear of the apple-mill.

He looked and smelt like Autumn's very brother, his face being sunburnt to wheat-colour, his eyes blue as corn-flowers, his sleeves and leggings dyed with fruit stains, his hands clammy with the sweet juice of apples, his hat sprinkled with pips, and everywhere about him that atmosphere of cider which at its first return each season has such an indescribable fascination for those who have been born and bred among the orchards. Her heart rose from its late sadness like a released bough; her senses revelled in the sudden lapse back to Nature unadorned. The consciousness of having to be genteel because of her husband's profession, the veneer of artificiality which she had acquired at the fashionable schools, were thrown off, and she became the crude country girl of her latent, early instincts.

Nature was bountiful, she thought. No sooner had she been cast aside by Edred Fitzpiers than another being, impersonating chivalrous and undiluted manliness, had arisen out of the earth, ready to her hand. This, however, was an excursion of the imagination which she did not wish to encourage, and she said suddenly, to disguise the confused regard which had followed her thoughts, "Did you meet my husband?"

Winterborne, with some hesitation: "Yes."

"Where did you meet him?"

"Near Reveller's Inn.—I come from Middleton Abbey; I have been making there for the last week."

"Haven't they a mill of their own?"

"Yes, but it's out of repair."

"I think—I heard that Mrs. Charmond had gone there to stay?"

"Yes. I have seen her at the windows once or twice."

Grace waited an interval before she went on, "Did Mr. Fitzpiers take the way to Middleton?"

"Yes . . . I met him on Darling." As she did not reply he added with a gentler inflection, "You know why the mare was called that?"

"Oh yes—of course," she answered quickly.

With their minds on these things they passed so far round the hill that the whole west sky was revealed. Between the broken clouds they could see far into the recesses of heaven as they mused and walked, the eye journeying on under a species of golden arcades, and past fiery obstructions, fancied cairns, logan-stones, stalactites and stalagmite of topaz. Deeper than this their gaze passed thin flakes of incandescence, till it plunged into a bottomless medium of soft green fire.

Her abandonment to the seductive hour and scene after her sense of ill-usage, her revolt for the nonce against social law, her passionate desire for primitive life, may have showed in her face. Winterborne was looking at her, his eyes lingering on a flower that she wore in her bosom. Almost with the abstraction of a somnambulist he stretched out his hand and gently caressed the flower.

She drew back. "What are you doing, Giles Winterborne!" she exclaimed with severe surprise. The evident absence of all premeditation from the act, however, speedily led her to think that it was not necessary to stand upon her dignity here and now. "You must bear in mind Giles," she said kindly, "that we are not as we were; and some people might have said that what you did was taking a liberty."

It was more than she need have told him; his action of forgetfulness had made him so angry with himself that he flushed through his tan. "I don't know what I am coming to!" he exclaimed savagely. "Ah—I was not once like this!" Tears of vexation were in his eyes.

"No, now—it was nothing. I was too reproachful."

"It would not have occurred to me if I had not seen something like it done elsewhere—at Middleton lately," he said thoughtfully after a while.

"By whom?"

"Don't ask it."

She scanned him narrowly. "I know quite well enough," she returned indifferently. "It was by my husband, and the woman was Mrs. Charmond. Association of ideas reminded you when you saw me. . . . Giles—tell me all you know about that.—Please do Giles!—But no—I won't hear it. Let the subject cease. And as you are my friend say nothing to my father."

They had descended into the vale again to a place where their ways divided. Winterborne continued along the highway which kept outside the copse, and Grace opened a gate that entered it.

XXIX

SHE walked up the soft grassy ride, screened on either hand by nut-bushes, just now heavy with clusters of twos and threes and fours. A little way on the track she pursued was crossed by a similar one at right angles. Here Grace stopped; some few yards up the transverse ride the buxom Suke Damson was visible—her gown tucked up high through her pocket-hole, and no bonnet on her head—in the act of pulling down boughs from which she was gathering and eating nuts with great rapidity, her lover Tim Tangs standing near her engaged in the same pleasant meal.

Crack, crack, went Suke's jaws every second or two. By an automatic leap of thought Grace's mind reverted to the tooth-drawing scene described by her husband; and for the first time she wondered if that narrative were really true, Susan's jaws being so obviously sound and strong. Grace turned up towards the nut-gatherers and conquered her reluctance to speak to the girl, who was a little in advance of Tim. "Good evening Susan," she said.

"Good evening Miss Melbury." (crack.)

"Mrs. Fitzpiers."

"Oh yes ma'am—Mrs. Fitzpiers," said Suke with a peculiar sniff and curtsey.

Grace, not to be daunted, continued, "Take care of your teeth Suke. That accounts for your toothache."

"O, I don't know what an ache is, either in tooth, ear, or head, thank the Lord." (crack.)

"Nor the loss of one, either?"

"See for yourself ma'am." She parted her red lips and exhibited the whole double row, full up and unimpaired.

"You have never had one drawn."

"Never."

"So much the better for your stomach," said Mrs. Fitzpiers in an altered voice. And turning away quickly she went on thinking what gall she could drop into poor Tim Tangs's honey if she chose.

As her husband's character thus shaped itself under the touch of time Grace was almost startled to find how little she suffered from that jealous excitement which is conventionally attributed to all wives in such circumstances. But though possessed by none of the feline wildness which it was her moral duty to experience, she did not fail to suspect that she had made a frightful mistake in her marriage. Acquiescence in her father's wishes had been degradation to herself. People are not given premonitions for nothing; she should have obeyed her impulse on that early morning when she peeped and saw the figure come from Fitzpiers's door, and have steadfastly refused her hand.

Oh that plausible tale which her then betrothed had told her about Suke—the dramatic account of her entreaties to him to draw the aching enemy, and the fine artistic finish he had given to the story by explaining that it was a lovely molar without a flaw!

She traced the remainder of the woodland track, dazed by the complications of her position. If his protestations to her before their marriage could be believed, her husband had felt affection of some sort for herself and this woman simultaneously; and was now again spreading the same conjoint emotion over Mrs. Charmond and herself, his manner being still kind and fond at times. But surely, rather than that, he must have played the hypocrite towards her in each case with elaborate completeness; and the thought of this sickened her, for it involved the conjecture that if he had not loved her his only motive for making her his wife must have been her little fortune. Yet here Grace made a mistake, for the love of men like Fitzpiers is unquestionably of such quality as to bear division and transference. He had indeed once declared, though not to her, that on one occasion he had noticed himself to be possessed by five distinct infatuations at the same time. If this were true, his differed from the highest affection as the lower orders of the animal world differ from advanced organisms, partition causing not death but a multiplied existence. He had loved her sincerely in his selfish way, and had by no means ceased to love her now. But such double and treble-barrelled hearts were naturally beyond her conception.

Of poor Suke Damson Grace thought no more. She had had her day.

"If he does not love me I will not love him!" said Grace proudly. And though these were mere words it was a somewhat formidable thing for Fitzpiers that her heart was approximating to a state in which it might be possible to carry them out. That very absence of hot jealousy in her which made his courses so easy, and on which, indeed, he congratulated himself, meant, unknown to either wife or husband, more mischief than the inconvenient watchfulness of a jaundiced eye.

Her sleep that night was nervous. The wing allotted to her and her husband had never seemed so lonely. At last she got up, put on her dressing-gown, and went downstairs. Her father, who slept lightly, heard her descend, and came to the stair-head. "Is that you, Grace? What's the matter?" he said.

"Nothing more than that I am restless. Edred is detained by a case in White-Hart Vale."

"But—how's that? I met the woman's husband going to Great Hintock just afore bed-time; and she was going on well, and the doctor gone then."

"Then he's detained somewhere else," said Grace. "Never mind me: he will soon be home. I expect him about one."

She went back to her room, and dozed and woke several times. One o'clock had been the hour of his return on the last occasion; but it had passed now by a long way, and still Fitzpiers did not come. Just before dawn she heard the men stirring in the yard; and the flashes of their lanterns spread every now and then through her window-blind. She remembered that her father had told her not to be disturbed if she noticed them, as they would be rising early to send off four loads of hurdles to a distant sheep-fair. Peeping out she saw them bustling about, the hollow-turner among the rest; he was loading his wares—wooden bowls, dishes, spigots, spoons, cheese-vats, funnels and so on—upon one of her father's waggons, who carried them to the fair for him every year out of neighbourly kindness.

The scene and the occasion would have enlivened her but that her husband was still absent; though it was now five o'clock. She could hardly suppose him, whatever his infatuation, to have prolonged to a later hour than ten an ostensibly professional call on Mrs. Charmond at Middleton; and he could have ridden home in two hours. What then had become of him? That he had been out the greater part of the two preceding nights added to her uneasiness.

She dressed herself, descended, and went out, the weird twilight of advancing day chilling the rays from the lanterns, and making the men's faces wan. As soon as Melbury saw her he came round, showing his alarm.

"Edred is not come," she said. "And I have reason to know that he's not attending anybody. He has had no rest for two nights before this. I was going to the top of the hill to look for him."

"I'll come with you," said Melbury.

She begged him not to hinder himself; but he insisted, for he saw a peculiar and rigid gloom in her face over and above her uneasiness, and did not like the look of it. Telling the men he would be with them again soon he walked beside her into the turnpike-road, and partly up the way whence she had watched Fitzpiers the night before as he skirted the Great Blackmoor or White-Hart Valley. They halted beneath a half-dead oak, hollow, and disfigured with white tumours, its roots spreading out like claws grasping the ground. A chilly wind circled round them, upon whose currents the seeds of a neighbouring lime-tree, supported parachute-wise by the wing attached, flew out of the boughs downward like fledglings from their nest. The vale was wrapped in a dim atmosphere of unnaturalness, and the east was like a livid curtain edged with pink. There was no sign nor sound of Fitzpiers.

"It is no use standing here," said her father. "He may come home fifty ways. . . . . Why, look here—here be Darling's tracks—

turned homeward and nearly blown dry and hard! He must have come in hours ago without your seeing him."

"He has not done that," said she.

They went back hastily. On entering their own gates they perceived that the men had left the waggons, and were standing round the door of the stable which had been appropriated to the doctor's use. "Is there anything the matter?" cried Grace.

"Oh no, ma'am. All's well that ends well," said old Timothy Tangs. "I've heard of such things before—amongst workfolk, though not amongst your gentlepeople—that's true."

They entered the stable, and saw the pale shape of Darling standing in the middle of her stall, with Fitzpiers on her back, sound asleep. Darling was munching hay as well as she could with the bit in her mouth, and the reins, which had fallen from Fitzpiers's hand, hung upon her neck.

Grace went and touched his hand; shook it, before she could arouse him. He moved, started, opened his eyes, and exclaimed, "Ah, Felice! . . . . . . Oh—it's Grace. I could not see in the gloom. What—am I in the saddle?"

"Yes," said she. "How do you come here?"

He collected his thoughts, and in a few minutes stammered as he began dismounting: "I was riding along homeward through the Vale, very very sleepy, having been up so much of late. When I came opposite Lydden Spring the mare turned her head that way as if she wanted to drink. I let her go in, and she drank; I thought she would never finish. While she was drinking the clock of Newland Buckton church struck twelve; I distinctly remember counting the strokes. From that moment I positively recollect nothing till I saw you here by my side."

"The name!—if it had been any other horse you'd have had a broken neck!" murmured Melbury.

"'Tis wonderful, sure, how a quiet hoss will bring a man home at such times!" said John Upjohn. "And what's more wonderful than keeping your seat in a deep, slumbering sleep, I've knowed men drowze off walking home from randies where the beer and other liquors have gone round well, and keep walking for more than a mile on end without waking.

Well doctor, 'tis a mercy you wasn't a drownded, or a splintered, or a hanged up to a tree like Absalont—also a handsome gentleman like yerself—as the prophets say."

"True," murmured old Timothy piously. "From the sole of his boots to the crown of his hat there was no blemish in him!"

"—Or leastwise you might ha' been a-wounded into tatters a'most, and no brother-tradesman to jine your few limbs together within seven mile!"

Whilst this impressive address was proceeding Fitzpiers had dismounted, and taking Grace's arm walked stiffly indoors with her. Melbury stood staring at the horse which, in addition to being very weary, was spattered with mud. Whilst they were rubbing down the mare Melbury's mind coupled with the mud, which was not local, the name he had heard unconsciously muttered by the surgeon when Grace took his hand—"Felice." Who was Felice? Why, Mrs. Charmond; and she, as he knew, was staying at Middleton.

Melbury had indeed pounced upon the image that filled Fitzpiers's half-awakened soul—wherein there had been a retrospect of a recent interview on a starlit lawn with a capriciously-passionate woman who had begged him not to come there again in tones whose modulation incited him to disobey. "What are you doing here? Why do you pursue me? Another belongs to you. If they were to see you getting over the fence they would seize you as a thief!" And she had turbulently admitted to his wringing questions that her visit to Middleton had been undertaken less because of the invalid relative than in shamefaced fear of her own weakness if she remained near his home. A triumph then it was to Fitzpiers poor and hampered as he had become to recognise his real conquest of this beauty, delayed so many years. His was the passion of Congreve's Millamant, whose delight lay in seeing "the heart which others bled for, bleed for me."

When the horse had been attended to Melbury stood uneasily here and there about his premises; he was rudely disturbed in the comfortable views which had lately possessed him on his domestic concerns. It is true that he had for some days discerned that Grace more and more sought his company, preferred supervising his kitchen and bakehouse with her step-mother to occupying herself with the lighter details of her own apartments. She seemed no longer able to find in her own hearth an adequate focus for her life, and hence, like a weak queen-bee after leading off to an independent home, had hovered again into the parent hive. But he had not construed these and other incidents of the kind till now.

Something was wrong in the homestead. A ghastly sense beset him that he alone would be responsible for whatever unhappiness should be brought upon her for whom he almost solely lived; whom to retain under his roof he had faced the numerous inconveniences involved in giving up the best part of his house to Fitzpiers. There was no room for doubt that, had he allowed events to take their natural course she would have accepted Winterborne, and realized his old dream of restitution to that young man's family.

That Fitzpiers would allow himself to look for a moment on any other creature than Grace filled Melbury with grief and astonishment. In the simple life he had led it had scarcely occurred to him that after marriage a man might be faithless. That he could sweep to the heights of Mrs. Charmond's position, lift the Veil of Isis, so to speak, would have amazed Melbury by its audacity if he had not suspected encouragement from that quarter. What could he and his simple Grace do to countervail the passions of those two sophisticated beings, versed in the world's ways, armed with every apparatus for victory? In such an encounter the homely timber-dealer felt as inferior as a savage with his bow and arrows to the precise weapons of modern warfare.

Grace came out of the house as the morning drew on. The village was silent, most of the folk having gone to the fair. Fitzpiers had retired to bed, and was sleeping off his fatigue. She went to the stable and looked at poor Darling: in all probability Giles Winterborne, by obtaining for her a horse of such intelligence and docility, had been the means of saving her husband's life. She paused over the strange thought; and then there appeared her father behind her. She saw that he knew things were not as they ought to be—from the troubled dulness of his eye, and from his face, different points of which had motions, twitchings, and tremblings, unknown to himself and involuntary.

"He was detained I suppose last night," said Melbury.

"Oh yes; a bad case in the Vale," she replied calmly.

"Nevertheless he should have stayed at home."

"But he couldn't, father."

Her father turned away. He could hardly bear to see his whilom truthful girl brought to the humiliation of having to talk like that.

That night carking care sat beside Melbury's pillow, and his stiff limbs tossed at its presence. "I can't lie here any longer," he muttered; striking a light he wandered about the room. "What have I done, what have I done for her!" he said to his wife. "I had long planned that she should marry the son of the man I wanted to make amends to—do ye mind how I told you all about it, Lucy, the night before she came home? Ah—but I was not content with doing right—I wanted to do more!"

"Don't raft yourself without good need, George," she replied. "I won't quite believe that things are so much amiss. I won't believe that Mrs. Charmond has encouraged him. Even supposing she has encouraged a great many, she can have no motive to do it now. What so likely as that she is not yet quite well, and doesn't care to let another doctor come near her?"

He did not heed. "Grace used to be so busy every day with fixing a curtain here, and driving a tin-tack there; but she cares for no employment now!"

"Do you know anything of Mrs. Charmond's past history?—perhaps that would throw some light upon things. Before she came here as the wife of old Charmond four or five years ago not a soul seems to have heard aught of her. Why not make inquiries? And then do ye wait and see more—there'll be plenty of opportunity. Time enough to cry when you know 'tis a crying matter; 'tis bad to meet troubles half way."

There was some good sense in the notion of seeing further. Melbury resolved to inquire, and wait—hoping still, but oppressed between whiles with much fear.

XXX

EXAMINE Grace as her father might, she would admit nothing. For the present therefore he simply watched.

The suspicion that his darling child was slighted wrought almost a miraculous change in Melbury's nature. No man so furtive for the time as the ingenuous countryman who finds that his ingenuousness has been abused. Melbury's heretofore confidential candour towards his gentlemanly son-in-law was displaced by a feline stealth that did injury to his every action, thought, and mood. He knew that a woman once given to a man for life took, as a rule, her lot as it came and made the best of it, without external interference; but for the first time he asked himself why this so generally should be done. Besides, this case was not, he argued, like ordinary cases. Leaving out the question of Grace being anything but an ordinary woman, her peculiar situation, as it were in mid-air between two storeys of society, together with the loneliness of Hintock, made a husband's neglect a far more tragical matter to her than it would be to one who had a large circle of friends to fall back upon. Wisely or unwisely, and whatever other fathers did, he resolved to fight his daughter's battle still.

Mrs. Charmond had returned. But Hintock House scarcely gave forth signs of life, so quietly had she re-entered it. He went to church at Great Hintock one afternoon as usual, there being no service at the smaller village. A few minutes before his departure he had casually heard Fitzpiers, who was no churchgoer, tell his wife that he was going to walk in the wood. Melbury entered the building and sat down in his pew; the parson came in, then Mrs. Charmond, then Mr. Fitzpiers.

The service proceeded, and the jealous father was quite sure that a mutual consciousness was uninterruptedly maintained between those two; he fancied that more than once their eyes met. At the end Fitzpiers so timed his movement into the aisle that it exactly coincided with Felice Charmond's from the opposite side, and they walked out with their garments in contact, the surgeon being just that two or three inches in her rear which made it convenient for his eyes to rest upon her cheek. The cheek warmed up to a richer tone.

This was a worse feature in the flirtation than he had expected. If she had been playing with him in an idle freak the game might soon have wearied her; but the smallest germ of passion—and women of the world do not change colour for nothing—was a threatening condition. The mere presence of Fitzpiers in the building, after his statement, was wellnigh conclusive as far as he was concerned; but Melbury resolved yet to watch.

He had to wait long. Autumn drew shiveringly to its end: one day something seemed to be gone from the gardens; the tenderer leaves of vegetables had shrunk under the first smart frost, and hung like faded linen rags; the forest leaves which had been descending at leisure descended in haste and in multitudes, and all the golden colours that had hung overhead were now crowded together in a degraded mass underfoot, where the fallen myriads got redder, and hornier, and curled themselves up to rot. The only suspicious features in Mrs. Charmond's existence at this season were two: the first that she lived with no companion or relative about her, which, considering her age and attractions, was somewhat unusual conduct for a young widow in a lonely country house; the other that she did not, as in previous years, start from Hintock to winter abroad. In Fitzpiers the only change from his last autumn's habits lay in his abandonment of night study: his lamp never shone from his new dwelling as from his old.

If the suspected ones met, it was by such adroit contrivances that even Melbury's vigilance could not encounter them together. A simple call at her house by the doctor had nothing irregular about it, and that he had paid two or three such calls was certain. What had passed at those interviews was known only to the parties themselves; but that Felice Charmond was under some one's influence Melbury soon had opportunity of perceiving.

Winter had come on. Owls began to be noisy in the mornings and evenings and flocks of wood-pigeons made themselves prominent again. On a day in February, about six

months after the marriage of Fitzpiers, Melbury was returning from Great Hintock on foot down to Little Hintock when
he saw before him the surgeon also walking. Melbury would
have overtaken him, but at that moment Fitzpiers turned in
through a gate to one of the rambling drives among the
trees at this side of the wood, which led to nowhere in particular, and the beauty of whose serpentine curves was the
only justification of their existence. Felice almost simultaneously trotted into the road ahead of the timber-dealer, in
a little basket-carriage which she sometimes drove about
the estate, unaccompanied by a servant. She turned in at
the same gate without having seen either Melbury or, apparently, Fitzpiers. Melbury was soon at the spot, despite his
aches and his sixty years. Mrs. Charmond had come up with
the doctor, inside the gate, who was standing immediately
behind the carriage. She had turned to him, her arm being
thrown carelessly over the back of the seat. They looked in
each other's faces without uttering a word, an arch yet gloomy
smile wreathing her lips. Fitzpiers clasped her hanging hand,
and, while she still remained in the same listless attitude, looking volumes into his eyes, he stealthily unbuttoned her glove,
and stripped her hand of it by rolling back the gauntlet over
the fingers, so that it came off inside out. He then raised her
hand to his mouth, she still reclining passively, watching him
as she might have watched a fly upon her dress. At last she
said, "Well, sir, what excuse for this disobedience?"

"I make none."

"Then go your way, and let me go mine." She snatched
away her hand, touched the pony with the whip, and left him
standing there, holding the reversed glove.

Melbury had not been seen, and his first impulse was to
reveal his presence to Fitzpiers, and upbraid him bitterly.
But a moment's thought was sufficient to show him the fu-
tility of any such simple proceeding. There was not, after all,
so much in what he had witnessed as in what that scene
might be the surface and froth of—probably a state of mind
which censure aggravates rather than cures. Moreover he
said to himself that the point of attack should be the woman
if either. He therefore kept out of sight, and musing sadly,

even tearfully—for he was meek as a child in matters concerning his daughter—continued his way towards Hintock.

The insight which is bred of deep sympathy was never more finely exemplified than in this instance. Through her guarded manner, her dignified speech, her placid countenance, he discerned the interior of Grace's life only too truly, hidden as were its incidents from every outer eye.

These incidents had become painful enough. Fitzpiers had latterly developed an irritable discontent which vented itself in monologues when Grace was present to hear them. The early morning of this day had been dull, after a night of wind, and on looking out of the window in the grey grim dawn Fitzpiers had observed some of Melbury's men dragging away a large limb which had been snapped off a beech tree. Everything was cold and colourless.

"My good God!" he said as he stood in his dressing-gown. "This is life!" He did not know whether Grace was awake or not, and he would not turn his head to ascertain. "Ah, Edred," he went on to himself, "to clip your own wings when you were free to soar! . . . But I could not rest till I had done it. Why do I never recognise an opportunity till I have missed it, nor the good or ill of a step till it is irrevocable? . . . I fell in love!"

Grace moved. He thought she had heard some part of his soliloquy. He was sorry—though he had not taken any precaution to prevent her.

He expected a scene at breakfast—but she only exhibited an extreme reserve. It was enough, however, to make him repent that he should have done anything to produce discomfort; for he attributed her manner entirely to what he had said. But Grace's manner had not its cause either in his sayings or in his doings. She had not heard a single word of his regrets. Something even nearer home than her husband's blighted prospects—if blighted they were—was the origin of her mood.

She had made a discovery; one which, to a girl of her nature was almost appalling. She had looked into her heart, and found that her early interest in Giles Winterborne had become revitalized into growth by her widening perceptions of what was great and little in life. His homeliness no longer offended her acquired tastes; his comparative want of so-called culture did not now jar on her intellect; his country dress even pleased her eye; his exterior roughness fascinated her. Having discovered by marriage how much that was humanly not great could co-exist with attainments of an exceptional order, there was a revulsion in her sentiments from all that she had formerly clung to in this kind: honesty, goodness, manliness, tenderness, devotion, for her only existed in their purity now in the breasts of unvarnished men; and here was one who had manifested such towards her from his youth up.

There was, further, that never ceasing pity in her soul for Giles as a man whom she had wronged, a man who had been unfortunate in his worldly transactions; who notwithstanding these things, had, like Hamlet's friend, borne himself throughout his scathing

> As one, in suffering all, that suffers nothing,

investing himself thereby with a real touch of sublimity. It was these perceptions, and no subtle catching of her husband's murmurs, that had bred the abstraction visible in her.

When her father approached the house after witnessing the interview between Fitzpiers and Mrs. Charmond, Grace was looking out of her sitting-room window, as if she had nothing to do, or think of, or care for. He stood still.

"Ah, Grace," he said regarding her fixedly.

"Yes, father," she murmured.

"Waiting for your dear husband?" he inquired, speaking with the sarcasm of pitiful affection.

"Oh no—not especially. He has a great many patients to see this afternoon."

Melbury came quite close. "Grace, what's the use of talking like that, when you know—. Here, come down and walk with me out in the garden, child."

He unfastened the door in the ivy-laced wall, and waited. This apparent indifference alarmed him. He would far rather that she had rushed in all the fire of jealousy to Hintock House regardless of conventionality, confronted and attacked

Felice Charmond *unguibus et rostro,* and accused her even in exaggerated shape of stealing away her husband. Such a storm might have cleared the air.

She emerged in a minute or two, and they went into the garden together. "You know as well as I do," he resumed, "that there is something threatening mischief to your life; and yet you pretend you do not. Do you suppose I don't see the trouble in your face every day? I am very sure that this quietude is wrong conduct in you. You should look more into matters."

"I am quiet because my sadness is not of a nature to stir me to action."

Melbury wanted to ask her a dozen questions: did she not feel jealous, was she not indignant; but a natural delicacy restrained him. "You are very tame and let-alone, I am bound to say," he remarked pointedly.

"I am what I feel, father," she repeated.

He glanced at her, and there returned upon his mind the scene of her offering to wed Winterborne instead of Fitzpiers in the last days before her marriage; and he asked himself if it could be the fact that she loved Winterborne now that she had lost him more than she had ever done when she was comparatively free to choose him.

"What would you have me do?" she asked in a low voice.

He recalled his mind from the retrospective pain to the practical matter before them. "I would have you go to Mrs. Charmond," he said.

"Go to Mrs. Charmond—what for?" said she.

"Well—if I must speak plain, dear Grace—to ask her, appeal to her in the name of your common womanhood, and your many like sentiments on things, not to make unhappiness between you and your husband. It lies with her entirely to do one or the other—that I can see."

Grace's face had heated at her father's words, and the very rustle of her skirts upon the box edging bespoke disdain. "I shall not *think* of going to her, father—of course I could not!" she answered.

"Why—don't 'ee want to be happier than you be at present?" said Melbury, more moved on her account than she was herself.

"I don't wish to be more humiliated. If I have anything to bear I can bear it in silence."

"But my dear maid you are too young—you don't know what the present state of things may lead to. Just see the harm done a'ready! Your husband would have gone away to Budmouth to a bigger practice if it had not been for this. Although it has gone such a little way it is poisoning your future even now. Mrs. Charmond is thoughtlessly bad, not bad by calculation; and just a word to her now might save 'ee a peck of woes."

"Ah—I loved her once," said Grace with a broken articulation; "and she would not care for me then! Now I no longer love her. Let her do her worst: I don't care."

"You ought to care. You have got into a very good position to start with. You have been well-educated, well tended, and you have become the wife of a professional man of unusually good family. Surely you ought to make the best of your position."

"I don't see that I ought. I wish I had never got into it. I wish you had never, never thought of educating me. I wish I worked in the woods like Marty South. I hate genteel life, and I want to be no better than she."

"Why?" said her amazed father.

"Because cultivation has only brought me inconveniences and troubles. I say again, I wish you had never sent me to those fashionable schools you set your mind on. It all arose out of that, father. If I had stayed at home I should have married——" She closed up her mouth suddenly and was silent; and he saw that she was not far from crying.

Melbury was much grieved. "What, and would you like to have grown up as we be here in Hintock—knowing no more, and with no more chance of seeing good life than we have here?"

"Yes. I have never got any happiness outside Hintock that I know of, and I have suffered many a heartache at being sent away. Oh the misery of those January days when I got back to school, and left you all here in the wood so happy. I used to wonder why I had to bear it. And I was always a little despised by the other girls at school, because they knew where I came from, and that my parents were not in so good a station as theirs."

Her poor father was much hurt at what he thought her ingratitude and intractability. He had admitted to himself bitterly enough that he should have let young hearts have their way, or rather should have helped on her affection for Winterborne, and given her to him according to his original plan; but he was not prepared for her deprecating those attainments whose completion had been a labour of years, and a severe tax upon his purse.

"Very well," he said with much heaviness of spirit. "If you don't like to go to her I don't wish to force you."

And so the question remained for him still, how should he remedy this perilous state of things. For days he sat in a moody attitude over the fire, a pitcher of cider standing on the hearth beside him, and his drinking-horn inverted upon the top of it. He spent a week and more thus, composing a letter to the chief offender, which he would every now and then attempt to complete, and suddenly crumple up in his hand.

XXXI

As February merged in March, and lighter evenings broke the gloom of the woodmen's homeward journey, the Hintocks Great and Little began to have ears for a rumour of the events out of which had grown the timber-dealer's trouble. It took the form of a wide sprinkling of conjecture, wherein no man knew the exact truth. Tantalizing phenomena, at once showing and concealing the real relationship of the persons concerned, caused a diffusion of excited surprise. Honest people as the woodlanders were, it was hardly to be expected that they could remain immersed in the study of their trees and gardens amid such circumstances, or sit with their backs turned like the good burghers of Coventry at the passage of the lady.

Rumour, for a wonder, exaggerated little. There threatened, in fact, in Grace's case as in thousands, the domestic disaster, old as the hills, which, with more or less variation, made a mourner of Ariadne, a byeword of Vashti, and a corpse of Amy Dudley. The incidents were rencounters accidental and contrived, stealthy correspondence, sudden misgivings on one side, sudden self-reproaches on the other. The inner state of the twain was one as of confused noise that would not allow the accents of politic reason to be heard. Determination to go in this direction, and headlong plunges in that; dignified safeguards, undignified collapses; not a single rash step by deliberate intention, and all against judgment.

It was all that Melbury had expected and feared. It was more, for he had overlooked the publicity that would be likely to result, as it now had done. What should he do? Appeal to Mrs. Charmond himself, since Grace would not? He bethought himself of Winterborne, and resolved to consult him, feeling the strong need of some friend of his own sex to whom he might unburden his mind.

He had entirely lost faith in his own judgment. That judgment on which he had relied for so many years seemed recently, like a false companion unmasked, to have disclosed unexpected depths of hypocrisy and speciousness where all had seemed solidity. He felt almost afraid to form a conjecture on the weather, or the time, or the fruit-promise, so great was his self-mistrust.

He set out to look for Giles on a rimy evening when the woods seemed to be in a cold sweat; beads of perspiration hung from every bare twig; the sky had no colour, and the trees rose before him as haggard grey phantoms whose days of substantiality were past. Melbury seldom saw Winterborne now, but he believed him to be occupying a lonely hut just beyond the boundary of Mrs. Charmond's estate, though still within the circuit of the woodland. The timber-merchant's thin legs stalked on through the pale damp scenery, his eyes declining on the dead leaves of last year; while every now and then a hasty "aye" escaped his lips in reply to some bitter mental proposition.

His notice was attracted by a thin blue haze of smoke, behind which arose sounds of voices and chopping: bending his steps that way he saw Winterborne just in front of him.

Though few knew of it, Giles had had a serious illness during the winter; but it just now happened that after being for a long time apathetic and unemployed on that account he had become one of the busiest men in the neighbourhood. It is often thus; fallen friends lost sight of we expect to find starving; we discover them going on fairly well. Without any solicitation, or desire to profit on his part, he had been asked to execute a very large order for hurdles and other copse-ware, for which purpose he had been obliged to buy several acres of hazel brushwood standing. He was now engaged in the cutting and manufacture of the same, proceeding with the work daily like an automaton.

The hazel tree did not belie its name to-day. The whole of the copse-wood where the mist had cleared returned purest tints of that hue, amid which Winterborne himself was in the act of making a hurdle, the stakes being driven firmly into the ground in a row, over which he bent and wove the twigs. Beside him was a square compact pile like the altar of Cain, formed of hurdles already finished, which bristled on all sides with the sharp points of their stakes. At a little distance the men in his employ were assisting him to carry out his contract. Rows of brushwood lay on the ground as it had fallen under the axe; and a shelter had been constructed near at hand in front of which burnt the fire whose smoke had attracted Melbury. The air was so dank that the smoke hung heavily, and crept away amid the bushes without rising from the ground.

After wistfully regarding the scene awhile Melbury drew nearer, and briefly inquired of Giles how he came to be so busily engaged, with an undertone of slight surprise that Winterborne could recommence thriving even to this degree after being deprived of Grace. Melbury was not without emotion at the meeting, for Grace's affairs had divided them, and ended their intimacy of old times.

Winterborne explained just as briefly, without raising his eyes from his occupation of chopping a bough that he held in front of him.

"'Twill be up in April before you get it all cleared," said Melbury.

"Yes—there, or there—abouts," said Winterborne, a chop of the bill-hook jerking the last word into two pieces.

There was another interval; Melbury still looked on, a chip from Winterborne's hook occasionally flying against the waistcoat or legs of his visitor, who took no heed.

"Ah Giles—you should have been my partner. You should have been my son-in-law," the old man said at last. "It would have been far better for her, and for me."

Winterborne saw that something had gone wrong with his former friend, and throwing down the switch he was about to interweave he responded only too readily to the mood of the timber-dealer. "Is she ill," he said hurriedly.

"No, no." Melbury stood without speaking for some minutes, and then, as though he could not bring himself to proceed, turned to go away.

Winterborne told one of his men to pack up the tools for the night and walked after Melbury. "Heaven forbid that I should seem too inquisitive sir," he said, "especially since we don't stand as we used to stand to one another; but I hope it is well with them all over your way?"

"No," said Melbury, "no." He stopped, and struck the smooth trunk of a young ash-tree with the flat of his hand. "I would that his ear had been where that rind is!" he exclaimed; "I should have treated him to little compared wi' what he deserves."

"Now," said Winterborne, "don't be in a hurry to go home. I've put some ale down to warm in my shelter here, and we'll sit and drink it and talk this over."

Melbury turned unresistingly as Giles took his arm, and they went back to where the fire was, and sat down under the screen, the other woodmen having gone. He drew out the ale-cup from the ashes, and they drank together.

"Giles you ought to have had her, as I said just now," repeated Melbury. "I'll tell you why for the first time."

He thereupon told Winterborne, as with great relief, the story of how he won away Giles's father's chosen one—by nothing worse than a lover's cajoleries, it is true; but by means which, except in love, would certainly have been pronounced cruel and unfair. He explained how he had always intended to make reparation to Winterborne the father by giving Grace to Winterborne the son; till the devil tempted him in the person of Fitzpiers and he broke his virtuous vow.

"How highly I thought of that man, to be sure! Who'd have supposed he'd have been so weak and wrong-headed as this! You ought to have had her Giles, and there's an end on't."

Winterborne knew how to preserve his calm under this unconsciously cruel tearing of a healing wound, to which Melbury's concentration on the more vital subject had blinded him. The young man endeavoured to make the best of the case, for Grace's sake. "She would hardly have been happy with me," he said in the dry unimpassioned voice under which he hid his feelings. "I was not well enough educated: too rough in short. I couldn't have surrounded her with the refinements she looked for, any how at all."

"Nonsense—you are quite wrong there," said the unwise old man doggedly. "She told me only this day that she hates refinements and such like. All that my trouble and money bought for her in that way is thrown away upon her quite. She'd fain be like Marty South—think o' that! That's the top of her ambition! Perhaps she's right. Giles, she loved you—under the rind; and what's more she loves 'ee still—worse luck for the poor maid!"

If Melbury only had known what fires he was recklessly stirring up he might have held his peace. Winterborne was silent a long time. The darkness had closed in round them, and the monotonous drip of the fog from the branches quickened as it turned to fine rain.

"Oh, she never cared much for me," Giles managed to say as he stirred the embers with a brand.

"She did, and does, I tell 'ee," said the other obstinately. "However, all that's vain talking now. What I come to ask you about is a more practical matter—how to make the best of things as they are. I am thinking of a desperate step—of calling on the woman Charmond. I am going to appeal to her, since Grace will not. 'Tis she who holds the balance in her hands—not he. While she's got the will to lead him astray he will follow—poor unpractical lofty-notioned dreamer—and how long she'll do it depends upon her whim. Did ye ever hear anything about her character before she came to Hintock?"

"She's been a bit of a charmer in her time, I believe," replied Giles with the same level quietude, as he regarded the red coals. "A body who has smiled where she has not loved, and loved where she has not married. Before Mr. Charmond made her his wife she was a play-actress a short while."

"Hey? But how close you have kept all this, Giles! What besides?"

"Mr. Charmond was a rich man engaged in the iron trade in the north—twenty or thirty years older than she. He married her, and retired, and came down here and bought this property, as they do nowadays."

"Yes, yes—I know all about that. But the other I did not know. I fear it bodes no good. For how can I go and appeal to the forbearance of a woman who made cross-loves and crooked passions her study for years? I thank ye, Giles, for finding it out; but it makes my plan the harder that she should have belonged to that unstable tribe."

Another pause ensued, and they looked gloomily at the smoke that beat about the roof of hurdles through whose weavings a large drop of rain fell at intervals and spat smartly into the fire. Mrs. Charmond had been no friend to Winterborne; but he was manly, and it was not in his heart to let her be condemned without a trial. "She is said to be generous," he answered. "You might not appeal to her in vain."

"It shall be done," said Melbury rising. "For good, or for evil, to Mrs. Charmond I'll go."

XXXII

AT nine o'clock the next morning Melbury dressed himself up in shining broadcloth, creased with folding, and smelling of camphor, and started for Hintock House. He was the more impelled to go at once by the absence of his son-in-law in London for a few days, to attend, really or ostensibly, some professional meetings. He said nothing of his destination either to his wife or to Grace, fearing that they might entreat

him to abandon so risky a project, and went out unobserved.
He had chosen his time with a view, as he supposed, of con-
veniently catching Mrs. Charmond when she had just finished
her breakfast, before any other business people should be
about, if any came. Plodding thoughtfully onward he crossed
a glade lying between Little Hintock woods and the plantation which abutted on the park. The spot being open he was
discerned there by Winterborne from the copse on the next
hill, where he and his men were working. Knowing his mission the younger man hastened down from the copse and
managed to intercept the timber-merchant.

"I have been thinking of this, sir," he said, "and I am of
opinion that it would be best to put off your visit for the
present."

But Melbury would not even stop to hear him. His mind
was fixed; the appeal was to be made; and Winterborne stood
and watched him sadly till he entered the second plantation
and disappeared.

Melbury rang at the tradesmen's door of the manor-house,
and was at once informed that the lady was not yet visible, as
indeed he might have guessed had he been anybody but the
man he was. Melbury said he would wait, whereupon the
young page informed him in a neighbourly way that between
themselves she was in bed and asleep.

"Never mind," said Melbury, retreating into the court, "I'll
stand about here." Charged so fully with his mission he shrank
from contact with anybody.

But he walked about the paved court till he was tired, and
nobody came to him. He entered the house and sat down in
a small waiting-room, from which he got glimpses of the
kitchen-corridor, and of the white-capped maids flitting jaun-
tily hither and thither. They had heard of his arrival, but had
not seen him enter, and, imagining him still in the court,
discussed freely the possible reason of his calling. They
marvelled at his temerity; for though most of the tongues
which had been let loose attributed the chief blame to
Fitzpiers, these of her household preferred to regard their
mistress as the deeper sinner.

Melbury sat with his hands resting on the familiar knobbed

thorn walking-stick whose growing he had seen before he enjoyed its use. The scene to him was not the material environment of his person, but a tragic vision that travelled with him like an envelope. Through this vision the incidents of the moment but gleamed confusedly here and there, as an outer landscape through the high-coloured scenes of a stained window. He waited thus an hour, an hour and a half, two hours. He began to look pale and ill, whereupon the butler who came in asked him to have a glass of wine. Melbury roused himself and said, "No, no. Is she almost ready?"

"She is just finishing breakfast, Mr. Melbury," said the butler. "She will soon see you now. I am just going up to tell her you are here."

"What, haven't you told her before?" said Melbury.

"Oh no," said the other. "You see you came so very early."

At last the bell rang: Mrs. Charmond could see him. She was not in her private sitting-room when he reached it, but in a minute he heard her coming from the front staircase, and she entered where he stood.

At this time of the morning Mrs. Charmond looked her full age and more. She might almost have been taken for the typical *femme de trente ans*, though she was really not more than seven- or eight-and-twenty. But the *édition définitive* of her beauty had been reached, even if it were not a little worn.

There being no fire in the room she came in with a shawl thrown loosely round her shoulders, and obviously without the least suspicion that Melbury had called upon any other errand than timber. Felice was, indeed, the only woman in the parish who had not heard the rumour of her own weaknesses; she was at this moment living in a fool's paradise in respect of that rumour, though not in respect of the weaknesses themselves, which, if the truth be told, caused her grave misgivings.

"Do sit down Mr. Melbury. You have felled all the trees that were to be purchased by you this season, except the oaks, I believe."

"Yes," said Melbury.

"How very nice! It must be so charming to work in the woods just now!"

She was too careless to affect an interest in an extraneous person's affairs so consummately as to deceive in the manner of the perfect social machine. Hence her words "very nice," "so charming," were uttered with a perfunctoriness that made them sound absurdly unreal.

"Yes, yes," said Melbury in a reverie. He did not take a chair, and she also remained standing. Resting upon his stick he began: "Mrs. Charmond, I have called upon a more serious matter—at least to me—than tree-throwing. And whatever mistakes I make in my manner of speaking upon it to you, Madam, do me the justice to set 'em down to my want of practice, and not to my want of care."

Mrs. Charmond looked ill at ease. She might have begun to guess his meaning; but apart from that she had such dread of contact with anything painful, harsh, or even earnest, that his preliminaries alone were enough to distress her. "Yes, what is it?" she said quickly.

"I am an old man," said Melbury, "that somewhat late in life God thought fit to bless with one child, and she a daughter. Her mother was a very dear wife to me; but she was taken away from us when the child was young; and the child became precious as the apple of my eye to me, for she was all I had left to love. For her sake entirely I married as second wife a homespun woman who had been kind as a mother to her. In due time the question of her education came on; and I said, 'I will educate the maid well, if I live upon bread to do it.' Of her possible marriage I could not bear to think, for it seemed like a death that she should cleave to another man, and grow to think his house her home rather than mine. But I saw it was the law of nature that this should be; and that it was for the maid's happiness that she should have a home when I was gone: and I made up my mind without a murmur to help it on for her sake. In my youth I had wronged my dead friend and to make amends I determined to give her, my most precious prize, to my friend's son, seeing that they liked each other well. Things came about which made me doubt if it would be for my daughter's happiness to do this, inasmuch as the young man was poor, and she was delicately reared. Another man came and paid court to her—

one her equal in breeding and accomplishments; in every
way it seemed to me that he only could give her the home
which her training had made a necessity a'most. I urged her
on, and she married him. But ma'am, a fatal mistake was at
the root of my reckoning: I found that this well-born gentleman I had calculated on so surely was not staunch of heart,
and that therein lay a danger of great sorrow for my daughter.
Madam, he saw you, and you know the rest. . . . I have come
to make no demands—to utter no threats; I have come simply
as a father in great grief about his only child, and I beseech
you to deal kindly with my daughter and to do nothing which
can turn her husband's heart away from her for ever. Forbid
him your presence ma'am, and speak to him on his duty as
one with your power over him well can do: and I am hopeful
that the rent between them may be patched up. For it is not
as if you would lose by so doing; your course is far higher
than the courses of a professional man; and the gratitude
you would win from me and mine by your kindness is more
than I can say!"

Mrs. Charmond had first rushed into a mood of indignation, on comprehending Melbury's story: hot and cold by
turns she had murmured, "Leave me, leave me!" But, as he
seemed to take no notice of this, his words began to influence her, and when he ceased speaking she said with hurried breath, "What has led you to think this of me? Who says
I have won your daughter's husband away from her? Some
monstrous calumnies are afloat—of which I have known
nothing until now!"

Melbury started, and looked at her simply: "But surely,
Ma'am, you know the truth better than I?"

Her features became a little pinched, and the touches of
powder on her handsome face for the first time showed
themselves as an extrinsic film. "Will you leave me to myself?" she said with a faintness which suggested a guilty conscience. "This is so utterly unexpected—you obtain admission
to my presence by misrepresentation——"

"As God's in heaven, Ma'am, that's not true. I made no
pretence; and I thought in reason you would know why I had
come. This gossip——"

"I have heard nothing of it. Tell me the gist of it, pray!"

"Tell you Ma'am—not I. What the gossip is, no matter. What really is, you know. Set facts right, and the scandal will right itself. But pardon me—I speak rough; and I came to speak gentle, to coax you, beg you to be my daughter's friend. She loved you once Ma'am; you began by loving her. Then you dropped her without a reason, and it hurt her warm heart more than I can tell ye. But you were within your right as the superior, no doubt. But if you would consider her position now—surely surely you would do her no harm!"

"Certainly I would do her no harm—I——" Melbury's eye met hers. It was curious, but the allusion to Grace's former love for her seemed to touch her more than all Melbury's other arguments. "Oh Melbury," she burst out, "you have made me so unhappy! How could you come to me like this! It is too dreadful. Now go away—go, go!"

"I will, and leave you to think," he said, in a husky tone.

As soon as he was out of the room she went to a corner and there burst into tears, and writhed, under an emotion in which hurt pride and vexation mingled with better sentiments.

Mrs. Charmond's mobile spirit was subject to these fierce periods of high-tide and storm. She had never so clearly perceived till now that her soul was being slowly invaded by a delirium which had brought about all this; that she was losing judgment and dignity under it, becoming an animated impulse only, a passion incarnate. A fascination had led her on: it was as if she had been seized by a hand of velvet; and this was where she found herself—overshadowed with sudden night, as if a tornado had passed.

While she sat, or rather crouched, unhinged by the interview, lunch time came, and then the early afternoon, almost without her consciousness. Then, "a strange gentleman who says it is not necessary to give his name," was suddenly announced.

Felice knew who the strange gentleman was—that Continental follower on whom she had once smiled, among others too numerous to name. But to meet this lover now—the thought made her sick.

"I cannot see him, whoever he may be. I am not at home to anybody."

She heard no more of her visitor; and shortly after in an attempt to recover some mental serenity by violent physical exercise, she put on her hat and cloak and went out of doors, taking a path which led her up the slopes to the nearest spur of the wood. She disliked the woods, but they had the advantage of being a place in which she could walk comparatively unobserved.

XXXIII

THERE was agitation that day in the lives of all whom these matters concerned. It was not till the Hintock dinner-time— one o'clock—that Grace discovered her father's absence from the house after a departure in the morning under somewhat unusual conditions. By a little reasoning and inquiry she was able to come to a conclusion on his destination, and to divine his errand.

Her husband, too, was away, and her father did not return. He had, in truth, gone on to Sherton after the interview, in the hope of calming himself by business; but this Grace did not know. In an indefinite dread that something serious would arise out of Melbury's visit by reason of the inequalities of temper and nervous irritation to which he was subject, something possibly that would bring her much more misery than accompanied her present negative state of mind, she left the house about three o'clock, and took a loitering walk in the woodland track by which she imagined he would come home. This track under the bare trees and over the cracking sticks, screened and roofed in from the outer world of wind by a network of boughs, led her slowly on till in time she had left the larger trees behind her and swept round into the coppice where Winterborne and his men were clearing the undergrowth.

Had Giles's attention been concentrated on his hurdles he would not have seen her; but ever since Melbury's passage across the opposite glade in the morning he had been as uneasy and unsettled as Grace herself; and her advent now was the one appearance which, since her father's avowal, could arrest him more than Melbury's return with his tidings. Fearing that something might be the matter he hastened up to her.

She had not seen her old lover for a long time, and too conscious of the late pranks of her heart she could not behold him calmly. "I am only looking for my father," she said in an unnecessary tone of apology.

"I was looking for him too," said Giles. "I think he may perhaps have gone on further."

"Then you knew he was going to the House, Giles?" she said turning her large tender eyes anxiously upon him. "Did he tell you what for?"

Winterborne glanced doubtingly at her, and softly hinted that her father had visited him the evening before, and that their old friendship was quite restored; on which she guessed the rest.

"Oh I am glad indeed that you two are friends again!" she cried. And then they stood facing each other, fearing each other, troubling each other's souls. Grace experienced acute regret at the sight of these wood-cutting scenes, because she had estranged herself from them, craving even to its defects and inconveniences that homely sylvan life of her father which in the best probable succession of events would shortly be denied her.

At a little distance, on the edge of the clearing, Marty South was shaping spar-gads to take home for manufacture during the evenings. Winterborne and Mrs. Fitzpiers stood looking at her in their mutual embarrassment at each other's presence, and while doing so they beheld approaching the girl a lady in a dark fur mantle and black hat having a white veil tied picturesquely round it. She spoke to Marty, who turned and curtsied, and the lady fell into conversation with her. It was Mrs. Charmond.

After leaving her house Mrs. Charmond had walked on under the fret and fever of her mind with more vigour than she was accustomed to show in her normal moods—a fever which the solace of a cigarette did not entirely allay. Reaching the coppice she had listlessly observed Marty at work, when she threw away her cigarette and drew near. Chop,

chop, chop, went Marty's little bill-hook with never more
assiduity, till Mrs. Charmond spoke.

"Who is that young lady I see talking to the woodman
yonder?" she asked.

"Mrs. Fitzpiers, ma'am," said Marty.

"Oh," said Mrs. Charmond, with something like a start; for
she had not recognised Grace at that distance. "And the man
she is talking to?"

"That's Mr. Winterborne."

A redness stole into Marty's face as she mentioned Giles's
name, which Mrs. Charmond did not fail to notice. "Are you
engaged to him?" she asked softly.

"No ma'am," said Marty. "*She* was once; and I think——"

But Marty could not possibly explain the complications of
her thought on this matter—a thought nothing less than one
of extraordinary acuteness for a girl so young and inexperienced—namely, that she saw danger to two hearts naturally
honest in Grace being thrown back into Winterborne's society
by the neglect of her husband. Mrs. Charmond however, with
the almost supersensory means to knowledge which women
have on such occasions, quite understood what Marty had
intended to convey; and the picture thus exhibited to her of
lives drifting awry, involving the wreck of poor Marty's hopes,
prompted her yet further in those generous resolves which
Melbury's remonstrances had stimulated.

Full of such feelings she bade the girl good-afternoon, and
went on over the stumps of hazel to where Grace and Winterborne were standing. They saw her approach, and Winterborne said, "She is coming to you: it is a good omen. She
dislikes me, so I'll go away." He accordingly retreated to
where he had been working before Grace came, and Grace's
formidable rival approached her, each woman taking the
other's measure as she drew near.

"Dear—Mrs. Fitzpiers," said Felice Charmond with some
inward turmoil which stopped her speech. "I have not seen
you for a long time."

She held out her hand tentatively, while Grace stood like
a wild animal on first confronting a mirror or other puzzling
product of civilization. Was it really Mrs. Charmond speaking

to her thus? If it was she could no longer form any guess as to what life signified.

"I want to talk to you," said Mrs. Charmond sensitively, for the gaze of the young woman had chilled her through. "Can you walk on with me till we are quite alone?"

Sick with distaste Grace nevertheless complied as by clock-work, and they moved evenly side by side into the deeper recesses of the woods. They went further, much further than Mrs. Charmond had meant to go; but mental indiscipline hindered her from beginning her conversation, and in default of it she kept walking.

"I have seen your father," she at length observed. "And—I am much troubled by what he told me."

"What did he tell you? I have not been admitted to his confidence on anything he may have said to you."

"Nevertheless, why should I repeat to you what you can easily divine."

"True—true," returned Grace mournfully. "Why should you repeat what we both have in our minds already."

"Mrs. Fitzpiers, your husband——" The moment that the speaker's tongue touched the dangerous subject a vivid look of self-consciousness flashed over her; in which her heart revealed, as by a lightning-gleam, what filled it to overflowing. So transitory was the expression that none but a quick-sensed woman, and she in Grace's position, would have had the power to catch its meaning. Upon her the phase was not lost.

"Then you *do* love him!" she exclaimed in a tone of much surprise.

"What do you mean, my young friend?"

"Why," cried Grace, "I thought till now that you had only been cruelly flirting with my husband, to amuse your idle moments—a rich lady with a poor professional gentleman whom in her heart she despised not much less than her who belongs to him. But I guess from your manner that you love him desperately; and I don't hate you as I did before.——Yes, indeed," continued Mrs. Fitzpiers with a trembling tongue, "since it is not sport in your case at all, but *real*—O I do pity you, more than I despise you. For *you* will suffer most!"

Mrs. Charmond was now as much agitated as Grace. "I

ought not to allow myself to argue about this," she exclaimed.
"I demean myself by doing it. But I liked you once, and for
the sake of that time I try to tell you how mistaken you are!"
Much of her confusion resulted from her wonder and alarm
at finding herself in a sense dominated mentally and emo-
tionally by this simple school-girl. "I do not love him," she
went on with insistent untruth. "It was a kindness—my making somewhat more of him than one usually does of one's
doctor. I was lonely; I talked—well, I trifled with him. I am
very sorry if such child's play, out of pure friendship, has
been a serious matter to you. Who could have expected it?
But the world is so simple here."

"O that's affectation," said Grace shaking her head. "It is
no use—you *love* him. I can see in your face that in this
matter of my husband you have not let your acts belie your
feelings. During these last four or six months you have been
terribly indiscreet; but you have not been insincere; and that
almost disarms me."

"I *have* been insincere—if you will have the word—I mean
I *have* coquetted, and do *not* love him!"

But Grace clung to her position like a limpet. "You may
have trifled with others; but him you love as you never loved
another man."

"Oh, well—I won't argue," said Mrs. Charmond, laughing
faintly. "And you come to reproach me for it, child."

"No," said Grace magnanimously. "You may go on loving him
if you like—I don't mind at all. You'll find it, let me tell you, a
bitterer business for yourself than for me in the end. He'll get
tired of you soon, as tired as can be—you don't know him so
well as I—and then you may wish you had never seen him!"

Mrs. Charmond had grown quite pale and weak under this
prophecy. It was extraordinary that Grace, whom almost every
one would have characterized as a gentle girl, should be of
tougher fibre than her interlocutor. "You exaggerate—cruel,
silly young woman," she reiterated, writhing with little agonies. "It is nothing but playful friendship—nothing. It will be
proved by my future conduct. I shall at once refuse to see
him more—since it will make no difference to my heart, and
much to my name."

"I question if you will refuse to see him again," said Grace drily, as she bent a sapling back. "But I am not incensed against you as you are against me," she added, abandoning the tree to its natural perpendicular. "Before I came I had been despising you for wanton cruelty; now I only pity your weakness for its misplaced affection. When Edred has gone out of the house in hope of seeing you, at seasonable hours and unseasonable; when I have found him riding miles and miles across the country at midnight, and risking his life, and getting covered with mud, to get a glimpse of you, I have called him a foolish man—the plaything of a finished co-quette. I thought that what was getting to be a tragedy to me was a comedy to you. But now I see that tragedy lies on your side of the situation no less than on mine, and more; that if I have felt trouble at my position you have felt anguish at yours, that if I have had disappointments you have had de-spairs. Philosophy may fortify *me*—God help *you!*"

"I cannot attempt to reply to your ravings," returned the other, struggling to restore a dignity which had completely collapsed. "My acts will be my proofs. In the world which you have seen nothing of friendships between men and women are not unknown, and it would have been better both for you and your father if you had each judged me more re-spectfully, and left me alone. As it is I wish never, never to see or speak to you madam any more!"

Grace bowed, and Mrs. Charmond haughtily turned away. The two went apart in directly opposite courses; and were soon hidden from each other by their umbrageous surround-ings and by the shadows of eve.

In the excitement of their long argument they had walked onward and zigzagged about without regarding direction or distance. All sound of the woodcutters had long since faded into remoteness, and even had not the interval been too great for hearing them they would have been silent and homeward bound at this twilight hour. But Grace went on her course without any misgiving, though there was much underwood here with only the narrowest passages for walking, across which brambles hung. She had not, however, traversed this the wildest part of the wood since her childhood, and the transformation of outlines had been great; old trees which once were landmarks had been felled or blown down, and the bushes which then had been small and scrubby were now large and overhanging. She soon found that her ideas as to direction were vague—that she had, indeed, no ideas as to direction at all. If the evening had not been growing so dark, and the wind had not put on its night moan so distinctly Grace would not have minded; but she was rather frightened now, and began to strike across hither and thither in random courses.

Denser grew the darkness, more developed the wind-voices, and still no recognisable spot or outlet of any kind appeared, nor any sound of the Hintocks floated near, though she had wandered probably between one and two hours, and began to be weary. She was vexed at her foolishness, since the ground she had covered, if in a straight line, must inevitably have taken her out of the wood to some remote village or other; but she had wasted her forces in countermarches; and now in much alarm wondered if she would have to pass the night here. She stood still to meditate, and fancied that between the soughing of the wind she heard shuffling footsteps on the leaves heavier than those of rabbits or other startled "beasts of beating heart" who lived there. Though fearing at first to meet anybody on the chance of his being a friend she decided that her fellow-noctambulist, even if a poacher, would not injure her, and that he might possibly be someone sent to search for her. She accordingly shouted a rather timid "Hoi!"

The cry was immediately returned by the other person; and Grace running at once in the direction whence it came beheld an indistinct figure hastening up to her as rapidly. They were almost in each other's arms before she recognised the outline and white veil of her whom she had parted from hours before—Mrs. Charmond.

"I have lost my way, I have lost my way!" cried the latter. "Oh—is it indeed you? I am so glad to meet you or anybody. I have been wandering up and down ever since we parted, and am nearly dead with terror and misery and fatigue!"

"So am I," said Grace. "What *shall* we—*shall* we do!"

"You won't go away from me?" asked her companion anxiously.

"No indeed.—Are you very tired?"

"I can scarcely move, and I am scratched dreadfully about the ancles."

Grace reflected. "Perhaps, as it is dry underfoot, the best thing for us to do would be to sit down for half-an-hour, and then start again when we have thoroughly rested. By walking straight we must come to a track leading somewhere, before the morning."

They found a clump of bushy hollies which afforded a shelter from the wind, and sat down under it, some tufts of dead fern, crisp and dry, that remained from the previous season forming a sort of nest for them. But it was cold nevertheless on this March night, particularly for Grace who, with the sanguine prematureness of youth in matters of dress had considered it springtime, and hence was not so warmly clad as Mrs. Charmond, who still wore her winter furs. But after sitting awhile the latter lady shivered no less than Grace as the warmth imparted by her hasty walking began to go off; and they felt the cold air drawing through the holly leaves which scratched their backs and shoulders. Moreover they could hear some drops of rain falling on the trees though none reached the nook in which they had ensconced themselves.

"If we were to cling close together," said Mrs. Charmond, "we should keep each other warm. . . . But," she added in an uneven voice, "I suppose you won't come near me for the world!"

"Why not?"

"Because—well, you know."

"Yes I will—I don't hate you at all."

They consequently crept up to one another, and, being in the dark, lonely, and weary, did what neither had dreamed of doing beforehand, clasped each other closely. Mrs. Charmond's furs consoled Grace's cold face, and each one's body as she breathed alternately heaved against that of her companion, while the funereal trees rocked and chanted dirges unceasingly.

When a few minutes had been spent thus Mrs. Charmond said—"I am so wretched!" in a heavy emotional whisper.

"You are frightened," said Grace. "But there is nothing to fear: I know these woods well."

"I am not at all frightened at the wood, but I am at other things." Mrs. Charmond embraced Grace more and more tightly, and put her face against that of her companion. The younger woman could feel her neighbour's breathings grow deeper and more spasmodic, as though uncontrollable feelings were germinating. "After I had left you," Felice went on, "I regretted something I had said. I have to make a confession—I must make it!" she whispered brokenly, the instinct to indulge in warmth of sentiment which had led this woman of passions to respond to Fitzpiers in the first place leading her now to find luxurious comfort in opening her heart to his wife. "I said to you I could give him up without pain or deprivation—that he had only been my pastime. That was absolutely untrue—it was said to deceive you. I could not do it without much pain; and what is more dreadful I cannot give him up—even if I would—of myself alone."

"Why? Because you love him, you mean."

Felice Charmond denoted assent by a movement.

"I knew I was right," said Grace exaltedly. "But that should not deter you," she presently added in a moral tone. "O do struggle against it, and you will conquer!"

"You are so simple, so simple!" cried Felice. "You think, because you guessed my assumed indifference to him to be a sham, that you know the extremes that people are capable of going to! But a good deal more may have been going on than you have fathomed with all your insight. I *cannot* give him up, until he chooses to give up me."

"But surely you are the superior in station and in every way, and the cut must come from you."

"Tchut! Must I tell verbatim, you simple child? O, I suppose I must! It will eat away my heart if I do not let out all, after meeting you like this and finding how guileless you are." She thereupon whispered a few words in the girl's ear, and burst into a violent fit of sobbing.

Grace started roughly away from the shelter of the furs, and sprang to her feet. "O my great God!" she exclaimed, thunderstruck at a revelation transcending her utmost suspicion. "He's had you! Can it be—can it be!"

She turned as if to hasten away. But Felice Charmond's sobs came to her ear: deep darkness circled her about, the cold lips of the wind kissed her where Mrs. Charmond's warm fur had been, and she did not know which way to go. After the moment of energy she felt mild again, and turned to the motionless woman at her feet.

"Are you rested?" she asked, in what seemed her own voice grown ten years older.

Without an answer Mrs. Charmond slowly rose. "You mean to betray me!" she asked out of the bitterest depths of her soul. "O fool, fool I!"

"No," said Grace shortly. "I mean no such thing. But let us be quick now. We have a serious undertaking before us. Think of nothing but going straight on."

They walked on in profound silence, pulling back boughs now growing wet, and treading down woodbine, but still keeping a pretty straight course. Grace began to be thoroughly worn out, and her companion too when, on a sudden, they broke into the deserted highway where the Sherton man had waited for Mrs. Dollery's van. Grace recognised the spot as soon as she looked around her.

"How we have got here I cannot tell," she said with cold civility. "We have made a complete circuit of Little Hintock. The hazel copse is quite on the other side. Now we have only to follow the road."

They dragged themselves onward, turned into the lane, passed the track to Little Hintock, and so reached the park. "Here I turn back," said Grace in the same passionless voice. "You are quite near home."

Mrs. Charmond stood inert, seeming appalled by her late admission. "I have told you something in a moment of irresistible desire to unburden my soul which all but a fool would have kept silent as the grave," she said. "I cannot help it now. Is it to be a secret, or do you mean war?"

"A secret, certainly," said Grace mournfully. "How can you expect war from such a helpless wretched being as me!"

"And I'll do my best not to see him. I am his slave; but I'll try."

Grace was naturally kind, but she could not help using a small dagger now. "Pray don't distress yourself," she said with

fine scorn. "You may see him as much as you like—for me."
Had she been wounded instead of mortified she could not
have used the words; but Fitzpiers's hold upon her heart just
now was slight.

They parted thus and there, kissing each other almost
unintentionally, and Grace went moodily homeward. Passing
Marty's cottage she observed through the window that the
girl was writing instead of chopping as usual, and wondered
what her correspondence could be. Directly afterwards she
met people in search of her, and reached the house to find
all in serious alarm. She soon explained that she had lost her
way; and her general depression was attributed to exhaustion on that account.

Could she have known what Marty was writing she would
have been surprised. The rumour which agitated the other
folk of Hintock had reached the young girl, and she was
penning a letter to Fitzpiers to tell him that Mrs. Charmond's
magnificent pile of hair was made up of the writer's more
largely than of her own. It was poor Marty's only card, and
she played it, knowing nothing of fashion, and thinking her
revelation a fatal one for a lover.

XXXIV

It was at the beginning of April, a few days after the meeting between Grace and Mrs. Charmond in the wood, that
Fitzpiers, just returned from London, was travelling from
Sherton-Abbas to Hintock in a hired carriage. In his eye
there was a doubtful light, and the lines of his fastidious face
showed a vague disquietude. He appeared like one of those
whose aspect seems to say to a beholder that they have suffered a certain wrong in being born.

His position was in truth gloomy, and to his impressible
mind it looked even gloomier than it was. His practice had
been slowly dwindling of late, and now threatened to die out
altogether, the undaunted old Doctor Jones capturing patients up to Fitzpiers's very door. Fitzpiers knew only too well
the latest and greatest cause of his unpopularity; and yet, so

illogical is man, the second branch of his sadness grew out of a remedial measure proposed for the first—a letter from Felice Charmond, imploring him not to see her again. To bring about their severance still more effectually, she added, she had decided upon almost immediate departure for the Continent.

The time was that dull interval in a woodlander's life which coincides with great activity in the life of the woodland itself —a period following the close of the winter tree-cutting, and preceding the barking season, when the saps are just begin-ning to heave with the force of hydraulic lifts, inside all the trunks of the forest.

Winterborne's contract was completed, and the plantations were deserted. It was dusk: there were no leaves as yet: the nightingales would not begin to sing for a fortnight; and "the Mother of the Months" was in her most attenuated phase —starved and bent to a mere bowed skeleton, which glided along behind the bare twigs in Fitzpiers's company.

When he reached home he went straight up to his wife's sitting-room. He found it deserted and without a fire. He had mentioned no day for his return; nevertheless he won-dered why she was not there waiting to receive him. On descending to the other wing of the house and enquiring of Mrs. Melbury he learnt with much surprise that Grace had gone on a visit to an acquaintance at Shottsford-Forum, three days earlier; that tidings had on this morning reached her father of her being very unwell there, in consequence of which he had ridden over to see her.

Fitzpiers went upstairs again, and the little drawing-room, now lighted by a solitary candle, was not rendered more cheerful by the entrance of Grammer Oliver with an apron full of wood, which she threw on the hearth while she raked out the grate and rattled about the fire-irons with a view to making things comfortable. Fitzpiers, guessing nothing of the revelations in the wood, considered that Grace ought to have let him know her plans more accurately before leaving home in a freak like this. He went desultorily to the window, the blind of which had not been pulled down, and looked out at the thin, fast-sinking moon, and at the stalk of smoke rising from the top of Suke Damson's chimney, signifying that the young woman had just lit her fire to prepare supper. He became conscious of a discussion in progress on the opposite side of the court. Somebody had looked over the wall to talk to the sawyers, and was telling them in a loud voice news in which the name of Mrs. Charmond soon arrested his ears.

"Grammer, don't make so much noise with that grate," said the surgeon; at which Grammer reared herself upon her knees and held the fuel suspended in her hand, while Fitzpiers half-opened the window.

"She is off to foreign lands again at last—have made up her mind quite sudden-like—and it is thoughted she'll leave in a day or two. She's been all as if her mind were low for some days past—with a sort of fret in her face, as if she chid her own soul. She's the wrong sort of woman for Hintock—hardly knowing a beech from a woak. But I don't care who the man is, she's been a very kind friend to me."

"Well—the day after to-morrow is the Sabbath day, and without charity we be but tinkling simples; but this I do say, that her going will be a blessed thing for a certain married couple who remain."

The fire was lighted, and Fitzpiers sat down in front of it, restless as the last leaf upon a tree. "A sort of fret in her face, as if she chid her own soul." Poor, poor Felice. How her frame must be pulsing under the conditions of which he had just heard the caricature; how her fair temples must ache, what a mood of wretchedness she must be in!—But for this mixing up of his name with hers, and her determination to sunder their too close acquaintance on that account, she would probably have sent for him professionally. She was now sitting alone, suffering, perhaps wishing she had not forbidden him to come again.

Unable to remain in this lonely room any longer, or to wait for the meal which was in course of preparation, he made himself ready for riding, descended to the yard, stood by the stable-door while Darling was saddled, and rode off down the lane. He would have preferred walking, but was weary with his day's travel.

As he approached the door of Marty South's cottage, which it was necessary to pass on his way, she came from the porch as if she had been awaiting him, and met him in the middle of the road, holding up a letter. Fitzpiers took it without stopping, and asked over his shoulder from whom it came.

Marty hesitated. "From me," she said with noticeable firmness.

This letter contained, in fact, Marty's declaration that she was the original owner of Mrs. Charmond's supplementary locks, and enclosed a sample from the native stock, which had grown considerably by this time. It was her long contemplated apple of discord, and much her hand trembled as she handed the document up to him.

But it was impossible on account of the gloom for Fitzpiers to read it then, while he had the curiosity to do so, and he put it in his pocket. His imagination having already centred itself on Hintock House, in his pocket the letter remained unopened and forgotten, all the while that Marty was hopefully picturing its excellent weaning effect upon him.

He was not long in reaching the precincts of the Manor House. He drew rein under a group of oaks commanding a view of the front, and reflected awhile. His entry would not be altogether unnatural in the circumstances of her possible indisposition; but upon the whole he thought it best to avoid riding up to the door. By silently approaching he could retreat unobserved in the event of her not being alone. He dismounted, hitched Darling to a stray bough hanging a little below the general browsing line of the trees, and proceeded to the door on foot.

In the meantime Melbury had returned from Shottsford Forum. The great court or quadrangle of the timber-merchant's house, divided from the shady lane by an ivy-covered wall, was entered by two white gates, one standing near each extremity of the wall. It had so happened that at the moment when Fitzpiers was riding out at the lower gate on his way to the Manor-House, Melbury was approaching the upper gate to enter it. Fitzpiers being in front of Melbury was seen by the latter, but the surgeon, never turning his head, did not observe his father-in-law, ambling up slowly and silently under the trees, though his horse too was a grey one.

"How is Grace?" said his wife, as soon as he entered.

Melbury looked gloomy. "She is not at all well," he said. "I don't like the looks of her at all. I couldn't bear the notion of her staying away in a strange place any longer, and I begged her to let me get her home. At last she agreed to it, but not till after much persuading. I was then sorry that I rode over instead of driving; but I have hired a nice comfortable carriage—the easiest-going I could get—and she'll be here in a couple of hours or less. I rode on ahead to tell you to get her room ready; but I see her husband has come back."

"Yes," said Mrs. Melbury. She expressed her concern that her husband had hired a carriage all the way from Shottsford. "What it will cost!" she said.

"I don't care what it costs," he exclaimed testily. "I was determined to get her home. Why she went away I can't think! She acts in a way that is not at all likely to mend matters as far as I can see." (Grace had not told her father of her interview with Mrs. Charmond and the disclosure that had been whispered in her startled ear.) "Since Edred is come," he continued, "he might have waited in till I got back, to ask me how she was, if only for a compliment. I saw him go out: where is he gone?"

Mrs. Melbury reminded her husband that there was not much doubt about the place of his first visit after an absence. She had, in fact, seen Fitzpiers take the direction of the Manor House.

Melbury said no more. It was exasperating to him that just at this moment, when there was every reason for Fitzpiers to stay in-doors, or at any rate to ride along the Shottsford road to meet his ailing wife, he should be doing despite to her by going elsewhere. The old man went out of doors again; and, his horse being hardly unsaddled as yet, he told Upjohn to re-tighten the girths; again mounting he rode off at the heels of the surgeon.

By the time that Melbury reached the park he was prepared to go any lengths in combating this rank and reckless errantry of his daughter's husband. He would fetch home Edred Fitzpiers to-night by some means, rough or fair: in his

view there could come of his interference nothing worse than
what existed at present. And yet to every bad there is a worse.

He had entered by the bridle-gate which admitted to the
park on this side, and cantered over the soft turf almost in
the tracks of Fitzpiers's horse, till he reached the clump of
trees under which his precursor had halted. The whitish object
that was indistinctly visible here in the gloom of the boughs
he found to be Darling, as left by Fitzpiers. "Damn him—why
did he not ride up to the house in an honest way?" said
Melbury. He profited by Fitzpiers's example; dismounting he
tied his horse under an adjoining tree, and went on to the
house on foot as the other had done. He was no longer
disposed to stick at trifles in his investigation, and did not
hesitate to gently open the front door without ringing. The
large square hall, with its oak floor, staircase, and wainscot,
was lighted by a dim lamp hanging from a beam. Not a soul
was visible. He went into the corridor and listened at a door
which he knew to be that of the drawing-room; there was no
sound, and on turning the handle he found the room empty.
A fire burning low in the grate was the sole light of the
apartment; its beams flashed mockingly on the somewhat
showy Versaillese furniture and gilding here, in style as unlike that of the structural parts of the building as it was
possible to be, and probably introduced by Felice to counter-
act the fine old-English gloom of the place. Disappointed in
his hope of confronting his son-in-law at once he went on to
the dining-room, which was without light or fire, and pervaded by a cold atmosphere signifying that she had not dined
there that day.

By this time Melbury's mood had a little mollified. Everything here was so pacific, so unaggressive in its repose, that
he was no longer incited to provoke a collision with Fitzpiers
or with anybody. The comparative stateliness of the apartments influenced him to an emotion, rather than to a belief,
that where all was outwardly so good and proper there could
not be quite that delinquency within which he had suspected.
It occurred to him, too, that even if his suspicion were justified his abrupt if not unwarrantable entry into the house
might end in confounding its inhabitant at the expense of

his daughter's dignity and his own. Any ill result would be pretty sure to hit Grace hardest in the long run. He would, after all, adopt the more rational course and plead with Fitzpiers privately, as he had pleaded with Mrs. Charmond.

He accordingly retreated as silently as he had come. Passing the door of the drawing-room anew he fancied that he heard a noise within which was not the crackling of the fire. Melbury gently re-opened the door to a distance of a few inches and saw at the opposite window two figures in the act of stepping out—a man and a woman, in whom he recognised the lady of the house and his son-in-law. In a moment they had disappeared amid the gloom of the lawn.

He drew back into the hall and let himself out by the carriage-entrance door, coming round to the lawn front in time to see the two figures parting at the railing which divided the precincts of the house from the open park. Mrs. Charmond turned to hasten back immediately that her lover had left her side; and Fitzpiers going onward was speedily absorbed into the duskiness of the trees.

Melbury waited till Mrs. Charmond had re-entered the drawing-room window, and then followed after Fitzpiers. He would give that precious young man a piece of his mind tonight, even if he were not tempted to give him more.

On plunging however into the thick shade of the clump of oaks he could not discover Fitzpiers; neither could he perceive his horse Blossom anywhere; but feeling his way carefully along he by-and-by discerned Fitzpiers's mare Darling still standing as before under the tree adjoining that to which he had hitched Blossom. For a moment Melbury thought that his own horse, being young and strong, had broken away from her fastening; but on listening intently he could hear her ambling comfortably along a little way ahead, and a creaking of the saddle which showed that she had a rider. Walking on as far as the small gate in the corner of the park he met a labourer, who, in reply to Melbury's inquiry if he had seen any person on a grey horse said that he had only met Dr. Fitzpiers.

It was just what Melbury had begun to suspect: Fitzpiers had mounted the mare which did not belong to him in mistake

for his own—an oversight easily explicable in a man ever un-
witting in horse-flesh by the gloom of the spot and the near
similarity of the animals in appearance, though Melbury's was
readily enough seen to be the darker horse by day. He
hastened back and did what seemed best in the circumstances—got upon old Darling and rode rapidly after Fitzpiers.

Melbury had just entered the wood, and was winding along
the cart-way which led through it, channelled deep in the
leaf-mould with large ruts that were formed by the timber-
waggons in fetching the spoil of the plantations, when all at
once he descried in front, at a point where the road took a
turning round a large chestnut tree, the form of his own
horse Blossom. Melbury quickened Darling's pace, thinking
to come up with Fitzpiers. Nearer view revealed that the
horse had no rider. At Melbury's approach it galloped friskily away under the trees in a homeward direction. Thinking
something was wrong the timber-merchant dismounted as
soon as he reached the chestnut, and after feeling about for
a minute or two discovered Fitzpiers lying on the ground.

"Here—help," cried the latter as soon as he felt Melbury's
touch; "I have been thrown off.... But there's not much
harm done I think."

Since Melbury could not now very well read the younger
man the lecture he had intended, and as friendliness would
be hypocrisy, his instinct was to speak not a single word to
his son-in-law. He raised Fitzpiers into a sitting-posture, and
found that he was a little stunned and stupefied, but, as he
had said, not otherwise hurt. How this fall had come about
was readily conjecturable: Fitzpiers, imagining there was only
old Darling under him, had been taken unawares by the
younger horse, anxious for the stable.

Melbury was a traveller of the old-fashioned sort; having
just come from Shottsford Forum he still had in his pocket
the pilgrim's flask of rum which he always carried on journeys
exceeding a dozen miles though he seldom drank much of
it. He poured it down the surgeon's throat with such effect
that he quickly revived. Melbury got him on his legs; but the
question was what to do with him. He could not walk more
than a few steps, and the other horse had gone away. With

great exertion Melbury contrived to get him astride Darling, mounting himself behind and holding Fitzpiers round his waist with one arm. Darling being broad, straight-backed, and high in the withers, was well able to carry double, at any rate the short distance to Hintock and at a gentle pace.

XXXV

THE mare paced along with firm and cautious tread through the copse where Winterborne had worked, and into the heavier soil where the oaks grew: thence towards Marshcombe Bottom, intensely dark now with overgrowth, and popularly supposed to be haunted by spirits. By this time Fitzpiers had quite recovered his physical strength. But he had eaten nothing since making a hasty breakfast in London that morning, his anxiety about Felice having hurried him away from home before dining: as a consequence the old rum administered by his father-in-law flew to the young man's head and loosened his tongue without his ever having recognised who it was that had lent him a kindly hand. He began to speak in desultory sentences, Melbury still supporting him.

"I've come all the way from London to-day," said Fitzpiers. "Ah—that's the place to meet your equals. I live at Hintock— worse, at Little Hintock—and I am quite wasted there. There's not a man within ten miles of Hintock who can comprehend me. . . . I tell you, Farmer What's-your-name, that I'm a man of education. I know several languages: the poets and I are familiar friends: I used to read more in metaphysics than anybody within fifty miles; and since I gave that up there's nobody can match me in the whole county of South Wessex as a scientist. . . . Yet I am doomed to live with tradespeople in a miserable little hole like Hintock!"

"Indeed!" muttered Melbury.

Here Fitzpiers, with alcoholic energy, reared himself up suddenly from the bowed posture he had hitherto held, thrusting his shoulders so violently against Melbury's breast as to make it difficult for the old man to keep a hold on the reins. "People don't appreciate me here!" the surgeon exclaimed;

then, lowering his voice he added softly and slowly, "except one—except one! .... A passionate soul, as warm as she is clever, as beautiful as she is warm, and as rich as she is beautiful.—I say, old fellow, those claws of yours clutch me rather tight—rather like the eagle's, you know, that ate out the liver of Pro—Pre—the man on Mount Caucasus. ... People don't appreciate me, I say, except *her!* ... Ah, God, I am an unlucky man! She would have been mine, she would have taken my name; but unfortunately it cannot be so. I stooped to mate beneath me; and now I rue it."

The position was becoming a very trying one for Melbury, corporeally and mentally. He was obliged to steady Fitzpiers with his left arm, and he began to hate the contact. He hardly knew what to do. It was useless to remonstrate with Fitzpiers in his intellectual confusion from the rum and from the fall. He remained silent, his hold upon his companion, however, being stern rather than compassionate.

"You hurt me a little, farmer. Though I am much obliged to you for your kindness. ... People don't appreciate me, I say. Between ourselves I am losing my practice here; and why? Because I see matchless attraction where matchless attraction is, both in person and position.—I mention no names, so nobody will be the wiser. ... But I have lost her, in a legitimate sense, that is. If I were a free man now, things have come to such a pass between us that she could not refuse me; while with her fortune (which I don't covet for itself) I should have a chance of satisfying an honourable ambition—a chance I have not had yet! ... and now never never shall have probably!"

Melbury, his heart throbbing against the other's backbone, and his brain on fire with indignation, ventured to mutter huskily, "Why?"

The horse ambled on some steps before Fitzpiers replied. "Because I am tied and bound to another by law, as tightly as I am to you by your arm—not that I complain of your arm—I thank you for helping me.—Well, where are we? Not nearly home yet? ... Home, say I. It *is* a home! When I might have been at the other house over there." In a stupefied way he flung his hand in the direction of the park. "I was just two months too early in committing myself. Had I only seen the other first——"

Here the old man's arm gave Fitzpiers a convulsive shake.

"What are you doing?" continued the latter. "Keep still, please, or put me down. . . . I was saying that I lost her by a mere little two months! There is no chance for me now in this world, and it makes me reckless—reckless! Unless, indeed, anything should happen to the other one. She is amiable enough; but if anything should happen to her—and I hear she is ill at this moment—well, if it *should*, I should be free—and my fame, my happiness, would be ensured."

These were the last words that Fitzpiers uttered in his seat in front of the timber-merchant. Unable longer to master himself Melbury whipt away his spare arm from Fitzpiers's waist, and seized him by the collar. "You heartless villain—After all that we have done for 'ee!" he cried with a quivering lip. "And the money of hers that you've had, and the roof we've provided to shelter 'ee!—It is to me, George Melbury, that you dare to talk like that!" The exclamation was accompanied by a powerful swing from the shoulder, which flung the young man headlong into the road.

Fitzpiers fell with a heavy thud upon the stumps of some brushwood which had been cut during the winter preceding. Darling continued her walk for a few paces further, and stopped. "God forgive me!" Melbury murmured, repenting of what he had done. "He tried me too sorely; and now perhaps I've murdered him!"

He turned round in the saddle and looked towards the spot on which Fitzpiers had fallen. To his great surprise he beheld the surgeon rise to his feet as if scarcely hurt, and walk away rapidly under the trees.

Melbury listened till the rustle of Fitzpiers's footsteps died away. "It might have been a crime, but for the mercy of Providence in providing leaves for his fall!" he said to himself. And then his mind reverted to the words of Fitzpiers, and his indignation so mounted within him that he almost wished the fall had put an end to the surgeon there and then.

He had not ridden far when he discerned his own grey mare standing under some bushes. Leaving Darling for a moment Melbury went forward and easily caught the younger animal, now disheartened at its freak. He made the pair of them fast to a tree, and turning back endeavoured to find some trace of Fitzpiers, feeling pitifully that, after all, he had gone further than he intended with the offender. But though he threaded the wood hither and thither, his toes ploughing layer after layer of the little horny scrolls that had once been leaves, he could not find him. He stood still, listening and looking round. The breeze was oozing through the network of boughs as through a strainer; the trunks and larger branches stood against the light of the sky in the forms of sentinels, gigantic candelabra, pikes, halberds, lances, and whatever else the fancy chose to make of them. Giving up the search Melbury came back to the horses, and walked slowly homeward leading one in each hand.

It happened that on the selfsame evening a boy had been returning through Hintock Park to Little Hintock about the time of Fitzpiers's passage home along that route. A horse-collar that had been left at the harness-mender's to be repaired was required for use at five o'clock next morning, and in consequence the boy had to fetch it overnight. He put his head through the collar, and the way of the park being a short cut he took it, whistling the one tune he knew as an antidote to fear.

The boy suddenly became aware of a horse brushing rather friskily along the track behind him. Not knowing whether to expect friend or foe prudence suggested that he should cease his whistling and retreat among the trees till the horse and his rider had gone by, a course to which he was still more inclined when he found how noiselessly they approached, and saw that the horse looked pale, and remembered what he had read about Death in the Revelation. He therefore deposited the collar by a tree and hid himself behind it. The horseman came on, and the youth, whose eyes were as keen as telescopes, to his great relief recognised the doctor.

As Melbury surmised Fitzpiers had in the darkness taken Blossom for Darling, and he had not discovered his mistake when he came up opposite the boy, though he was somewhat surprised at the liveliness of his usually placid mare. The only other pair of eyes on the spot whose vision was keen as the young carter's were those of the horse; and, with that strongly conservative objection to the unusual which animals show, Blossom, on eyeing the collar under the tree—quite invisible to Fitzpiers—exercised none of the patience of the older horse, but shied sufficiently to unseat so second-rate an equestrian as the surgeon.

He fell, and did not move, lying as Melbury afterwards found him. The boy ran away, salving his conscience for the desertion by thinking how vigorously he would spread the alarm of the accident when he got to Hintock—which he uncompromisingly did, encrusting the skeleton event with a load of dramatic horrors.

Grace had returned, and the fly hired on her account, though not by her husband, at the Crown Hotel, Shottsford Forum, had been paid for and dismissed. The long drive had somewhat revived her, her illness being a feverish intermittent nervousness which had more to do with mind than body, and she walked about her sitting-room in something of a hopeful mood. Mrs. Melbury had told her as soon as she arrived that her husband had returned from London. He had gone out, she said, to see a patient as she supposed, and he must soon be back, since he had had no dinner or tea. Grace would not allow her mind to harbour any suspicion of his whereabouts, and her step-mother said nothing of Mrs. Charmond's rumoured sorrows, and plans of departure.

So the young wife sat by the fire, waiting silently. She had left Hintock in a turmoil of aversion from her husband, after the revelation of Mrs. Charmond, and had intended not to be at home when he returned. But she had thought the matter over, and had allowed her father's influence to prevail and bring her back; and now somewhat regretted that Edred's arrival had preceded hers. By and by Mrs. Melbury came upstairs with a slight air of flurry and abruptness. "I have something to tell—some bad news," she said. "But you must not be alarmed, as it is not so bad as it might have been. Edred has been thrown off his horse. We don't think he is hurt much. It happened in the wood the other side of

Marshcombe Bottom." She went on to give a few of the particulars, but none of the invented horrors that had been communicated by the boy. "I thought it better to tell you at once," she added, "in case he should not—be very well able to walk home, and somebody should bring him."

Mrs. Melbury really thought matters much worse than she represented, and Grace knew that she thought so. She sat down dazed for a few minutes, returning a negative to her step-mother's inquiry if she could do anything for her. "Ah— yes—please go into the bedroom," Grace said on second thoughts, "and see if all is ready there—in case it is serious." Mrs. Melbury thereupon called Grammer, and they did as directed, supplying the room with everything they could think of for the accommodation of an injured man.

Nobody was left in the lower part of the house. Not many minutes had passed when Grace heard a knock at the door— a single knock, not loud enough to reach the ears of those in the bedroom. She went to the top of the stairs and said faintly, "Come up," knowing that the door stood, as usual in such houses, wide open. Retreating into the gloom of the broad landing she saw rise up the stairs a woman whom at first she did not recognise, till her voice revealed her to be Suke Damson in great fright and sorrow. A streak of light from the partially closed door of Grace's room fell upon her face as she came forward; and it was drawn and pale.

"Oh Miss Melbury—I would say Mrs. Fitzpiers," she said wringing her hands. "This terrible news—is he dead? Is he hurted very bad? Tell me! I couldn't help coming—please forgive me Miss Melbury—Mrs. Fitzpiers I would say!"

Grace sank down on the oak chest which stood on the landing, and put her hands to her now flushed face and head. Ought she not to order Suke Damson downstairs and out of the house? Her husband might be brought in at any moment, and what would happen? But could she order this genuinely grieved woman away? There was a dead silence of half a minute or so, till Suke said, "Why don't ye speak? Is he here? Is he dead? If so, why can't I see him—would it be so very wrong?"

Before Grace had answered somebody else came to the

door below—a footfall light as a roe's. There was a hurried tapping upon the panel, as if with the impatient tips of fingers whose owner thought not whether a knocker were there or no. Without a pause, and possibly guided by the stray beam of light on the landing, the new-comer ascended the staircase as the first had done. Grace started: it was a lady. Grace was sufficiently visible, and the lady came to her side.

"I could make nobody hear downstairs," said Felice Charmond with lips whose dryness could almost be heard, and panting as she stood ready to sink on the floor with distress. "What is—the matter—tell me the worst! Can he live?" She looked at Grace imploringly, without perceiving poor Suke who, dismayed at such a presence, had shrunk away into the shade. Mrs. Charmond's little feet were covered with mud; she was quite unconscious of her appearance now. "I have heard such a dreadful report," she went on. "I came to ascertain the truth of it. Is he—killed?"

"She won't tell us—he's dying—he's in that room!" burst out Suke, regardless of consequences, as she heard the distant movements of Mrs. Melbury and Grammer in the bedroom at the end of the passage.

"Where?" said Mrs. Charmond; and on Suke pointing out the direction she made as if to go thither.

Grace barred the way. "He is not there," she said. "I have not seen him any more than you. I have heard a report only—not so bad as you think. It must have been exaggerated to you."

"Please do not conceal anything—let me know all!" said Felice doubtingly.

"You shall know all I know. Indeed, you have a perfect right to go into his bedroom; who can have a better than either of you?" said Grace with a delicate sting which was lost upon them now as, ceasing to obstruct the way, she led on to the chamber door, and flung it open. "Wives all, let's enter together! . . . I repeat, I have only heard a less alarming account than you have heard—how much it means, and how little, I cannot say. I pray God that it means not much—in common humanity. You probably pray the same—*for other reasons.*"

Then she regarded them there in the dim light awhile, as, gathering with her round the empty bed of Fitzpiers they stood dumb in their trouble, staring at it, and at his night-shirt lying on the pillow; not stinging back at her; not heed-ing her mood. A tenderness spread over Grace like a dew. It was well enough, conventionally, to address either one of them in the wife's regulation terms of virtuous sarcasm, as woman, creature, or thing. But life, what was it, after all? She had, like the singer of the Psalm of Asaph, been plagued and chastened all the day long; but could she, by retributive words, in order to please herself the individual, "offend against the generation," as that singer would not?

"He is dying, perhaps!" blubbered Suke Damson, putting her apron to her eyes.

In their gestures and faces there were anxieties, affection, agony of heart—all for a man who had wronged them—had never really behaved towards either of them anyhow but selfishly. Neither one but would have well-nigh sacrificed half her life to him, even now. The tears which his possibly crit-ical situation could not bring to her eyes surged over at the contemplation of these fellow-women whose relations with him were as close as her own without its conventionality. She went out to the balustrade, bent herself upon it, and wept.

Thereupon Felice following began to cry also, without using her handkerchief, letting the tears run down silently. While the three stood together thus, pitying another though most to be pitied themselves, the pacing of a horse or horses became audible in the court, and in a moment Melbury's voice was heard calling to his stableman. Grace at once started up, ran down the stairs, and out into the quadrangle as her father crossed it towards the door. "Father—what is the matter with him!" she cried.

"Who—Edred?" said Melbury abruptly. "Matter? Nothing.— What, my dear, and have you got home safe? Why you are better already! But you ought not to be out in the air like this."

"But he has been thrown off his horse!"

"I know—I know. I saw it. He got up again, and walked off as well as ever—a fall on the leaves didn't hurt a spry fellow like him. He did not come this way," he added significantly. "I suppose he went to look for his horse. I tried to find him, but could not. But after seeing him go away under the trees I found the horse, and have led it home for safety. So he must walk. Now, don't you stay out here in this night air."

She returned to the house with her father. When she had again ascended to the landing and to her own rooms beyond, it was a great relief to her to find that both Petticoat the First and Petticoat the Second of her *Bien-aimé* had silently disappeared. They had in all probability heard the words of her father, and departed with their anxieties relieved.

Presently her parents came up to Grace, and busied themselves to see that she was comfortable. Perceiving soon that she would prefer to be left alone they went away.

Grace waited on. The clock raised its voice now and then, but her husband did not return. At her father's usual hour for retiring he again came in to see her. "Do not stay up," she said as soon as he entered. "I am not at all tired. I will sit up for him."

"I think it will be useless, Grace," said Melbury slowly.

"Why?"

"I have had a bitter quarrel with him. And on that account I hardly think he will return to-night."

"A quarrel? Was that after the fall seen by the boy?"

Melbury nodded an affirmative—without taking his eyes off the candle. "Yes—it was as we were coming home together," he said.

Something had been swelling up in Grace while her father was speaking. "How could you want to quarrel with him!" she cried suddenly. "Why could you not let him come home quietly, if he were inclined to? He is my husband; and now you have married me to him surely you need not provoke him unnecessarily. First you induce me to accept him; and then you do things that divide us more than we should naturally be divided!"

"How can you speak so unjustly to me, Grace!" said Melbury, with indignant sorrow. "*I* divide you from your husband, indeed! You little think——"

He was inclined to say more—to tell her the whole story

of the encounter, and that the provocation he had received had lain entirely in hearing her despised. But it would have greatly distressed her; and he forebore. "You had better lie down—You are tired," he said soothingly. "Good-night."

The household went to bed, and a silence fell upon the dwelling, broken only by the occasional skirr of a halter in Melbury's stables. Despite her father's advice Grace still waited up. But nobody came.

It was a critical time in Grace's emotional life, that night. She thought of her husband a good deal, and for the nonce forgot Winterborne. "How these unhappy women must have admired Edred!" she said to herself. "How attractive he must be to everybody—and, indeed, he is attractive." The possibility is that, piqued by rivalry, these ideas might have been transmuted into their corresponding emotions by a show of the least reciprocity in Fitzpiers. There was, in truth, a love-bird yearning to fly from her heart; and it wanted a lodging badly.

But no husband came. The fact was that Melbury had been much mistaken about the condition of Fitzpiers. People do not fall headlong on stumps of underwood with impunity. Had the old man been able to watch Fitzpiers narrowly enough he would have observed that, on rising and walking into the thicket he dropped blood as he went; that he had not proceeded fifty yards before he showed signs of being dizzy, and, raising his hands to his head, reeled and fell.

XXXVI

GRACE was not the only one who watched and meditated in Hintock that night.

Felice Charmond was in no mood to retire to rest at a customary hour; and over her drawing-room fire at the Manor House she sat as motionless and in as deep a reverie as Grace in her little chamber at the homestead.

Having caught ear of Melbury's intelligence while she had stood on the landing at his house, and been eased of much of her mental distress, her sense of personal decorum had

returned upon her with a rush. She descended the stairs and
left the door like a ghost, keeping close to the walls of the
building till she got round to the gate of the quadrangle,
through which she noiselessly passed almost before Grace
and her father had finished their discourse. Suke Damson
had thought it well to imitate her superior in this respect,
and, descending the back stairs as Felice descended the front,
went out at the side door and home to her cottage.

Once outside Melbury's gates Mrs. Charmond ran with all
her speed to the Manor House without stopping or turning
her head, and splitting her thin boots in her haste. She
entered her own dwelling as she had emerged from it—by
the drawing-room window. In other circumstances she would
have felt some timidity at undertaking such an unpremeditated excursion alone; but her anxiety for another had cast
out her fear for herself.

Everything in her drawing-room was just as she had left
it—the candles still burning, the casement closed, and the
shutters gently pulled to, so as to hide the state of the window from the cursory glance of a servant entering the apartment. She had been gone about three-quarters of an hour
by the clock, and nobody seemed to have discovered her
absence. Tired in body but tense in mind she sat down,
palpitating, round-eyed, bewildered at what she had done.

She had been betrayed by affrighted love into a visit which,
now that the emotion instigating it had calmed down under
her belief that Fitzpiers was in no danger, was the saddest
surprise to her. This was how she had set about doing her
best to escape her passionate bondage to him! Somehow, in
declaring to Grace and to herself the unseemliness of her
infatuation she had grown a convert to its irresistibility. If
Heaven would only give her strength; but Heaven never did.
One thing was indispensable; she must go away from Hintock
if she meant to withstand further temptation. The struggle
was too wearying, too hopeless, while she remained. It was
but a continual capitulation of conscience to what she dared
not name.

By degrees, as she sat on and on, Felice's mind—helped
perhaps by the anti-climax of supposing that her lover was

unharmed after all her fright about him—grew wondrously strong in wise resolve. For the moment she was in a mood, in the words of Mrs. Elizabeth Montagu, "to run mad with discretion"; and was so persuaded that discretion lay in departure that she wished to set about going that very minute. Jumping up from her seat she began to gather together some small personal knicknacks scattered about the room, to feel that preparations were really in train.

While moving here and there she fancied that she heard a slight noise out of doors; and stood still. Surely it was a tapping at the window. A thought entered her mind, and burnt her cheek. He had come to that window before; yet was it possible that he should dare to do so now! All the servants were in bed, and in the ordinary course of affairs she would have retired also. Then she remembered that on stepping in by the casement and closing it she had not fastened the window-shutter, so that a streak of light from the interior of the room might have revealed her vigil to an observer on the lawn. How all things conspired against her keeping faith with Grace! The tapping re-commenced, light as from the bill of a little bird: her illegitimate hope overcame her discretion: she went and pulled back the shutter, determining however to shake her head at him and keep the casement securely closed.

What she saw outside might have struck terror into a heart stouter than a helpless woman's at midnight. In the centre of the lowest pane of the window, close to the glass, was a human face which she barely recognised as the face of Fitzpiers. It was surrounded with the darkness of the night without, corpse-like in its pallor, and covered with blood. As disclosed in the square area of the pane it met her frightened eyes like a replica of the Sudarium of St. Veronica.

He moved his lips and looked at her imploringly. Her rapid mind pieced together in an instant a possible concatenation of events which might have led to this tragical issue. She unlatched the casement with a terrified hand, and bending down to where he was crouching pressed her face to his with passionate solicitude. She assisted him into the room without a word, to do which it was almost necessary to lift him bodily.

Quickly closing the window and fastening the shutters she bent over him breathlessly.

"Are you hurt much, much?" she cried faintly. "Oh, Oh, how is this!"

"Rather much—but don't be frightened," he answered in a difficult whisper, and turning himself to obtain an easier position if possible. "A little water, please."

She ran across into the dining-room, and brought a bottle and glass, from which he eagerly drank. He could then speak much better, and with her help got upon the nearest couch.

"Are you dying, Edred?" she said. "Do speak to me!"

"I am half dead," gasped Fitzpiers. "But perhaps I shall get over it. . . . It is chiefly loss of blood."

"But I thought your fall did not hurt you?" said she. "Who did this?"

"Felice—my father-in-law! . . I have crawled to you more than a mile on my hands and knees—God, I thought I should never have got here! . . . . I have come to you—because you are the only friend—I have in the world now. . . . . I can never go back to Hintock—never—to the roof of the Melburys! . . . . Not poppy nor mandragora will ever medicine this bitter feud! . . . If I were only well again——"

"Let me bind your head, now that you have rested."

"Yes—but wait a moment—it stopped bleeding, fortunately, or I should be a dead man before now! While in the wood I managed to make a tourniquet of some halfpence and my handkerchief, as well as I could in the dark. . . . But listen, dear Felice! Can you hide me till I am well? Whatever comes, I can be seen in Hintock no more. My practice is nearly gone you know—and after this I would not care to recover it if I could."

By this time Felice's tears began to blind her. Where were now her discreet plans for sundering their lives for ever? To administer to him in his pain, and trouble, and poverty, was her single thought. The first step was to hide him, and she asked herself where. A place occurred to her mind.

She got him some wine from the dining-room, which strengthened him much. Then she managed to remove his boots, and, as he could now keep himself upright by leaning upon her on one side and a walking-stick on the other, they went thus in slow march out of the room and up the stairs. At the top she took him along a gallery, pausing whenever he required rest, and thence up a smaller staircase to the least used part of the house, where she unlocked a door. Within was a lumber-room, containing abandoned furniture of all descriptions, built up in piles which obscured the light of the windows, and formed between them nooks and lairs in which a person would not be discerned even should an eye gaze in at the door. The articles were mainly those that had belonged to the previous owner of the house, and had been bought in by the late Mr. Charmond at the auction; but changing fashion, and the tastes of a young wife, had caused them to be relegated to this dungeon.

Here Fitzpiers sat on the floor against the wall till she had hauled out materials for a bed, which she spread on the floor in one of the aforesaid nooks. She obtained water and a basin, and washed the dried blood from his face and hands; and when he was comfortably reclining fetched food from the larder. While he ate her eyes lingered anxiously on his face, following its every movement with such lovingkindness as only a fond woman can show.

He was now in better condition, and discussed his position with her.

"What I fancy I said to Melbury must have been enough to enrage any man, if uttered in cold blood, and with knowledge of his presence. But I did not know him, and I was stupefied by what he had given me, so that I hardly was aware of what I said. Well—the veil of that temple is rent in twain! . . . As I am not going to be seen again in Hintock, my first efforts must be directed to allay any alarm that may be felt at my absence, before I am able to get clear away. Nobody must suspect that I have been hurt, or there will be a country talk about me. Felice, I must at once concoct a letter to check all search for me. I think if you can bring me a pen and paper I may be able to do it now. I could rest better if it were done. Poor thing—how I tire her with running up and down!"

She fetched writing-materials and held up the blotting-book as a support to his hand, while he penned a brief note to his nominal wife.

"The animosity shown towards me by your father," he wrote in this coldest of marital epistles, "is such that I cannot return again to a roof which is his, even though it shelters you. A parting is unavoidable, as you are sure to be on his side in this division. I am starting on a journey which will take me a long way from Hintock, and you must not expect to see me there again for some time."

He then gave Grace a few directions bearing upon his professional engagements and other practical matters, concluding without a hint of his destination, or a notion of when she would see him again. He offered to read the note to Felice before he closed it up; but she would not hear or see it: that side of his obligations distressed her beyond endurance. She turned away from Fitzpiers and sobbed bitterly.

"If you can get this posted at a place some miles away," he whispered, exhausted by the effort of writing. "At Sherton Abbas, or Port-Bredy, or still better, Budmouth, it will divert all suspicion from this house as the place of my refuge."

"I will drive to one or other of the places myself—anything to keep it unknown!" she murmured, her voice weighted with vague foreboding, now that the excitement of helping him had passed away.

Fitzpiers told her that there was yet one thing more to be done. "In creeping over the fence on to the lawn," he said, "I made the rail bloody, and it shows rather too plainly on the white paint—I could see it in the dark. At all hazards it should be washed off. Could you do that also, Felice?"

What will not women do on such devoted occasions? Weary as she was she went—all the way down the rambling staircases to the ground floor, then to search for a lantern, which she lighted and hid under her cloak; then for a wet sponge, and next forth into the night. The white railing stared out in the darkness at her approach, and a ray from the enshrouded lantern fell upon the blood—just where he had told her it would be found. She shuddered. It was almost too much to bear in one day—but with a shaking hand she sponged the rail clean, and returned to the house.

The time occupied by these several proceedings was not much less than two hours. When all was done, and she had smoothed his extemporized bed, and kissed him, and placed everything within his reach that she could think of, she took her leave of him and locked him in.

XXXVII

WHEN her husband's letter reached Grace's hands, bearing upon it the postmark of a distant town, it never once crossed her mind that Fitzpiers was lying wounded within a mile or two of her still. She felt relieved that he did not write more bitterly of the quarrel with her father, whatever its nature might have been; but the general frigidity of his communication quenched in her the incipient spark that events had kindled so shortly before.

From this centre of information it was made known in Hintock that the doctor had gone away, and as none but the Melbury household was aware that he did not return on the night of his accident, no excitement manifested itself in the village.

Thus the early days of May passed by. None but the nocturnal birds and animals observed that late one evening, towards the middle of the month, a closely wrapped figure with a crutch under one arm and a stick in his hand, crept out from Hintock House across the lawn to the shelter of the trees, taking thence a slow and laborious walk to the nearest point of the turnpike road. The mysterious personage was so disguised that his own wife would hardly have known him. Felice Charmond was a practised hand at such work, as well she might be; and she had done her utmost in padding and painting Fitzpiers with the old materials of her art in recesses of that lumber-room.

In the highway he was met by a covered carriage which conveyed him to Sherton Abbas, whence he proceeded to the nearest port on the south coast, and immediately crossed the Channel.

But it was known to everybody that three days after this time Mrs. Charmond executed her oft-deferred plan of setting out for a long term of travel and residence on the Continent.

She went off one morning as unostentatiously as could be, and took no maid with her, having, she said, engaged one to meet her at a point further on in her route. After that Hintock House, so frequently deserted, was to be let. Spring had not merged in summer when a clinching rumour, founded on the best of evidence, reached the parish and neighbourhood. Mrs. Charmond and Fitzpiers had been seen together in Baden, in relations which set at rest the question that had agitated the little community ever since the winter.

Melbury had entered the Valley of Humiliation even further than Grace. His spirit seemed broken.

But once a week he mechanically went to market as usual, and here, as he was passing by the conduit one day, his mental condition expressed largely by his gait, he heard his name spoken by a voice formerly familiar. He turned and saw a certain Fred Beaucock—once a promising lawyer's clerk and local dandy, who had been called the cleverest fellow in Sherton, without whose brains the firm of solicitors employing him would be nowhere. But later on Beaucock had fallen into the mire. He was invited out a good deal, sang songs at agricultural meetings and burgesses' dinners; in sum, victualled himself with spirits more frequently than was good for the clever brains or body either. He lost his post, and after an absence spent in trying his powers elsewhere came back to his native town, where, at the time of the foregoing events in Hintock, he gave legal advice for astonishingly small fees— mostly carrying on his profession in public-house settles, in whose recesses he might often have been overheard making country-people's wills for half-a-crown; calling with a learned voice for pen-and-ink and a halfpenny sheet of paper, on which he drew up the testament while resting it in a little space wiped with his hand on the table amid the liquid circles formed by the cups and glasses. An idea implanted early in life is difficult to uproot, and many elderly tradespeople still clung to the notion that Fred Beaucock knew a great deal of law.

It was he who had called Melbury by name. "You look very down, Mr. Melbury—very, if I may say as much," he observed, when the timber-merchant turned. "But I know—I know. A very sad case—very. I was bred to the law, as you are aware, and am professionally no stranger to such matters. Well, Mrs. Fitzpiers has her remedy."

"How—what—a remedy?" said Melbury.

"Under the new law, sir. A new court was established last year, and under the new statute, twenty and twenty-one Vic., Cap. eighty-five, unmarrying is as easy as marrying. No more Acts of Parliament necessary, no longer one law for the rich and another for the poor—but come inside—I was just going to have a nipperkin of rum-hot—I'll explain it all to you."

The intelligence amazed Melbury, who saw little of newspapers. And though he was a severely correct man in his habits, and had no taste for entering a tavern with Fred Beaucock—nay, would have been quite uninfluenced by such a character on any other matter in the world—such fascination lay in the idea of delivering his poor girl from bondage that it deprived him of the critical faculty. He could not resist the ex-lawyer's clerk, and entered the inn.

Here they sat down to the rum, which Melbury paid for as a matter of course, Beaucock leaning back on the settle with a legal gravity that would hardly allow him to be conscious of the spirits before him, which nevertheless disappeared with mysterious quickness.

How much of the exaggerated information on the then new divorce laws imparted by Beaucock to his listener was the result of ignorance, and how much of dupery, was never ascertained. But he related such a plausible story of the ease with which Grace could become a free woman that her father was irradiated with the project, and though he scarcely wetted his lips Melbury never knew how he came out of the inn, or when, or where he mounted his gig to pursue his way homeward. But home he found himself, his brain having all the way seemed to ring sonorously as a gong in the intensity of its stir. Before he had seen Grace, he was accidentally met by Winterborne, who found him as Stephen was beheld by the Council, with a face like the face of an angel.

He relinquished his horse and took Winterborne by the arm to a heap of rendlewood—as barked oak was here called—which lay under a privet-hedge.

"Giles," he said, when they had sat down upon the logs, "there's a new law in the land! Grace can be free quite easily. I only knew it by the merest accident. I might not have found it out for the next ten years. She can get rid of him—d'ye hear—get rid of him. Think of that, my friend Giles!"

He related what he had learnt of the new legal remedy. A subdued tremulousness about the mouth was all the response that Winterborne made; and Melbury added, "My boy—you shall have her yet—if you want her." His feelings had gathered volume as he said this, and the articulate sound of the old idea drowned his sight in mist.

"Are you sure—about this new law?" asked Winterborne, so disquieted by a gigantic exultation which loomed alternately with fearful doubt that he evaded the full acceptance of Melbury's last statement.

Melbury said that he had no manner of doubt, for since his talk with Beaucock it had come into his mind that he had seen some time ago in the weekly paper an allusion to such a legal change; but having no interest in those desperate remedies at the moment he had passed it over. "But I'm not going to let the matter rest doubtful for a single day," he continued. "I am going to London. Beaucock will go with me, and we shall get the best advice as soon as we possibly can. Beaucock is a thorough lawyer—nothing the matter with him but a fiery palate. I knew him as the stay and refuge of Sherton in knots of law at one time."

Winterborne's replies were of the vaguest. The new possibility was almost unthinkable at the moment. He was what was called at Hintock "a solid-going fellow"; he maintained his abeyant mood not from want of reciprocity, but from a taciturn hesitancy taught by life as he knew it.

"But," continued the timber-merchant, a temporary crease or two of anxiety supplementing those already established in his forehead by time; "Grace is not at all well. Nothing constitutional you know; but she has been in a low nervous state ever since that night of fright. I don't doubt but that she will be all right soon. . . . I wonder how she is this evening." He rose with the words as if he had too long forgotten her personality in the excitement of her previsioned career.

They had sat till evening was beginning to dye the garden brown, and now went towards Melbury's house, Giles a few steps in the rear of his old friend, who was stimulated by the enthusiasm of the moment to outstep the more ordinary pace of Winterborne. He felt shy of entering Grace's presence as her reconstituted lover—which was how her father's manner would be sure to present him—before definite information as to her future state was forthcoming; it seemed too nearly like the act of those who rush in where angels fear to tread.

A chill to counterbalance all the glowing promise of the day was prompt enough in coming. No sooner had he followed the timber-merchant in at the door than he heard Grammer inform him that Mrs. Fitzpiers was still more unwell than she had been in the morning. Old Doctor Jones being in the neighbourhood they had called him in, and he had instantly directed them to get her to bed. They were not however to consider her illness serious—a feverish nervous attack, the result of recent events, was what she was suffering from—and she would doubtless be well in a few days.

Winterborne therefore did not remain, and his hope of seeing her that evening was disappointed. Even this aggravation of her morning condition did not greatly depress Melbury. He knew, he said, that his daughter's constitution was sound enough. It was only these domestic troubles that were pulling her down. Once free she would be blooming again. Melbury diagnosed rightly, as parents usually do.

He set out for London the next morning, Jones having paid another visit and assured him that he might leave home without uneasiness, especially on an errand of that sort, which would the sooner put an end to her suspense.

The timber-merchant had been away only a day or two when it was told in Hintock that Mr. Fitzpiers's hat had been found in the wood. Later on in the afternoon the hat was brought to Melbury's, and, by a piece of ill-fortune, into Grace's presence. It had doubtless lain in the wood ever since his fall from the horse, but it looked so clean and uninjured —the summer weather and leafy shelter having much favoured its preservation—that Grace could not believe it had remained so long concealed. A very little fact was enough to set her fevered fancy at work at this juncture; she thought him still in the neighbourhood; she feared his sudden appearance; and her nervous malady developed consequences so grave that Doctor Jones began to look serious, and the household was alarmed.

It was the beginning of June, and the cuckoo at this time of the summer scarcely ceased his cry for more than a couple of hours during the night. The bird's note, so familiar to her ears from infancy, was now absolute torture to the poor girl. On the Friday following the Wednesday of Melbury's departure, and the day after the discovery of Fitzpiers's hat, the cuckoo began at two o'clock in the morning with a sudden cry from one of Melbury's appletrees, not three yards from the window of Grace's room.

"Oh—he is coming!" she cried, and in her terror sprang clean out of the bed upon the floor.

These starts and frights continued till noon; and when the doctor had arrived and had seen her, and had talked with Mrs. Melbury, he sat down and meditated. That ever present terror it was indispensable to remove from her mind at all hazards; and he thought how this might be done.

Without saying a word to anybody in the house, or to the disquieted Winterborne waiting in the lane below, Dr. Jones went home and wrote to Mr. Melbury at the address in London he had obtained from his wife. The gist of his communication was that Mrs. Fitzpiers should be assured as soon as possible that steps were taken to sever the bond which was becoming a torture to her; that she would soon be free; and was even then virtually so. "If you can say it *at once* it may be the means of averting much harm," he said. "Write to herself; not to me."

On Saturday he drove over to Hintock, and assured her with mysterious pacifications that in a day or two she might expect to receive some good news. So it turned out. When Sunday morning came there was a letter for Grace from her father. It arrived at seven o'clock, the usual time at which the toddling postman passed by Hintock; at eight Grace awoke—having slept an hour or two for a wonder, and Mrs. Melbury brought up the letter.

"Can you open it yourself?" said she.

"Oh yes, yes!" said Grace with feeble impatience. She tore the envelope, unfolded the sheet, and read; when a creeping blush tinctured her white neck and cheek.

Her father had exercised a bold discretion. He informed her that she need have no further concern about Fitzpiers's return; that she would shortly be a free woman; and therefore if she should desire to wed her old lover—which he trusted was the case, since it was his own deep wish—she would be in a position to do so. In this Melbury had not written beyond his belief. But he very much stretched the facts in adding that the legal formalities for dissolving her union were practically settled. The truth was that on the arrival of the doctor's letter poor Melbury had been much agitated, and could with difficulty be prevented by Beaucock from returning to her bedside. What was the use of his rushing back to Hintock? Beaucock had asked him. The only thing that could do her any good was a breaking of the bond. Though he had not as yet had an interview with the eminent solicitor they were about to consult he was on the point of seeing him; and the case was clear enough. Thus the simple Melbury, urged by his parental alarm at her danger, by the representations of his companion, and by the doctor's letter, had yielded, and sat down to tell her roundly that she was virtually free.

"And you'd better write also to the gentleman," suggested Beaucock, who scenting fame and the germ of a large practice in the case, wished to commit Melbury to it irretrievably; to effect which he knew that nothing would be so potent as awakening the passion of Grace for Winterborne, so that her father might not have the heart to withdraw from his attempt to make her love legitimate when he discovered that there were difficulties in the way.

The nervous, impatient Melbury was much pleased with the idea of "starting them at once," as he called it. To put his long-delayed reparative scheme in train had become a passion with him now. He added to the letter addressed to his daughter a passage hinting that she ought to begin to encourage Winterborne, lest she should lose him altogether;

and he wrote to Giles that the path was virtually open for him at last. Life was short, he declared; he, her father, was getting old; there were slips betwixt the cup and the lip; her interest in him should be reawakened at once, that all might be ready when the good time came for uniting them.

XXXVIII

At these warm words Winterborne was much moved. The novelty of the avowal rendered what it carried with it inapprehensible by him all at once. Only a few short months ago completely estranged from this family—beholding Grace going to and fro in the distance, clothed with the alienating radiance of obvious superiority, the wife of the then popular and fashionable Fitzpiers, hopelessly outside his social boundary down to so recent a time that flowers then folded were hardly faded yet—he was now asked by that jealously guarding father of hers to take courage; to get himself ready for the day when he should be able to claim her.

The old times came back to him in dim procession. How he had been snubbed; how Melbury had despised his Christmas party; how that sweet, coy Grace herself had looked down upon him, and his household arrangements, and poor Creedle's contrivances!

Well, he could not believe it. Surely the adamantine barrier of marriage with another could not be pierced like this. It did violence to custom. Yet a new law might do anything. But was it at all within the bounds of probability that a woman who, over and above her own attainments, had been accustomed to those of a cultivated professional man, could ever be the wife of such as he?—that the ceorl Giles Winterborne would be able to make such a dainty girl happy now that she stood in a position further removed from his own than at first? He was full of doubt.

Nevertheless it was not in him to show backwardness. To act so promptly as Melbury desired him to act seemed, indeed, scarcely wise, because of the uncertainty of events. Giles knew nothing of legal procedure, but he did know that for him to step up to Grace as a lover before the bond which bound her was actually dissolved was simply an extravagant dream of her father's overstrained mind. He pitied Melbury for his almost childish enthusiasm, and saw that the ageing man must have suffered acutely to be weakened to this unreasoning desire.

Winterborne was far too magnanimous to harbour any cynical conjecture that the timber-merchant, in his intense affection for Grace, was courting him now because that young lady when disunited would be left in an anomalous position to escape which a bad husband was better than none. He felt quite sure that his old friend was simply on tenterhooks of anxiety to repair the almost irreparable error of dividing two whom nature had striven to join together in earlier days, and that in his ardour to do this he was oblivious of formalities. The cautious supervision of his past years had overleapt itself at last. Hence Winterborne perceived that, in this new beginning, the necessary care not to compromise Grace by too early advances must be exercised by himself.

There is no such thing as a stationary love; men are either loving more or loving less; but Giles recognised no decline in his sense of her dearness. He had been labouring ever since his rejection and her marriage to reduce his former passion to a docile friendship, out of pure regard to its expediency; but hitherto he had experienced no great success in his attempt.

A week and more passed, and there was no further news of Melbury. But the effect of the intelligence he had already transmitted upon the elastic-nerved daughter of the woods had been much as the old surgeon Jones had surmised. It had soothed her perturbed spirit better than all the opiates in the pharmacopœia. She had slept unbrokenly a whole night and a day. The "new law" was to her a mysterious, beneficent, godlike entity, lately descended upon earth, that would make her as she once had been without trouble or annoyance. Her position fretted her, its abstract features rousing an aversion which was greater than her aversion to the personality of him who had caused it. It was mortifying, productive of slights, undignified. Him she could forget; her circumstances she had always with her.

She saw nothing of Winterborne during the days of her recovery; and perhaps on that account her fancy wove about him a more romantic tissue than it could have done if he had stood before her with all the specks and flaws inseparable from concrete humanity. He rose upon her memory as the fruit-god and the wood-god in alternation; sometimes leafy, and smeared with green lichen, as she had seen him amongst the sappy boughs of the plantations; sometimes cider-stained and starred with apple-pips, as she had met him on his return from cidermaking in Blackmoor Vale, with his vats and presses beside him. In her secret heart she approximated to her father's enthusiasm in wishing to show Giles once for all how she still regarded him. The question whether the future would indeed bring them together for life was a standing wonder with her. She knew that it could not with any propriety do so just yet. But reverently believing in her father's sound judgment and knowledge, as good girls are wont to do, she remembered what he had written about her giving a hint to Winterborne lest there should be risk in delay, and her feelings were not averse to such a step, so far as it could be done without danger at this early stage of the proceedings.

From being but a frail phantom of her former self she returned in bounds to a condition of passable hopefulness. She bloomed again in the face in the course of a few days, and was well enough to go about as usual. One day Mrs. Melbury proposed that for a change she should be driven in the gig to Sherton market, whither Melbury's man was going on other errands. Grace had no business whatever in Sherton; but it crossed her mind that Winterborne would probably be there, and this made the thought of such a drive interesting.

On the way she saw nothing of him; but when the horse was walking slowly through the obstructions of Sheep Street she discerned the young man on the pavement. She thought of that time when he had been standing under his appletree on her return from school, and of the tender opportunity then missed through her fastidiousness. Her heart rose in her throat. She abjured all fastidiousness now. Nor did she forget the last occasion on which she had beheld him in that town, making cider in the courtyard of the Earl of Wessex hotel, while she was figuring as a fine lady in the balcony above.

Grace directed the man to set her down there in the midst, and immediately went up to her lover. Giles had not before observed her, and his eyes now suppressedly looked his pleasure, without, perhaps, quite so much embarrassment as had formerly marked him at such meetings.

When a few words had been spoken she said invitingly, "I have nothing to do. Perhaps you are deeply engaged?"

"I? Not a bit. My business now at the best of times is small, I am sorry to say."

"Well, then—I am going into the Abbey. Come along with me."

The proposition had suggested itself as a quick escape from publicity, for many eyes were regarding her. She had hoped that sufficient time had elapsed for the extinction of curiosity; but it was quite otherwise. The people looked at her with tender interest as the deserted girl-wife—without obtrusiveness, and without vulgarity; but she was ill-prepared for scrutiny in any shape.

They walked about the Abbey aisles, and presently sat down. Not a soul was in the building save themselves. She regarded a high marble tomb to the last representative of an extinct Earldom, without a thought that it was the family with which Fitzpiers was maternally connected; and with her head sideways tentatively asked her companion if he remembered the last time they were in that town alone.

He remembered it perfectly, and remarked, "You were a proud damsel then, and as dainty as you were high. Perhaps you are now."

Grace slowly shook her head. "Affliction has taken all that out of me," she answered impressively. "Perhaps I am too far the other way now." As there was something lurking in this that she could not explain she added so quickly as not to allow him time to think of it, "Has my father written to you at all?"

"Yes," said Winterborne.

She glanced ponderingly up at him. "Not about me?"

"Yes."

She saw that he had been bidden to take the hint as to the future which she had been bidden to give, and the discovery sent a scarlet pulsation through her for the moment. However it was only Giles who sat there, of whom she had no fear; and her self-possession returned.

"He said I was to sound you with a view to—what you will understand, if you care to," continued Winterborne in a low voice. Having been put on this track by herself he was not disposed to abandon it in a hurry.

They had been children together, and there was between them that familiarity as to personal affairs which only such acquaintanceship can give. "You know, Giles," she answered, speaking in a very practical tone, "that that is all very well; but I am in a very anomalous position at present, and I cannot say anything to the point about such things as those."

"No?" he said, with a stray air as regarded the subject. He was looking at her with a curious consciousness of discovery. He had not been imagining that their renewed intercourse would show her to him thus. For the first time he realized an unexpectedness in her, which after all should not have been unexpected. She before him was not the girl Grace Melbury whom he had used to know. Of course he might easily have prefigured as much; but it had never occurred to him. She was a woman who had been married; she had moved on; and without having lost her girlish modesty she had lost her girlish shyness. The inevitable change, though known to him, had not been heeded; and it struck him into a momentary fixity. The truth was that he had never come into close comradeship with her since her engagement to Fitzpiers, with the brief exception of the evening encounter under High-Stoy Hill, when she met him with his cider apparatus; and that interview had been of too cursory a kind for insight.

Winterborne had advanced, too. Shy though he was he could criticise her somewhat. Times had been when to criticise a single trait in Grace Melbury would have lain as far beyond his powers as to criticise a deity. And this thing was sure as the result of his criticism: it was a new woman in many ways whom he had come out to see; a creature of more ideas, more dignity, and, above all, more assurance, than the original Grace had been capable of. He could not at first decide whether he were pleased or displeased at this. But upon the whole the novelty attracted him.

She was so sweet and sensitive that she feared his silence betokened something in his brain of the nature of an enemy to her. "What are you thinking of that makes those lines come in your forehead?" she asked. "I did not mean to offend you by speaking of the time being premature."

Touched by the genuine lovingkindness which had lain at the foundation of these words, and much moved, Winterborne turned his face aside as he took her by the hand. He was grieved that he had criticised her.

"You are very good, dear Grace," he said in a low voice. "You are better, much better, than you used to be."

"How?"

He could not very well tell her how, and said with an evasive smile, "You are prettier," which was not what he really had meant. He then remained still holding her right hand in his own right, so that they faced in opposite ways; and as he did not let go she ventured upon a tender remonstrance.

"I think we have gone as far as we ought to go at present—and far enough to satisfy my poor father that we are the same as ever. You see Giles, my case is not settled yet, and if. . . . . . Oh, suppose I *never* get free! . . . . . . there should be any hitch or informality——"

She drew a catching breath and turned pale. The duologue had been affectionate comedy up to this point. The gloomy atmosphere of the past, and the still gloomy horizon of the present, had been for the interval forgotten. Now the whole environment came back, the due balance of shade among the light was restored.

"It is sure to be all right, I trust?" she resumed in uneasy accents. "What did my father say the solicitor had told him?"

"Oh—that all is sure enough. The case is so clear—nothing could be clearer. But the legal part is not yet quite done and finished, as is natural."

"Oh no—of course not," she said sunk in meek thought. "But father said it was *almost*—did he not? Do you know anything about the new law that makes these things so easy?"

"Nothing—except the general fact that it enables ill-assorted husbands and wives to part in a way they could not formerly do without an Act of Parliament."

"Have you to sign a paper, or swear anything? Is it something like that?"

"Yes I believe so."

"How long has it been introduced?"

"About six months or a year the lawyer said, I think."

To hear these two Arcadian innocents talk of imperial law would have made a humane person weep who should have known what a dangerous structure they were building up on their supposed knowledge. They remained in thought, like children, in the presence of the incomprehensible.

"Giles," she said at last, "it makes me quite weary when I think how serious my situation is, or has been.—Shall we not go out from here now, as it may seem rather fast of me—our being so long together I mean—if anybody were to see us? . . . I am almost sure," she added uncertainly, "that I ought not to let you hold my hand yet, knowing that the documents—or whatever it may be—have not been signed; so that I am still as married as ever—or almost. My dear father has forgotten himself. Not that I feel morally bound to any one else after what has taken place; no woman of spirit could—now, too, that several months have passed. But I wish to keep the proprieties as well as I can."

"Yes; yes. Still, your father reminds us that life is short. I myself feel that it is; that is why I wished to understand you in this that we have begun. At times, dear Grace, since receiving your father's letter, I am as uneasy and fearful as a child at what he said. If one of us were to die before the formal signing and sealing that is to release you have been done—if we should drop out of the world and never have made the most of this little, short, but real opportunity, I should think to myself as I sank down dying, 'Would to my God that I had spoken out my whole heart—given her one poor little kiss when I had the chance to give it! But I never did, although she had promised to be mine some day; and now I never can.' That's what I should think."

She had begun by watching the words from his lips with a

mournful regard, as though their passage were visible; but as he went on she dropped her glance. "Yes," she said. "I have thought that too. And because I have thought it I by no means meant, in speaking of the proprieties, to be reserved and cold to you who loved me so long ago, or to hurt your heart as I used to do at that thoughtless time. O not at all, indeed! But—ought I to allow you—O it is too quick—surely!" Her eyes filled with tears of bewildered, alarmed emotion.

Winterborne was too straightforward to influence her further against her better judgment. "Yes—I suppose it is," he said repentantly. "I'll wait till all is settled. What has your father said in his letters to you?"

He meant about his progress with the petition, but she, mistaking him, frankly spoke of the personal part. "He says— what I have implied. Should I tell more plainly?"

"O no—don't, if it is a secret."

"Not at all. I will tell every word straight out, Giles, if you wish. He says I am to encourage you. There. But I cannot obey him further to-day. Come, let us go now." She gently slid her hand from his and went in front of him out of the Abbey.

"I was thinking of getting some dinner," said Winterborne, changing to the prosaic as they walked. "And you too must require something. Do let me take you to a place I know?"

Grace was almost without a friend in the world outside her father's house; her life with Fitzpiers had brought her no society; had sometimes indeed brought her deeper solitude than any she had ever known before. Hence it was a treat to her to find herself again the object of thoughtful care. But she questioned if to go publicly to dine alone with Giles Winterborne were not a proposal due rather to his unsophistication than to his prudence. She said gently that she would much prefer his ordering her lunch at some place, and then coming to tell her it was ready while she remained in the Abbey porch. Giles saw her secret reasoning, thought how hopelessly blind to propriety he was beside her, and went to do as she wished.

He was not absent more than ten minutes, and found Grace where he had left her. "It will be quite ready by the time you get there," he said, and told her the name of the inn at which the meal had been ordered, which was one that she had never heard of.

"I'll find it by inquiry," said Grace, setting out.

"And shall I see you again?"

"Oh yes—come to me there. It will not be like going to-gether. I shall want you to find my father's man and the gig for me."

He waited on some ten minutes or a quarter of an hour, till he thought her lunch ended, and that he might fairly take advantage of her invitation to start her on her way home. He went straight to where he had sent her, an old commercial tavern, scrupulously clean, but humble and inexpensive. On his way he had an occasional misgiving as to whether the place had been elegant enough for her; and as soon as he entered it, and saw her ensconced there, he perceived that he had blundered.

Grace was seated in the only dining-room that the simple old hostelry could boast of, which was also a general parlour on market-days—a long low apartment with a sanded floor herring-boned with a broom; a wide red-curtained window to the street, and another to the garden. Grace had retreated to the end of the room looking out upon the latter, the front part being full of a mixed company of dairymen and butchers which had, to be just to him, dropped in since he was there.

She was in a mood of the greatest depression. On arriving and seeing what the tavern was like she had been taken by surprise; but having gone too far to retreat she had heroically entered and sat down on the well-scrubbed settle, opposite the narrow table with its knives and steel forks, tin pepper-boxes, blue salt-cellars, and posters advertising the sale of bullocks against the wall. The last time that she had taken any meal in a public place it had been with Fitzpiers at the dignified Earl of Wessex hotel in that town, after a two months' roaming and sojourning at the gigantic hotels of the Continent. How could she have expected any other kind of accommodation in present circumstances than such as Giles had provided? And yet how unprepared she was for this change! The tastes that she had acquired from Fitzpiers had been imbibed so subtly that she hardly knew she possessed them till confronted by this contrast. The elegant Fitzpiers, in fact, at that very moment owed a long bill at the above-mentioned hotel for the luxurious style in which he used to put her up there whenever they drove to Sherton. But such is social sentiment that she had been quite comfortable under those debt-impending conditions, whilst she felt humiliated by her present situation, which Winterborne had paid for honestly on the nail.

He had noticed in a moment that she shrank from her position, and all his pleasure was gone. It was the same susceptibility over again which had spoiled his Christmas party long ago.

But he did not know that this recrudescence was only the casual result of Grace's apprenticeship to what she was determined to learn in spite of it—a consequence of one of those sudden surprises which confront everybody bent upon turning over a new leaf. She had finished her lunch, which he saw had been a very mincing performance; and he brought her out of the house as soon as he could.

"Now," he said, with great sad eyes, "you have not finished at all well, I know. Come round to the Earl of Wessex. I'll order a tea there. I did not remember that what was good enough for me was not good enough for you."

Her face faded into an aspect of deep distress when she saw what had happened. "Oh no Giles," she said with extreme earnestness: "certainly not. Why do you—say that, when you know better? You *ever* will misunderstand me."

"Indeed that's not so, Mrs. Fitzpiers. Can you deny that you felt out of place at that tavern?"

"I don't know! . . . Well since you make me speak, I do not deny it."

"And yet I have felt at home there these twenty years. Your husband used always to take you to the Earl of Wessex, did he not?"

"Yes," she reluctantly admitted. How could she explain in the street of a market-town that it was her superficial and transitory taste which had been offended, and not her nature or her affection? Fortunately, or unfortunately, at that moment they saw Melbury's man driving vacantly along the street in search of her, the hour having passed at which he had been told to take her up. Winterborne hailed him, and she was powerless then to prolong the discourse. She entered the vehicle sadly, and the horse trotted away.

XXXIX

ALL night did Winterborne think over that unsatisfactory ending of a pleasant time, forgetting the pleasant time itself. He feared anew that they could never be happy together, even should she be free to choose him. She was accomplished: he was unrefined. It was the original difficulty, which he was too thoughtful to recklessly ignore as some men would have done in his place.

He was one of those silent unobtrusive beings who want little from others in the way of favour or condescension, and perhaps on that very account scrutinize those others' behaviour too closely. He was not versatile, but one in whom a hope or belief which had once had its rise, meridian, and decline, seldom again exactly recurred, as in the breasts of more sanguine mortals. He had once worshipped her, laid out his life to suit her, wooed her, and lost her. Though it was with almost the same zest it was with not quite the same hope that he had begun to tread the old tracks again, and had allowed himself to be so charmed with her that day.

Move another step towards her he would not. He would even repulse her—as a tribute to conscience. It would be sheer sin to let her prepare a pitfall for her happiness not much smaller than the first by inveigling her into a union with such as he. Her poor father was now blind to these subtleties, which he had formerly beheld as in noontide light. It was his own duty to declare them—for her dear sake.

Grace too had a very uncomfortable night, and her solicitous embarrassment was not lessened the next morning when another letter from her father was put into her hands. Its tenor was an intenser strain of the one that had preceded it.

After stating how extremely glad he was to hear that she was better, and able to get out of doors, he went on:

"This is a wearisome business, the solicitor we have come to see being out of town. I do not know when I shall get home. My great anxiety in this delay is still lest you should lose Giles Winterborne. I cannot rest at night for thinking that while our business is hanging fire, he may become estranged, or in his shyness go away from the neighbourhood. I have set my heart upon seeing him your husband, if you ever have another. Do then Grace give him some temporary encouragement, even though it is over-early. For when I consider the past I do think God will forgive me and you for being a little forward. I have another reason for this my dear. I feel myself going rapidly down hill, and late affairs have still further helped me that way. And until this thing is done I cannot rest in peace."

He added a postscript:

"I have just heard that the solicitor is to be seen to-morrow. Possibly therefore I shall return in the evening after you get this."

The paternal longing ran on all fours with her own desire; and yet in forwarding it yesterday she had been on the brink of giving offence. While craving to be a country girl again just as her father requested; to put off the old Eve, the fastidious Miss—or rather Madam—completely, her first attempt had been beaten by the unexpected vitality of that fastidiousness. Her father on returning and seeing the trifling coolness of Giles would be sure to say that the same perversity which had led her to make difficulties about marrying Fitzpiers was now prompting her to blow hot and cold with poor Winterborne.

If the latter had been the most subtle hand at touching the stops of her delicate soul instead of one who had just bound himself to let her be mute on all that appertained to his personality, he could not have acted more seductively than he did that day. He chanced to be superintending some temporary work in a field opposite her windows. She could not discover what he was doing, but she read his mood keenly and truly: she could see in his coming and going an air of determined abandonment of the whole prospect that lay in her direction.

O how she longed to make it up with him! Her father coming in the evening—which meant, she supposed, that all formalities would be in train, her marriage virtually annulled, and she be free to be won again—how could she look him in the face if he should see them estranged thus?

It being a fair green afternoon in June she seated herself in the garden, in the rustic chair which stood under the laurel-bushes; made of peeled oak branches that came to Melbury's premises as refuse after barking-time. The mass of full-juiced leafage on the heights around her was just swayed into faint gestures by a nearly spent wind which, even in its enfeebled state, did not reach her shelter. She had expected Giles to call—to inquire how she had got home, or something or other; but he did not come. And he still tantalized her by going athwart and across that orchard opposite. She could see him as she sat.

A slight diversion was presently created by Creedle bringing him a letter. She knew from this that Creedle had just come from Sherton, and had called as usual at the post-office for anything that had arrived by the afternoon post, of which there was no delivery at Hintock. She pondered on what the letter might contain—particularly whether it were a second refresher for Winterborne from her father, like her own of the morning.

But it appeared to have no bearing upon herself whatever. Giles read its contents and almost immediately turned away to a gap in the hedge of the orchard—if that could be called a hedge which, owing to the drippings of the trees, was little more than a bank with a bush upon it here and there. He entered the plantation, and was no doubt going that way homeward to the mysterious hut he occupied on the other side of the woodland.

The sad sands were running swiftly through Time's glass; she had often felt it in these latter days; and, like Giles, she felt it doubly now after the solemn and pathetic reminder in her father's communication. Her freshness would pass, the long-suffering devotion of Giles might suddenly end—might end that very hour. Men were so strange. The thought took away from her all her former reticence and made her action bold. She started from her seat. If the little breach, quarrel, or whatever it might be called, of yesterday, was to be healed up it must be done by her on the instant. She crossed into the orchard and clambered through the gap after Giles, just as he was diminishing to a faun-like figure under the green canopy and over the brown floor.

Grace had been wrong—very far wrong—in assuming that the letter had no reference to herself because Giles had turned away into the wood after its perusal. It was, sad to say, because the missive had so much reference to herself that he had thus turned away. He feared that his grieved discomfiture might be observed. The letter was from Beaucock, written a few hours later than Melbury's to his daughter. It announced failure.

Giles had once done that thriftless man a good turn, and now was the moment when Beaucock had chosen to remember it, in his own way. During his absence in town with Melbury the lawyer's-clerk had naturally heard a great deal of the timber-merchant's family scheme of justice to Giles; and his communication was to inform Winterborne at the earliest possible moment that their attempt had failed, in order that the young man should not place himself in a false position towards Grace in the belief of its coming success. The news was, in sum, that Fitzpiers's conduct had not been sufficiently cruel to Grace to enable her to snap the bond. She was apparently doomed to be his wife till the end of the chapter.

Winterborne quite forgot his superficial differences with the poor girl under the warm rush of deep and distracting love for her which the almost tragical information engendered.

To renounce her for ever—that was then the end of it for him, after all. There was no longer any question about suitability, or room for tiffs on petty tastes. The curtain had fallen again between them. She could not be his. The cruelty of their late revived hope was now terrible. How could they all have been so simple as to suppose this thing could be done!

It was at this moment that, hearing some one coming behind him, he turned and saw her hastening on between the thickets. He perceived in an instant that she did not know the blighting news.

"Giles—why didn't you come across to me?" she asked with arch reproach. "Didn't you see me sitting there ever so long?"

"Oh yes," he said in unprepared provisional tones, for her unexpected presence caught him without the slightest plan of behaviour in the conjuncture. His manner made her think that she had been too chiding in her speech; and a mild scarlet wave passed over her as she resolved to soften it.

"I have had another letter from my father," she hastened to continue. "He thinks he may come home this evening. And—in view of his hopes—it will grieve him if there is any little difference between us, Giles."

"There is none," he said, sadly regarding her from the face downwards as he pondered how to lay the cruel truth bare.

"Still—I fear you have not quite forgiven me about my being uncomfortable at the inn."

"I have, I'm sure."

"But you speak in quite an unhappy way," she returned, coming up quite close to him with the most winning of the many pretty airs that appertained to her. "Don't you think you will ever be happy, Giles?"

He did not reply for some instants. "When the sun shines flat on the north front of Sherton Abbey—that's when my happiness will come to me!" said he, staring as it were into the earth.

"But—then that means that there is something more than my offending you in not liking the Sherton tavern. . . . . If it is because I—did not like to let you kiss me in the Abbey— well, you know, Giles, that it was not on account of my cold feelings, but because I did certainly, just then, think it was rather premature, in spite of my poor father. That was the true reason—the sole one. But I do not want to be hard— God knows I do not," she said, her voice fluctuating. "And perhaps—as I am on the verge of freedom—I am not right, after all, in thinking there is any harm in your kissing me."

"O Heaven!" groaned Winterborne to himself.

His head was turned askance, as he still resolutely regarded the ground. For the last several minutes he had seen this great temptation approaching him in regular siege; and now it had come. The wrong, the social sin, of now taking advantage of the offer of her lips, had a magnitude, in the eyes of one whose life had been so primitive, so ruled by household laws as Giles's, which can hardly be explained.

"Did you say anything?" she asked timidly.

"O no—only that. . . . ."

"You mean that it must be settled, since my father is coming home?" she said gladly.

"Ah—yes."

"Then why don't you do what you want to?" She was almost pouting at his hesitation.

Winterborne, though fighting valiantly against himself all this while—though he would have protected Grace's good repute as the apple of his eye, was a man; and, as Desdemona said, men are not gods. In face of the agonizing seductiveness shown by her, in her unenlightened school-girl simplicity about the laws and ordinances, he betrayed a man's weakness. Since it was so—since it had come to this, that Grace, deeming herself free to do it, was virtually asking him to demonstrate that he loved her—since he could demonstrate it only too truly—since life was short and love was strong—he gave way to the temptation, notwithstanding that he perfectly well knew her to be wedded irrevocably to Fitzpiers. Indeed he cared for nothing past or future, simply accepting the present and what it brought, deciding once in his life to clasp in his arms her he had watched over and loved so long.

She looked up suddenly from his long embrace and passionate kiss, influenced by a sort of inspiration. "O—I suppose," she stammered, "that I am really free?—that this is right? Is there *really* a new law? Father cannot have been too sanguine in saying——"

He did not answer, and a moment afterwards Grace burst into tears in spite of herself. "Oh, why does not my father come home and explain," she sobbed upon his breast, "and let me know clearly what I am! It is too trying, this, to ask me to—and then to leave me so long in so vague a state that I do not know what to do, and perhaps do wrong!"

Winterborne felt like a very Cain, over and above his previous sorrow. How he had sinned against her in not telling her himself only knew. He lifted her up and turned aside;

the feeling of his cruelty mounted higher and higher. How could he have dreamt of kissing her? He could hardly refrain from tears. Surely nothing more pitiable had ever been known than the condition of this poor young thing, now as heretofore the victim of her father's well-meant but blundering policy.

Even in the hour of Melbury's greatest assurance Winterborne had harboured a suspicion that no law, new or old, could undo Grace's marriage without her appearance in public; though he was not sufficiently sure of what might have been enacted to destroy by his own words her pleasing idea that a mere dash of the pen, on her father's testimony, was going to be sufficient. But he had never suspected the sad fact that the position was irremediable.

Poor Grace, perhaps feeling that she had indulged in too much fluster for a mere embrace, even though it had been prolonged an unconscionable time, calmed herself at finding how grave he was. "I am glad we are friends again, anyhow," she said smiling through her tears. "Giles, if you had only shown half the boldness before I married that you show now you would have carried me off for your own first instead of second. If we do marry I hope you will never think badly of me for encouraging you a little, but my father is *so* impatient, you know, as his years and infirmities increase, that he will wish to see us a little advanced when he comes. That is my only excuse."

To Winterborne all this was sadder than it was sweet. How could she so trust her father's conjectures! He did not know how to tell her the truth, and shame himself. And yet he felt that it must be done.

To hasten the revelation, however, was beyond even him. The endearments that had been begun between them were repeated as they walked, and the afternoon was far advanced before he could actually set about opening her eyes.

"We may have been wrong," he began, almost fearfully, "in supposing that it can all be carried out whilst we stay here at Hintock. I am not sure but that people may have to appear in a public court even under the new Act; and if there should be any difficulty and we cannot marry after all——"

Her cheeks became slowly bloodless. "O Giles," she said grasping his arm, "you have heard something! What—cannot my father conclude it there and now? Surely he has done it? O Giles, Giles, don't deceive me. After letting you go on like this—what terrible position am I in?"

He could not tell her, try as he would. The sense of her implicit trust in his honour disabled him. "I cannot inform you," he murmured, his voice as husky as that of the leaves under foot. "Your father will soon be here. Then we shall know. I will take you home."

Inexpressibly dear as she was to him he offered her his arm with the most reserved air as he added correctingly, "I will take you at any rate into the drive."

Thus they walked on together, Grace vibrating between happiness and misgiving. It was only a few minutes' walk to where the drive ran, and they had hardly descended into it when they heard a voice behind them cry, "Take out that arm!"

For a moment they did not heed, and the voice repeated more loudly and hoarsely,

"Take out that arm!"

It was Melbury's. He had returned sooner than they expected and now came up to them. Grace's hand had been withdrawn like lightning on her hearing the second command. "I don't blame you, I don't blame you," he said, in the weary cadence of one broken down with scourgings. "But you two must walk together no more. . . . . I have been surprised—I have been cruelly deceived. . . . . Giles, don't say anything to me; but go away!"

He was evidently not aware that Winterborne had known the truth before he brought it; and Giles would not stay to discuss it with him then. When the younger man had gone Melbury took his daughter indoors to the room he used as his office. There he sat down and bent over the slope of the bureau, her bewildered gaze fixed upon him.

When Melbury had recovered a little he said, "You are now as ever Fitzpiers's wife. I was deluded. He has not done you *enough* harm. You are still subject to his beck and call."

"Then let it be, and never mind, Father," she said with

dignified sorrow. "I can bear it. It is your trouble that grieves
me most." She stooped over him, and put her arm round his
neck, which distressed Melbury still more. "I don't mind at
all what comes to me," Grace continued; "whose wife I am,
or whose I am not. I do love Giles; I cannot help that; and
I have gone farther with him than I should have done if I
had known exactly how things were. But I do not reproach
you."

"Then Giles did not tell you?" said Melbury.

"No," said she. "He could not have known it. His behaviour to me proved that he did not know."

Her father said nothing more, and Grace went away to the
solitude of her chamber.

Her heavy disquietude had many shapes; and for a time
she put aside the dominant fact to think of her too free
conduct towards Giles. His love-making had been brief as it
was sweet; but would he on reflection contemn her for forwardness? How could she have been so simple as to suppose
she was in a position to behave as she had done! Thus she
mentally blamed her ignorance; and yet in the centre of her
heart she blessed it a little for what it had momentarily
brought her.

XL

LIFE among the people involved in these events seemed to
be suppressed and hide-bound for a while. Grace seldom
showed herself outside the house, never outside the garden;
for she feared she might encounter Giles Winterborne; and
that she could not bear.

This pensive intramural existence of the self-constituted
nun appeared likely to continue for an indefinite time. She
had learnt that there was one possibility in which her formerly imagined position might become real, and only one;
that her husband's absence should continue long enough
to amount to positive desertion. But she never allowed her
mind to dwell much upon the thought; still less did she deliberately hope for such a result. Her regard for Winterborne

had been rarefied by the shock which followed its avowal into an ethereal emotion that had little to do with living and doing.

As for Giles he was lying—or rather sitting—ill at his distant hut. A feverish indisposition which had been hanging about him for some time, the result of a chill caught the previous winter, seemed to acquire virulence with the prostration of his hopes. But not a soul knew of his languor, and he did not think the case serious enough to send for a medical man. After a few days he was better again, and crept about his home in a great-coat, attending to his simple wants as usual with his own hands.

So matters stood when the inertion of Grace's pool-like existence was disturbed as by a geyser. She received a letter from Fitzpiers.

A startling letter it was in its import, though couched in the gentlest language. In his absence Grace had grown to regard him with toleration, and her relation to him with equanimity; till she had almost forgotten how trying his presence would be. He wrote briefly and unaffectedly; he made no excuses, but informed her that he was living quite alone, and had been led to think that they ought to be together, if she would make up her mind to forgive him. He therefore purported to cross the Channel to Budmouth by the steamer on a day he named, which she found to be three days after the time of her present reading.

He said that he could not come to Hintock for obvious reasons, which her father would understand even better than herself. As the only alternative she was to be on the quay to meet the steamer when it arrived from the opposite coast, probably about half an hour before midnight, bringing with her any luggage she might require; join him there, and pass with him into the twin-vessel, which left immediately the other entered the harbour; returning thus with him to his Continental dwelling-place, which he did not name. He had no intention of showing himself on land at all.

The troubled Grace took the letter to her father, who now continued for long hours by the fireless summer chimney-corner as if he thought it were winter, the pitcher of cider standing beside him, mostly untasted, and coated with a film of dust. After reading it he looked up.

"You shan't go," said he.

"I had felt I would not," she answered. "But I did not know what you would say."

"If he comes and lives in England, not too near here, and in a respectable way, and wants you to come to him, I am not sure that I'll oppose him in wishing it," muttered Melbury. "I'd stint myself to keep you both in a genteel and seemly style. But go abroad you never shall with my consent."

There the question rested that day. Grace was unable to reply to her husband in the absence of an address, and the morrow came, and the next day, and the evening on which he had requested her to meet him. Throughout the whole of it she remained within the four walls of her room.

The sense of her harassment, carking doubt of what might be impending, hung like a cowl of blackness over the Melbury household. They spoke almost in whispers, and wondered what Fitzpiers would do next. It was the hope of everyone that, finding she did not arrive, he would return again to France; and as for Grace, she was willing to write to him on the most kindly terms if he would only keep away.

The night passed, Grace lying tense and wide awake, and her relatives in great part likewise. When they met the next morning they were pale and anxious, though neither speaking of the subject which occupied all their thoughts. The day passed as quietly as the previous ones; and she began to think that in the rank caprice of his moods he had abandoned the idea of getting her to join him as quickly as it was formed. All on a sudden some person who had just come from Casterbridge entered the house with the news that Mr. Fitzpiers was on his way home to Hintock. He had been seen hiring a carriage at the King's Arms hotel.

Her father and Grace were both present when the intelligence was announced. "Now," said Melbury, "we must make the best of what has been a very bad matter. The man is repenting: the partner of his folly, I hear, is gone away from him to Switzerland; so that chapter of his life is probably over. If he chooses to make a home for 'ee I think you should not say him nay, Grace. Certainly, he cannot very well live at Hintock without a blow to his pride; but if he can bear that, and likes Hintock best—why, there's the empty wing of the house as it was before."

"O father!" said Grace, turning white with dismay.

"Why not?" said he, a little of his former doggedness returning. He was, in truth, disposed to somewhat more leniency towards her husband just now than he had shown formerly, from a conviction that he had treated him over roughly in his anger. "Surely it is the most respectable thing to do?" he continued. "I don't like this state that you are in—neither married nor single. It hurts me, and it hurts you, and it will always be remembered against us in Hintock. There has never been any scandal like it in the Melbury family before."

"He will be here in less than an hour," murmured Grace. The twilight of the room prevented her father seeing the despondent misery of her face. The one intolerable condition, the condition she had deprecated above all others, was that of Fitzpiers's reinstatement there. "O I won't, I won't see him," she said sinking down. She was almost hysterical.

"Try if you cannot," he returned moodily.

"O yes, I will, I will," she went on inconsequently, "I'll try"; and jumping up suddenly she left the room.

In the darkness of the apartment to which she flew nothing could have been seen during the next half hour; but from a corner a quick breathing was audible from this impressionable creature, who combined modern nerves with primitive feelings, and was doomed by such co-existence to be numbered among the distressed, and to take her scourgings to their exquisite extremity.

The window was open. On this quiet late-summer evening whatever sound arose in so secluded a district—the chirp of a bird, a call from a voice, the turning of a wheel—extended over bush and tree to unwonted distances. Very few sounds did arise. But as Grace invisibly breathed in the brown glooms of the chamber the small remote noise of light wheels came to her, accompanied by the trot of a horse on the turnpike-road. There seemed to be a sudden hitch or pause in the progress of the vehicle, which was what first drew her attention to it. She knew the point whence the sound proceeded—the upper ground down which travellers came on their way hitherward from the south—the place at which she had emerged from the wood with Mrs. Charmond. Grace slid along the floor and bent her head over the window-sill, listening with open lips. The carriage had stopped, and she heard a man use exclamatory words. Then another said, "What the devil is the matter with the horse?" She recognised the voice as her husband's.

The accident, such as it had been, was soon remedied, and the carriage could be heard resuming its descent, soon to turn into the lane leading out of the high-way, and then into the "drong" which led to the house where she was.

A spasm passed through Grace. The Daphnean instinct, exceptionally strong in her as a girl, had been revived by her widowed seclusion; and it was not lessened by her affronted sentiments towards the comer, and her regard for another man. She opened some little ivory tablets that lay on the dressing-table, scribbled in pencil on one of them, "I am gone to visit one of my school friends," gathered a few toilet necessaries into a hand-bag; and, not three minutes after that voice had been heard, her slim form, hastily wrapped up from observation, might have been seen passing out of the back door of Melbury's house. Thence she skimmed up the garden-path, through the gap in the hedge, and into the mossy cart-track under the trees which led into the depth of the woods.

The leaves overhead were now in their latter green—so opaque that it was darker at some of the densest spots than in winter-time, scarce a crevice existing by which a ray could get down to the ground. But in open places she could see well enough. Summer was ending; in the daytime singing insects hung in every sunbeam; vegetation was heavy nightly with globes of dew; and after showers creeping damps and twilight chills came up from the hollows. The plantations were always weird at this hour of eve—more spectral far than in the leafless season, when there were fewer masses and more minute lineality. The smooth surfaces of glossy plants came out like weak lidless eyes; there were strange faces and figures from expiring lights that had somehow wandered into the canopied obscurity; while now and then low peeps of the sky between the trunks were like sheeted shapes, and on the tips of boughs sat faint cloven tongues.

But Grace's fear just now was not imaginative or spiritual; and she heeded these impressions but little. She went on as silently as she could, avoiding the hollows wherein leaves had accumulated, and stepping upon soundless moss and grass-tufts. She paused breathlessly once or twice, and fancied that she could hear, above the sound of her strumming pulse, the vehicle containing Fitzpiers turning in at the gate of her father's premises. She hastened on again.

The Hintock woods owned by Mrs. Charmond were presently left behind, and those into which she next plunged were divided from the latter by a highway. It was with some caution that Grace now walked, though she was quite free from any of the commonplace timidities of her ordinary pilgrimages to such spots. She feared no lurking harms, but that her effort would be all in vain, and her return to the house rendered imperative.

She had walked three or four miles westward when that prescriptive comfort and relief to wanderers in woods—a distant light—broke at last upon her searching eyes. It was so very small as to be almost sinister to a stranger, but to her it was what she sought. She pushed forward and the dim outline of a dwelling was disclosed. It was the place she sought.

The house was a square cot of one storey only, sloping up on all sides to a chimney in the midst. It had formerly been the home of a charcoal-burner, in times when that fuel was still used in the county-houses. Its only appurtenance was a paled enclosure, there being no garden, the shade of the trees preventing the growth of vegetables. She advanced to the window whence the rays of light proceeded, and the shutters being as yet unclosed she could survey the whole interior through the panes.

The room within was kitchen, parlour, and bed-chamber all in one: the natural sandstone floor was worn into hills and dales by long treading, so that none of the furniture stood level, and the table slanted like a desk. A fire burnt on the hearth, in front of which revolved the skinned carcase of a very small rabbit, suspended by a string from a nail. Leaning with one arm on the mantel-shelf stood Winterborne, his eyes on the roasting animal, his face so rapt that speculation could build nothing on it concerning his thoughts, more than that they were not with the scene before him. She thought his features had changed a little since she saw them last. The firelight did not enable her to perceive that they were positively haggard.

Grace's throat emitted a gasp of relief at finding the result so nearly as she had hoped. She went to the door and tapped lightly.

He seemed to be accustomed to the noises of woodpeckers, squirrels, and such small creatures, for he took no notice of her tiny signal; and she knocked again. This time he came and opened the door. When the light of the room fell upon her face he started; and, hardly knowing what he did, crossed the threshold to her, placing his hands upon her two arms; while surprise, joy, alarm, sadness, chased through him by turns. With Grace it was the same: even in this stress there was the fond fact that they had met again. Thus they stood:

> Long tears upon their faces, waxen white
> With extreme sad delight,

till he broke the silence by saying in a whisper, "Come in."

"No no, Giles," she answered, hurriedly stepping yet further back from the door. "I am passing by—and I have called on you—I won't enter. Will you help me? I am afraid. I want to get by a roundabout way to Ivell, and so to Exonbury. I have a schoolfellow there—but I cannot get to Ivell alone. O if you will only accompany me a little way! Don't condemn me Giles, and be offended! I was obliged to come to you because—I have no other help here. Three months ago you were my lover: now you are only my friend. The law has stepped in and forbidden what we thought of. It must not be. But we can act honestly, and yet you can be my friend for one little hour? I have no other——"

She could get no further. Covering her eyes with one hand,

by an effort of repression she wept silent tears without a sigh
or sob. Winterborne took her other hand in both his. "What
has happened?" he said.

"He has come."

There was a stillness as of death, till Winterborne asked,
"You mean this, Grace—that I am to help you to get away?"

"Yes," said she. "Appearance is no matter, when the reality
is right. I have said to myself I can trust you."

Giles knew from this that she did not suspect his treachery—if it could be called such—earlier in the summer, when
they met for the last time as lovers; and in the intensity of his
contrition for that tender wrong he determined to deserve her
faith now at least, and so wipe out that reproach from his
conscience. "I'll come at once," he said. "I'll light a lantern."

He unhooked a dark lantern from a nail under the eaves,
and she did not notice how his hand shook with the slight
strain, or dream that in making this offer he was taxing a
convalescence which could ill-afford such self-sacrifice. The
lantern was lit and they started.

XLI

The first hundred yards of their course lay under motionless
trees, whose upper foliage began to hiss with falling drops of
rain. By the time that they emerged upon a glade it rained
heavily.

"This is awkward," said Grace, with a forced little laugh to
hide her concern.

Winterborne stopped. "Gracie," he said, preserving a strictly
business manner which belied him; "you cannot go to Ivell
to-night."

"But I must!"

"Why? It is seven or eight miles from here. It is almost an
impossibility in this rain."

"True—*why*," she replied mournfully at the end of a silence. "What is reputation to me?"

"Now hearken," said Giles. "You won't—go back to your——"

"No, no, no! Don't make me!" she cried piteously.

"Then let us turn." They slowly retraced their steps, and again stood before his door. "Now this house from this moment is yours, and not mine," he said deliberately. "I have a place near by where I can stay very well."

Her face had dropped. "Oh," she murmured as she saw the dilemma. "What have I done!"

There was a smell of something burning within, and he looked through the window. The young rabbit that he had been cooking to coax a weak appetite was beginning to char. "Please go in and attend to it," he said. "Do what you like. Now I leave. You will find everything about the hut that is necessary."

"But Giles—your supper," she exclaimed. "An outhouse would do for me—anything—till to-morrow at daybreak!"

He signified a negative. "I tell you to go in—you may catch agues out here in your weakly state. You can give me my supper through the window, if you feel well enough. I'll wait a while."

He gently urged her to pass the doorway, and was relieved when he saw her within sitting down on his bed. Without so much as crossing the threshold himself he closed the door upon her, and turned the key in the lock. Tapping at the window he signified that she should open the casement, and when she had done this he handed in the key to her.

"You are locked in," he said; "and your own mistress."

Even in her trouble she could not refrain from a faint smile at his scrupulousness, as she took the door-key.

"Do you feel better?" he went on. "If so, and you wish to give me some of your supper, please do. If not it is of no importance. I can get some elsewhere."

The grateful sense of his kindness stirred her to action, though she only knew half what that kindness really was. At the end of some ten minutes she again came to the window, pushed it open, and said in a whisper "Giles!" He at once emerged from the shade, and saw that she was preparing to hand him his share of the meal upon a plate.

"I don't like to treat you so hardly," she murmured with deep regret in her words as she heard the rain pattering on the leaves. "But—I suppose it is best to arrange like this?"

"O yes," he said quickly.

"I feel that I could never have reached Ivell."

"It was impossible."

"Are you sure you have a snug place out there?" (with renewed misgiving.)

"Quite. Have you found everything you want? I am afraid it is rather rough accommodation."

"Can I notice defects? I have long passed that stage, and you know it, Giles, or you ought to."

His eyes contemplated her face as its responsiveness modulated through a crowd of expressions that showed only too clearly to what a pitch she was strung. If ever Winterborne's heart chafed his bosom it was at this sight of a perfectly defenceless creature conditioned by such harsh circumstances. He forgot his own agony in the satisfaction of having at least found her a shelter. He took his plate and cup from her hands, saying, "Now I'll push the shutter to, and you will find an iron pin on the inside, which you must fix into the bolt. Do not stir in the morning till I come and call you."

She expressed an alarmed hope that he would not go very far away.

"O no—I shall be quite within hail," said Winterborne.

She bolted the window as directed, and he retreated. His snug place without the hut proved to be a wretched little shelter of the roughest kind, formed of four hurdles thatched with brake-fern. Underneath were dry sacks, hay, and other litter of the sort, upon which he sat down; and there in the dark tried to eat his meal. But his appetite was quite gone.

He pushed the plate aside, and shook up the hay and sacks, so as to form a rude couch, on which he flung himself down to sleep, for it was getting late.

But sleep he could not for many reasons, of which not the least was thought of his charge. He sat up, and looked towards the cot through the damp obscurity. With all its external features the same as usual he could scarcely believe that it contained the dear friend—he would not use a warmer name—who had come to him so unexpectedly and, he could not help admitting, so rashly.

He had not ventured to ask her any particulars; but the

position was pretty clear without them. Though social law had negatived for ever their opening paradise of the previous June, it was not without stoical pride that he accepted the present trying conjuncture. There was one man on earth in whom she believed absolutely, and he was that man. That this crisis could end in nothing but sorrow was a view for a moment effaced by his triumphant thought of her trust in him; and the purity of the affection with which he responded to that trust rendered him more than proof against any frailty that besieged him in relation to her.

The rain, which had never ceased, now drew his attention by beginning to drop through the meagre screen that covered him. He rose to attempt some remedy for this discomfort, but the trembling of his knees and the throbbing of his pulse told him that in his weakness he was unable to fence against the storm, and he lay down to bear it as best he might. He was angry with himself for his feebleness—he who had been so strong. It was imperative that she should know nothing of his present state, and to do that she must not see his face by daylight, for its thinness would inevitably betray him.

The next morning accordingly, when it was hardly light, he rose and dragged his stiff limbs about the precincts, preparing for her everything she could require for getting breakfast within. On the bench outside the window-sill he placed water, wood, and other necessaries, writing with a piece of chalk beside them, "It is best that I should not see you. Put my breakfast on the bench."

At seven o'clock he tapped at her window as he had promised, retreating at once that she might not catch sight of him. But from his shelter under the boughs he could see her very well, when, in response to his signal, she opened the window and the light fell upon her face. The languid largeness of her eyes showed that her sleep had been little more than his own, and the pinkness of their lids that her waking hours had not been free from tears.

She read the writing, seemed, he thought, disappointed, but took up the materials he had provided, evidently thinking him some way off. Giles waited on, assured that a girl who, in spite of her culture, knew what country life was, would find no difficulty in the simple preparation of their food.

Within the cot it was all very much as he conjectured, though Grace had slept much longer than he. After the loneliness of the night she would have been glad to see him, but appreciating his feeling when she read the request she made no attempt to recall him. She found abundance of provisions laid in, his plan being to replenish his buttery weekly, and this being the day after the victualling-van had called from Ivell. When the meal was ready she put what he required outside, as she had done with the supper, and notwithstanding her longing to see him, withdrew from the window promptly, and left him to himself.

It had been a leaden dawn, and the rain now steadily renewed its fall. As she heard no more of Winterborne she concluded that he had gone away to his daily work and forgotten that he had promised to accompany her to Ivell—an erroneous conclusion, for he remained all day by force of his condition within fifty yards of where she was. The morning wore on, and in her doubt when to start, and how to travel, she lingered yet, keeping the door carefully bolted lest an intruder should discover her. Locked in this place she was comparatively safe at any rate, and doubted if she would be safe elsewhere.

The humid gloom of an ordinary wet day was doubled by the shade and drip of the leafage. Autumn this year was coming in with rains. Gazing in her enforced idleness from the one window of the single room, she could see various small members of the animal community that lived unmolested there—creatures of hair, fluff, and scale; the toothed kind and the billed kind; underground creatures jointed and ringed—circumambulating the hut under the impression that Giles having gone away, nobody was there; and eyeing it inquisitively with a view to winter quarters. Watching these neighbours who knew neither law nor sin distracted her a little from her trouble; and she managed to while away some portion of the afternoon by putting Giles's home in order, and making little improvements which she deemed that he would value when she was gone.

Once or twice she fancied that she heard a faint noise amid the trees resembling a cough; but as it never came any nearer she concluded that it was a squirrel or a bird.

At last the daylight lessened and she made up a larger fire, for the evenings were chilly. As soon as it was too dark—which was comparatively early—to discern the human countenance in this place of shadows there came to the window, to her great delight, a tapping which she knew from its method to be Giles's.

She opened the casement instantly, and put out her hand to him, though she could only just perceive his outline. He clasped her fingers, and she noticed the heat of his palm, and its shakiness.

"He has been walking fast in order to get here quickly," she thought. How could she know that he had just crawled out from the straw of the shelter hard by; and that the heat of his hand was feverishness?

"My dear good Giles!" she burst out impulsively.

"Anybody would have done it for you," replied Winterborne, with as much matter-of-fact as he could summon.

"About my getting to Ivell and Exonbury?" she said.

"I have been thinking," responded Giles with tender deference, "that you had better stay where you are for the present, if you wish not to be caught. I need not tell you that the place is yours as long as you like; and perhaps in a day or two, finding you absent, he will go away. At any rate in two or three days I could do anything to assist—such as make inquiries, or go a great way towards Ivell with you; for the cider-season will soon be coming on, and I want to run down that way to see how the crops are. But for a day or two I am busy here." (He was hoping that by the time mentioned he would be strong enough to engage himself actively on her behalf.) "I hope you do not feel over-much melancholy in being a prisoner?"

She declared that she did not mind it; but she sighed.

From long acquaintance they could read each other's heart-symptoms like books of large type. "I fear you are sorry you came," said Giles, "and that you think I should have advised you more firmly than I did not to stay."

"O no, dear dear friend," answered Grace, with a heaving bosom. "Don't think that that is what I regret. What I regret is my enforced treatment of you—dislodging you, excluding you from your own house. Why should I not speak out? You know what I feel for you—what I have felt for no other living man, what I shall never feel for a man again! But as I have vowed myself to somebody else than you, and cannot be released, I must behave as I do behave, and keep that vow. I am not bound to him by any divine law, after what he has done; but I have promised, and I will pay."

The rest of the evening was passed in his handing her such things as she would require the next day, and casual remarks thereupon, an occupation which diverted her mind to some degree from pathetic views of her attitude towards him and of her life in general. The only infringement—if infringement it could be called—of his predetermined bearing towards her was an involuntary pressing of her hand to his lips when she put it through the casement to bid him good-night. He knew she was weeping, though he could not see her tears.

She again entreated his forgiveness for so selfishly appropriating the cottage. But it would only be for a day or two more, she thought, since go she must.

He yearningly replied. "I—I don't like you to go away!"

"O Giles," said she, "I know—I know! But—I am a woman, and you are a man. I cannot speak more plainly. I yearn to let you in, but—you know what is in my mind, because you know me so well."

"Yes Gracie, yes. I do not at all mean that the question between us has not been settled by your marriage turning out hopelessly unalterable. I merely meant—well, a feeling— no more."

"In a week, at the outside, I should be discovered if I stayed here; and I think that by law he could compel me to return to him."

"Yes. Perhaps you are right. Go when you wish, dear Grace."

His last words that evening were a hopeful remark that all might be well with her yet; that Mr. Fitzpiers would not intrude upon her life, if he found that his presence cost her so much pain. Then the window was closed, the shutters folded, and the rustle of his footsteps died away.

No sooner had she retired to rest that night than the wind began to rise, and after a few prefatory blasts to be accompanied by rain. The wind grew more violent, and as the storm went on it was difficult to believe that no opaque body, but only an invisible colourless thing was trampling and climbing over the roof, making branches creak, springing out of the trees upon the chimney, popping its head into the flue; and shrieking and blaspheming at every corner of the walls. As in the grisly story, the assailant was a spectre which could be felt but not seen. She had never before been so struck with the devilry of a gusty night in a wood, because she had never been so entirely alone in spirit as she was now. She seemed almost to be apart from herself—a vacuous duplicate only. The recent self of physical animation and clear intentions was not there.

Sometimes a bough from an adjoining tree was swayed so low as to smite the roof in the manner of a gigantic hand smiting the mouth of an adversary, to be followed by a trickle of rain, as blood from the wound. To all this weather Giles must be more or less exposed; how much she did not know.

At last Grace could hardly endure the idea of such a hardship in relation to him. Whatever he was suffering it was she who had caused it; he had vacated his single-roomed hut on account of her. She was not worth such self-sacrifice; she should not have accepted it of him. And then, as her anxiety increased with increasing thought, there returned upon her mind some incidents of her late intercourse with him, which she had heeded but little at the time. The look of his face— what had there been about his face which seemed different from its appearance of yore? Was it not thinner, less rich in hue, less like that of ripe Autumn's brother to whom she had formerly compared him? And his voice; she had distinctly noticed a change in tone. And his gait; surely it had been feebler, stiffer, more like the gait of a weary man. That slight occasional noise she had heard in the day, and attributed to squirrels; it might have been his cough after all.

Thus conviction took root in her perturbed mind that

Winterborne was unwell, or had been so, and that he had carefully concealed his condition from her that she might have no scruples about accepting a hospitality which by the nature of the case expelled her entertainer.

"My own own, true love—my dear kind friend!" she cried to herself. "O it shall not be—it shall not be!"

She hastily got out of bed, obtained a light, and partially dressed herself; and taking the key went at once to the door, which was close at hand, the cot possessing only one floor. Before turning the key in the lock she paused, her fingers still clutching it; and pressing her other hand to her forehead she fell into agitating thought.

A tattoo on the window, caused by the tree-droppings blowing against it, brought her indecision to a close. She turned the key, and opened the door.

The darkness was intense, seeming to touch her pupils like a substance. She only now became aware how heavy the rainfall had been and was; the dripping of the eaves splashed like a fountain. She stood listening with parted lips, and holding the door in one hand, till her eyes growing accustomed to the obscurity she discerned the wild brandishing of their arms by the adjoining trees. At last she cried loudly, with an effort, "Giles! You must come in!"

There was no answer to her cry, and, overpowered by her own temerity, Grace retreated quickly, shut the door, and stood looking on the floor with flushed cheeks. Perhaps he was very well after all. But this mood was not for long. She again lifted the latch, and with far more determination than at first.

"Giles, Giles!" she cried with the full strength of her voice, and without any of the shamefacedness that had characterized her first cry; "O come in—come in! Where are you? . . . . . I have been wicked. I have thought too much of myself. . . . . Do you hear? I don't want to keep you out any longer—I cannot bear that you should suffer so. . . . . I want you here! Gi-i-iles!"

A reply?—it was a reply! Through the darkness and wind a feeble voice reached her, floating upon the weather as though a part of it.

"Here I am—all right! Don't trouble about me."

"Don't you want to come in? Are you not wet? *Come to me, dearest! I don't mind what they say, or what they think of us any more.*"

"I am all right," he repeated. "It is not necessary for me to come. Good night, good night!"

Grace sighed, turned and shut the door slowly. Could she have shocked him by her impulsive words? Perhaps, after all, she had perceived a change in him because she had not seen him for so long. Time sometimes did his ageing work in jerks, as she knew. Well, she had done all she could. He would not come in. She retired to rest again.

XLII

THE next morning Grace was at the window early. She felt determined to see him somehow that day, and prepared his breakfast eagerly. Eight o'clock struck, and she then remembered that he had not come to arouse her by a knocking as usual, her own anxiety having caused her to stir.

His breakfast was set in its place without. But he did not appear to take it; and she waited on. Nine o'clock arrived, and the breakfast was cold; and still there was no Giles. A thrush who had been repeating himself a good deal on an opposite bush for some time, came and took a morsel from the plate, bolted it, waited, looked around, and took another. At ten o'clock she drew in the tray and sat down to her own solitary meal. He must have been called away on business early, the rain having cleared off.

Yet she would have liked to assure herself by thoroughly exploring the precincts of the hut, that he was nowhere in its vicinity; but as the day was comparatively fine the dread lest some stray passenger or woodman should encounter her in such a reconnoitre paralyzed her wish. The solitude was further accentuated to-day by the stopping of the clock for want of winding, and the fall into the chimney-corner of flakes of soot loosened by the rains. At noon she heard a slight rustling outside the window, and found that it was

caused by an eft which had crept out of the leaves to bask in
the last sun-rays that would be worth having till the following
May.

She continually peeped out through the lattice, but could
see little. In front lay the brown leaves of last year, and upon
them some yellowish-green ones of this season, that had been
prematurely blown down by the gale. Above stretched an old
beech, with vast arm-pits, and great pocket-holes in its sides,
where branches had been removed in past times; a black
slug was trying to climb it. Dead boughs were scattered about
like ichthyosauri in a museum, and beyond them were perishing wood-bine stems resembling old ropes.

From the other window all she could see were more trees,
in jackets of lichen, and stockings of moss. At their roots
were stemless yellow fungi like lemons and apricots, and tall
fungi with more stem than stool. Next were more trees close
together, wrestling for existence, their branches disfigured
with wounds resulting from their mutual rubbings and blows.
It was the struggle between these neighbours that she had
heard in the night. Beneath them were the rotting stumps of
those of the group that had been vanquished long ago, rising from their mossy setting like black teeth from green
gums. Further on were other tufts of moss in islands divided
by the shed leaves—variety upon variety, dark green and pale
green; moss like little fir-trees, like plush, like malachite stars;
like nothing on earth except moss.

The strain upon Grace's mind in various ways was so great
on this the most desolate day she had passed there, that she
felt it would be well-nigh impossible to spend another in
such circumstances. The evening came at last; the sun, when
its chin was on the earth, found an opening through which
to pierce the shade, and stretched irradiated gauzes across
the damp atmosphere, making the wet trunks shine, and
throwing splotches of such ruddiness on the leaves beneath
the beech that they were turned to gory hues. When night at
last arrived, and with it the time for his return, she was nearly
broken down with suspense.

The simple evening meal, partly tea, partly supper, which
Grace had prepared, stood waiting upon the hearth; and yet

Giles did not come. It was now nearly twenty-four hours since
she had seen him. As the room grew darker, and only the
fire-light broke against the gloom of the walls, she was convinced that it would be beyond her staying power to pass the
night without hearing from him or from somebody. Yet eight
o'clock drew on, and his form at the window did not appear.

The meal remained untasted. Suddenly rising from before
the hearth of smouldering embers, where she had been
crouching with her hands clasped over her knees, she crossed
the room, unlocked the door, and listened. Every breath of
wind had ceased with the decline of day, but the rain had
resumed the steady dripping of the night before. Grace might
have stood there five minutes when she fancied she heard
that old sound, a cough, at no great distance; and it was
presently repeated. If it were Winterborne's he must be near
her; why then had he not visited her?

A horrid misgiving that he could not visit her took possession of Grace, and she looked up anxiously for the lantern,
which was hanging above her head. To light it and go in the
direction of the sound would be the obvious way to solve the
dread problem; but the conditions made her hesitate, and in
a moment a cold sweat pervaded her at further sounds from
the same quarter.

They were low mutterings; at first like persons in conversation, but gradually resolving themselves into varieties of
one voice. It was an endless monologue, like that we sometimes hear from inanimate nature in deep secret places where
water flows, or where ivy leaves flap against stones; but by
degrees she was convinced that the voice was Winterborne's.
Yet who could be his listener, so mute and so patient? for
though he argued rapidly and persistently nobody replied.

A dreadful enlightenment spread through the mind of
Grace. "Oh," she cried in her anguish as she hastily prepared
herself to go out; "how selfishly correct I am always—too, too
correct! Can it be that cruel propriety is killing the dearest
heart that ever woman clasped to her own!"

While speaking thus to herself she had lit the lantern, and
hastening out without further thought took the direction
whence the mutterings had proceeded. The course was

marked by a little path, which ended at a distance of about forty yards in a small erection of hurdles, not much larger than a shock of corn, such as were frequent in the woods and copses when the cutting season was going on. It was too slight even to be called a hovel, and was not high enough to stand upright in; appearing in short to be erected for the temporary shelter of fuel. The side towards Grace was open, and turning the light upon the interior she beheld what her prescient fear had pictured in snatches all the way thither.

Upon the hay within her lover lay in his clothes, just as she had seen him during the whole of her stay here, except that his hat was off, and his hair matted and wild.

Both his clothes and the hay were saturated with rain. His arms were flung over his head; his face was flushed to an unnatural crimson. His eyes had a burning brightness, and, though they met her own, she perceived that he did not recognize her.

"O my Giles," she cried, "what have I done to you!"

But she stopped no longer even to reproach herself. She saw that the first thing to be thought of was to get him in-doors.

How Grace performed that labour she never could have exactly explained. But by dint of clasping her arms round him, rearing him into a sitting posture and straining her strength to the uttermost, she put him on one of the hurdles that was loose alongside, and taking the end of it in both her hands dragged him along the path to the entrance of the hut and, after a pause for breath, in at the doorway.

It was somewhat singular that Giles in his semi-conscious state acquiesced unresistingly in all that she did. But he never for a moment recognised her, continuing his rapid conversation to himself and seeming to look upon her as some angel, or other supernatural creature of the visionary world in which he was mentally living. The undertaking occupied her more than ten minutes; but by that time, to her great thankfulness, he was in the hut lying in her bed, his damp clothing removed.

Then the unhappy Grace regarded him by the light of the candle. There was something in his look which agonized her, in the rush of his thoughts, accelerating their speed from

minute to minute. His soul seemed to be passing through
the universe of ideas like a comet; erratic, inapprehensible,
untraceable.

Grace's distraction was almost as great as his. In a few
moments she firmly believed he was dying. Unable to withstand her impulse she knelt down beside him, kissed his
hands, and his face, and his hair, moaning in a low voice,
"how could I—how could I!"

Her timid morality had, indeed, underrated his chivalry
till now, though she knew him so well. The purity of his
nature, his freedom from the grosser passions, his scrupulous delicacy, had never been fully understood by Grace till
this strange self-sacrifice in lonely juxtaposition to her own
person was revealed. The perception of it added something
that was little short of reverence to the deep affection for
him of a woman who herself had more of Artemis than of
Aphrodite in her constitution.

All that a tender nurse could do Grace did; and the power
to express her solicitude in action, unconscious though the
sufferer was, brought her mournful satisfaction. She bathed
his hot head, clasped his twitching hands, moistened his lips,
cooled his fiery eyelids, sponged his heated skin and administered whatever she could find in the house that the imagination could conceive as likely to be in any way alleviating. That
she might have been the cause, or partially the cause, of all
this, interfused misery with her sorrow.

Six months before this date a scene almost similar in its
mechanical parts had been enacted at Hintock House. It was
between a pair of persons most intimately connected in their
lives with these. Outwardly like as it had been, it was yet
infinite in spiritual difference; though a woman's devotion
had been common to both.

Grace rose from her attitude of affection and bracing her
energies saw that something practical must immediately be
done. Much as she would have liked, in the emotion of the
moment, to keep him entirely to herself, medical assistance
was necessary whilst there remained a possibility of preserving him alive. Such assistance was fatal to her own concealment; but even had the chance of benefiting him been less

than it was she would have run the hazard for his sake. The question was where should she get a medical man, competent and near.

There was one such man, and only one, within accessible distance; a man who, if it were possible to save Winterborne's life, had the brain most likely to do it. If human pressure could bring him that man ought to be brought to the sick Giles's side. Though completely stultifying her flight the attempt should be made.

Yet she dreaded to leave her patient, and the minutes raced past, and still she postponed her departure. At last, when it was after eleven o'clock, Winterborne fell into a fitful sleep, and it seemed to afford her an opportunity.

She hastily made him as comfortable as she could, put on her things, cut a new candle from the bunch hanging in the cupboard, and having set it up and placed it so that the light did not fall upon his eyes she closed the door and started, there being now no rain.

The spirit of Winterborne seemed to keep her company, and banish all sense of darkness from her mind. The rains had imparted a phosphorescence to the pieces of touchwood and rotting leaves that lay about her path, which, as scattered by her feet, spread abroad like luminous milk. She would not run the hazard of losing her way by plunging into any short unfrequented track through the woodland; but followed a more open course round by the highway. She went along with great speed, animated by a devoted purpose which had much about it that was stoical; and it was with scarcely any faltering of spirit that, after an hour's progress, she saw High-Stoy Hill and drew onward towards that same Hintock and that same house out of which she had fled a few days before in irresistible alarm. But that had happened which, above all other things of chance and change, could make her deliberately frustrate her plan of flight, and sink all regard of personal consequences.

One speciality of Fitzpiers was respected by Grace as much as ever: his professional skill. In this she was right. Had his persistence equalled his insight instead of being the spasmodic and fitful thing it was, fame and fortune need never have remained a wish with him. His freedom from conventional errors and crusted prejudices had indeed been such as to retard rather than accelerate his advance in Hintock and its neighbourhood, where people could not believe that Nature herself effected cures, and that the doctor's business was only to smooth the way.

It was past midnight when Grace arrived opposite her father's house, now again temporarily occupied by her husband, unless he had already gone away. Ever since her emergence from the denser plantations about Winterborne's residence a pervasive lightness had hung in the damp autumn sky in spite of the vault of cloud, signifying that a moon of some age was shining above its arch. The two white gates were distinct, and the white balls on the pillars, and the puddles and damp ruts left by the recent rain had a cold corpse-eyed luminousness. She entered by the lower gate and crossed the quadrangle to the wing wherein the apartments that had been hers since her marriage were situate, till she stood under a window which, if her husband were in the house, gave light to his bed-chamber.

She faltered, and paused with her hand on her heart, in spite of herself. Could she call to her presence the very cause of all her foregoing troubles! Alas—old Jones was many miles off, Giles was possibly dying; what else could she do?

It was in a perspiration wrought even more by consciousness than by exercise that she picked up some gravel, threw it at the panes, and waited to see the result. The night-bell which had been fixed when Fitzpiers first took up his residence there still remained; but as it had fallen into disuse with the collapse of his practice, and his elopement, she did not venture to pull it now.

Whoever slept in the room had heard her signal, slight as it was. In half a minute the window was opened, and a voice said "Yes?" inquiringly. Grace recognised her husband in the speaker at once. Her effort was now to disguise her own accents.

"Doctor," she said in as unusual a tone as she could command, "a man is dangerously ill in One-Chimney Hut, by Delborough, and you must go to him at once in all mercy!"

"I will, readily."

The alacrity, surprise, and even pleasure, expressed in his reply, amazed her for a moment. But in truth they denoted the sudden relief of a man who, having got back, in a mood of contrition, from erratic abandonment to doubtful joys, found the soothing routine of professional practice unexpectedly opening anew to him. The highest desire of his soul just now was for a respectable life of painstaking. If this, his first summons since his return, had been to attend upon a cat or dog, he would scarcely have refused it in the circumstances.

"Do you know the way?" she asked.

"Yes, I think," said he.

"One-Chimney Hut—in King's-Hintock Wood, by Delborough," she repeated. "And immediately!"

"Yes; yes," said Fitzpiers.

Grace remained no longer. She passed through the white gate without slamming it, and hastened on her way back. Her husband, then, had re-entered her father's house. How he had been able to effect a reconciliation with the old man, what were the terms of the treaty between them, she could not so much as conjecture. Some sort of truce must have been entered into; that was all she could say. But close as the question lay to her own life there was a more urgent one which banished it, and she traced her steps quickly along the meandering trackways.

Meanwhile Fitzpiers was preparing to leave the house. The state of his mind, over and above his professional zeal, was peculiar. At Grace's first remark he had not recognised or suspected her presence; but as she went on he was awakened to the great resemblance of the speaker's voice to his wife's. He had taken in such good faith the statement of the household on his arrival, that she had gone on a visit for a time, because she could not at once bring her mind to be reconciled to him, that he could not quite believe this neighbour to be she. It was one of the features of Fitzpiers's repentant humour at this date that on receiving the explanation of her absence he had made no attempt to outrage her feelings by following her; though nobody had informed him how very shortly her departure had preceded his entry, and of all that might have been inferred from her precipitancy.

Melbury, after much alarm and consideration, had decided not to follow her either. He sympathized with her flight, much as he deplored it; moreover the tragic colour of the antecedent events that he had been a great means of creating checked his instinct to interfere. He prayed and trusted that she had got into no danger on her way (as he supposed) to Ivell, and thence to Exonbury, if that were the place she had gone to, forbearing all inquiry which the strangeness of her departure would have made natural. A few months before this time a performance by Grace of one-tenth the magnitude of this would have aroused him to unwonted investigation.

It was in the same spirit that he had tacitly assented to Fitzpiers's domiciliation there. The two men had not met face to face, but Mrs. Melbury had proposed herself as an intermediary who made the surgeon's re-entrance comparatively easy to him. Everything was provisional, and nobody asked questions. Fitzpiers had come in the performance of a plan of penitence which had originated in circumstances hereafter to be explained; his self-humiliation to the very bass-string was deliberate; and as soon as a voice reached him from the bedside of a dying man his desire was to set to work and do as much good as he could with the least possible fuss or show. He therefore refrained from calling up a stableman to get ready any horse or gig, and set out for One-Chimney Hut on foot as Grace had done.

XLIII

SHE re-entered the hut, flung off her bonnet and cloak, and approached the sufferer. He had begun anew those terrible mutterings, and his hands were cold. As soon as she saw him there returned to her that agony of mind which the stimulus of her journey had thrown off for a time.

Could he really be dying? She bathed him, kissed him, forgot all things but the fact that lying there before her was he who had loved her more than the mere lover would have loved; had immolated himself for her comfort, cared more for her self-respect than she had thought of caring. This mood continued till she heard quick smart footsteps without; she knew whose footsteps they were.

Grace sat on the inside of the bed against the wall, holding her lover's hand, so that when her husband entered the patient lay between herself and him. He stood transfixed at first, noticing Grace only. Slowly he dropped his glance; and discerned who the prostrate man was. Strangely enough, though Grace's distaste for her husband's company had amounted almost to dread, and culminated in actual flight, at this moment her last and least feeling was personal. Sensitive femininity was eclipsed by devoted purpose; and that it was a husband who stood there was forgotten. The first look that possessed her face was relief; satisfaction at the presence of the physician obliterated thought of the man, which only returned in the form of a sub-consciousness that did not interfere with her words.

"Is he dying—is there any hope?" she asked.

"Grace!" said Fitzpiers in an indescribable whisper—more than invocating—if not quite deprecatory.

He was arrested by the spectacle, not so much in its intrinsic character—though that was striking enough to a man who called himself the husband of the sufferer's friend and nurse—but in its character as the counterpart of one that had had its run many months before, in which he had figured as the patient, and the woman had been Felice Charmond.

"Is he in great danger—can you save him?" she asked again.

Fitzpiers aroused himself, came a little nearer, and examined Winterborne as he stood. His inspection was concluded in a mere glance. Before he spoke he looked at her contemplatively as to the effect of his coming words.

"He is dying," he said with dry precision.

"What?" said she.

"Nothing can be done, by me or any other man. It will soon be all over. The extremities are dead already." His eyes still remained fixed on her, the conclusion to which he had come seeming to end his interest, professional and otherwise, in Winterborne for ever.

"But it cannot be! He was well a week ago."

"Not well I suspect. This seems like what we call a sequel,

which has followed some previous disorder—possibly typhoid —it may have been months ago, or recently."

"Ah—he was ill last year—you are right. And he must have been ill when I came."

There was nothing more to do or say. She crouched down at the side of the bed, and Fitzpiers took a seat. Thus they remained in silence, and long as it lasted she never turned her eyes, or apparently her thoughts, at all to her husband. He occasionally murmured, with automatic authority, some slight directions for alleviating the pain of the dying man, which she mechanically obeyed; bending over him during the intervals in silent tears.

Winterborne never recovered consciousness of what was passing; and that he was going became soon perceptible also to her. In less than an hour the delirium ceased; then there was an interval of somnolent painlessness and soft breathing, at the end of which Winterborne passed quietly away.

Then Fitzpiers broke the silence. "Have you lived here long?" he said.

Grace was wild with sorrow—bitter with all that had befallen her—with the cruelties that had attacked her—with life—with Heaven. She answered at random: "Yes. By what right do you ask?"

"Don't think I claim any right," said Fitzpiers. "It is for you to do and say what you choose. I admit, quite as much as you feel, that I am a vagabond—a brute—not worthy to possess the smallest fragment of you. But here I am; and I have happened to take sufficient interest in you to make that inquiry."

"He is everything to me!" said Grace, hardly heeding her husband, and laying her hand reverently on the dead man's eyelids, where she kept it a long time, pressing down their lashes with gentle touches, as if she were stroking a little bird.

He watched her awhile; and then glanced round the chamber where his eyes fell upon a few dressing necessaries that she had brought.

"Grace—if I may call you so," he said, "I have been already humiliated almost to the depths. I have come back, since you refused to join me elsewhere,—I have entered your father's house—and borne all which that cost me without flinching, because I have felt I deserved humiliation. But is there a yet greater humiliation in store for me? You say you have been living here with him—that he was everything to you. Am I to draw from that the obvious, the extremest inference?"

Triumph at any price is sweet to men and women—especially the latter. It was her first and last opportunity of repaying him for the slights which she had borne at his hands so docilely.

"Yes," she answered; "the extremest inference"; and there was that in her subtly compounded nature which made her feel a thrill of pride as she did so.

Yet the moment after she had so mightily belied her conduct she half repented. Her husband had turned as white as the wall behind him. It seemed as if all that remained to him of hope and spirit had been abstracted at a stroke. Yet he did not move, and in his efforts at self-control closed his mouth together as a vice. His determination was fairly successful, though she saw how very much greater than she had expected her triumph had been. Presently he looked across at Winterborne.

"Would it startle you to hear," he said, as if he hardly had breath to utter words, "that she who was to me what he was to you is dead also?"

"Dead—*she* dead?" exclaimed Grace.

"Yes. Felice Charmond is where this young man is."

"Never!" said Grace vehemently.

He went on without heeding the insinuation: "And I came back to try to make it up with you—but——"

Fitzpiers rose, and moved across the room to go away, looking downwards with the droop of a man whose hope was turned to apathy if not despair. In going round the door his eye fell upon her once more. She was still bending over the body of Winterborne, her face close to his.

"Have you been kissing him during his illness?" asked her husband.

"Yes."

"Since his fevered state set in?"

"Yes."

"On his lips?"

"Yes, a hundred times!"

"Then you will do well to take a few drops of this in water as soon as possible." He drew a small phial from his pocket, and returned to offer it to her.

Grace shook her head.

"If you don't do as I tell you you may soon be like him."

"I don't care. I wish to die."

"I'll put it here," said Fitzpiers, placing the bottle on a ledge beside him. "The sin of not having warned you will not be upon my head at any rate, amongst my other sins. I am now going, and I will send somebody to you. Your father does not know that you are here, so I suppose I shall be bound to tell him."

"Certainly."

Fitzpiers left the cot, and the stroke of his feet was soon immersed in the silence that pervaded the spot. Grace remained kneeling and weeping she hardly knew how long, and then she sat up, covered Giles's fixed statuesque features, and went towards the door where her husband had stood. No sign of any other comer greeted her ear, the only perceptible sounds being the tiny cracklings of the dead leaves which, like a feather bed, had not yet done rising to their normal level where indented by the pressure of her husband's receding footsteps. It reminded her that she had been struck with the change in his aspect; the extremely intellectual look that had always been in his face was wrought to a finer phase by thinness; and a careworn dignity had been superadded. She returned to Winterborne's side, and during her meditations another tread drew near the door, entered the room, and halted at the foot of the bed.

"What—Marty!" said Grace.

"Yes. I have heard," said Marty, whose demeanour had lost all its girlishness under the stroke that seemed almost literally to have bruised her.

"He died for me!" murmured Grace heavily.

Marty did not fully comprehend and she answered, "He belongs to neither of us now, and your beauty is no more

powerful with him than my plainness. I have come to help
you, ma'am. He never cared for me, and he cared much for
you; but he cares for us both alike now."

"Oh don't, don't, Marty!"

Marty said no more, but knelt over Winterborne from the
other side.

"Did you meet my hus—Mr. Fitzpiers?"

"No."

"Then what brought you here?"

"I come this way sometimes. I have got to go to the further
side of the wood at this time o' year, and am obliged to get
there before four o'clock in the morning, to begin heating
the oven for the early baking. I have passed by here often at
this time."

Grace looked at her quickly. "Then did you know I was
here?"

"Yes ma'am."

"Did you tell anybody?"

"No. I knew you lived in the hut, that he had gied it up
to 'ee, and lodged out himself."

"Did you know where he lodged?"

"No. That I couldn't find out. Was it at Delborough?"

"No. It was not there, Marty. Would it had been! It would
have saved—saved——" To check her tears she turned, and
seeing a book in the window-bench took it up. "Look Marty,
this is a Psalter. He was not an outwardly religious man; but
he was pure and perfect in his heart. Shall we read a psalm
over him?"

"O yes—we will—with all my heart!"

Grace opened the thin brown book which poor Giles had
kept at hand mainly for the convenience of whetting his
penknife upon its leather covers. She began to read in that
rich devotional voice peculiar to women on such occasions.
When it was over Marty said, "I should like to pray for his
soul."

"So should I," said her companion. "But we must not."

"Why? Nobody would know."

Grace could not resist the argument, influenced as she was
by the sense of making amends for having neglected him in

the body: and their tender voices united and filled the narrow room with supplicatory murmurs that a Calvinist might have countenanced. They had hardly ended when new and more numerous footfalls were audible; also persons in conversation, one of whom Grace recognised as her father.

She rose and went to the outside of the hut, where there was only such light as beamed from the doorway. Melbury and Mrs. Melbury were standing there.

"I don't reproach you, Grace," said her father with an estranged manner and in a voice not at all like his old voice. "What has come upon you and us through you giving up yourself to him is beyond reproach, beyond weeping and beyond wailing. Perhaps I drove you to it. But I am hurt, I am scourged, I am astonished. In the face of this there is nothing to be said."

Without replying Grace turned and glided back to the chamber. "Marty," she said quickly, "I cannot look my father in the face until he knows the true circumstances of my life here. Go and tell him—what you have told me—what you saw—that he gave up his house to me."

She sat down, her face buried in her hands, and Marty went, and after a short absence returned. Then Grace rose, and going out asked her father if he had talked to Marty.

"Yes," said Melbury.

"And you know all that has happened? I will let my husband think the utmost, but not you."

"I do.—Forgive me Grace for suspecting 'ee of worse than rashness—I ought to know 'ee better. Are you coming with me to what was once your home?"

"No. I stay here with *him*. Take no account of me any more."

The tender, perplexing, agitating relations in which she had stood to Winterborne quite lately—brought about by Melbury's own contrivance—could not fail to soften the natural anger of a parent at her more recent doings. "My daughter, things are bad," he rejoined. "But why do you persevere to make 'em worse? What good can you do to Giles by staying here with him? Mind, I ask no questions. I don't inquire why you decided to come here, or anything as to what your course would have been if he had not died, though

I know there's no deliberate harm in 'ee. As for me, I have lost all claim upon you; and I make no complaint. But I do say that by coming back with me now you will show no less kindness to him, and escape any sound of shame."

"But I don't wish to escape it?"

"If you don't on your own account cannot you wish to on mine and hers? Nobody except our household knows that you have left home. Then why should you by a piece of perverseness bring down my hairs with sorrow to the grave."

"If it were not for my husband——" she began, moved by his words. "But how can I meet him there? How can any woman who is not a mere man's creature live with him after what has taken place?"

"He would go away again rather than keep you out of my house."

"How do you know that, father?"

"We met him on our way here, and he told us so," said Mrs. Melbury. "He had said something like it before. He seems very much upset altogether."

"He declared to her when he came to our house that he would wait for time and devotion to bring about his forgiveness," said Melbury. "That was it, wasn't it Lucy?"

"Yes. That he would not intrude upon you, Grace, till you gave him absolute permission," Mrs. Melbury added.

This antecedent considerateness in Fitzpiers was as welcome to Grace as it was unexpected; and though she did not desire his presence she was sorry that by her retaliatory fiction she had given him a different reason for avoiding her. She made no further objections to accompanying her parents, taking them into the hut to give Winterborne a last look, and gathering up the two or three things that belonged to her. While she was doing this the two women came who had been called by Melbury and at their heels poor Creedle.

"Forgive me, but I can't rule my mourning nohow as a man should, Mr. Melbury," he said. "I ha'n't seen him since Thursday se'night, and have wondered for days and days where he's been keeping. There was I expecting him to come and tell me to wash out the cider-barrels against the making, and here was he. . . . . Well, I've knowed him from table-high;

I knowed his father—used to bide about upon two sticks in the sun afore he died!—and now I've seen the end of the family, which we can ill afford to lose, wi' such a scanty lot of good folk in Hintock as we've got. And now Robert Creedle will be nailed up in parish boards 'a b'lieve; and nobody will glutch down a sigh for he!"

They started for home, Marty and Creedle remaining behind. For a time Grace and her father walked side by side without speaking. It was just in the blue of the dawn and the chilling tone of the sky was reflected in her cold wet face. The whole wood seemed to be a house of death, pervaded by loss to its uttermost length and breadth. Winterborne was gone and the copses seemed to show the want of him; those young trees, so many of which he had planted, and of which he had spoken so truly when he said that he should fall before they fell, were at that very moment sending out their roots in the direction that he had given them with his subtle hand.

"One thing made it tolerable to us that your husband should come back to the house," said Melbury at last. "The death of Mrs. Charmond."

"Ah, yes," said Grace, arousing slightly to the recollection, "he told me so."

"Did he tell you how she died? It was no such death as Giles's. She was shot—by a disappointed lover. It occurred in Germany. The unfortunate man shot himself afterwards. He was that South Carolina gentleman of very passionate nature, who used to haunt this place to force her to favour him, and followed her about everywhere. So ends the brilliant Felice Charmond—once a good friend to me—but no friend to you."

"I can forgive her," said Grace absently. "Did Edred tell you this?"

"No. But he put a London newspaper, giving an account of it, on the hall table, folded in such a way that we should see it. It will be in the Sherton paper this week no doubt. To make the event more solemn still to him he had just before had sharp words with her, and left her. He told Lucy this, as nothing about him appears in the newspaper. And the cause of the quarrel was, of all people, she we've left behind us."

"Do you mean Marty?" Grace spoke the words; but perfunctorily. For, pertinent and pointed as Melbury's story was, she had no care for it now.

"Yes. Marty South." Melbury persisted in his narrative, to divert her from her present grief if possible. "Before he went away she wrote him a letter, which he kept in his pocket a long while before reading. He chanced to pull it out in Mrs. Charmond's presence, and read it out loud. It contained something which teased her very much, and that led to the rupture. She was following him to make it up, when she met with her terrible death."

Melbury did not know enough to give the gist of the incident, which was that Marty South's letter had been concerning a certain personal adornment common to herself and Mrs. Charmond. Her bullet reached its billet at last. The scene between Fitzpiers and Felice had been sharp as only a scene can be which arises out of the mortification of one woman by another in the presence of a lover. True, Marty had not effected it by word of mouth; the charge about the locks of hair was made simply by Fitzpiers reading her letter to him aloud to Felice in the playfully ironical tones of one who had become a little weary of his situation, and was finding his friend, in the phrase of George Herbert, a "flat delight." He had stroked those false tresses with his hand many a time without knowing them to be transplanted, and it was impossible when the discovery was so abruptly made, to avoid being finely satirical, despite his generous disposition.

That was how it had begun; and tragedy had been its end. On his abrupt departure she had followed him to the station; but the train was gone; and in travelling to Homburg in search of him she had met his rival, whose reproaches led to an altercation, and the death of both. Of that precipitate scene of passion and crime Fitzpiers had known nothing till he saw an account of it in the papers, where, fortunately for himself, no mention was made of his prior acquaintance with the unhappy lady; nor was there any allusion to him in the subsequent inquiry, the double death being attributed to some gambling losses, though in point of fact neither one of them had visited the tables.

Melbury and his daughter drew near their house having seen but one living thing on their way, a squirrel, which did not run up its tree, but, dropping the sweet chestnut which it carried, cried chut-chut-chut and stamped with its hind legs on the ground. When the roofs and chimneys of the homestead began to emerge from the screen of boughs Grace started, and checked herself in her abstracted advance.

"You clearly understand," she said to her step-mother, some of her old misgiving returning, "that I am coming back only on condition of his leaving as he promised. Will you let him know this, that there may be no mistake?"

Mrs. Melbury, who had had some long private talks with Fitzpiers, assured Grace that she need have no doubts on that point, and that he would probably be gone by the evening. Grace then entered with them into Melbury's wing of the house, and sat down listlessly in the parlour while her step-mother went to Fitzpiers.

The prompt obedience to her wishes which the doctor showed did honour to him, if anything could. Before Mrs. Melbury had returned to the room Grace, who was sitting on the parlour window-bench, saw her husband go from the door under the increasing light of morning, with a bag in his hand. While passing through the gate he turned his head. The firelight of the room she sat in threw her figure into dark relief against the window as she looked through the panes, and he must have seen her distinctly. In a moment he went on, the gate fell to, and he disappeared. At the hut she had declared that another had usurped his rights; now she had banished him.

XLIV

Fitzpiers had hardly been gone an hour when Grace began to sicken. The next day she kept her room. Old Jones was called in: he murmured some statements in which the words "feverish symptoms" occurred. Grace heard them, and guessed the means by which she had brought this visitation upon herself.

One day while she still lay there with her head throbbing, wondering if she were really going to join him who had gone before, Grammer Oliver came to her bedside. "I don't know whe'r this is meant for you to take Ma'am," she said. "But I have found it on the table. It was left by Marty, I think, when she came this morning."

Grace turned her hot eyes upon what Grammer held up. It was the phial, left at the hut by her husband when he had begged her to take some drops of its contents if she wished to preserve herself from falling a victim to the malady which had pulled down Winterborne. She examined it as well as she could. The liquid was of a brownish hue, and bore a label with an inscription in Italian. He had probably got it in his wanderings abroad. She knew but little Italian, but could understand that the cordial was a febrifuge of some sort. Her father, her mother, and all the household were anxious for her recovery, and she resolved to obey her husband's directions. Whatever the risk, if any, she was prepared to run it. A glass of water was brought and the drops dropped in.

The effect, though not miraculous, was remarkable. In less than an hour, she felt calmer, cooler, better able to reflect, less inclined to fret and chafe and wear herself away. She took a few drops more. From that time the fever retreated and went out like a damped conflagration.

"How clever he is!" she said regretfully. "Why could he not have had more principle so as to turn his great talents to good account! Perhaps he has saved my useless life. But he doesn't know it, and doesn't care whether he has saved it or not; and on that account will never be told by me. Probably he only gave it to me in the arrogance of his skill, to show the greatness of his resources beside mine, as Elijah drew down fire from Heaven."

As soon as she had quite recovered from this foiled attack upon her life Grace went to Marty South's cottage. The current of her being had again set towards the lost Giles Winterborne.

"Marty," she said, "we both loved him. We will go to his grave together."

The church stood somewhat outside the village, and could be reached without passing through the street. In the dusk of the late September day they went thither by secret ways, walking mostly in silence side by side, each busied with her own thoughts. Grace had a trouble exceeding Marty's—that haunting sense of having put out the light of his life by her own hasty doings. She had tried to persuade herself that he might have died of his illness even if she had not taken possession of his house. Sometimes she succeeded in her attempt; sometimes she did not.

They stood by the grave together, and though the sun had gone down they could get glimpses over the woodland for miles and along the Vale in which he had been accustomed to descend every year with his portable mill and press to make cider about this time.

Perhaps Grace's first grief, the discovery that if he had lived he could never have claimed her, had some power in softening this, the second. On Marty's part there was the same consideration; never would she have been his. As no anticipation of gratified affection had been in existence while he was with them there was none to be disappointed now that he had gone.

Grace was abased when by degrees she found that she had never understood Giles as Marty had done. Marty South alone, of all the women in Hintock and the world, had approximated to Winterborne's level of intelligent intercourse with Nature. In that respect she had formed his true complement in the other sex, had lived as his counterpart, had subjoined her thoughts to his as a corollary.

The casual glimpses which the ordinary population bestowed upon that wondrous world of sap and leaves called the Hintock woods had been with these two, Giles and Marty, a clear gaze. They had been possessed of its finer mysteries as of commonplace knowledge; had been able to read its hieroglyphs as ordinary writing; to them the sights and sounds of night, winter, wind, storm, amid those dense boughs, which had to Grace a touch of the uncanny, and even of the supernatural, were simple occurrences whose origin, continuance, and laws they foreknew. They had planted together, and together they had felled; together they had, with the run of the years, mentally collected those remoter signs and symbols which seen in few were of runic obscurity, but all together made an alphabet. From the light lashing of the twigs upon their faces when brushing through them in the dark either could pronounce upon the species of the tree whence they stretched; from the quality of the wind's murmur through a bough either could in like manner name its sort afar off. They knew by a glance at a trunk if its heart were sound, or tainted with incipient decay, and by the state of its upper twigs the stratum that had been reached by its roots. The artifices of the seasons were seen by them from the conjuror's own point of view, and not from that of the spectator.

"He ought to have married *you*, Marty, and nobody else in the world!" said Grace with conviction, after thinking in the above strain.

Marty shook her head. "In all our outdoor days and years together, ma'am," she replied, "the one thing he never spoke of to me was love; nor I to him."

"Yet you and he could speak in a tongue that nobody else knew—not even my father, though he came nearest knowing —the tongue of the trees and fruits and flowers themselves."

She could indulge in mournful fancies like this to Marty; but the hard core to her grief—which Marty's had not— remained. Had she been sure that Giles's death resulted entirely from his exposure it would have driven her well-nigh to insanity, but there was always the bare possibility that his exposure had only precipitated what was inevitable. She longed to believe that it had not done even this.

There was only one man whose opinion on the circumstances she would be at all disposed to trust. Her husband was that man. Yet to ask him it would be necessary to detail the true conditions in which she and Winterborne had lived during these three or four critical days that followed her flight; and in withdrawing her original defiant announcement on that point there seemed a weakness she did not care to show. She never doubted that Fitzpiers would believe her if she made a clean confession of the actual situation; but to volunteer the correction would seem like signalling for a truce, and that in her present frame of mind was what she did not feel the need of.

*

It will probably not appear a surprising statement, after what has been already declared of Fitzpiers, that the man whom Grace's matrimonial fidelity could not keep faithful was stung into passionate throbs of interest concerning her by her avowal of the contrary.

He declared to himself that he had never known her dangerously full compass if she were capable of such a reprisal; and, melancholy as it may be to admit the fact, his own humiliation and regret engendered a smouldering admiration of her.

He passed a month or two of nervous misery at some midland town—the place to which he had retired—quite as much misery indeed as Grace, could she have known of it, would have been inclined to inflict upon any living creature, how much soever he might have wronged her. Then a sudden hope dawned upon him; he wondered if her affirmation were true. He asked himself whether it were not the act of an innocent woman whose pique had for the moment blinded her to the contingencies of such an announcement. His wide experience of the sex had taught him that, in many cases, women who ventured on hazardous phrases did so because they lacked an imagination gross enough to feel their full force. In this light Grace's bold avowal might merely have denoted the desperation of one who was a child to the realities of faithlessness.

Fitzpiers's mental sufferings and suspense led him at last to take a melancholy journey to the neighbourhood of Little Hintock; and here he hovered for hours around the scene of the purest emotional experiences that he had ever known in his life. He walked about the woods that surrounded Melbury's house, keeping out of sight like a criminal. It was a fine evening, and on his way homeward he passed near Marty South's cottage. As usual she had lighted her candle without closing her shutters; he saw her within as he had seen her many times before.

She was polishing tools, and though he had not wished to show himself he could not resist speaking to her through the half-open door. "What are you doing that for, Marty?"

"Because I want to clean them. They are not mine." He could

see indeed that they were not hers, for one was a spade, large and heavy, and another was a bill-hook which she could only have used with both hands. The spade though not a new one had been so completely burnished that it was bright as silver.

Fitzpiers somehow divined that they were Giles Winterborne's, and he put the question to her.

She replied in the affirmative. "I am going to keep 'em," she said, "but I can't get his apple-mill and press. I wish I could; it is going to be sold, they say."

"Then I will buy it for you," said Fitzpiers. "That will be making you a return for a kindness you did me." His glance fell upon the girl's rare-coloured hair, which had grown again. "O Marty those locks of yours—and that letter! . . . . But it was a kindness to send it, nevertheless," he added musingly.

After this there was confidence between them—such confidence as there had never been before. Marty was shy, indeed, of speaking about the letter and her motives in writing it; but she thanked him warmly for his promise of the cider-press. She would travel with it in the autumn season, as poor Giles had done, she said. She would be quite strong enough with old Creedle as an assistant.

"Ah—there was one nearer to him than you," said Fitzpiers, referring to Grace. "One who lived where he lived, and was with him when he died."

Then Marty, suspecting that he did not know the true circumstances, from the fact that Mrs. Fitzpiers and himself were living apart, told him of Giles's generosity to Grace in giving up his house to her, at the risk, and possibly the sacrifice, of his own life. When the surgeon heard it he almost envied Giles his chivalrous character. He expressed a wish to Marty that his visit to her should be kept secret, and went home thoughtful, feeling that in more than one sense his journey to Hintock had not been in vain.

He would have given much to win Grace's forgiveness then. But whatever he dared hope for in that kind from the future there was nothing to be done yet, while Giles Winterborne's memory was green. To wait was imperative. "A little time might melt her frozen thoughts"; and lead her to look on him with toleration, if not with love.

XLV

WEEKS and months of mourning for Winterborne had been passed by Grace in the soothing monotony of the memorial act to which she and Marty had devoted themselves. Twice a week the pair went in the dusk to Hintock Churchyard and, like the two mourners in *Cymbeline*, sweetened his sad grave with their flowers and their tears. Nothing ever had brought home to her with such force as this death how little acquirements and culture weigh beside sterling personal character. While her simple sorrow for his loss took a softer edge with the lapse of the Autumn and winter seasons, her self-reproach at having had a possible hand in causing it knew slight abatement.

Little occurred at Hintock during these months of the fall and decay of the leaf. Discussion of the almost contemporaneous death of Mrs. Charmond abroad had waxed and waned. There was a rumour that her death had resulted less from the shot than from the effect of fright upon her personal condition at the time; but this was never verified. Fitzpiers had had a fortunate escape from being dragged into the enquiry which followed the catastrophe, through the accident of having parted from his mistress just before it, under the influence of Marty South's letter—the tiny instrument of a cause deep in nature.

Her body was not brought home. It seemed to accord well with the fitful fever of that impassioned woman's life that she should not have found an English grave. She had enjoyed but a life-interest in the estate, which after her death passed to a relative of her husband's—one who knew not Felice, one whose purpose seemed to be to blot out every vestige of her.

On a certain day in February—the cheerful day of St. Valentine—a letter reached Mrs. Fitzpiers which had been mentally promised her for that particular day a long time before.

Her husband announced that he was living at some midland town where he had obtained a temporary practice as assistant to a local medical man whose curative principles were all wrong, though he dared not set them right. He had thought fit to communicate with her on that day of tender traditions to inquire if, in the event of his obtaining a substantial practice that he had in view elsewhere, she could forget the past and bring herself to join him.

There the practical part ended: he then went on:—

"My last year of experience has added ten years to my age, dear Grace and dearest wife that ever erring man undervalued. You may be absolutely indifferent to what I say, but let me say it, I have never loved any woman alive or dead as I love, respect, and honour you at this present moment. What you told me in the pride and naughtiness of your heart I never believed [this by the way was not strictly true]; but even if I had believed it, it could never have estranged me from you. Is there any use in telling you—no, there is not—that I dream of your fresh lips more frequently than I say my prayers: that the old familiar rustle of your dress often returns upon my mind till it distracts me. If you could condescend even only to see me again you would be breathing life into a corpse. My pure, pure Grace, modest as a turtle-dove, how came I ever to possess you? For the sake of being present in your mind on this lovers' day I think I would almost rather have you hate me a little than not think of me at all. You may call my fancies whimsical; but remember, sweet lost one, that 'nature is fine in love, and where 'tis fine it sends some instance of itself.'—I will not intrude upon you further now. Make me a little bit happy by sending back one line to say that you will consent at any rate to a short interview. I will meet you and leave you as a mere acquaintance, if you will only afford me this slight means of making a few explanations, and of putting my position before you. Believe me, in spite of all you may do or feel,

"Your lover always (once your husband),
"E.F."

It was, oddly enough, the first occasion, or nearly the first on which Grace had ever received a love-letter from him, his courtship having taken place under conditions which rendered letter-writing unnecessary. Its perusal, therefore, had a certain novelty for her. She thought that, upon the whole, he wrote love-letters very well. But the chief rational interest of the letter to the reflective Grace lay in the chance that such a meeting as he proposed would afford her of setting her doubts at rest one way or the other on her actual share in Winterborne's death. The relief of consulting a skilled mind, the one professional man who had seen Giles at that time, would be immense. As for that statement that she had uttered in her disdainful grief, which at the time she had regarded as her triumph, she was quite prepared to admit to him that his belief was the true one; for in wronging herself as she did when she made it she had done what to her was a far more serious thing, wronged Winterborne's memory.

Without consulting her father, or anyone in the house or out of it, Grace replied to the letter. She agreed to meet Fitzpiers on two conditions, of which the first was that the place of meeting should be the top of High-Stoy Hill, the second that he would not object to Marty South accompanying her.

Whatever art, much or little, there may have been in Fitzpiers's so-called valentine to his wife, he felt a delight as of the bursting of Spring when her brief reply came. It was one of the few pleasures that he had experienced of late years at all resembling those of his early youth. He promptly replied that he accepted the conditions, and named the day and hour at which he would be on the spot she mentioned.

A few minutes before three on the appointed day found him climbing the well-known hill, which had been the axis of so many critical movements in their lives during his residence at Hintock.

The sight of each homely and well-remembered object swelled the regret that seldom left him now. Whatever paths might lie open to his future the soothing shades of Hintock were forbidden him for ever as a permanent dwelling-place.

He longed for the society of Grace. But to lay offerings on her slighted altar was his first aim, and until her propitiation was complete he would constrain her in no way to return to him. The least reparation that he could make, in a case where he would gladly have made much, would be to let her feel herself absolutely free to choose between living with him and without him.

Moreover, a subtlist in emotions, he cultivated as under glasses strange and mournful pleasures that he would not willingly let die just at present. To show any forwardness in suggesting a *modus vivendi* to Grace would be to put an end to these exotics. To be the vassal of her sweet will for a time—he demanded no more, and found solace in the contemplation of the soft miseries she caused him.

Approaching the hill with a mind strung to these notions Fitzpiers discerned a gay procession of people coming down the way, and was not long in perceiving it to be a wedding-party. Though the wind was keen the women were in light attire, and the flowered waistcoats of the men had a pleasing vividness of pattern. Each of the gentler ones clung to the arm of her partner so tightly as to have with him one step, rise, swing, gait, almost one centre of gravity. In the buxom bride Fitzpiers recognised no other than Suke Damson, who in a light gown looked a giantess; the small husband beside her he saw to be Tim Tangs.

Fitzpiers could not escape, for they had seen him; though of all the beauties of the world whom he did not wish to meet Suke was the chief. But he put the best face on the matter that he could and came on, the approaching company evidently discussing him and his separation from Mrs. Fitzpiers. As the couples closed upon him he expressed his congratulations.

"We be just walking round the parishes to show ourselves a bit," said Tim. "First we het across to Great Hintock, then back to here, and from here we go to Revellers Inn and Marshwood, and then round by the cross-roads home. Home says I, but it won't be that long. We be off in a couple of months."

"Indeed. Where to?"

Tim informed him that they were going to New Zealand. Not but that he would have been contented with Hintock, but his wife was ambitious and wanted to leave; so he had given way.

"Then good-bye," said Fitzpiers. "I may not see you again." He shook hands with Tim and turned to the bride. "Good-bye, Suke," he said taking her hand also. "I wish you and your husband prosperity in the country you have chosen." With this he left them, and hastened on to his appointment.

The wedding-party re-formed and resumed march likewise. But in restoring his arm to Suke Tim noticed that her full and blooming countenance had undergone a change. "Hullo, me dear—what's the matter?" said Tim.

"Nothing to speak o'," said she. But to give the lie to her assertion she was seized with lachrymose twitches, that soon produced a dribbling face.

"How—what the devil's this about!" exclaimed the bridegroom.

"She's a little wee bit overcome, poor dear!" said the first bridesmaid, unfolding her handkerchief and wiping Suke's eyes.

"I never did like parting from people!" said Suke as soon as she could speak.

"Why him in particular?"

"Well—he's such a clever doctor that 'tis a thousand pities we sha'n't see him any more! There'll be no such clever doctor as he in New Zealand, if I should be wanting one in a few months; and the thought o't got the better of my feelings!"

They walked on, but Tim's face had grown rigid and pale, for he recalled slight circumstances disregarded at the time of their occurrence. The former boisterous laughter of the wedding-party at the groomsman's jokes was heard rising between the hedges no more.

By this time Fitzpiers had advanced on his way to the hill, where he saw two figures emerging from the bank on the right hand. These were the expected ones, Grace and Marty South, who had evidently come there by a short and secret path through the wood. Grace was muffled up in her winter dress, and he thought that she had never looked so seductive as at this moment, in the noontide bright but heatless sun, and the keen wind, and the purplish-grey masses of brushwood around. Fitzpiers continued to regard the nearing picture, till at length their glances met for a moment, when she demurely sent off hers at a tangent and gave him the benefit of her three-quarter face, while with courteous completeness of conduct he lifted his hat in a large arc. Marty dropped behind, and when Fitzpiers held out his hand Grace touched it with her fingers.

"I have agreed to be here mostly because I wanted to ask you something important," said Mrs. Fitzpiers, her intonation modulating in a direction that she had not quite wished it to take.

"I am most attentive," said her husband. "Shall we take to the trees for privacy?"

Grace demurred; and Fitzpiers gave in, and they kept outside by the gate.

At any rate she would take his arm? This also was gravely negatived, the refusal being audible to Marty.

"Why not?" he inquired.

"Oh Mr. Fitzpiers—how can you ask!"

"Right, right," said he, his effusiveness shrivelled up.

As they walked on she returned to her inquiry. "It is about a matter that may perhaps be unpleasant to you. But I think I need not consider that too carefully."

"Not at all," said Fitzpiers heroically.

She then took him back to the time of poor Winterborne's death, and related the precise circumstances amid which his fatal illness had come upon him, particularizing the dampness of the shelter to which he had betaken himself, his concealment from her of the hardships that he was undergoing, all that he had put up with, all that he had done for her in his scrupulous considerateness. The retrospect brought her to tears as she asked him if he thought that the sin of having driven him to his death was upon her.

Fitzpiers could hardly help showing his satisfaction at what her narrative indirectly revealed, the actual harmlessness of an escapade with her lover which had at first, by her own showing, looked so grave, and he did not care to inquire whether that harmlessness had been the result of aim or of accident. With regard to her question he declared that in his judgment no human being could answer it. He thought that upon the whole the balance of probabilities turned in her favour. Winterborne's apparent strength, during the last months of his life, must have been delusive. It had often occurred that after a first attack of that insidious disease a person's apparent recovery was a physiological mendacity.

The relief which came to Grace lay almost as much in

sharing her knowledge of the particulars with an intelligent mind as in the assurances Fitzpiers gave her. "Well then, to put this case before you and obtain your professional opinion was chiefly why I consented to come here to-day," said she, when he had reached the aforesaid conclusion.

"For no other reason at all?" he asked ruefully.

"It was nearly the whole."

They stood and looked over a gate at twenty or thirty starlings feeding in the grass, and he started the talk again by saying in a low voice, "And yet I love you more than ever I loved you in my life."

Grace did not move her eyes from the birds, and folded her delicate lips as if to keep them in subjection.

"It is a different kind of love altogether," said he. "Less passionate; more profound. It has nothing to do with the material conditions of the object at all; much to do with her character and goodness, as revealed by closer observation. 'Love talks with better knowledge, and knowledge with dearer love.'"

"That's out of *Measure for Measure*," said she slily.

"Oh yes—I meant it as a citation," blandly replied Fitzpiers. "Well then, why not give me a very little bit of your heart again?"

The crash of a felled tree in the depths of the nearest wood recalled the past at that moment, and all the homely faithfulness of Winterborne. "Don't ask it. My heart is in the grave with Giles," she replied staunchly.

"Mine is with you—in no less deep a grave I fear, according to that."

"I am very sorry; but it cannot be helped."

"How can you be sorry for me, when you wilfully keep open the grave?"

"Oh no—that's not so," returned Grace quickly; and moved to go away from him.

"But dearest Grace!" said he. "You have condescended to come; and I thought from it that perhaps when I had passed through a long state of probation you would be generous. But if there can be no hope of our getting completely reconciled treat me gently—wretch though I am."

"I did not say you were a wretch, nor have I ever said so."

"But you have such a contemptuous way of looking at me that I fear you think so."

Grace's heart struggled between the wish not to be harsh and the fear that she might mislead him. "I cannot look contemptuous unless I feel contempt," she said evasively. "And all I feel is lovelessness."

"I have been very bad I know," he returned. "But unless you can really love me again, Grace, I would rather go away from you for ever. I don't want you to receive me again for duty's sake, or anything of that sort. If I had not cared more for your affection and forgiveness than my own personal comfort I should never have come back here. I could have obtained a practice at a distance, and have lived my own life without coldness or reproach. But I have chosen to return to the one spot on earth where my name is tarnished—to enter the house of a man from whom I have had worse treatment than from any other man alive. All for you."

This was undeniably true, and it had its weight with Grace, who began to look as if she thought she had been shockingly severe.

"Before you go," he continued, "I want to know your pleasure about me: what you wish me to do, or not to do."

"You are independent of me, and it seems a mockery to ask that. Far be it from me to advise. But I will think it over. I rather need advice myself than stand in a position to give it."

"*You* don't need advice, wisest, dearest woman that ever lived. If you did. . . ."

"Would you give it to me?"

"Would you act upon what I gave?"

"That's not a fair inquiry," said she smiling despite her gravity. "I don't mind hearing it—what you do really think the most correct and proper course for me."

"It is so easy for me to say, and yet I dare not, for it would be provoking you to remonstrances."

Knowing of course what the advice would be she did not press him further, and was about to beckon Marty forward and leave him, when he interrupted her with, "O one moment dear Grace—you will meet me again?"

She eventually agreed to see him that day fortnight. Fitzpiers expostulated at the interval, but the half-alarmed earnestness with which she entreated him not to come sooner made him say hastily that he submitted to her will—that he would regard her as a friend only, anxious for his reform and well-being, till such time as she might allow him to exceed that privilege.

All this was to assure her; it was only too clear that he had not won her confidence yet. It amazed Fitzpiers and overthrew all his deductions from previous experience, to find that this girl, though she had been married to him, could yet be so coy. Notwithstanding a certain fascination that it carried with it his reflections were sombre as he went homeward; he saw how deep had been his offence to produce so great a wariness in a gentle and once unsuspicious soul.

He was himself too fastidious to care to coerce her. To be an object of misgiving or dislike to a woman who shared his home was what he could not endure the thought of. Life as it stood was more tolerable.

When he was gone Marty joined Mrs. Fitzpiers. She would fain have consulted Marty on the question of platonic relations with her former husband, as she preferred to regard him. But Marty showed no great interest in their affairs, so Grace said nothing. They came onward and saw Melbury standing at the scene of the felling which had been audible to them, when, telling Marty that she wished her meeting with Mr. Fitzpiers to be kept private, she left the girl to join her father. At any rate she would consult him on the expediency of occasionally seeing her husband.

Her father was cheerful, and walked by her side as he had done in earlier days. "I was thinking of you when you came up," he said. "I have considered that what has happened is for the best. Since your husband is gone away and seems not to wish to trouble you, why, let him go, and drop out of your life. Many women are worse off. You can live here comfortably enough, and he can emigrate, or do what he likes for his good. I wouldn't mind sending him the further sum of money he might naturally expect to come to him, so that you may not be bothered with him any more. . . . . He could hardly have gone on living here without speaking to me, or meeting me; and that would have been very unpleasant on both sides."

These remarks checked her intentions. There was a sense of weakness in following them by saying that she had just met her husband by appointment. "Then you would advise me not to communicate with him?" she observed.

"I shall never advise 'ee again. You are your own mistress—do as you like. But my opinion is that if you don't live with him you had better live without him, and not go shilly-shallying and playing bo-peep. You sent him away; and now he's gone. Very well; trouble him no more."

Grace felt a guiltiness—she hardly knew why—and made no confession.

XLVI

THE woods were uninteresting, and Grace stayed indoors a great deal. She became quite a student, reading more than she had done since her marriage. But her seclusion was always broken for the periodical visit to Winterborne's grave with Marty, which was kept up with pious strictness for the purpose of putting snowdrops, primroses, and other vernal flowers thereon as they came.

One afternoon at sunset she was standing under the trees just at the back of her father's garden which like the rest of the Hintock enclosures abutted into the wood. A slight footpath led along here, forming a secret way to either of the houses by getting through its boundary hedge. Grace was about to adopt this mode of entry when a figure approached along the path and held up his hand to detain her. It was her husband.

"I am delighted," he said coming up out of breath; and there seemed no reason to doubt his words. "I saw you some way off—I was afraid you would go in before I could reach you."

"It is a week before the time," said she reproachfully. "I said a fortnight from the last meeting."

"My dear, you don't suppose I could wait a fortnight without trying to get a glimpse of you, even though you had declined to meet me! Would it make you angry to know that I have been along this path at dusk three or four times since our last meeting? Well, how are you?"

She did not refuse her hand, but when he showed a wish to retain it a moment longer than mere formality required she made it smaller so that it slipped away from him, with again that same alarmed look which always followed his attempts in this direction. He saw that she was not yet out of the elusive mood; not yet to be treated presumingly; and he was correspondingly careful to tranquillize her.

His assertion had seemed to impress her somewhat. "I had no idea you came so often," she said. "How far do you come from?"

"From Sherton Abbas where I am temporarily staying. I always walk the distance here, for if I hire people will know that I come; and my success with you so far has not been great enough to justify such overtness. Now, my dear one—as I *must* call you—I put it to you: will you see me a little oftener as the spring advances?"

Grace lapsed into unwonted sedateness and avoiding the question said, "I wish you would concentrate on your profession, and give up those strange studies that used to distract you so much. I am sure you would get on."

"It is the very thing I am doing. I was going to ask you to burn—or at least get rid of—all my philosophical literature. It is in the bookcases in your rooms. The fact is I never cared much for abstruse studies."

"I am so glad to hear you say that. And those other books—those piles of old plays—what good are they to a medical man?"

"None whatever!" he replied cheerfully. "Sell them at Sherton for what they will fetch."

"And those dreadful old French romances with their horrid spellings of 'filz' and 'ung' and 'ilz' and 'mary' and 'ma foy'."

"You haven't been reading them, Grace?"

"Oh no—I just looked into them, that was all."

"Make a bonfire of 'em directly you get home. I meant to do it myself. I can't think what possessed me ever to collect them. I have only a few professional handbooks now, and am quite a practical man. I am in hopes of having some good news to tell you soon, and then do you think you could—come to me again?"

"I would rather you did not press me on that just now," she replied with some feeling. "You have said you mean to lead a new, useful, effectual life; but I should like to see you put it in practice for a little while before you address that query to me. Besides—I could not live with you."

"Why not?"

Grace was silent a few instants. "I go with Marty to Giles's grave. I almost worship him. We swore we would show him that devotion. And I mean to keep it up."

"Well—I wouldn't mind that at all. I have no right to expect anything else, and I will not wish you to keep away. I liked the man as well as any I ever knew. In short I would accompany you a part of the way to the grave, and smoke a cigar on the stile while I waited till you came back——"

"Then you haven't given up smoking?"

"Well—ahem—no. I have thought of doing so, but——"

His extreme complaisance had rather disconcerted Grace, and the question about smoking had been to effect a diversion. Presently she said firmly, and with a moisture in her eye that he could not see, as her mind returned to poor Giles's "frustrate ghost"; "I don't like you—to speak lightly on that subject, if you did speak lightly. To be frank with you—quite frank—I think of him as my betrothed lover still. I cannot help it. So that it would be wrong for me to join you."

Fitzpiers was now uneasy. "You say your betrothed lover still," he rejoined. "When then were you betrothed to him, or engaged as we common people say?"

"When you were away."

"How could that be?"

Grace would have avoided this; but her natural candour led her on. "It was when I was under the impression that my marriage with you was about to be dissolved, and that he could then marry me. So I encouraged him to love me."

Fitzpiers winced visibly; and yet upon the whole she was right in telling it. Indeed, his perception that she was right in her absolute sincerity kept up his affectionate admiration for her under the pain of the rebuff. Time had been when the avowal that Grace had deliberately taken steps to replace him would have brought him no sorrow. But she so far dominated him now that he could not bear to hear her words, although the object of her high regard was no more.

"It is rough upon me—that!" he said bitterly. "O Grace— I did not know you—tried to get rid of me! I suppose it is of no use, but I ask, cannot you hope to—find a little love in your heart for me again?"

"If I could I would oblige you; but I fear I cannot!" she replied with illogical ruefulness. "And I don't see why you should mind my having had one lover besides yourself in my life when you have had so many."

"But I can tell you honestly that I love you better than all of them put together, and that's what you will not tell me."

"I am sorry; but I fear I cannot," she said sighing again.

"I wonder if you ever will!" He looked musingly into her indistinct face as if he would read the future there. "Now have pity, and tell me: will you try?"

"To love you again?"

"Yes, if you can."

"I don't know how to reply," she answered, her embarrassment proving her truth. "Will you promise to leave me quite free as to seeing you or not seeing you?"

"Certainly. Have I given any ground for you to doubt my first promise in that respect?"

She was obliged to admit that he had not.

"Then I think you might get your heart out of that grave," said he with playful sadness. "It has been there a long time."

She faintly shook her head, but said, "I'll try to think of you more, if I can."

With this Fitzpiers was compelled to be satisfied, and he asked her when she would meet him again.

"As we arranged—in a fortnight."

"If it must be a fortnight it must!"

"This time at least. I'll consider by the day I see you again if I can shorten the interval."

"Well, be that as it may, I shall come at least twice a week to look at your window."

"You must do as you like about that. Good-night."

"Say 'husband.'"

She seemed almost inclined to give him the word; but exclaiming, "No, no—I cannot," slipped through the garden-hedge and disappeared.

Fitzpiers did not exaggerate when he told her that he should haunt the precincts of the dwelling. But his persistence in this course did not result in his seeing her much oftener than at the fortnightly interval which she had herself marked out as proper. At these times, however, she punctually appeared, and as the spring wore on the meetings were kept up, though their character changed but little with the increase in their number.

The small garden of the cottage occupied by the Tangs family—father, son, and now son's wife—aligned with the larger one of the timber-dealer at its upper end; and when young Tim, after leaving work at Melbury's, stood at dusk in the little bower at the corner of his enclosure to smoke a pipe, he frequently observed the surgeon pass along the outside track before-mentioned. Fitzpiers always walked loiteringly, pensively, looking with a sharp eye into the gardens one after another as he proceeded; for Fitzpiers did not wish to leave the now absorbing spot too quickly after travelling so far to reach it, hoping always for a glimpse of her whom he passionately desired to take to his arms anew.

Now Tim began to be struck with these loitering progresses along the garden boundaries in the gloaming, and wondered what they boded. It was, naturally, quite out of his power to divine the singular, sentimental revival in Fitzpiers's heart: the fineness of tissue which could take a deep emotional—almost also an artistic—pleasure in being the yearning *innamorato* of a woman he once had deserted would have seemed an absurdity to the young sawyer. Mr. and Mrs. Fitzpiers were separated; therefore the question of affection as between them was settled. But his Suke had, since that meeting on their marriage-day, repentantly admitted, to the urgency of his questioning, a good deal concerning her past levities. Putting all things together he could hardly avoid connecting Fitzpiers's mysterious visits to this spot with Suke's residence under his roof. But he made himself fairly easy: the vessel in which they were about to emigrate sailed that month; and then Suke would be out of Fitzpiers's way for ever.

The interval at last expired, and the eve of their departure arrived. They were pausing in the room of the cottage allotted to them by Tim's father, after a busy day of preparation which left them weary. In a corner stood their boxes, crammed and corded, their large case for the hold having already been sent away. The firelight shone upon Suke's plump face and form as she stood looking into it, and upon the face of Tim seated in a corner, and upon the walls of his father's house, which he was beholding that night almost for the last time.

Tim Tangs was not happy. This scheme of emigration was dividing him from his father—for old Tangs would on no account leave Hintock—and had it not been for Suke's reputation and his own dignity Tim would at the last moment have abandoned the project. As he sat in the back part of the room he regarded her moodily, and the fire, and the boxes. One thing he had particularly noticed this evening—she was very restless; fitful in her actions, unable to remain seated, and in a marked degree depressed.

"Sorry that you be going, after all, Suke?" he said.

She sighed involuntarily. "I don't know but that I be," she answered. "'Tis natural, isn't it, when one is going away?"

"But you wasn't born here as I was."

"No."

"There's folk left behind that you'd fain have with 'ee, I reckon?"

"Why do you think that?"

"I've seen things, and I've heard things; and Suke, I say 'twill be a good move for me to get 'ee away. . . . I don't mind his leavings abroad, but I do mind 'em at home."

Suke's face was not changed from its aspect of listless indifference by the words. She answered nothing; and shortly after he went out for his customary pipe of tobacco at the top of the garden.

The restlessness of Suke had indeed owed its presence to the gentleman of Tim's suspicions, but in a different—and it must be added in justice to her—more innocent sense than he supposed, judging from former doings. She had accidentally discovered that Fitzpiers was in the habit of coming secretly once or twice a week to Hintock, and knew that this evening was a favourite one of the seven for his journey. As she was going next day to leave the country Suke thought there could be no great harm in giving way to a little sentimentality by obtaining a glimpse of him quite unknown to himself or to anybody, and thus taking a silent last farewell. Awaré that Fitzpiers's time for passing was at hand she thus betrayed her feeling. No sooner, therefore, had Tim left the room than she let herself noiselessly out of the house and hastened to the corner of the garden whence she could witness the surgeon's transit across the scene—if he had not already gone by.

Her light cotton dress was visible to Tim lounging in the arbour of the opposite corner, though he was hidden from her. He saw her stealthily climb into the hedge, and so ensconce herself there that nobody could have the least doubt her purpose was to watch unseen for a passer-by.

He went across to the spot and stood behind her. Suke started, having, in her blundering way, forgotten that he might be near. She at once descended from the hedge.

"So he's coming to-night," said Tim laconically. "And we be always anxious to see our dears."

"He *is* coming to-night," she replied with defiance. "And we *be* anxious for our dears."

"Then will you step indoors, where your dear will soon jine 'ee? We've to mouster by half-past-three to-morrow, and if we don't get to bed by eight at latest our faces will be as long as clock-cases all day."

She hesitated for a minute but ultimately obeyed, going slowly down the garden to the house, where he heard the door-latch click behind her.

Tim was incensed beyond measure. His marriage had so

far been a total failure, a source of bitter regret; and the only course for improving his case, that of leaving the country, was a sorry, and possibly might not be a very effectual one. Do what he would his domestic sky was likely to be overcast to the end of the day. Thus he brooded, and his resentment gathered force. He craved a means of striking one blow back at the cause of his cheerless plight while he was still on the scene of his discomfiture. For some minutes no method suggested itself; and then he had an idea.

Coming to a sudden resolution he hastened along the garden, and entered the one attached to the next cottage, which had formerly been the dwelling of a gamekeeper. Tim descended the path to the back of the house, where only an old woman lived at present, and reaching the wall he stopped. Owing to the slope of the ground the roof-eaves of the linhay were here within touch, and he thrust his arm up under them, feeling about in the space on the top of the wall-plate.

"Ah—I thought my memory didn't deceive me!" he lipped silently.

With some exertion he drew down a cobwebbed object curiously framed in iron; which clanked as he moved it. It was about three feet in length and half as wide. Tim contemplated it as well as he could in the dying light of day, and raked off the cobwebs with his hand.

"That will spoil his pretty shins for'n, I reckon!" he said.

It was a man-trap.

XLVII

Were the inventors of automatic machines to be ranged according to the excellence of their devices for producing sound, artistic torture, the creator of the man-trap would occupy a very respectable, if not a very high place.

It should rather, however, be said, the inventor of the particular form of man-trap of which this found in the keeper's outhouse was a specimen. For there were other shapes and other sizes; instruments which, if placed in a row beside one of the type disinterred by Tim, would have worn the subordinate

aspect of the bears, wild boars, or wolves in a travelling mena-
gerie as compared with the leading lion or tiger. In short,
though many varieties had been in use during those centuries
which we are accustomed to look back upon as the true and
only period of merry England—in the rural districts more
especially—and onward down to the third decade of the nineteenth century, this model had borne the palm, and had been
most usually followed when the orchards and estates required
new ones.

There had been the toothless variety used by the softer-
hearted landlords—quite contemptible in their clemency.
The jaws of these resembled the jaws of an old woman to
whom time has left nothing but gums. There were also the
intermediate or half-toothed sorts, probably devised by the
middle-natured squires, or those under the influence of their
wives—two inches of mercy, two inches of cruelty, two inches
of mere nip, two inches of probe, and so on through the
whole extent of the jaws. There were also, as a class apart,
the bruisers, which did not lacerate the flesh, but only crushed
the bone.

The sight of one of these gins when set produced a vivid
impression that it was endowed with life. It exhibited the
combined aspects of a shark, a crocodile, and a scorpion.
Each tooth was in the form of a tapering spine two-and-a-
quarter inches long, which when the jaws were closed stood
in alternation from this side and from that. When they were
open the two halves formed a complete circle between two
and three feet in diameter, the plate or treading-place in the
midst being about a foot square, while from beneath extended in opposite directions the soul of the apparatus, the
pair of springs, each one having been in its prime of a stiffness
to render necessary a lever, or the whole weight of the body,
when forcing it down, though rust had weakened it somewhat now.

There were men at this time still living at Hintock who
remembered when the gin and others like it were in use. Tim
Tang's great-uncle had endured a night of six hours in this
very trap, which lamed him for life. Once a keeper of Hintock
woods set it on the track of a poacher, and afterwards coming

back that way, forgetful of what he had done, walked into it himself. The wound brought on lock-jaw of which he died. This event occurred during the thirties, and by the year 1840, the use of such implements was well-nigh discontinued in the neighbourhood. But being made entirely of iron they by no means disappeared, and in almost every village one could be found in some nook or corner as readily as this was found by Tim. It had indeed been a fearful amusement of Tim and other Hintock lads—especially those who had a dim sense of becoming renowned poachers when they reached their prime—to drag out this trap from its hiding, set it, and throw it with billets of wood, which were penetrated by the teeth to the depth of near an inch.

As soon as he had examined the trap and found that the hinges and springs were fairly perfect, he shouldered it without more ado and returned with his burden to his own garden, passing on through the hedge to the path immediately outside the boundary. Here by the help of a stout stake he set the trap and laid it carefully behind a bush while he went forward to reconnoitre. As has been stated, nobody passed this way for days together sometimes; but there was just a possibility that some other pedestrian than the one in request might arrive, and it behoved Tim to be careful as to the identity of his victim.

Going about a hundred yards along the rising ground to the right he reached a ridge whereon a large and thick holly grew. Beyond this for some distance the wood was more open, and the course which Fitzpiers must pursue to reach the point, if he came to-night, was visible a long way forward.

For some time there was no sign of him, or of anybody. Then there shaped itself a spot out of the dim mid-distance, between the masses of brushwood on each hand. It enlarged, and Tim could hear the brushing of feet over the tufts of sour grass. The airy gait revealed Fitzpiers even before his exact outline could be seen.

Tim Tangs turned about and ran down the opposite side of the hill till he was again at the head of his own garden. It was the work of a few moments to drag out the man-trap very gently—that the plate might not be disturbed sufficiently to throw it—to a space between a pair of young oaks which, rooted in contiguity, grew apart upward, forming a V-shaped opening between; and, being backed up by bushes, left this as the only course for a foot passenger. In it he laid the trap with the same gentleness of handling, locked the chain round one of the trees, and finally slid back the guard which was placed to keep the gin from accidentally catching the arms of him who set it, or—to use the local and better word— "toiled" it. Having completed these arrangements Tim sprang through the adjoining hedge of his father's garden, ran down the path, and softly entered the house.

Obedient to his order, Suke had gone to bed, and as soon as he had bolted the door Tim unlaced and kicked off his boots at the foot of the stairs and retired likewise, without lighting a candle. His object seemed to be to undress as soon as possible. Before, however, he had completed the operation a long cry resounded without—penetrating, but indescribable.

"What's that?" said Suke, starting up in bed.

"Sounds as if somebody had caught a hare in his gin."

"O no," said she. "It was not a hare. 'Twas louder. Hark!"

"Do 'ee get to sleep!" said Tim. "How be you going to wake at half-past-three else?"

She lay down and was silent. Tim stealthily opened the window and listened. Above the low harmonies produced by the instrumentation of the various species of tree around the premises he could hear the twitching of a chain from the spot whereon he had set the man-trap. But further human sound there was none.

Tim was puzzled. In the haste of his project he had not calculated upon a cry; but if one, why not more? He soon ceased to essay an answer; for Hintock was dead to him already. In half-a-dozen hours he would be out of its precincts for life, on his way to the antipodes. He closed the window, and lay down.

The hour which had brought these movements of Tim to birth had been operating actively elsewhere. Awaiting in her father's house the minute of her appointment with her husband Grace Fitzpiers deliberated on many things. Should she inform her father before going out that the estrangement of herself and Edred was not so complete as he had imagined and deemed desirable for her happiness? If she did so she must in some measure become the apologist of her husband, and she was not prepared to go so far.

As for him, he kept her in a mood of considerate gravity. He certainly had changed. He had at his worst times always been gentle in his manner towards her. Could it be that she might make of him a true and worthy husband yet? She had married him; there was no getting over that; and ought she any longer to keep him at a distance. His suave deference to her lightest whim on the question of his comings and goings, when as her lawful husband he might show a little insistence, was a trait in his character as unexpected as it was engaging. If she had been his empress, and he her thrall, he could not have exhibited a more sensitive care to avoid intruding upon her against her will.

Impelled by a remembrance she took down a prayer-book and turned to the marriage-service. Reading it slowly through she became quite appalled at her recent offhandedness, when she rediscovered what awfully solemn promises she had made him at Hintock chancel steps not so very long ago. She became lost in long ponderings on how far a person's conscience might be bound by vows made without at the time a full recognition of their force. That particular sentence, beginning, "Whom God hath joined together," was a staggerer for a gentle woman of strong devotional sentiment. She wondered whether God really did join them together. Before she had done deliberating the time of her engagement drew near, and she went out of the house almost at the moment that Tim Tangs retired to his own.

The position of things at that critical juncture was as follows. Two hundred yards to the right of the upper end of Tangs's garden Fitzpiers was still advancing, having now nearly reached the summit of the wood-clothed ridge, the path being the actual one which further on passed between the two young oaks. Thus far it was according to Tim's conjecture. But about two hundred yards to the left, or rather less, was arising a condition which he had not divined, the emergence of Grace as aforesaid from the upper corner of her father's garden, with the view of meeting Tim's intended victim. Midway between husband and wife was the diabolical trap, silent, open, ready.

Fitzpiers's walk that night had been cheerful, for he was convinced that the slow and gentle method he had adopted was promising success. The very restraint that he was obliged to exercise upon himself, so as not to kill the delicate bud of returning confidence, fed his flame. He walked so much more rapidly than Grace that, if they continued advancing as they had begun, he would reach the trap a good half-minute before she could reach the same spot. But here a new circumstance came in: to escape the unpleasantness of being watched or listened to by lurkers—naturally curious by reason of their strained relations—they had arranged that their meeting for to-night should be at the holm-tree on the ridge above-named. So soon, accordingly, as Fitzpiers reached the tree he stood still to await her.

He had not paused under the prickly foliage more than two minutes when he thought he heard a scream from the other side of the ridge. Fitzpiers wondered what it could mean; but such wind as there was just now blew in an adverse direction, and his mood was light. He set down the origin of the sound to one of the superstitious freaks or frolicsome scrimmages between sweethearts that still survived in Hintock from old-English times; and waited on where he stood till ten minutes had passed. Feeling then a little uneasy his mind reverted to the scream; and he went forward over the summit and down the embowered incline till he reached the pair of sister oaks with the narrow opening between them.

Fitzpiers stumbled and all but fell. Stretching down his hand to ascertain the obstruction it came in contact with a confused mass of silken drapery and ironwork, that conveyed absolutely no explanatory idea to his mind at all. It was but the work of a moment to strike a match; and then he saw a sight which congealed his blood.

The man-trap was thrown; and between its jaws was part of a woman's clothing—a patterned silk skirt—gripped with such violence that the iron teeth had passed through it, skewering its tissue in a score of places. He immediately recognised the skirt as that of one of his wife's gowns—the gown that she had worn when she met him on the very last occasion.

Fitzpiers had often studied the effect of these instruments when examining the collection at Hintock House; and the conception instantly flashed through him that Grace had been caught, taken out mangled by some chance passer, and carried home, some of her clothes being left behind in the difficulty of getting her free. The shock of this conviction, striking into the very current of high hope, was so great that he cried out like one in corporal agony, and in his misery bowed himself down to the ground.

Of all the degrees and qualities of punishment that Fitzpiers had undergone since his sins against Grace first began, not any even approximated in intensity to this. "O my own— my darling—O cruel Heaven—it is too much this!" he cried, writhing and rocking himself over the sorry accessories of her he deplored.

The voice of his distress was sufficiently loud to be audible to any one who might have been there to hear it; and one there was. Right and left of the narrow pass between the oaks were dense bushes; and now from behind these a female figure glided, whose appearance even in the gloom was though graceful in outline noticeably strange.

She was in white up to the waist, and figured above. She was, in short, Grace his wife, lacking the portion of her dress which the gin retained.

"Don't be grieved about me—don't, dear Edred!" she exclaimed, rushing up and bending over him. "I am not hurt a bit! I was coming on to find you after I had released myself, but I heard footsteps, and I hid away, because I was without some of my clothing and I did not know who the person might be."

Fitzpiers had sprung to his feet, and his next act was no less unpremeditated by him than it was irresistible by her, and would have been so by any woman not of Amazonian strength. He clasped his arms completely round her, pressed her to his breast, and kissed her passionately.

"You are not dead!—you are not hurt! Thank God—thank God!" he said almost sobbing in his delight and relief from the horror of his apprehension. "Grace, my wife, my love, how is this—what has happened?"

"I was coming on to you," she said as distinctly as she could in the half-smothered state of her face against his. "I was trying to be as punctual as possible, and as I had started a minute late I ran along the path very swiftly—fortunately for myself. Just when I had passed between these trees I felt something clutch at my dress from behind with a noise, and the next moment I was pulled backwards by it, and fell to the ground. I screamed with terror—thinking it was a man lying down there to murder me—but the next moment I discovered it was iron, and that my clothes were caught in a trap. I pulled this way and that, but the thing would not let go, drag it as I would, and I did not know what to do. I did not want to alarm my father, or anybody, as I wished nobody to know of these meetings with you; so I could think of no other plan than slipping off my skirt, meaning to run on and tell you what a strange accident had happened to me. But when I had just freed myself by leaving the dress behind I heard steps, and not being sure it was you I did not like to be seen in such a pickle so I hid away."

"It was only your speed that saved you! One or both of your legs would have been broken if you had come at ordinary walking pace."

"Or yours, if you had got here first!" said she, beginning to realise the whole ghastliness of the possibility, or what seemed a possibility to them, though whether the old springs would have done quite so much mischief may be doubted. "O Edred, there has been an Eye watching over us to-night, and we should be thankful indeed."

He continued to press his face to hers. "You are mine, mine again now."

She owned that she supposed she was. "I heard what you said when you thought I was injured," she went on shyly, "and I know that a man who could suffer as you were suffering must have a tender regard for me. But how does this awful thing come here?"

"I suppose it has something to do with poachers." Fitzpiers was still so shaken by the sense of her danger that he was obliged to sit awhile and it was not until Grace said, "If I could only get my skirt out nobody would know anything about it," that he bestirred himself.

By their united efforts, each standing on one of the springs of the trap, they pressed them down sufficiently to insert across the jaws a billet which they dragged from a faggot near at hand: and it was then possible to extract the silk mouthful from the monster's bite, creased and pierced with small holes, but not torn. Fitzpiers assisted her to put it on again; and when her customary contours were thus restored they walked on together, Grace taking his arm till he effected an improvement by passing it round her waist.

The ice having been broken in this unexpected manner she made no further attempt at reserve. "I would ask you to come into the house," she said; "but my meetings with you have been kept secret from my father, and I should like to prepare him."

"Never mind, dearest. I could not very well have accepted the invitation. I shall never live here again—as much for your sake as for mine. I have news to tell you on this very point, but my alarm had put it out of my head. I have bought a practice, or rather a partnership, in the Midlands, and I must go there in a week to take up permanent residence. My poor old great-aunt died about eight months ago, and left me enough to do this. I have taken a little furnished house for a time, till we can get one of our own."

He described the place, and the surroundings, and the view from the windows; and Grace became much interested. "But why are you not there now?" she said.

"Because I cannot tear myself away from here till I have your promise. Now, darling, you will accompany me there soon—will you not? To-night has settled that?"

Grace's tremblings had gone off, and she did not say nay. They went on together. The adventure, and the emotions consequent upon the reunion which that event had forced on, combined to render Grace oblivious of the direction of their desultory ramble, till she noticed they were in an encircled glade in the densest part of the wood. The moon, that had imperceptibly added her rays to the scene, shone almost vertically.

It was an exceptionally soft balmy evening for the time of year, which was just that transient period in the May month when beech trees have suddenly unfolded large limp young leaves of the softness of butterflies' wings. Boughs bearing such leaves hung low around and completely enclosed them, so that it was as if they were in a great green vase, which had moss for its bottom and leaf sides. Here they sat down.

The clouds having been packed in the west that evening so as to retain the departing glare a long while, the hour had seemed much earlier than it was. But suddenly the question of time occurred to her.

"I must go back!" she said, springing up; and without further delay they set their faces towards Hintock. As they walked he examined his watch by the aid of the now strong moonlight.

"By the gods I think I have lost my train!" said Fitzpiers.

"Dear me—whereabouts are we?" said she.

"Two miles in the direction of Sherton."

"Then do you hasten on, Edred. I am not in the least afraid. I recognise now the part of the wood we are in, and I can find my way back quite easily. I'll tell my father that we have made it up—I wish I had not kept our meetings so private, for it may vex him a little to know I have been seeing you. He is getting old and irritable; that was why I did not. Good-bye."

"But—as I must stay at the Earl of Wessex to-night, for I cannot possibly catch the train, I think it would be safer for you to let me take care of you."

"But what will my father think has become of me! He does not know in the least where I am—he thinks I only went into the garden for a few minutes."

"He will surely guess—somebody has seen me for certain. I'll go all the way back with you to-morrow."

"But that newly done-up place the Earl of Wessex!"

"If you are so very particular about the publicity I will stay at a little quiet one."

"O no—it is not that I am particular—but I haven't a brush or comb or anything!"

XLVIII

ALL the evening Melbury had been coming to his door saying, "I wonder where in the world that girl is! Never in all my born days did I know her bide out like this. She surely said she was going into the garden to get some parsley."

Melbury searched the garden, the outbuildings, and the orchard, but could find no trace of her, and then he made inquiries at the cottages of such of his workmen as had not gone to bed, avoiding Tangs's because he knew the young people were to rise early to leave. In these inquiries one of the men's wives somewhat incautiously let out the fact that she had heard a scream in the wood, though from which direction she could not say.

This set Melbury's fears on end. He told the men to light lanterns, and headed by himself they started, Creedle following at the last moment with a bundle of grapnels and ropes which he could not be persuaded to leave behind, and the company being joined by the hollow-turner and Cawtree as they went along.

They explored the precincts of the village, and in a short time lighted upon the man-trap. Its discovery simply added an item of fact without helping their conjectures; but Melbury's indefinite alarm was greatly increased when, holding a candle to the ground, he saw in the teeth of the instrument some frayings from Grace's clothing. No intelligence of any kind was gained till they met a woodman of Delborough, who said that he had seen a lady answering to the description her father gave of Grace, walking through the wood on a gentleman's arm in the direction of Sherton.

"Was he supporting her?" said Melbury.

"Well—rather," said the man.

"Did she walk lame?"

"Well 'tis true her head hung over towards him a bit."

Creedle groaned tragically. Melbury, not suspecting the presence of Fitzpiers, coupled this account with the man-trap and the scream; he could not understand what it all meant, but the sinister event of the trap made him follow on. Accordingly they bore away towards the town shouting as they went, and in due course emerged upon the highway.

Nearing Sherton-Abbas the previous information was confirmed by other strollers, though the gentleman's supporting arm had disappeared from these later accounts. At last they were so near Sherton that Melbury informed his faithful followers that he did not wish to drag them further at so late an hour, since he could go on by himself and inquire if the woman who had been seen were really Grace. But they would not leave him alone in his anxiety, and trudged onward till the lamplight from the town began to illuminate their faces. At the entrance to the borough they got fresh scent of the pursued, but coupled with the new condition that the lady in the costume described had been going up the street alone.

"Faith—I believe she's mesmerised, or walking in her sleep!" said Melbury.

However, the identity of this woman with Grace was by no means certain; but they plodded along the street. Percomb the hairdresser, who had despoiled Marty of her tresses, was standing at his door, and they duly put inquiries to him.

"Ah—how's Little Hintock folk by now!" he cried before replying. "Never have I been over there since one winter night some three year ago—and then I lost myself finding it. How can ye live in such a one-eyed place? Great Hintock is bad enough—but Little Hintock—the bats and owls would drive me melancholy-mad! It took two days to raise my sperrits to their true pitch again after that night I went there. Mr. Melbury sir, as a man that's put by money why not retire and live here, and see something of the world?" The responses at last given by him to their queries guided them to the building that offered the best accommodation in Sherton—having been rebuilt contemporaneously with the construction of the railway—namely, the Earl of Wessex Hotel.

Leaving the others without Melbury made prompt inquiry here. His alarm was lessened, though his perplexity was increased, when he received a brief reply that such a lady was in the house.

"Do you know if it is my daughter?" asked Melbury.

The waiter did not.

"Do you know the lady's name?"

Of this, too, the household was ignorant, the hotel having been taken by bran-new people from a distance. They knew the gentleman very well by sight, and had not thought it necessary to ask him to enter his name.

"Oh—the gentleman appears again now," said Melbury to himself. "Well—I want to see the lady," he declared.

A message was taken up, and after some delay the shape of Grace appeared descending round the bend of the staircase, looking as if she lived there, but in other respects rather guilty and frightened.

"Why—what the name—" began her father. "I thought you went out to get parsley!"

"O yes—I did—but it is all right," said Grace in a flurried whisper. "I am not alone here. I am here with Edred. It is entirely owing to an accident, father."

"Edred—an accident? How does he come here? I thought he was two hundred mile off!"

"Yes—so he is—I mean, he has got a beautiful practice two hundred miles off—he has bought it with his own money— some that came to him. But he travelled here, and I was nearly caught in a man-trap, and that's how it is I am here. We were just thinking of sending a messenger to let you know."

Melbury did not seem to be particularly enlightened by this explanation.

"You were caught in a man-trap?"

"Yes—my dress was—that's how it arose."

"Oh."

"Edred is upstairs in the sitting-room," she went on. "He would not mind seeing you, I am sure."

"O faith, I don't want to see him—I have seen him too often a'ready. . . . . I'll see him another time, perhaps, if 'tis to oblige 'ee."

"He came to see me—he wanted to consult me about this large partnership I speak of—as it is very promising."

"Oh—I am glad to hear it," said Melbury drily.

A pause ensued, during which the inquiring faces and whitey-brown clothes of Melbury's companions appeared in the doorway.

"Then bain't you coming home with us?" he asked.

"I—I think not," said Grace blushing.

"H'm—very well—you are your own mistress," he returned in tones which seemed to assert otherwise. "Good-night." And Melbury retreated towards the door.

"Don't be angry, father," she said following him a few steps. "I have done it for the best."

"I am not angry—though it is true I have been a little misled in this. However, good-night. I must get home-along."

He left the hotel, not without relief; for to be under the eyes of strangers while he conversed with his lost child had embarrassed him much. His search-party, too, had looked awkward there—having rushed to the task of investigation some in their shirt-sleeves, others in their leather-aprons, and all much stained, just as they had come from their work of barking, and not in their Sherton marketing attire; while Creedle, with his ropes and grapnels and air of impending tragedy had added melancholy to gawkiness.

"Now, neighbours," said Melbury on joining them, "as it is getting late we'll leg it home again as fast as we can. I ought to tell you that there has been some mistake—some arrangement entered into between Mr. and Mrs. Fitzpiers which I didn't quite understand—an important practice in the Midland Counties had come to him, which made it necessary for her to join him to-night—so she says. That's all it was—and I'm sorry I dragged you out."

"Well," said the hollow-turner, "here be we seven mile from home, and night-time, and not a hoss or four-footed creeping thing to our name. I say we'll have a mossel and a drop o' summat to strengthen our nerves afore we vamp all the way back again? My throat's as dry as a kex. What d'ye say, so's?"

They all concurred on the need for sustenance, and proceeded to the antique back street in which the red curtain of the tavern to which Winterborne had taken Grace was the only radiant object. As soon as they had stumbled down into the room Melbury ordered them to be served, when they made themselves comfortable by the long table, and stretched out their legs upon the herring-boned sand of the floor. Melbury himself, restless as usual, walked to the door while he waited for them, and looked up and down the street.

"Well—he's her husband," Melbury said to himself, "and let her take him back to her bed if she will! . . . But let her bear in mind that the woman walks and laughs somewhere at this very moment whose neck he'll be coling next year as he does hers to-night; and as he did Felice Charmond's last year; and Suke Damson's the year afore! . . . It's a forlorn hope for her; and God knows how it will end!"

Inside the inn the talk was also of the reunited pair.

"I'd gie her a good shaking if she were my maid, pretending to go out in garden, and leading folk a dozen-mile traipse that have got to get up at five o'clock to-morrow," said a bark-ripper who, not working regularly for Melbury, could afford to indulge in strong opinions.

"I don't speak so warm as that," said the hollow-turner, "but if 'tis right for couples to make a country talk about their parting for ever, and excite the neighbours, and then make fools of 'em like this, why, I haven't stood upon one leg for five-and-twenty year."

All his listeners knew that when he alluded to his foot-lathe in these enigmatic terms the speaker meant to be impressive; and Creedle chimed in with, "Ah, young women do wax wanton in these days! Why couldn't she ha' bode with her father, and been faithful." Poor Creedle was thinking of his old employer.

"But this deceiving of folks is nothing unusual in matrimony," said Farmer Cawtree. "I know'd a man and wife—faith, I don't mind owning as there's no strangers here, that the pair were my own relations—they'd be at it that hot one hour that you'd hear the poker, and the tongs, and the bellows, and the warming-pan, flee across the house with the movements of their vengeance; and the next hour you'd hear 'em singing 'The Spotted Cow' together as peaceable as two holy twins; yes—and very good voices they had, and would strike in like street ballet-singers to one another's support in the high notes."

"'Tis so with couples: they do make up differences in all manner of queer ways," said the bark-ripper. "I knowed a woman; and the husband o' her went away for four-and-twenty year. And one night he came home when she was sitting by the fire, and thereupon he sat down himself on the other side of the chimney-corner. 'Well,' says she, 'have ye got any news?'—'Don't know as I have,' says he. 'Have you?'—'No,' says she, 'except that my daughter by the husband that succeeded 'ee was married last month, which was a year after I was made a widow by him.'—'Oh—Anything else?' he says.—'No,' says she. And there they sat one on each side of that chimney-corner, and were found by the neighbours sound asleep in their chairs, not having known what to talk about at all."

"Well, I don't care who the man is," said Creedle, "it took a good deal to interest 'em, and that's true. It won't be the same with these."

"No—He is such a projick, you see. And she is a wonderful scholar, too!"

"What women do know nowadays!" observed the hollow-turner. "You can't deceive 'em as you could in my time."

"What they knowed then was not small," said John Upjohn. "Always a good deal more than the men. Why, when I was courting my wife that is now, the skilfulness that she would show in keeping me on her pretty side as she walked was beyond all belief—perhaps you've noticed that she's got a pretty side to her face as well as a plain one?"

"I can't say I've noticed it particular much," said the hollow-turner blandly.

"Well," continued Upjohn, not disconcerted, "she has. All women under the sun be prettier one side than t'other. And, as I was saying, the pains she would take to make me walk on the pretty side were unending! I warrant that whether we were going with the sun or against the sun, uphill or down-hill, in wind or in lewth, that wart of hers was always towards the hedge, and that dimple towards me. There was I, too

simple to see her wheelings and turnings; and she so artful,
though two years younger, that she could lead me with a
cotton thread, like a blind ram; for that was in the third
climate of our courtship. . . . . No—I don't think the women
have got cleverer, for they was never otherwise."

"How many climates may there be in courtship, Mr.
Upjohn?" inquired a youth—the same who had assisted at
Winterborne's Christmas party.

"Five—from the coolest to the hottest—leastwise there was
five in mine."

"Can ye give us the chronicle of 'em, Mr. Upjohn?"

"Yes—I could. I could certainly. But 'tis quite unnecessary.
They'll come to ye by nater, young man, too soon for your
good."

"At present Mrs. Fitzpiers can lead the doctor as your mis'ess
could lead you," the hollow-turner remarked. "She's got him
quite tame. But how long 'twill last I can't say. I happened
to be setting a wire on the top of my garden one night when
he met her on the other side of the hedge; and the way she
queened it, and fenced, and kept that poor feller at a distance was enough to freeze yer blood. I should never have
supposed it of such a girl."

Melbury now returned to the room, and the men having
declared themselves refreshed they all started on the homeward journey, which was by no means cheerless under the
rays of the high moon. Having to walk the whole distance
they came by a footpath rather shorter than the highway,
though difficult except to those who knew the country well.
This brought them by way of the church; and passing the
graveyard they observed as they talked a motionless figure
standing by the gate.

"I think it was Marty South," said the hollow-turner paren-
thetically.

"I think 'twas: 'a was always a lonely maid," said Upjohn.
And they passed on homeward, and thought of the matter
no more.

It was Marty, as they had supposed. That evening had been
the particular one of the week upon which Grace and herself
had been accustomed to privately deposit flowers on Giles's

grave, and this was the first occasion since his death eight months earlier on which Grace had failed to keep her appointment. Marty had waited in the road just outside Melbury's, where her fellow pilgrim had been wont to join her, till she was weary; and at last, thinking that Grace had missed her and gone on alone, she followed the way to the church, but saw no Grace in front of her. It got later, and Marty continued her walk till she reached the churchyard gate; but still no Grace. Yet her sense of comradeship would not allow her to go on to the grave alone, and, still thinking the delay had been unavoidable she stood there with her little basket of flowers in her clasped hands, and her feet chilled by the damp ground, till more than two hours had passed. She then heard the footsteps of Melbury's men, who presently passed on their return from the search. In the silence of the night Marty could not help hearing fragments of their conversation, from which she acquired a general idea of what had occurred, and that Mrs. Fitzpiers was by that time in the arms of another man than Giles.

Immediately they had dropped down the hill she entered the churchyard, going to a secluded corner behind the bushes where rose the unadorned stone that marked the last bed of Giles Winterborne. As this solitary and silent girl stood there in the moonlight, a straight slim figure, clothed in a plaitless gown, the contours of womanhood so undeveloped as to be scarcely perceptible in her, the marks of poverty and toil effaced by the misty hour, she touched sublimity at points, and looked almost like a being who had rejected with indifference the attribute of sex for the loftier quality of abstract humanism. She stooped down and cleared away the withered flowers that Grace and herself had laid there the previous week, and put her fresh ones in their place.

"Now, my own own love," she whispered, "you are mine, and only mine; for she has forgot 'ee at last, although for her you died. But I—whenever I get up I'll think of 'ee, and whenever I lie down I'll think of 'ee again. Whenever I plant the young larches I'll think that none can plant as you planted; and whenever I split a gad, and whenever I turn the cider-wring I'll say none could do it like you. If ever I forget your name let me forget home and heaven. . . . But no, no, my love, I never can forget 'ee; for you was a good man, and did good things!"

THE END

EXPLANATORY NOTES

THESE notes combine textual notes and explanatory notes in one
list. To save space, the textual notes use the following sigla to identify the different versions of the novel from which variants are being
cited. In quotations from the MS, angled brackets enclose material
deleted within the MS, and slanted lines enclose material added
within the MS, usually interlineally.

MS   Manuscript (in the Dorset County Museum, Dorchester)
HB   *Harper's Bazar* (weekly, 15 May 1886–9 April 1887)
A1   American first edition (one volume, Harper & Brothers), 1887
MM   *Macmillan's Magazine* (monthly, May 1886–April 1887)
87a English first edition (three volumes, Macmillan), 1887
Col Colonial Library Edition (Macmillan), 1887
87b English one-volume, or six-shilling, edition (Macmillan), 1887
96   Wessex Novels collected edition (Osgood, McIlvaine), 1896
12pc Printer's copy for the Wessex Edition (a 1906 copy of the
     1903 Uniform Edition, with Hardy's handwritten revisions),
     1911
12   Wessex Edition (Macmillan), 1912

For help on several of these notes I thank Doug Corcoran, Simon
Gatrell, Marianne Kalinke, Jana Kramer, and Robert Rogers.

    TITLE PAGE. *'Not boskiest . . . the wind!'*: the four-line poem was
written by Hardy for the Osgood, McIlvaine edition of the
novel (96).

3 PREFACE. *one or two others of this series*: nearly all of Hardy's
greater novels deal with this theme; but perhaps Hardy has in
mind primarily *Tess of the d'Urbervilles* and *Jude the Obscure*.

    "the duty . . . controversy": from Chapter 15 of *The History of the
Decline and Fall of the Roman Empire*, by Edward Gibbon (1737–
94). Like Hardy, Gibbon treated religion ironically and was a
religious sceptic while remaining an Anglican. Hardy claimed
Gibbon was one of the writers whose style he considered while
developing his own ideas about writing (*Life and Work of Thomas
Hardy*, p. 108).

4 *"copsework"*: products made from the branches of trees grown
for the purpose of pollarding (periodical cutting), to obtain
shoots of the desired lengths. The passage on p. 10 (see note)

describes some of the activities that come under this general term; and p. 17 names some of the products.

5 *meridional*: pertaining to the meridians, imaginary lines running due north and south used in navigation.

   incubus: demon or evil spirit that appears in a nightmare. An incubus can have sexual intercourse with sleeping women. It is not inappropriate for this word to appear in a context close to a description of Fitzpiers as a worker of black magic.

6 *Eastern plain*: Hardy seems to be suggesting that the horse is Arabian.

7 *crupper*: a leather loop that passes under the horse's tail. By means of a vertical connecting strap, the crupper helps hold straight the breeching, which passes lower down on the horse's buttocks.

   Dumpy level: a long spirit-level connected to a telescope, so that when the bubble is centred the line of sight is horizontal; used in surveying for measuring elevations.

   tilt: a coarse cloth, canvas canopy or awning.

   catenary curve: 'The curve formed by a chain or rope of uniform density hanging freely from two fixed points not in the same vertical line' (*OED*, which gives this line from *The Woodlanders* as an example). Strictly speaking the line formed by the reins is not a catenary curve, in that neither the end attached to the horse nor to the hook is perfectly 'fixed' in relation to each other.

   waxen woman: the wax bust on which wigs are displayed.

   journeyman hair-cutter . . . master-barber: a journeyman has completed his apprenticeship and is an employee; a master is in business, employing journeymen.

   that's left off his pole because 'tis not genteel: a barber's pole would mean he was open for public business; as it is, Percomb has a private clientele.

8 *and High-Stoy . . . At length*: in MS-87b, this was 'till they turned into a half-invisible little lane, whence, as it reached the verge of an eminence,'. The revision is one of those by which Hardy transferred the action from the Bubb Down Hill area to that of High-Stoy Hill.

   flitches: sides of bacon.

   dramas of a grandeur and unity truly Sophoclean . . . therein: Sophocles (497[495?]–406 BC), Greek writer of tragedies. His

Oedipus Rex is praised by Aristotle in the *Poetics* as the supreme instance of organization aimed to achieve a single powerful effect.

9 *pomace*: pulpy substance resulting from crushing or grinding apples.

10 *bill-hook . . . spars . . . spar-gads*: a bill-hook is a sharp hooked instrument used in pruning. A spar is a pointed stick used to fasten thatching to roofs. Spar-gads are peeled sticks that are made from gads (stout straight sticks) by the procedure described in the paragraph.

coffin-stool: a small stool used for general purposes, including holding the coffin when the burial service begins from the home.

deal: fir or pine.

tenure . . . by copy of court-roll: a court-roll is a record of rents and holdings on a manor, 'a copy of which constitutes the tenant's title to his holding' (*OED*). Such a tenant is known as a 'copyholder'. Although technically held at the will of the lord of the manor, such tenancy—controlled by customary practice in the neighbourhood and not subject to arbitrary decisions by the landowner—amounted to securely held property. (Copyhold and other residual feudal forms of tenure ownership were abolished in 1925, and replaced by the single concept of 'socage'—that is, 'ownership', or fee simple.) A 'cotter' (or 'cottar'), on the other hand, held only temporary possession, subject to a lease, usually requiring labour in payment.

changes had led: in MS, this read 'for the last generation or two a feeling of *carpe diem* had led'. In HB-MM, '*carpe diem*' was changed to '*cui bono*'. Both terms are Latin. *Carpe diem* means 'enjoy the present day'. A common poetic equivalent is 'Gather ye rosebuds while ye may'. *Cui bono* can be translated as 'to whose advantage' and refers to the principle that the value of a practice depends upon its utility or usefulness.

subdued it to what it worked in: from Shakespeare's Sonnet 111:

> O, for my sake do you with Fortune chide,
> The guilty goddess of my harmful deeds,
> That did not better for my life provide
> Than public means which public manners breeds.
> Thence comes it that my name receives a brand,
> And almost thence my nature is subdu'd
> To what it works in, like the dyer's hand.
> Pity me then, and wish I were renew'd,

> Whilst like a willing patient I will drink
> Potions of eisel 'gainst my strong infection,
> No bitterness that I will bitter think,
> Nor double penance, to correct correction.
> > Pity me then, dear friend, and I assure ye,
> > Even that your pity is enough to cure me.

11 *an impression-picture*: Impressionist painters such as Edouard Manet (1832–83) and Claude Monet (1840–1926) manipulated light for special effects, and drew attention to particular features of their subjects through careful details surrounded by more general shapes. Impressionism was gaining adherents in England during the 1880s; that Hardy for the three-volume first edition changed the phrasing from 'a post-Raffaelite picture' may have been a result of his attending the Society of British Artists Exhibition of Impressionist pictures in London in December 1886: 'The impressionist school is strong. It is even more suggestive in the direction of literature than in that of art. As usual it is pushed to absurdity by some. But their principle is, as I understand it, that what you carry away with you from a scene is the true feature to grasp; or in other words, *what appeals to your own individual eye and heart in particular* amid much that does not so appeal, and which you therefore omit to record' (*Life and Work of Thomas Hardy*, p. 191; italics Hardy's).

13 *Doctor Faustus*: the best-known versions of the Doctor Faustus legend, a man who sells his soul, are by Christopher Marlowe and Goethe, but many writers of 'penny books' or inexpensive chapbooks distributed by religious bodies also used the story.

15 *lifehold*: a lifehold is a lease held for the duration of specific persons' lives, usually members of one family or of three generations of a single family, sometimes simply three persons. As is evident in *The Woodlanders*, a lifehold is a tenuous holding (see pp. 99–100). The best-known lifehold in a Hardy novel is that which lapses on the death of Mr Durbeyfield, causing the expulsion of Tess and the remainder of her family, and leading to her eventual return to Alec. Both the Souths and the Durbeyfields have come down in the world. Their ancestors were once copyholders (see note to p. 10), and probably gave up to the lords of their manors their permanent tenure for a limited tenure in exchange for cash or for repairs to their residences which they could not otherwise afford (see p. 99).

16 *Ginnung-Gap*: in Norse mythology, the void that was all that existed at the beginning of time.

17 *ancient lines . . . Trafalgar line-of-battle ships*: Trafalgar, the 1805 battle in which Napoleon lost much of his sea-power and Admiral Nelson his life, was fought with ships broad in the beam, which increased their stability as gun platforms. Hardy's namesake Admiral Thomas Masterson Hardy was the captain of Nelson's flagship.

18 *turnpike bonds*: bonds sold to finance the construction of turnpike roads, the interest costs being met by tolls charged to the users of the turnpikes (see p. 201).

"The ghosts of the Two Brothers?": for this story, see Chapter XIX (p. 137).

20 *"buffeting at will by rain and storm"*: William Wordsworth, 'The Small Celandine' (1804, 1807) has 'buffeted'. The poem, as the passage indicates, describes a flower which in youth has the ability to open and close itself according to the amount of light and the air's temperature, losing this ability as it ages.

"I had half thought so.": not in MS-96.

21 *Loke*: Loki, the crafty, cowardly, and destructive giant of Norse mythology. He cut off the hair of Sif, the wife of Thor. In at least one tale, he also seduces her.

22 *from the White Sea to Cape Horn*: the White Sea is part of the Arctic Ocean in the north-west part of Russia; Cape Horn is on an island at the southernmost point of South America.

24 *early Georgian time*: in Georgian architecture (1702–1830), the house generally consisted of a symmetrical square or rectangle with or without wings. The centre of the main block usually contained a large entrance hall with a single or double staircase to the first floor. Early Georgian architecture was more classical and restrained than the later, which became more varied under the influence of Robert Adams's studies of Pompeii.

25 *Hapsburgian frequency*: the Hapsburg, or Habsburg, family of Austria controlled at various times the thrones of Austria, Hungary, Bohemia, Spain, and the Holy Roman Empire, among others. Many of their claims were created through intermarriages, including marriages within royal lines lacking male issue; and before the Hapsburg male line itself died out in 1740 its last member, Charles VI, secured the succession to his daughter Maria Theresa, and the family continued as Hapsburg-Lorraine. (Maria Theresa had married Francis Stephen, Duke of Lorraine, afterwards the Holy Roman Emperor.) A similar suzerainty is not maintained in *The Woodlanders*. The Melbury and Winterborne

names will die out, and Grace's exogamous marriage removes her from the scene.

26 *hollow-turnery trade*: making hollow wooden objects (such as bowls), mostly for household use, by turning wood on a lathe.

top and bottom sawyers: one technique for sawing large logs was with a two-handled saw, with one sawyer standing in a deep pit and a second, on the other end of the saw, atop a platform above the log.

27 *the Table o' Sundays*: the Communion Table. There is irony, of course, in the contrast between piety and genteel fashionableness.

28 *black-pudding*: a highly spiced sausage made with blood and suet.

pattens: 'a kind of overshoe or sandal worn to raise the ordinary shoes out of mud or wet; consisting, since 17th c., of a wooden sole secured to the foot by a leather loop passing over the instep' (*OED*).

29 *sea of troubles*: from *Hamlet*, III. i. 59 (the 'To be, or not to be' soliloquy). The deliberateness, and even strain, of Hardy's style of allusions are seen in the linking of scientific ('specific gravity' means 'relative density') and literary-philosophical imagery.

30 *'Who dragged Whom . . . What?'*: the allusion is to Achilles dragging the body of Hector around the walls of Troy, in *The Iliad*, Book 22.

Doctor What's-his-name: in MS, this was written '⟨land agent at my lords⟩ /Doctor What's-his-name/'. (For a discussion of this alteration, see Note on the Text.)

31 *pollard*: the trunk of a tree stripped of its branches. Melbury's carrying one testifies to his strength.

34 *he felt doubtful*: in MS-MM, this was followed by: '—perhaps a trifle cynical, for that strand was wound into him with the rest.'

but said nothing: in MS-MM, this was: 'then with indifference.'

noted it not: in MS-MM, this was followed by: 'Neither did he observe what was also the fact, that though he cherished a true and warm feeling towards Grace Melbury, he was not altogether her fool just now. It must be remembered that he had not seen her for a year.'

36 *those houses which I should lose by his death*: properties that were lifehold (see note to p. 15) could be in the effective control or 'possession' of someone whose life is not one of those which determine the length of the lease. This is the case with Giles's

properties (see pp. 90–1, 99–100), which have come to him through his parents (his mother had been a South). When John South dies, Giles's houses revert to their permanent owner, who is—by inheritance from her husband—Mrs Charmond.

Perruquier: wigmaker; barber, hairdresser.

39 *transcendentalism*: an idealistic perspective upon experience; the individual is of a 'type' as well as being unique in him or herself. Philosophers drawn upon by Hardy in this novel—Spinoza, Schleiermacher, Shelley—all dealt with issues centring on the relations between the ideal and the real, between reason and nature. Pure transcendentalism posits an absolute unity of, or correspondence between, thought and reality, mind and matter.

reductio ad absurdum: the refutation of a proposition by showing its absurdity if taken to its logical conclusion.

gentleness . . . good: in MS, this was 'latent sauciness that might never actually show itself.'

Prout's or Vandyke brown: Samuel Prout (1783–1852), English water-colour painter, known for paintings of picturesque architecture in shaded colours, one of which he developed himself with a mixture of brown and grey inks; Anthony van Dyck (1599–1641), Flemish painter famous for his portraits of Charles I. 'Vandyke brown' is an earth colour popular in the eighteenth and nineteenth centuries for its clear, non-chalky character, less used now because one of its ingredients, organic matter (usually humus or coal), causes it to decay and fade, although it is more permanent in oil than in water-colour.

41 *Olympian*: in Greek mythology, Mount Olympus is the home of the gods.

Tempe-vale: a valley sacred to Apollo between Mount Olympus and Mount Ossa.

43 *And she looked at him affectionately*: not in MS-MM.

45 *fire-dog*: one of a pair of supports for burning wood in a fireplace.

50 *and I'm not rich*: not in MS-96.

Everything . . . hands of a clock: the idea that the life of humanity is understood by examining the relationship of ego and non-ego can be found in many eighteenth-century and nineteenth-century writers, including Johann Gottlieb Fichte (1761–1814), Thomas Carlyle (1795–1881), and Friedrich Schleiermacher (1768–1834). The basis of this idea can be found in the idealism or transcendentalism of Immanuel Kant (1724–1804) and

Spinoza (see note to p. 116). Spinoza also argued that the universe reveals the mechanical operation of fixed laws.

52 *shy self-control*: in MS-MM, this was 'dry self-control'.

53 *pari passu*: at an equal pace (Latin).

the Unfulfilled Intention: the term seems to take something from Arthur Schopenhauer's (1788–1860) *Wille*—a force 'without knowledge, . . . merely a blind incessant impulse' (*The World as Will and Idea*). Hardy's view was evolving at the time of *The Woodlanders*. In time he came to think that the Immanent Will, the term he gave to his life-force in *The Dynasts* (1902–6), might be slowly growing self-conscious and aware of its effect on living creatures—but not so aware that it was actively benevolent. Rather, it was indifferent, although by the time of *The Dynasts*, possibly reflecting his reading in the works of Eduard von Hartmann (1842–1906), Hardy had become optimistic about the direction of the Will's ultimate development. The First World War destroyed Hardy's optimism.

sheet-iron foliage of the fabled Jarnvid wood: the literal translation of 'Jarnvid' is 'Iron Wood'. The iron forest of Scandinavian mythology, located east of Midgard (the world of men), is the birthplace of wolves.

obviously not local: this was followed in MS-Col by: 'for Winterborne knew all the cobblers' patterns in that district, because they were very few to know.'

54 *Peripatetic school*: the most famous philosopher of this school, who delivered 'lectures in the shady groves of the Lyceum', a public walk near the temple of Apollo in Athens, is Aristotle (384–322 BC).

57 *free-masonry*: reference to membership of a secret order, the Free and Accepted Masons; the term now stands for a tacit and instinctive sympathy.

frills and furbelows: pleated or gathered fabric, used in edgings and flounces or ruffles; thus, Grace's most elaborate clothing is being tried on.

58 *cheval glass*: a full-length mirror that can be tilted in a frame.

battlemented . . . Elizabethan windows: Elizabethan architecture (1558–1603) marked a transition between medieval features—such as parapets, and windows that were mullioned (their panels separated by vertical posts) and hooded (protected from rain by projecting mouldings)—and Renaissance details and exterior decoration (such as bay and oriel windows).

laps, rolls: a method of waterproofing a roof by overlapping the lead sheets and rolling the joined edges in a semicircular shape.

ashlar: stone masonry smoothed to make an even facing to be set in mortar; the outer face may be rough or smooth.

plinth: the projecting base of a wall.

60 *man-traps*: a man-trap is a large spring-type trap with a tread trigger used to catch poachers. Man-traps fell out of use after the early part of the nineteenth century.

gin: tool or mechanical device, such as a trap for game.

the instruments: in MS-MM, this was: 'these instruments of torture, some with semi-circular jaws, some with rectangular; most of them with long sharp teeth, but a few with none, so that their jaws looked like the blank gums of old age.'

61 *New Sentimental Journey*: Laurence Sterne's *Sentimental Journey*, an account of travels on the Continent, was published in 1768. The journey is a flight from death by a sentimentalist, and Sterne died shortly after the book was published. Since Mrs Charmond dies on a trip to the Continent, Hardy may intend both irony and foreshadowing here.

62 *which her adaptable . . . neighbours*: in MS, this was written: 'which she could not claim, either on her own account or her late husband's. / The daughter of an eminent painter she might have said she could claim more./' In HB-MM, it became: 'which, though she herself could claim it, her adaptable, wandering, *weltbürgerliche* nature had grown tired of caring about—a peculiarity that made her a contrast to her neighbours'. From 87a to 12pc, the passage was as here, lacking only the word 'piquant'.

weltbürgerliche: cosmopolitan (German).

67 *"Your face is like . . . Mount"*: Moses's face 'shone' while he talked with God on Mount Sinai and when he came down from the Mount with the Ten Commandments (Exodus 34: 29–35). Giles, unlike the children of Israel with Moses, is not afraid of the transfigured Grace. (Moses veiled his face while talking to humans when in this state.)

Dumas, and Méry, and Sterne: all wrote books based on their travels—Alexandre Dumas (1802–70), *Impressions de voyage: De Pairs à Cadix* (1847–8); François Méry (1797–1866), *Scènes de la vie italienne* (1837); Laurence Sterne (1713–68), *A Sentimental Journey* (1768) (see note to p. 61).

70 *modesty*: in MS-MM, this was 'modesty, or indifference'.

to the Melburys . . . guests: not in MS-MM.

71 *fender*: a sturdy metal frame before an open fireplace to keep back falling coals.

hob: a projection or shelf at the back or side of a fireplace on which something to be kept warm could be set.

74 *Flemish Last-Suppers*: the 'Flemish school' of painting can be said to have lasted from the late fourteenth to the early nineteenth centuries. Presumably Hardy has in mind those Flemish painters working in the shadow and influence of Van Dyck (cf. note to p. 39) and Peter Paul Rubens (1577–1640), who gave particular attention to detail, such as garments and drapery, and in general stressed literal representation. Although many Flemish painters both before and after this time dealt with religious subjects in this style (e.g. Theodor Rombouts (1597–1637) and Abraham Janssens (1567–1637), only Rubens and Frans Pourbus the Younger (1569–1662) painted Last Suppers.

75 *hang-fair*: a public execution, frequently a festive occasion for a community.

76 *langterloo*: a popular card game of the nineteenth century. As the jingle on this page suggests, it could be played with thirty-two cards.

77 *phrenologists*: phrenology is the study of the shape of the skull for indications of mental and moral qualities.

78 *"... said she, ... orange tree!"*: in MS-87b, the song of the langterloo players was:

> 'She may go, oh!
> She may go, oh!
> She may go to the d— ['devil' in 87a–87b] for me!'

Both songs are probably Dorset versions, with which Hardy would have been familiar, of widespread folk songs.

79 *egg-flip*: egg-nog.

criddled: in MS-MM, this was 'curdled'.

81 *Cause*: in MS, this was written '⟨Eventuality⟩ /Causality/'. In HB-MM, it was printed 'Causality'. A concern of Hardy's in many of his novels, but one about which he is not consistent, is the personalization of the force that shapes men's lives. In this passage, the differences among the terms are slight.

83 *post hoc*: the logic fallacy of arguing that because one event occurs after another the first event must be the cause of the second.

85 *plane*: in MS-MM, the chapter contained two further paragraphs:

'He could not forget that Mrs. Charmond had apparently abandoned all interest in his daughter as suddenly as she had conceived it, and was as firmly convinced as ever that the comradeship which Grace had shown with Giles and his crew by attending his party had been the cause.

Matters lingered on thus. And then, as a hoop by gentle knocks on this side and on that is made to travel in specific directions, the little touches of circumstance in the life of this young girl shaped the curves of her career.'

86 *gentleman-farmer*: in MS-MM, this was 'farmer'.

Acteonic excitement: in Greek mythology, the hunter Acteon was changed into a stag and killed by his own hounds for having spied upon Diana bathing.

the Greek poet: Menander (342–291 BC), a Greek dramatist, who was famous for his maxims.

88 *Port-Breedy Harbour bonds*: see the explanation for turnpike bonds, note to p. 18.

90 *"Can I be a prophet in Hintock?"*: in MS-A1, it was 'Israel' not 'Hintock'. Evidently an allusion to 2 Kings 5: 8. The King of Israel has mistaken a request from the King of Syria to cure him of leprosy, and reacts in despair. He is admonished by Elisha: 'And it was so, when Elisha the man of God had heard that the king of Israel had rent his clothes, that he sent to the king, saying, Wherefore hast thou rent thy clothes? let him come now to me, and he shall know that there is a prophet in Israel.'

the words of the faithful be only as wind: i.e. words have no effect if the hearer won't act on them. Perhaps a paraphrase of Job 6: 26: 'Do ye imagine to reprove words, and the speeches of one that is desperate, which are as wind?' Job is lamenting the inadequacy of language to convey the extent of and to grasp the purpose of his suffering. Creedle speaks as if he is praising himself; but in placing himself in the position of the 'faithful' (who are not up to the task of helping Job), Creedle is unintentionally slighting himself. Hardy's ability to incorporate a few words from this passage (and later on p. 100) into the speech of one of his rustics reveals his thorough familiarity with biblical phraseology, as well as his probable enjoyment of ironic inversions of the passages' meanings.

92 *Gregorian melodies*: liturgical music to accompany services and rituals; named after Pope Gregory I (540–604; Pope from 590 to 604). A Gregorian chant is monophonic, developing a single line of melody, and the same phrase is repeated over and over.

fugleman: a trained soldier placed in front of other soldiers as a model.

94 *in an enfeebled voice*: in MS-MM, this was 'as if without surprise, in a voice'.

95 *Niflheim or fog-land*: in Norse mythology, Niflheim is the dark, misty world that existed before the formation of earth, and into which men pass from the world of death (i.e. a kind of second death).

96 *The trunks were chained down*: in MS-MM, this was: 'The proud trunks were taken up from the silent spot which had known them through the buddings and sheddings of their growth for the foregoing hundred years; chained down, like slaves,'.

skid: a shoe or brake that prevents wheels from turning, as when the vehicle is descending a hill.

98 *lofty voice*: in MS-96, this was 'soft voice'.

tournure: silhouette, shape, appearance, 'turn-out' (French).

99 *to exchange their old copyholds for life-leases*: see notes to pp. 10 and 15 for explanations of the forms of control of property.

100 *'the sword of the Lord and of Gideon'*: Judges 7: 13–20. A dream of a cake of barley bread tumbling into the multitude of Midianites and Amalekites was interpreted by Gideon as 'the sword of Gideon'; and the cry 'the sword of the Lord and of Gideon' by Gideon's 300 men routed the Midianite host, who in their terror battled each other. South's biblical quotation ironically identifies his own self-destructive adherence to a fantastic image.

101 *de rigueur*: indispensable, obligatory. Also, according to good form, or required by etiquette (French).

102 *that it has got human sense*: this was added within MS.

on purpose . . . Hintock: this was added within MS.

104 *Dismissing . . . remember*: not in MS-MM.

105 *and was left practically penniless*: not in MS-96.

106 *firmly believing it to be a last blow for Grace*: not in MS-Col.

107 *answer*: this was followed in MS-MM by: 'Fitzpiers too, though he did not personally appear, was much interested, and not altogether easy in his mind; for he had been informed by an authority of what he had himself conjectured, that if the tree had been allowed to stand the old man would have gone on complaining, but might have lived for twenty years.'

"Pulling down is always the game.": not in MS-96.

entirely to himself: this was followed in MS-MM by: 'There could be no doubt that, up to this last moment, he had nourished a feeble hope of regaining Grace in the event of this negociation [*sic*] turning out a success. Not being aware of the fact that her father could have settled upon her a fortune sufficient to enable both to live in comfort, he deemed it now an absurdity to dream any longer of such a vanity as making her his wife; and sank into silence forthwith.'

108 *Encountering Melbury one day*: in MS-MM, this was much longer, reading: 'Mr. Melbury, in his compunction, thought more of the matter than any one else, except his daughter. Had Winterborne been going on in the old fashion Grace's father could have alluded to his disapproval of the alliance every day with the greatest frankness; but to speak any further on the subject he could not find it in his heart to do now. He hoped that Giles would of his own accord make some final announcement that he entirely withdrew his pretensions to Grace, and so get the thing past and done with. For though Giles had in a measure acquiesced in the wish of her family, he could make matters unpleasant if he chose to work upon Grace; and hence, when Melbury saw the young man approaching along the road one day, he kept friendliness and frigidity exactly balanced in his eye till he could see ['find' in MM] whether Giles's manner were ['was' in HB-A1] presumptive or not.'

109 *for he knew . . . work upon Grace*: not in MS-MM.

110 *because it was the truth*: in MS-MM this was followed by: ' "I didn't mean to let it stay Mr. Winterborne; but when I was going to rub it out you came, and I was obliged to run off." '

112 *a Dutch designer of the time of William and Mary*: William of Orange (the Dutch Republic) reigned as King of England 1689–1702; his wife Mary was co-reigning Queen 1689–94. Both house and garden in Dutch design were characterized by rigorous symmetry.

112 *Fitzpiers knew her as Suke Damson*: this sentence first appeared in MM, where Suke's last name was 'Sengreen'. It became 'Damson' in 87a.

114 *a German metaphysician*: see notes to pp. 50 and 140.

115 *grimness*: in MS-MM, this was 'grimness, partly in his character, partly'.

116 *"She moved . . . stream"*: these lines are from Percy Bysshe Shelley, *The Revolt of Islam*, II, stanza 23. Laon is describing Cythna, who is his 'second self' and one of the manifestations of the Ideal.

Leyden jar: a glass jar partly filled with water, used to store static electricity, discovered in 1746 by Pieter van Musschoenbroek of Leiden. Its relevance as a metaphor for Fitzpiers's affections is that it holds a charge for only a brief time.

Spinoza: Baruch Spinoza (1632–77). Dutch philosopher. He proposed a correspondence between, or unity of, the body and mind, the physical and mental. The principle here is that knowable reality exists only within the human mind through its awareness of itself and 'its' body (*ipsa hominis essentia* means, as the text says, 'the essence itself of man').

117 *Socratic εἰρωνεία*: 'irony', or Socrates' manner of asking simple questions and then demonstrating the shallowness or contradictoriness of the answers he had elicited. Also, Socrates' manner of deprecating his own merits.

118 *"who hath gathered the wind in his fists? who hath bound the waters in a garment?"*: Proverbs 30: 4, in Agur's confession of faith and contentment with the incomplete knowledge God has allowed him.

122 *a remorseless Jehovah of the sciences*: presumably the Old Testament deity of strict law in contrast to the God of the New Testament who sent his Son to suffer for mankind's sins. The idea is that Grammer thinks that Fitzpiers will require the bargain to be carried out to the letter.

Jehovah: in MS-MM, this was 'Jove'.

123 *at times*: not in MS-87a.

125 *glued up by frozen thawings*: this allusion to the first stanza of Keats's 'In drear nighted December' plays upon Keats's contrast of appropriate seasonal event in nature and humanity's sexual unhappiness unlimited by season; Hardy here as elsewhere in the novel suggests natural as well as human propagation is

attended by mischance and frustration. The first and third stanzas of Keats's poem:

> In drear nighted December,
>   Too happy, happy tree,
> Thy branches ne'er remember
>   Their green felicity—
> The north cannot undo them
> With a sleety whistle through them,
> Nor frozen thawings glue [i.e. prevent] them
>   From budding at the prime.
>
>   .   .   .
>
> Ah! would 'twere so with many
>   A gentle girl and boy—
> But were there ever any
>   Writh'd not of passed joy?
> The feel of not to feel it,
> When there is none to heal it,
> Nor numbed sense to steel it,
>   Was never said in rhyme.

(*Keats: Complete Poems*, ed. Jack Stillinger (Cambridge, Mass., 1978, 1982), p. 163)

126 *some canopied mural tomb of the fifteenth century*: tombs of this sort are usually set within a recess in a wall, or placed against a wall so that in either case the effigy is enclosed except for one side open for viewing. The area within the enclosure is customarily elaborately carved.

130 *Nature has at last . . . Idea!*: according to Plato, there is an irreducible chasm between the physical, or the temporal, and the Ideal, which is eternal. The 'transcendental philosopher' (who would support the idea of union of or the correspondence between the physical and the Ideal) could be any of several thinkers (e.g. see note to p. 39).

132 *idealist*: the starting point for most considerations of idealism is Plato's belief that there is a world of abstract Ideals of which material manifestations on earth are only imperfect copies; the principal tenet of idealism is thus that thought is the fundamental reality. Idealism and transcendentalism are often hard to distinguish, though there is a thin but significant difference between idealism and the transcendentalism of the eighteenth and nineteenth centuries (which premised unity and coherence:

see note to p. 39). That Fitzpiers here thinks in Platonic terms, and elsewhere (e.g. pp. 50, 140) expounds transcendental ideas, suggests an intellectual opportunism rather than an ability to synthesize.

Hardy implies in this passage that there is a schism between science and idealism, but several philosophers with whose work he was familiar stressed their indivisibility, and such early formulators of the distinctions between dualism and idealism as Descartes and Spinoza advocated the application of scientific and mathematical methods to 'prove' their perceptions.

132 *recreative . . . acquaintance*: in MS-MM, this was 'ethereal character of my regard'.

133 *nightingale*: one of the sure signs of spring.

134 *"little toilette" of the executioner's victim*: preparing the back of the neck of the person to be guillotined by shaving or arranging the hair so that the blade would not be interfered with.

137 *King's Hintock Court*: in MS-87b, this was 'Hintock House'.

Old Style: before the calendar reform in 1752, New Year's Day was 25 March.

138 *madder hues*: reddish. A red dye is made from the roots of the madder plant.

140 *Crusoe's island*: Robinson Crusoe, in the book (1718) by Daniel Defoe, lived alone on an island for years after being shipwrecked, and several years further with a native companion before being rescued.

Schleiermacher: Friedrich Schleiermacher (1768–1834), Prussian theologian. An admirer of Kant and Spinoza but disciple of neither, he was also influenced by such German Romantics as Karl Friedrich Schlegel (1772–1829) and Friedrich Schelling (1775–1854), and not least of all by Plato. More than any other transcendental philosopher, Schleiermacher advocated the concept of the *summum bonum*, or highest good, and stipulated that the individual must perform the virtues not in isolation but in relation to family, state, and society. (Hardy, who knew little German, in the MS and HB translated the first two virtues as 'fortitude' and 'discretion'.) Fitzpiers's familiarity with idealist thinkers is used ironically by Hardy, for despite knowing the precepts Fitzpiers is not guided by the rigorous selflessness and detachment of his favourite writers.

142 *night-hawk*: nightjar, a grey-brown nocturnal bird (see also p. 149).

Midsummer eve: Midsummer Day (24 June) is the feast, or day of birth, of John the Baptist. Hardy frequently draws upon the ironic perpetuation of pagan rituals within a Christian context: thus Fitzpiers's landlady's condemnation of it as 'an ungodly performance' (p. 143).

143 *swarthy faces and funereal figures*: in MS-MM, this was: 'strange faces and figures shaped by the dying lights; the surfaces of the holly leaves would here and there shine like peeping eyes, while such fragments of the sky as were visible between the trunks assumed the aspect of sheeted forms and cloven tongues.'

spell or enchantment: two folk rituals are referred to in this scene: a young woman who digs a hole will hear the sounds that characterize her future husband's occupation if at high noon (pp. 144–5) she places her ear close to the fresh hole; the sowing of hemp-seed (p. 145) stems from a vegetation myth intended to ensure a good crop, but in one version its aim is to bring into material form a 'reaper' (i.e. lover).

144 *fell into hand*: that is, back into the possession of the lord of the manor. See note to p. 36.

148 *local ballad*: that is, the local variant of the widespread folk-song.

with a laugh, and: not in MS-96.

same: in MS-87b, this was 'next'.

149 *Fitzpiers kissed her again*: not in MS-MM.

and pressed her close to him: not in MS-87b.

It was daybreak . . . Hintock: not in A1-MM. The MS is marked 'Omit for mag.'

151 *Southern cause*: that of the Confederacy during the American war between the States, 1861–5.

152 *and seemed wandering in his mind*: not in MS-12pc.

157 *pettishly*: in MS-Col, this was 'coquettishly'.

shyly: not in MS-Col.

she had experienced: this was followed in MS-MM by '—still more if she reflected on the silent, almost sarcastic, criticism apparent in Winterborne's air towards her—'.

159 *"Why, on the mother's side . . . Sherton"*: Fitzpiers's connection with a specific (fictional) aristocratic family was added in 12pc and 12. The version in 12pc lacked 'of Sherton'.

160 *Sherton Castle*: Sherborne Castle, home of the Bixby family. The identification of Fitzpiers's relation to this family, at this and other places in the novel, was made for the 1912 Wessex Edition.

160 *crochet capital*: a Gothic carving at the top of a column, characterized by stylized leaves.

Norman carving: the Norman, or Romanesque, style developed
around the eleventh and twelfth centuries, before the development of the Gothic. Norman carving is profusely ornamented,
and employs several geometric designs, including zigzags,
crenellations, and chains. It appears that the castle was built
in a mixture of both the Norman and Gothic styles, not an unusual occurrence.

Galen, Hippocrates, and Herophilus: Galen (AD 129–*c*.199), Greek
physician, founder of experimental physiology; Hippocrates
(*c*.460–*c*.377 BC), Greek physician, the 'father of modern medicine'; Herophilus (*c*.335–*c*.280 BC), Alexandrian physician,
performer of public dissections of human corpses (cf. Fitzpiers's
wish to dissect Grammer Oliver). These physicians were dominant influences on medical practice until fairly recent times.

dogmatic: 'Proceeding upon *a priori* principles accepted as true,
instead of being founded upon experience or induction, as
dogmatic philosophy, medicine. . . . 1883: an ancient sect of physicians, so called because they endeavoured to discover, by reasoning, the essence and the occult causes of diseases' (*OED*).

empiric: medical practice opposed to the elaborate theories of
Galen and to the dogmatists, preferring to rely solely on evidence of clinical effectiveness.

hermetical: a kind of alchemy, or magical medicine, based on
'works of revelation' attributed to Hermes Trismegistos, a
legendary figure identified with the Egyptian god Thoth.

by copious bleeding: not in MS-96.

161 *sweeping . . . at the Interpreter's which well-nigh choked the Pilgrim*:
Pilgrim's Progress, Part 1 (1678), by John Bunyan. The parlour
is the heart that has not received Grace; the dust is Original
Sin and inner corruption. The Interpreter settles the dust with
water (the Gospel), an action not taken by the Melburys, either
literally or metaphorically, in their welcome for Fitzpiers.

169 *had come half-dressed to beg me*: in MS-87b, this was 'begged me'.

intimacy established in the hayfield: in MS-87b, this was 'incident
in the wood'.

libration: an oscillation in a secondary body, such as a planet,
as seen from the body around which it revolves. Also, however,
balance—a moving from side to side. Hardy's word-choice

suggests at one stroke Grace's subsidiary role in the courtship, an apparent movement or shift from her objection (which Fitzpiers seizes upon), and a balance or acceptance of her marriage.

"To holy . . . us": this was added within the MS.

170 *spokeshaved*: used a curved two-handled knife to make convex or concave surfaces. Most likely the specific products were axe handles and wheel spokes, whose ends had to be precisely shaped to fit into the axe head or wheel rim. These could be made at inactive times, and stored for use at busier seasons.

173 *When the fair apples . . . eyes around*: Thomas Chatterton, stanza 33 of *Ælla*, the third minstrel's song at the celebration of the marriage of Ælla and Bertha.

"marvellous boy": in MS-12pc, it was 'youthful Chatterton'. Thomas Chatterton (1752–70) imitated medieval verse, and published it as the work of the monk Rowley. Unable to make a living with his writing, he committed suicide at seventeen. He was much admired by the Romantics, being called the 'marvellous boy' by Wordsworth in 'Resolution and Independence'.

"cheeses": so called because their cylindrical shapes resembled the large cakes of curd produced in dairies after separation from the whey.

Pomona's plain: in Roman mythology, Pomona is the goddess of fruit trees.

175 *sapphire and opal*: the legendary 'meaning' of these gems conveys the ambiguity of Grace's and Fitzpiers's relationship. The sapphire connotes loyalty and chastity, while the opal primarily connotes an ill omen.

176 *If I forget . . . you forget*: the poem is 'Two Points of View' (1885) by Edmund Gosse (1849–1928). Gosse's poem reads 'flows', not 'flowed', and 'lord', not 'queen'.

178 *It was two months since he married her*: not in MS-MM.

179 *locum tenens*: someone temporarily taking another's place, especially that of a clergyman or a doctor (Latin).

180 *relieving officer*: administrator of the poor-relief in a parish or union (see note to p. 182).

181 *a handwriting on the wall*: an allusion to the mysterious but ominous writing that appeared on the wall during Balshazzar's feast, which when interpreted was found to pronounce his downfall (Daniel 5).

182 *Board of Guardians*: this Board oversaw the operations of a workhouse, which was often maintained by a 'union' of several parishes.

183 *Winterborne had given up his house*: in MS-MM, this was 'Winterborne's house had been pulled down.'

pinion: gable-end.

according to the landlords' principle at this date of getting rid of cottages whenever possible: not in MS-96.

184 *great November gale of 1824 . . . Chesil Bank*: the 1824 gale was a memorable storm, causing many deaths and much damage to property along the coast. Local residents still point out where the brig came to rest, well inland from the Bank. Chesil Bank is a beach and ridge of pebbles erected by the action of the waves, extending for miles along the coast of Dorset from Portland Bill to Abbotsbury.

phaeton: a light four-wheeled carriage, usually with two seats.

185 *elegant*: in MS-87b, this was 'full round'.

delicately curled: in MS-87b, this was 'plump'.

186 *court plaster*: a cotton adhesive, faced with silk on one side, with a preparation of isinglass and glycerine on the other, to cover small wounds; equivalent to a modern Elastoplast or Band-Aid.

187 *trouvaille*: windfall, lucky find (French).

knowing my face was my only fortune: in MS-A1, this was 'knowing my disposition'.

Baden: at the time of the novel a grand duchy in south-west Germany. Also, a spa town in the Aargau canton of Switzerland. Both Badens are south of Heidelberg.

188 *While you have grown rich*: in MS-A1, this was 'You are still rich, and'.

189 *blasphemer*: this was followed in MS-Col by 'She broke into a low musical laugh at the idea.'

191 *gold-beater's skin*: prepared from the large intestine of the ox, and laid between leaves of gold when they are being beaten. Its nearness to the colour of flesh made it a cosmetic covering for a wound.

192 *Neckar*: the Neckar flows through Heidelberg.

194 *Achillean moodiness*: Achilles sulked in his tent at Troy because he felt slighted by Agamemnon. He re-entered battle to avenge the death of Patroclus.

folding star: the evening star, Venus, so called because with its appearance in the sky the shepherds put their flocks in the fold.

195 *Why should Death alone lend what Life is compelled to borrow—rest?*: this amplifies Shelley's *Adonais*, stanza 21: 'Great and mean | Meet massed in death, who lends what life must borrow.'

196 *a second tree of knowledge*: the first tree of knowledge is that from which Eve and Adam ate, and brought woe upon mankind. Fitzpiers's comment is, then, ominous.

pretendedly: not in MS-MM.

In reality he thought: in MS-A1, this was 'In reality he knew'.

198 *my agent*: in MS-96, this was 'I'.

199 *dozen miles*: in MS-87b, this was 'twenty miles'.

a little less: in MS-87b, this was 'eighteen'.

High-Stoy: in MS-MM, this was 'Rub-Down'; in 87a–87b, it became 'Rubdon'. (Similar revisions of place-names occur in this chapter and elsewhere in the novel's text, but in order to conserve space they are only infrequently listed.)

Sherton Abbas: in MS-87b, this was 'Buckbury'; in 96–12pc, it became 'Oakbury'.

201 *turnpike-ticket*: see note to p. 18.

203 *Tannhäuser*: a German poet (*c.*1200–*c.*1270) who according to legend was enticed to live with Venus; after seven years, he felt remorse and left, but—assured by the Pope that he cannot be forgiven—he returned to Venus in despair.

the load-star of my one desire: Percy Bysshe Shelley, *Epipsychidion*, ll. 219–21. The lines refer to an Ideal, or a Platonic perfection in life. A load-star, or lodestar, serves as a guide or as a point on which to fix one's attention, such as the North Star.

Wouvermans: Philips Wouverman(s) (1619–68), Dutch painter in the Baroque style. His 'eccentricity' is that his favourite subject was horses. James Gibson has pointed out that in the National Gallery in London his painting 'A View on a Seashore, with Fishwives offering Fish to a Horseman' presents 'a back view of a white horse against a vast sky', almost exactly the image Hardy, who surely had seen this picture, presents from Grace's perspective.

malic acid: an acid in the juice of various plants, especially apples (*malum* = apple (Latin)).

204 *cast aside*: in MS-Col, this was 'starved off'.

   chivalrous: in MS-Col, this was 'bare'.

207 *thinking what gall . . . if she chose*: not in MS-87b.

208 *in his selfish way*: not in MS-Col.

210 *All's well that ends well*: Shakespeare's play of this name in which a low-born woman marries above her station. The husband Bertram is a lecher, and as in *The Woodlanders* the abruptness of the ending implicitly queries their conventional reconciliation.

211 *Absalont*: in MS-MM, this was 'Absalom'. Absalom, the son of David who rebelled, was caught by his head in an oak-tree while fleeing, and was killed by Joab and Joab's armour-bearers. 2 Samuel 18: 9–15.

   "From the sole . . . no blemish in him": 2 Samuel 14: 25. 'But in all Israel there was none to be so much praised as Absalom for his beauty: from the sole of his foot even to the crown of his head there was no blemish in him.' MM changes 'foot' to 'boots' and 'head' to 'hat', in keeping with the unlikelihood that Timothy could have quoted the Bible with precision.

   getting over the fence: not in MS-Col.

   Congreve's Millamant: William Congreve (1670–1729), a writer of comedies during the Restoration. His best-known work is *The Way of the World*, whose heroine is the affected Millamant. Hardy twice quotes (see note to p. 217) her 'Song' from Act III:

> Love's but the frailty of the mind
> When 'tis not with ambition joined;
> A sickly flame which, if not fed, expires,
> And feeding, wastes in self-consuming fires!
>
> 'Tis not to wound a wanton boy
> Or amorous youth, that gives the joy,
> But 'tis the glory to have pierced a swain,
> For whom inferior beauties sighed in vain.
>
> Then I alone the conquest prize,
> When I insult a rival's eyes;
> If there's delight in love, 'tis when I see
> That heart, which others bleed for, bleed for me.

212 *lift the Veil of Isis*: connotes the violation of a holy mystery. Isis is a principal goddess of Egypt, the wife of Osiris. A protean deity, she is a temptress, a life-giver or mother-figure, a protectress,

and a controller of death. Her statue bore the inscription, 'I am that which is, has been, and shall be. My veil no one has lifted.' It is doubtful that Melbury would have been familiar with such minutiae of mythology; as elsewhere (e.g. p. 219), Hardy's putting classical allusions within Melbury's frame of reference strikes a false note.

214–15 *He went to church . . . He had to wait long*: this description of the meeting in church of Fitzpiers and Mrs Charmond was deleted from MM to fit the instalment into available space and was not reinstated until the 1981 Clarendon Edition.

217 *I fell in love*: this was followed in MS-MM by the first stanza of 'Song' from *The Way of the World* (see note to p. 211). In A1 only, this stanza was followed by an apostrophe from Fitzpiers: 'Ah, old author of "The Way of the World," you knew—you knew!'

origin of her mood: this was followed in MS-MM by 'a mood that was the mere continuance of what her father had noticed when he would have preferred a passionate jealousy in her as the more natural.'

218 *Hamlet's friend*: Hardy's connecting Winterborne and Horatio is the more relevant in that Hardy, quoting the passage from the play in which this line occurs, claimed that his father was exactly like Horatio (*Life and Work of Thomas Hardy*, p. 262).

219 *unguibus et rostro*: with claws and beak (Latin).

221 *For days he sat . . . crumple up in his hand*: not in MS-HB.

lady: in MS-Col, this was 'beautiful lady'—i.e. Lady Godiva. The legend is that her husband Leofric, exasperated at her pleas for a reduction in taxes for Coventry, agreed to lower them if she would ride naked through the town's marketplace. She agreed, but required that the residents stay indoors and not watch her pass by. All obeyed except Peeping Tom.

222 *Ariadne*: in Greek mythology Ariadne, the daughter of Minos, king of Crete, helped Theseus escape from the Labyrinth. According to one version of the legend, she was afterwards abandoned by Theseus.

Vashti: when she refused to show her beauty at a great feast, her husband Ahasuerus deposed her and chose Esther to be his new queen (Esther 1–2).

Amy Dudley: in MS-A1, this was 'the Countess Amy'. Her death from a fall in 1560 gave rise to rumours that her husband

Robert (later the Earl of Leicester) had killed her in the hope that Queen Elizabeth would marry him.

223 *Though few knew . . . winter; but*: not in MS-MM. The phrase 'on that account' was also not in MS-MM.

the altar of Cain: Cain's altar is not described in Genesis 4: 3–5, but Canaanite altars were square. Giles is scarcely a defier of God, but his 'offering', like Cain's, is fruit of the ground, and had been refused by Melbury and Grace.

226 *smiled*: in MS-HB, this was 'often smiled'.

passions her study: in MS-Col, it was 'entanglements her trade'.

228 *femme de trente ans*: woman of thirty years. The age of a woman of experience. Balzac's novel of this name (1831–4) portrays a woman torn between passion and social convention.

édition définitive: definitive edition, i.e. highest state. The use of French here is probably intended to emphasize Mrs Charmond's role as a *femme fatale*.

But the édition définitive . . . little worn: not in MS-MM.

228–9 *"Yes," said Melbury. . . . absurdly unreal*: These paragraphs appeared only in A1 until the 1981 Clarendon Edition, having been removed from the novel's text at the time of the British serialization for reasons of space (see p. xxxiv). This material, concerned with Mrs Charmond's language, enhances Hardy's portrayal of her as someone trivial but also essentially honest and in her own way innocent.

231 *Felice knew who . . . made her sick*: not in MS-MM. The point of adding the paragraph is to make more evident the relationship of Mrs Charmond with the South Carolinian gentleman, who later affects the plot so strongly. In the MS, he had upset Mrs Charmond and thus brought about Fitzpiers's catastrophic late-night visit (see note to pp. 244–6), but when Hardy decided that Mrs Charmond's unhappiness should be caused by a weakness in her own character he needed to compensate for the resulting diminution of the South Carolinian as a character. The phrase 'among others too numerous to name' first appeared in 96.

240 *put her face against that of her companion*: not in MS-MM.

"He's had you!": not in MS-87b.

242 *kissing each other almost unintentionally*: not in MS-12pc.

fastidious face: in MS-Col, this was 'refined face'.

243 *the Mother of the Months*: the moon; from the first Chorus of Swinburne's *Atalanta in Calydon* (1865).

244–6 Lengthy cancelled passages in the MS indicate that Mrs Charmond's moodiness, which led to Fitzpiers's nocturnal visit, originally was caused by a visit from her South Carolinian lover, who evidently threatened her.

247 *And yet to every . . . worse*: this was added within MS.

Versaillese furniture: French furniture, presumably of the delicate style of the eighteenth century.

251 *Pro—Pre—*: i.e. Prometheus, who stole fire from Zeus and gave it to mankind. For punishment, Zeus had him chained to a rock in the Caucasus Mountains; an eagle came each day to eat his liver, which regenerated each night.

253 *Death in the Revelation*: 'And I looked, and behold a pale horse: and his name that sat on him was Death'. Revelation 6: 8.

256 *to go into his bedroom*: in MS-MM, this was 'to know—'; in 87a–87b, it became 'to go in there'.

"Wives all, let's enter together! . . .": not in MS-87b.

257 *empty bed . . . pillow*: the reference to the 'empty bed' first appeared in 87a; it was identified ('of Fitzpiers') in 96. 'his night-shirt lying on the pillow' also first appeared in 96.

Psalm of Asaph: Psalm 73. Lines 14–15 are paraphrased and quoted by Hardy here. Several Psalms are attributed to Asaph.

whose relations with him were as close as her own without its conventionality: not in MS-87b.

While the three: in MS-87b, this was 'While these three poor women'; in 96, it became 'the three women'. In 12pc, Hardy wrote 'the three virtual wives of one husband', crossed out 'virtual', then on proofs deleted 'wives of one husband'.

258 *Bien-aimé*: well-beloved (French).

260 *timidity . . . cast out*: MS contained a deletion referring to the frightening visit from Mrs Charmond's 'other admirer . . . earlier in the evening' (see note to pp. 244–6).

261 *Mrs. Elizabeth Montagu*: 1720–1800. One of the first 'bluestockings', friend of Samuel Johnson and Horace Walpole, and the hostess of an intellectual salon, as well as author. The source of 'to run mad with discretion' has not been located.

Sudarium of St. Veronica: an instance of Hardy's ironic handling of religious images. Taking pity on Christ carrying his Cross to

Golgotha, Veronica gave him her sudarium (handkerchief) so
he could wipe his face. When Christ returned the cloth to her
it bore his image. Thus Fitzpiers is connected to Christ, and
Mrs Charmond, who washes Fitzpiers's face (p. 263), to a saint.

262 *Not poppy nor mandragora will ever medicine this bitter feud*: a quotation and paraphrase of *Othello*, III. iii. 330–3:

> Not poppy, nor mandragora,
> Nor all the drowsy syrups of the world
> Shall ever medicine thee to that sweet sleep
> Which thou ow'dst yesterday.

Poppy is the plant source of opium; mandragora, or mandrake,
is of the nightshade family: as sources of narcotics and sopor-
ifics, they are images of forgetfulness.

263 *the veil of that temple is rent in twain!*: at the death of Christ on
the Cross, 'the veil of the temple was rent in twain from the top
to the bottom' (Matthew 27: 51). The image is of an irreparable breach between a former and a present way of life.

266 *Valley of Humiliation*: in *Pilgrim's Progress*, Christian passes through
the Valley of Humiliation while moving from the City of De-
struction to the City of Zion. Prudence, who sets him on his
way, says: 'It is an hard matter for a man to go down into the
valley of *Humiliation*, as thou art now, and to catch no slip by
the way.' Christian meets the fiend Apollyon; Melbury meets
Beaucock.

267 *new law*: the details Hardy gives clearly point to the Matrimonial Causes Act of 1857, deliberated and passed in the 20th
and 21st years of Parliament during Victoria's reign. The 1857
Act created a new court that permitted petitioners for divorce
to pursue a less expensive and complicated course than secur-
ing a special Parliamentary Act, as this passage states, and taking the proceedings into an Ecclesiastical Court. Divorce under
this Act required not only a husband's adultery but some further offence such as violence, incest, sodomy, or desertion without reasonable cause for over two years. This is the condition
which Grace's situation seems *not* to meet (see pp. 285 and
289). Scholars have used Beaucock's reference to the law as a
recent one to attempt to date the novel's action and to characterize Beaucock's behaviour as a lawyer. Since the South
Carolinian had fought in the American Civil War and has afterwards been in Europe long enough to become Italianized
(see p. 151 and note), the novel's action must occur well after
1857; and so the Act so concretely identified by Beaucock

cannot be a 'new' law at the time of the novel. Another Act, of 1878, allowed separate maintenance (although not divorce) for wives whose husbands had been found guilty of aggravated assault to the extent that the wife's future safety was in peril. The 1878 Act scarcely applies to Grace's situation, since she and Melbury wish for her complete freedom from Fitzpiers, but perhaps Hardy intends to suggest that Beaucock is so befuddled that the passing of the recent 1878 Act has jogged his memory of what had been current legal news during his sober years.

nipperkin: 'a measure or vessel of small capacity used for liquors, containing half-a-pint or less' (*OED*). In MS-96, this was 'nibleykin'.

as Stephen was beheld by the Council, with a face like the face of an angel: in Acts 6–7, Stephen is accused of 'blasphemous words against Moses'. Despite his transfigured appearance he is stoned, becoming the first Christian martyr. In MS-Col, it was 'the Lawgiver' whose face is 'shining' after conversing with an angel. This is an allusion to Exodus 34; probably noticing that he had already drawn upon this passage in Giles's sarcastic remark to Grace (see p. 67 and note), Hardy altered the reference to a similar occurrence in the Bible.

269 *rush in where angels fear to tread*: Alexander Pope, *Essay on Criticism*, Part III, line 625.

270 *cuckoo*: an implied connection with Fitzpiers might be intended with the cuckoo's practice of laying eggs in other birds' nests, a metaphor for devious husbandry and infidelity.

272 *the wife of such as he?*: this was followed in MS-Col by: 'Since the date of his rejection he had almost grown to see the reasonableness of that treatment. He had said to himself again and again that her father was right.'

ceorl: 'an OE [Old English] freeman of the lowest class, opposed on one side to a *thane* or nobleman, on the other to the servile classes' (*OED*). In using this word, Hardy connects Giles to a long-vanished traditional social designation.

273 *There is no such thing*: this was preceded in MS-MM by 'Perhaps Winterborne was not quite so ardent as heretofore.'

dearness: this was followed in MS-MM by: 'If the flame did indeed burn lower now than when he had fetched her from Sherton at her last return from school the marvel was small.'

273 *but hitherto he had experienced no great success in his attempt*: in MS-MM, this was 'and their separation may have helped him to a partial success.'

  all the opiates in the pharmacopœia: for 'opiate' see note to p. 262. By causing dullness a narcotic can quiet the emotions and induce sleep. A pharmacopoeia can be either a collection or stock of drugs or a book that describes drugs and tells how to prepare them for use.

275 *invitingly*: in MS-MM, this was 'archly'.

  last representative ... maternally connected: the reference to the marble tomb of an extinct earldom was added in 12pc; its connection with Fitzpiers's family was added in 12.

276 *Shy though he was*: not in MS-MM.

278 *Arcadian innocents*: Arcadia was a mountainous region of ancient Greece, the scene of many pastorals. The image is of rural isolation and contented lack of sophistication.

287 *"Ah—yes" ... hesitation*: not in MS-MM.

  men are not gods: *Othello*, III. iv. 148. The passage suggests that bad temper in men can alternate with devotedness:

> Nay, we must think men are not gods,
> Nor of them look for such observancy
> As fits the bridal.

  as Desdemona said, men are not gods: not in MS-HB.

  She looked up ... passionate kiss: the description of the 'embrace' and 'kiss' was modified several times. In MS-Col, the clause was 'She started back suddenly from his embrace'; the embrace became 'long' in 87b; 96 included the 'kiss' for the first time; 'passionate' was added in 12pc.

  upon his breast: not in MS-Col.

  lifted her up and: not in MS-Col.

288 *even though it had been prolonged an unconscionable time*: not in MS-MM.

  To hasten ... eyes: this paragraph, indicating that Giles and Grace kissed frequently after Giles knew her marriage could not be ended, was not in MS-MM.

289 *After letting you go on like this—*: not in MS-MM.

290 *"... His behaviour ... not know."*: not in MS-HB.

  said nothing more: in MS-HB, this was 'suspected the accuracy of this, for he knew that Beaucock had written. But he said nothing.'

291 *As for Giles . . . his own hands*: this paragraph, which details Giles's illness before Grace's coming to him for help, is added within the MS.

292 *Casterbridge*: in MS-87b, this was 'Sherton'.

294 *Daphnean instinct*: in Greek mythology, Daphne rejected all lovers. Fleeing from an amorous Apollo, she called for rescue and was changed into a laurel, which became Apollo's sacred shrub. Another of Daphne's lovers, Leucippus, was killed owing to Apollo's jealousy. (Allowing that Apollo was, among other things, the god of crops and a bulwark against disease, Hardy's allusion is complex.)

295 *It was the place she sought*: not in MS-12pc.

     paled: fenced, as with stakes.

     bed-chamber: in MS-87b, this was 'scullery'. There are numerous alterations nearby in the text which reduce Giles's hut to one room; I do not include all of them in this listing for reasons of space. (Some relevant passages were not corrected until 12.)

296 *She thought his features . . . positively haggard*: this was added within the MS.

     Long tears . . . sad delight: from stanza 6 of Swinburne's 'A Ballad of Life', a poem portraying the transfiguring power of ideal love in a context of what conventionally is a matter of Lust, Shame, and Pity. Swinburne's poem reads 'men's faces', not 'their faces'.

     Three months ago . . . my lover: this was originally 'Three hours', revised to 'months' within the MS, in conjunction with the addition of Giles's illness (see note to p. 291).

302 *Once or twice . . . or a bird*: this paragraph was not in MS.

303 *I yearn . . . but*: in MS-MM, this was '"Whatsoever things are pure, whatsoever things are of good report"'; in 87a-12pc, it became: '"Whatsoever things are pure"'. Philippians 4: 8: 'Finally, brethren, whatsoever things are true, whatsoever things are honest, whatsoever things are just, whatsoever things are pure, whatsoever things are lovely, whatsoever things are of good report; if there be any virtue, and if there be any praise, think on these things.'

304 *grisly story*: sometimes identified as Edgar Allan Poe's 'The Fall of the House of Usher', but possibly Hardy has in mind only a story written in the Gothic manner. MS-MM had 'old' instead of 'grisly'.

305 *I want you here!*: not in MS-87b.

306 *Come to me, dearest!*: not in MS-87b; 96 reads '*Come to me!*'

I don't mind . . . any more: in MS-MM, this passage was not italicized.

shocked him by her impulsive words?: in MS-Col, this was 'been mistaken about his health?'

307 *malachite*: a green mineral that shines brightly when polished; used for ornamental objects.

309 *shock*: 'A group of sheaves of grain placed upright and supporting each other in order to permit the drying and ripening of the grain before carrying' (*OED*).

310 *His soul seemed*: in MS-A1, this was 'He seemed'.

Artemis: the twin sister of Apollo (see note to p. 294), the goddess of chastity, vegetation, and wild animals. She is identified with the Roman goddess Diana, and associated with the moon. Aphrodite, or Venus, is the goddess of sexual love and beauty.

311 *Though completely stultifying her flight*: not in MS-MM.

touchwood: 'The soft white substance into which wood is converted by the action of certain fungi . . . and has the property of burning for many hours when once ignited, and is occasionally self-luminous' (*OED*, which gives this passage from *The Woodlanders* as an example).

314 *loved her more than the mere lover would have loved; had*: added within the MS.

317 *with him*: not in MS-87b.

"the extremest inference": not in MS-96.

318 *"a hundred times"*: not in MS-96.

Giles's fixed statuesque features: in MS-96, this was 'poor Giles's features'.

320 *Calvinist*: some branches of Calvinism urged that the tenets of predestination and irresistible grace made prayers for the souls of the dead both unnecessary and impious.

through you giving up yourself to him: not in MS-87b.

I will let my husband think the utmost, but not you: not in MS-A1.

321 *bring down my hairs with sorrow to the grave*: Genesis 42: 38 has the phrase 'grey hairs', which also appeared in A1.

323 *"flat delight"*: from George Herbert (1593–1663), 'Vanitie (II)', where the phrase suggests earthly as opposed to spiritual values.

325 *febrifuge*: something that reduces or dispels a fever.

as Elijah drew down fire from Heaven: in 2 Kings 1: 1–16, the prophet twice calls down fire to destroy forces whose captains had ordered him in the king's name to come down from a hill in order to go to the king to give counsel. The third captain begs to be spared, and Elijah comes down.

326 *hieroglyphs*: hieroglyphic symbols or writing; or, more generally, a figure with a hidden meaning or writing difficult to decipher. In MS, this was 'hieroglyphics'.

327 *runic*: reference to an alphabet of uncertain origin (probably Etruscan) in use in Northern Europe from the third to the seventeenth century AD. Magical powers were attributed to the symbols as carved on jewellery and tombstones. The alphabet was probably once used for all purposes, secular (literature, law, and business) as well as religious, but in its last centuries mostly for charms and memorial inscriptions.

328 *an innocent woman whose pique had for the moment*: in MS-A1, this was 'a woman whose natural purity and innocence had'.

330 *the two mourners in Cymbeline*: in Shakespeare's *Cymbeline*, IV. ii. 218–20, Arviragus vows to mourn for the supposedly dead Fidele (Imogen disguised) 'While summer lasts and I live here.' Guiderius, impatient with Arviragus's 'wench-like words' (l. 230), is ready to bury Fidele/Imogen. The ironic suggestions of short-lived grief are carried out in the novel, at least by Grace.

Nothing ever had brought home to her: this was preceded in MS-A1 by: 'Sometimes Grace thought that it was a pity neither one of them had been his wife for a little while, and given the world a copy of him who was so valuable in their eyes.'

There was a rumour . . . verified: the rumour about Mrs Charmond's condition at the time of her death (presumably pregnancy) was not in MS-MM.

331 *'nature is fine in love, and where 'tis fine it sends some instance of itself'*: *Hamlet*, IV. v. 162–3. The following line in the play concludes the expression: 'After the thing it loves.' The speaker is Laertes upon first seeing the mad Ophelia. Frank Kermode glosses this passage, 'So delicate is Ophelia's love for her father that her sanity has pursued him to the grave' (note in *The Riverside Shakespeare*, ed. G. Blakemore Evans, Boston, 1974). Fitzpiers's drawing upon this allusion to grief but placing himself in the role of the sufferer would seem somewhat tasteless in the context of Grace's own grief. Since Hardy has Grace admire the letter, however, he was either merely using the

sentiment for its own sake or implying Grace's own essential (if natural) self-centredness.

333 *modus vivendi*: literally, mode of living (Latin). A temporary arrangement or practical compromise pending an agreement about matters in dispute.

336 *'Love talks . . . with dearer love'*: *Measure for Measure*, III. ii. 150–1. The disguised Duke is defending his character from Lucio's imputations of lechery and superficiality. Immediately preceding, Pompey has just been jailed as a bawd. Overall, Fitzpiers's allusion counteracts his professed ethereal love for Grace.

340 *'filz'. . . 'ung' . . . 'ilz' . . . 'mary' . . . 'ma foy'*: 'filz' = son; 'ung' = one; 'ilz' = they; 'mary' = married person; 'ma foy' = my faith.

341 *'I almost worship him*: not in MS-87b.

"frustrate ghost": in Browning's 'The Statue and the Bust' (1855) a couple shrink from an adulterous elopement. Browning does not admire their conventionality, thinking it denies them their only chance for true life. The allusion to Browning's couple suggests that when writing the novel Hardy felt both Giles and Grace were to blame. By 1893, however, he seems to shift most of the blame to Grace: Rebekah Owen recorded on an end-paper of her copy of the novel a conversation in which Hardy told her that 'Grace never interested him much; he was provoked with her all along: if she would have done a really self-abandoned, impassioned thing (gone off with Giles), he could have made a fine tragic ending to the book, but she was too commonplace and straightlaced and he could not make her.' Miss Owen's reply was to the point: Grace 'was "willin'"' when he [Giles] was not.'

343 *innamorato*: a (male) lover (Italian).

347 *though rust had weakened it somewhat now*: not in MS-96.

350 *She wondered whether God really did join them together*: added within the MS.

352 *Fitzpiers had often studied . . . Hintock House*: in MS-HB, this was: 'Although he had never seen a man-trap before, Fitzpiers could not help perceiving that this instrument was one.'

Amazonian strength: in Greek mythology, the Amazons were female warriors.

353 *or what seemed . . . may be doubted*: not in MS-96.

360 *"Well—he's her husband,"... reunited pair*: in MS-Col, there was
no paragraph at this location. In 87b the paragraph read:
'"Well—he's her husband," Melbury said to himself. "But it's
a forlorn hope for her; and God knows how it will end!" Inside
the inn the talk was also of the reunited pair.'

'The Spotted Cow': a traditional country song, evidently from
the early nineteenth century; also appears in *Tess of the
d'Urbervilles*.

363 *that Mrs. Fitzpiers was by that time in the arms of another man than
Giles*: in MS-96, this was 'where Mrs. Fitzpiers then was'.

DIALECT GLOSSARY

This list excludes most dialectical spellings of standard English words.

a-croupied several possible meanings; crept, crouched, or raked together (69)

apple-booth apple-blossom (138)

bruckle het unfortunate mischance (**bruckle** means uncertain, precarious, untrustworthy) (73)

chevy pursue (120)

chick nor chiel children (50)

chimmer chamber (120)

'Ch woll I will (119, etc.)

coling embracing (360)

criddled curdled (79)

drong a narrow lane between two hedges (294)

eft newt (307)

fay flourish, prosper (41)

glutch swallow with difficulty (322)

het struck (333)

huffed reprimanded, scolded (28)

kex dry hollow stalk of any umbelliferous plant like cowparsley, teazle, or wild carrot (359)

larries excited scenes (from alarums) (145)

lewth shelter (361)

linhay shed or open building, usually with a lean-to roof (346)

mawn-baskets deep round two-handled wickerwork baskets (173)

mossel morsel (345)

mouster be moving (359)

natomy anatomical specimen (50)

nesh delicate, tender (28)

projick either prodigy, or projector (speculator) (50, etc.)

raft disturb, upset (213)

randy-voo, randy party (72, 80, etc.)

rozums strange tales (50)

shail and wamble Hardy defined this as "An uneven unsteady gait"; when used separately there is a distinction between them; **shail** means walk crookedly or awkwardly; **wamble** means wander about aimlessly. (81)

skiver skewer (72)

squat crush, flatten (91)

teuny weak, sickly, undersized, mostly used of children (28)

tole entice, attract, beguile (146)

uppingstock horse mounting-block (161)

vamped tramped (13, etc.)

wherrit worry (120)

woak oak (244)

The Oxford World's Classics Website

www.worldsclassics.co.uk

- Information about new titles
- Explore the full range of Oxford World's Classics
- Links to other literary sites and the main OUP webpage
- Imaginative competitions, with bookish prizes
- Peruse *Compass*, the Oxford World's Classics magazine
- Articles by editors
- Extracts from Introductions
- A forum for discussion and feedback on the series
- Special information for teachers and lecturers

www.worldsclassics.co.uk

American Literature

British and Irish Literature

Children's Literature

Classics and Ancient Literature

Colonial Literature

Eastern Literature

European Literature

History

Medieval Literature

Oxford English Drama

Poetry

Philosophy

Politics

Religion

The Oxford Shakespeare